MONDAY TO FRIDAY

COOKBOOK

MICHELE URVATER

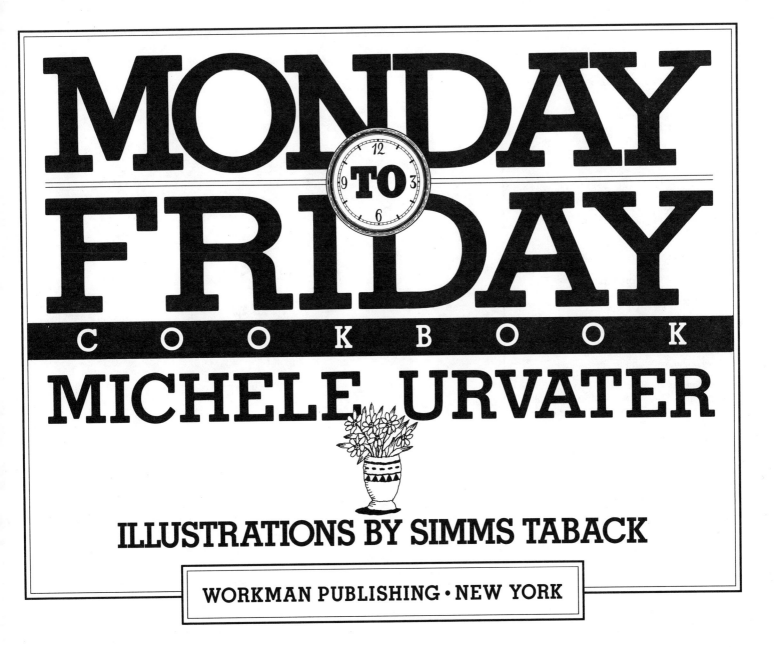

ILLUSTRATIONS BY SIMMS TABACK

WORKMAN PUBLISHING · NEW YORK

Library of Congress Cataloging-in-Publication Data
Urvater, Michèle.
    The Monday-to-Friday cookbook / by Michèle
Urvater.
        p.   cm.
    Includes index.
    ISBN 1-56305-035-8
        —ISBN 0-89480-764-1 (pbk.)
    1. Cookery.   I. Title
TX652.U783   1991
641.5-dc20   90-50947
                                            CIP
Book design by Lisa Hollander with Lori S. Malkin
Cover and book illustrations by Simms Taback
Back cover photo by Walt Chrynwski

Workman books are available at special discounts
when purchased in bulk for premiums and sales
promotions as well as for fund-raising or educa-
tional use. Special editions or book excerpts can
also be created to specification. For details, contact
the Special Sales Director at the address below.

Workman Publishing Company, Inc.
708 Broadway
New York, NY 10003

Manufactured in the United States of America

First printing June 1991
10 9 8 7 6 5 4 3

FOR ALESSIA

ACKNOWLEDGMENTS

A million thanks to: Workman Publishing for the timely, wonderful Monday-to-Friday concept.

Peter Workman for wanting me as his Monday-to-Friday Cookbook writer.

Suzanne Rafer, my tireless and inspiring editor, whose suggestions were so helpful, and who demonstrated time and again, unending patience and creativity in dealing with the myriad details involved in producing such a complicated book.

Barbara Ottenhoff for her painstaking and meticulous copyediting.

Lisa Hollander for her terrific book and cover design and Lori S. Malkin for making the book lay out so well.

Andrea Glickson, in publicity, for her cheerful encouragement, and Bert Snyder and Janet Harris, in sales, for all their hard work.

Susan Ginsburg, my agent, for her extraordinary professionalism and competence, and mostly for her support and friendship.

Mary Bralove, for her help in writing the proposal, for her invaluable suggestions and constructive criticism about my writing, for her inexhaustible enthusiasm for my work, and especially for her love and belief in me.

Hans Mautner, for his special dietary needs, which led to my discovery of new, more healthful cooking techniques, and for his sincere encouragement of this work.

Michael Cook, my husband, for his unwavering love and support, and for his honest critique of the recipes.

And lastly to my daughter, Alessia, whose birth changed my life for the better in countless ways, great and small, and who unknowingly led me to come up with culinary solutions for everyday family dinners.

CONTENTS

INTRODUCTION
CONFESSIONS OF A PROFESSIONAL COOK

As soon as people hear I am a professional cook, they often sigh with envy at what they imagine my family dinners are like. They envision a pleasant, relaxed family chat over a four-course dinner of roasted duck, scalloped potatoes, seasonal vegetables, and an extravagant dessert. Sometimes they start angling for a dinner invitation or, better still, adoption, for they think that at last they have found someone who rustles up those dinners they see on food pages but never have time or energy to fix themselves. After all, if a professional chef can't manage it, who can?

Beats me. I can't do it, and most people I know—food professionals included—can't either. My day is as harried and hectic as any other working person's. And, in my case, as the chef of the executive dining room of a New York real estate firm and freelance recipe developer and food writer, the last thing in the world I want to do when I come home is cook.

Yet the myth remains that civilized people sit down to effortlessly produced dinners every night of the week. They don't dash out to the deli. They don't bake a potato in the oven and call it a meal. They don't have the phone number of the local pizzeria indelibly inked on the kitchen wall. But, take it from me, they do. My family and I dined on every neighborhood take-out food until I couldn't bear another Chinese noodle, piece of sushi, or salad-to-go. I finally had to face facts. I love to eat and eat well, but I'm frequently too busy, too tired, or too lazy to cook during the week. I'm old enough to be concerned about my cholesterol level but too young to forgo three-star taste. My husband is as pressed for time as I am, and my daughter's idea of fine dining is a bowl of elbow macaroni. I live in a small New York City apartment with a kitchen the size of a closet, and I don't have lots of kitchen gadgets or a maid to clean up after me.

I wrote *The Monday-to-Friday Cookbook* for people like me—those with complicated lives and sophisticated tastes who haven't time to fuss. We watch our diets and avoid high-cholesterol foods when we can. We may be single, married, with children or without, but what we share is the desire to put a tasty, nourishing dinner on the table and no time to do it.

MONDAY-TO-FRIDAY EATING

Monday-to-Friday recipes are designed for a minimum of equipment and a maximum of flexibility. These are meals created for how people really live. Life is infinitely more complicated than most dinner-in-minutes cookbooks would have us believe. For instance, sometimes you come home stuffed from a business lunch, and other times you've barely managed to grab a yogurt at your desk. You may want to go for a run after work but lengthy dinner preparations will make it too late to go and postponing them will make it too late to eat. Other household members may be on different schedules or diets: A child's stomach may start to grumble a good three hours before a grown-up's. You may like cooked carrots but your partner hates them, or you both adore black olives but your kids can't stand the sight of them.

The *Monday-to-Friday Cookbook* is written for real people and real-life situations. Many of my dishes can be started, stopped in the middle, and finished later. None require split-

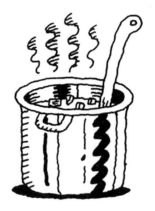

second timing, special skills, or equipment. Most can be eaten piping hot, warm, or even at room temperature without losing their delicious flavors. In other words, they fit the fractured nature of Monday-to-Friday living.

My emphasis is on flexibility and ease, not necessarily speed. Some weeks you're better off planning and cooking ahead. Knowing what you'll be eating on Thursday when it's still Monday can be a great comfort. Other weeks you may not have time to think about Thursday's dinner until Thursday evening. *The Monday-to-Friday Cookbook* covers every situation from best-case to worst-case scenarios.

MONDAY-TO-FRIDAY RECIPES

The recipes offered here make this book comprehensive enough to function as a basic everyday cookbook. My weekday dinners are inviting and uncomplicated. The recipes are healthy and based on my preference for lots of grains, vegetables, and beans, and for reduced-fat and low-cholesterol foods. But I've left plenty of room for people who couldn't care less with suggestions for adding cheese, butter, or sour cream when appropriate. While most of my desserts are fruit based, some are downright decadent. After all, at the end of a hard workday, you deserve some pampering.

Monday-to-Friday recipes are designed to guide, not dictate to you. Think of each recipe as a tune—I may hum a few bars but feel free to take it from there. If I suggest an ingredient not to your taste, use another. If I call for fresh red peppers and you've run out, use roasted peppers from a jar or just skip them altogether.

Monday-to-Friday recipes require no precooking before you get down to business, and you'll find no last-minute surprises. I don't waste time. While the water is heating for

the pasta, I'll move you along to the next step. You'll also find that whatever preparation is called for is essential to the taste of the recipe; there's no froufrou here. If the dish requires herbs, it is because they are intrinsic to the flavor of the dish, not its look.

I am also unapologetically expedient. If a can of stewed tomatoes will do just as nicely as peeled and seeded fresh ones, I'll use them. If I can get away with frozen vegetables, I am happy to do so. Remember, the only food critics you need to please are you and your family.

During the week I avoid making dishes that require special finessing, but I do emphasize cooking techniques. It takes just as much time to cook a dish badly as it does well, and the results are far more delicious when it's done right.

Most of my dishes serve four people, a number that is as easy to halve (for couples or singles) as it is easy to double (for those who like to cook in large batches, or who have bigger families to feed, or who have invited guests during the week—yes, it's possible).

A FINAL WORD

These days food has assumed a glamour once reserved for haute couture. Glossy magazines feature dazzling culinary feats. Chefs are cult figures. Restaurant dining is an aesthetic experience and a popular indoor entertainment. As a result, many home cooks feel compelled to replicate the most complicated restaurant dishes before they deem themselves good cooks. These cooks devote weekends to whipping up complex sauces. They weigh and measure

precisely. They follow recipes slavishly and yet feel inadequate and perplexed when confronted with the basic task of everyday cooking. Somewhere along the line, they've forgotten how to relax and how to improvise. They don't know when it's okay to cut corners or what corners to cut.

The Monday-to-Friday Cookbook is for all those who want to be good weekday cooks. This is a kitchen artistry of a different sort. It calls for Grandma's nearly lost art of simple, solid cooking. It calls for thrift and organization as well as flexibility, good nutrition, and ease. It calls for knowing how to rummage in the pantry and forage through the refrigerator. Come with me and I'll show you how.

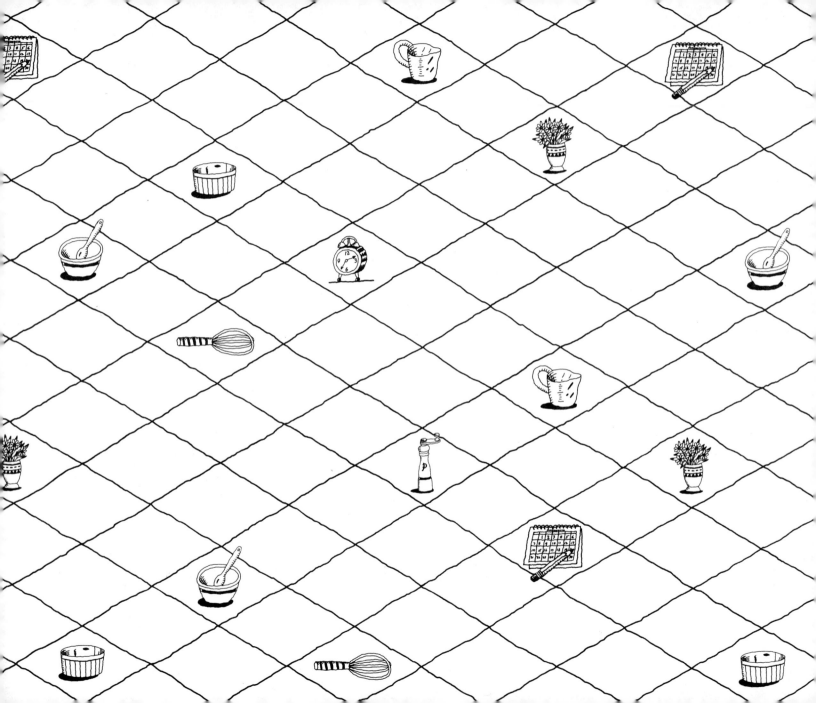

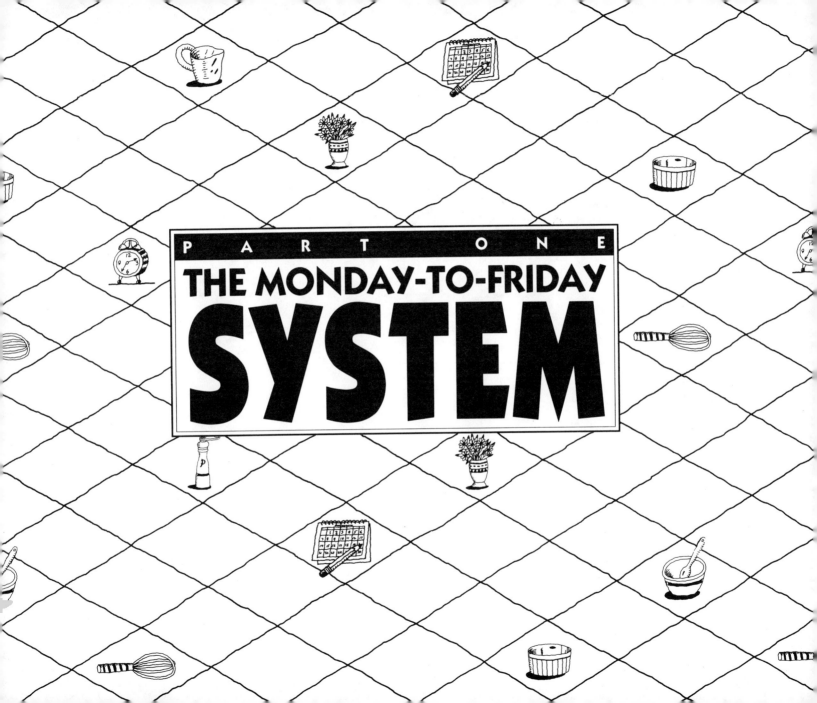

PART ONE

THE MONDAY-TO-FRIDAY
SYSTEM

SETTING UP THE PANTRY
THE MONDAY-TO-FRIDAY KEY

Setting up the pantry is the essential key to easy Monday-to-Friday cooking. You're familiar with the feeling—it usually occurs around 4 or 5 in the afternoon—you can't think of what to make for dinner and know you've got nothing in the house. Even though you may have time to pick up a couple of ingredients, you certainly don't carry around a cookbook to guide you. The final scene of this scenario finds you eating tuna straight from the can or a bowlful of pasta, again. Pasta and tuna are dandy, but you could have more.

At work in my corporate kitchen and at home, I've a stash of staple dried and canned goods in the cupboard, fresh items in the refrigerator, and a variety of seasonings and frozen foods. They inspire me and take the worry out of everyday cooking because I know that I always have something in the house from which I can rustle up a dinner in a flash.

Now please don't be alarmed by this pantry list. It may seem formidable, but it simply is an extensive overview of what most of you probably already stock, with explanations of the whys of each entry and the advance preparation involved, if any. This is all to make your future as easy as possible, for after you have set up the initial pantry, all you need do is replace items as you run out.

Nor does this pantry presume you've loads of storage space. My family of three lives in a very small Manhattan apartment where the pantry space is bigger than a bread box but not much. Refrigerator and freezer space are also at a premium in my house. I imagine the average American cook has the luxury of space and can afford to pick up several varieties of each item and buy them in large sizes, but I can only fit a single variety and a small quantity of each.

It seems every time I use an ingredient, I need to replenish it immediately. And yet my system works. For small apartment dwellers like me, it is no harder than keeping a shopping list nearby.

Stocking your pantry should take just one trip to the supermarket where you can find the serious basics and even some ethnic and specialty items. If you can't find these extras in your supermarket, a shopping trip to your local health food store and perhaps one to a gourmet shop will help you fill in the gaps.

A final word. The pantry list does not include some of the basics for a well-stocked household like flour, milk, soda, coffee, and tea nor items each household will stock according to its specific needs, like breakfast cereal, butter, or margarine, nor the variable fresh foods like broccoli, lamb chops, or fish that fill out a week.

Of course, you'll adjust the items in my suggested pantry to fit your space and palate. But you'll find

that a well-stocked pantry will make your work-week dinners infinitely easier and tastier.

SUPERMARKET TRIP

All the recipes in this book were developed and tested with the assumption you have a pantry much like the one I suggest.

Just a few fresh items like poultry, fish, meat, vegetables, and fruit are needed to complete the recipes. Most of these fresh ingredients store well in the refrigerator for at least a couple of days, keeping your weekday shopping to a minimum. Instead of a frantic last-minute trip to the grocery store, use the time between work and dinner to unwind.

DRIED GOODS

GRAINS: Most of us accept the notion that dinner can be a plateful of pasta with sauce and steamed vegetables, but we have trouble with the idea that a plateful of grains can be anything more than a side dish.

My job, which requires preparing lunches high in complex carbohydrates and low in meat, forced me to explore the different culinary properties of various grains. Their distinctive rich flavors and nubby textures have so amazed and delighted me that they've become main meals at home. A plateful of rice, kasha, cornmeal, or cracked wheat accompanied by a pasta sauce will expand your dinner repertoire too. Whenever you think of having pasta for dinner, consider serving a grain instead.

RICE: 1 to 2 pounds long-grain white, preferably converted; 1 pound aromatic rice, such as basmati or Texmati, either brown or white; and 1 pound short-grain brown rice (optional)

While there are numerous varieties of rice on the market, two or three types in your pantry are sufficient. But first you need to understand a little about the differences among rices (see box, this page).

CORNMEAL: 2 pounds yellow

Strange as it sounds, I enjoy cornmeal mush (polenta) for dinner. I dress it with either a chili sauce or a stir-fry of vegetables, or I simply chop in some green chilies and stir in grated Cheddar cheese. Voilà—dinner in minutes.

I am partial to yellow cornmeal because I love its golden hue. When it is available, I buy stone-ground cornmeal—it is more nutritious.

KASHA (buckwheat kernels): 1 box (13 ounces) roasted, medium grain

Kasha has an earthy, nutty flavor that may be an acquired taste. It is especially good when complemented by other winter flavors such as wild mushrooms, root vegetables, sage, and marjoram. In supermarkets you can purchase it plain or roasted in boxes. It is also available in three different grinds: fine, medium, and

CHOOSING RICE

Parboiled rice, the generic name for white rice usually called "converted," is my choice for a standard white long-grain rice. Before milling, the rice is processed so that nutrients from its hull are forced into the core. This makes it more nutritious than ordinary polished white rice, which is milled to remove the outer germ and bran layers. Converted rice also tends to hold its shape better than ordinary white rice.

Brown rice is rice with its outer shell removed but most of the bran left on. Brown rice is more nutritious than white rice and has a more earthy flavor. It is wonderful with hearty stews or sauces, but it takes 35 minutes to cook, so it isn't my first choice for most Monday-to-Friday meals.

It is also helpful to know that the length of the kernels, long or short, affects the texture of the rice dish. Long-grain rice, brown or white, cooks up fluffy and separate and is good for side dishes, pilafs, and salads. Medium- or short-grain white rice is sticky, and short-grain brown rice is chewy. Short-grain white rice is traditionally used in risottos, Oriental cooking as in sushi, and rice puddings.

Confusing the issue even more is that there has been an influx of imported rices and new domestic aromatic rices, each one with its own special name. For example, there is "basmati" rice, a long-grain white rice imported from India, and "Arborio" rice, a short-grain white rice imported from Italy to make risotto. There are new domestic "aromatic" rices—some brown, some white— all nutty smelling and flavorful. For example, "Texmati" is an aromatic long-grain white rice and "Wehani" an aromatic long-grain brown rice. When trying to select the right one for a dish, bear in mind that no matter how they are marketed every rice can be classified as either long or short grain, brown or white. Let your own taste guide your selections.

In my pantry, I store converted white rice because it cooks quickly, holds its shape, and is as nutritious as brown rice. I might have on hand a short-grain brown rice (available in health food stores only) because I love its chewy texture. And, if I have the room, I like to have Texmati around, for its wonderful nutty flavor transforms the plainest of rice dishes into something festive.

coarse. Cooking time varies, depending on the grind, but the medium grind takes only 12 to 15 minutes to cook.

❧

OTHER NICE BUT NOT NECESSARY GRAINS: While not essential, the grains that follow are terrific to have on hand because, without much fuss or preparation, they can add variety to your meals. Some of these can be prepared almost instantly and thus qualify as perfect weekday dinner fare.

You may not have to go farther than your local supermarket to find them. Many stores carry a line of grains and legumes packaged in boxes under the label "Near East." While I am delighted that supermarkets carry more grains, it is unfortunate that this particular company adds spices and seasonings. They aren't necessary, and they jack up the price of what should be an inexpensive food. Don't discard these seasoning packets. Instead, check the Index for the list of recipes in this book that can be enhanced by these premixed spices.

CRACKED WHEAT: 1 box (6 ounces) Near East wheat pilaf

I love the flavor of cracked wheat (like that of whole wheat bread) and substitute it at times for rice in pilafs or salads.

Near East wheat pilaf is a fancy name for cracked wheat, which is the wheat berry, coarsely milled. The grind is medium. If you buy cracked wheat in bulk from a health food store, you can choose a fine, medium, or coarse grind. Cooking time depends upon the grind, but even the coarsest grind cooks in 25 minutes. I prefer to buy my cracked wheat from a health food store because I can get a finer grind, which means faster cooking. But I've often purchased the boxed "pilaf" when I didn't have time to do more than supermarket shopping.

While cracked wheat is often confused with its sister, bulgur wheat (see below), the two cannot be used interchangeably. Cracked wheat needs to be cooked; bulgur wheat doesn't.

BULGUR WHEAT: 1 box (5¼ ounces) Near East tabouleh

This is wheat that has been steamed and then dried before cracking. It is the perfect Monday-to-Friday grain because you need only rehydrate it. You cover it with water (hot or cold) and let it stand 15 minutes until the grains swell and become tender!

If you want, you may cook bulgur wheat, but it isn't necessary. Rehydrated, it can be thrown in salads or reheated in hot dishes.

Under the Near East label, bulgur wheat is called "tabouleh," the name for a Middle Eastern salad of bulgur, mint, and parsley. Like cracked wheat, you may purchase it in bulk from a health food store and choose among three different grinds. I prefer the finer grind for salads and the medium or coarse grind for hot dishes. The Near East variety, however, comes only in medium grind.

COUSCOUS: 1 box (10 ounces) Near East couscous

Technically couscous is a form of pasta—pasta pellets really. However,

I've included it under the grain section because its grainlike shape places it alongside tabouleh and wheat pilaf on the supermarket shelves.

Couscous is tiny pasta beads made from semolina (durum wheat) and water. According to Paula Wolfert's book *Couscous and Other Good Foods From Morocco*, the authentic way of preparing couscous involves steaming it for an hour over a fragrant broth, raking it with your fingers to break up clumps, and doing the whole procedure all over again.

Although the boxed kind is precooked, when cooked properly it works well. I don't follow the package directions because I find the couscous comes out too soggy. Each of my couscous recipes describes a preferred cooking method.

PEARL BARLEY: 1 box (16 ounces)

Barley has a lovely gentle flavor

and adds body to soups and stews. It is also very good for you and widely available in supermarkets.

Although barley is a grain, it is usually found alongside the dried beans, lentils, and peas. Sometimes it is labeled simply "barley" and sometimes "pearl" or "pearled" barley. All of these, however, are barley grains that have been refined to remove the husk and endosperm of the grain.

I had always thought that barley, even pearl barley, took about a day to cook. I never considered it a possibility for Monday-to-Friday cooking. But once I began to work with it, I discovered that boiling it rapidly in plenty of water or stock tenderized the grain in 25 minutes. Thus barley is yet another perfect grain to add to soups and hearty stews in which the other ingredients take at least as long to cook.

❧

PASTAS: Even though I occasionally use the domestic variety of pasta, I try to buy imported Italian pasta made from semolina (durum wheat). I find it tastier, and it doesn't disintegrate as quickly as domestic pasta. I

like the Italian DeCecco pastas, which are available in some supermarkets, but other imported Italian pastas are just fine.

SHORT AND TUBULAR: 1 pound elbow macaroni, penne, or fusilli; and 1 pound orzo or acini pepe

I have at least one type of short and tubular-shaped pasta on hand to eat with chunky meat, bean, and fish sauces, as their nooks and crannies catch bits and pieces of sauce. Elbows, penne, or fusilli are my favorites. Indulge your own quirks and buy the shape that suits your fancy.

LONG NOODLES: 1 pound linguine fini

I prefer the flat shape of linguine to the round one of spaghetti, but either of these, or even fettuccine (for those who like a broader noodle), is terrific when you want a simple dish of pasta tossed with a smooth sauce.

SKINNY LONG NOODLES:
1 pound capellini

Capellini, the skinniest of noodles, is a boon for those times when you are starving and need an instant fix. This pasta cooks in 2 to 3 minutes.

❀

LEGUMES: Legumes—beans, lentils, and split peas—are becoming more popular. They're fabulous flavor absorbers, with the kind of texture that makes them the perfect addition to hearty stews and soups where you want lots of body. They're also an inexpensive source of protein and high in vitamins and fiber. When paired with a grain or swept into a few ounces of meat, they're a wholesome alternative to a dairy or meat-centered meal.

From Monday to Friday, rely on canned beans. (See Cans and Jars on this page to find out which ones and how much to buy.) Most dried beans take at least 1 hour of soaking before you even begin the 1½ to 2 hours of cooking. (When I'm in the mood, I'll cook dried beans in a pressure cooker, which cuts down considerably on the time.)

LENTILS: *1 pound*

SPLIT GREEN PEAS: *1 pound*

Lentils and split peas (the green ones; the yellow ones take an hour to cook) are the only dried legumes that I stock in my pantry. Their robust flavor adds soul-warming heft to main-course soups and stews. And, unlike dried beans, they don't require presoaking and cook in a mere 30 minutes.

❀

DRIED FRUITS: Dried fruits always come in handy. They are taste counterpoints in pilafs and stews and main-course salads and add panache to a fresh fruit salad. They're also good for snacking: a handful will stave off hunger until you can get dinner on the table.

Stock one or two of each kind.

RAISINS: 1 box (12 ounces)

CURRANTS: 1 box (10 ounces)

APRICOTS: 1 box (12 ounces)

PITTED PRUNES: 1 box (10 ounces) or 1 can (8 ounces)

CANS AND JARS

LEGUMES: I use beans with abandon, stirring them into stews, soups, and casseroles. Most canned beans, though, are too mushy for cold salads except for chick-peas (or garbanzos as they are known to some) and the S & W brand of red kidney beans.

Here are the basic four types of beans I keep on my shelf; they're widely available and canned by several manufacturers.

BEANS (black beans, red kidney beans, chick-peas, and white cannellini beans): 1 or 2 cans (16 to 19 ounces each) of each variety

If you find the Goya brand, you may want to stock the following for those occasions when you want a smaller bean.

Small pink beans for kidney beans and small white beans for white cannellini beans

❧

VEGETABLES: I prefer fresh vegetables. Although there are a few frozen vegetables I think are acceptable (see the frozen food section), the only canned vegetables I use are canned tomatoes and canned beets.

TOMATOES: 2 or 3 cans (14½ or 16 ounces each) peeled whole; 1 can (28 ounces) Italian plum tomatoes or 1 can (28 ounces) Redpack whole tomatoes in tomato purée; 2 or 3 cans (14½ ounces each) stewed tomatoes; and 2 or 3 cans (14½ ounces each) Italian-style stewed tomatoes

Even in summer, the flavor of locally grown fresh tomatoes leaves a lot to be desired. Cooked in stews, sauces, and soups, canned tomatoes are infinitely better. The only problem is that the best canned varieties come in large sizes. The imported plum tomatoes from Italy are canned in 28-ounce containers as are Redpack (the best domestic variety) whole tomatoes in tomato purée. As a result, I often end up with opened cans of tomatoes in the refrigerator, which forces me to make a succession of tomato-based dishes, and so I mostly stick to the smaller sized cans. However, if your pantry is large enough, you should stock a few large sizes of canned tomatoes.

Besides plain stewed tomatoes, I like to store the Italian-style stewed tomatoes which include onions and peppers in addition to the tomatoes. These additional ingredients bring a depth of flavor to a dish without my having to do any more work.

TOMATO PASTE: 1 tube (4½ ounces)

Avoid canned tomato paste if you can. Whenever I use tomato paste, I use such a small quantity that the remainder sits in the can only to develop a layer of mold on top within a couple of weeks. So I use tomato paste in a tube instead.

If you can't find tube tomato paste on the regular shelves in your supermarket, try the ethnic department or a gourmet grocery. Sometimes, if I've run out of tomato paste, I'll substitute a tablespoonful of ketchup. This works fine in many recipes.

BEETS: 1 jar (1 pound) pickled or 1 can (14 ounces) sliced

Although their slightly soft texture isn't ideal, canned sliced or pickled beets are fine for salads or other cold dishes.

❧

FRUITS (packed in water, no sugar added; or packed in "lite" syrup):

I prefer to buy the more expensive canned fruit packed without added sugar (usually found in the diet section of a supermarket) because it allows more of the fruit flavor to shine through and it isn't too sweet.

1 can each (8 ounces) apricots or peaches, pears, and crushed pineapple

I find mixing canned fruit with fresh fruit makes a tangy, more varied fruit salad. Moreover a purée of canned fruit is a wonderful quick fruit sauce. I selected these particular canned fruits because the fresh fruits aren't available in winter except at exorbitant prices. Even in season some fruits, like apricots, are so flavorless that the unsweetened canned variety is infinitely better.

❧

SAUCES: Of course there's no substitute for the flavor of a long-simmering homemade spaghetti sauce, but a good-quality jarred variety is just fine for weekday cooking. While some of you may devote weekend hours to the preparation of such a luxury item, it should be for fun not need.

SPAGHETTI SAUCE: 2 jars (1 pound each) or 2 jars (2 pounds each) (Newman's Own is my favorite)

APPLESAUCE: 1 jar (16 ounces)

I like having applesauce around to mix into fruit for dessert, but I also add it to flavor other dishes, such as Stir-fried Greens and Cabbage (see Index) to give it an unexpected note of fruity sweetness.

BABY FOOD FRUIT PUREES: 1 or 2 jars (either 4 or 6 ounces each; the choice is yours) apple "purée," peach "purée," or pear "purée"

From my daughter's infancy I learned that apple and pear purées make wonderful ready-made sauces to pour over cut-up fresh fruit or delicious spreads between layers of pound cake. These fruit purées are also great no-cook soufflé bases.

❧

BROTHS AND JUICES: Keeping broths and juices in the house is a wonderful way to add more flavor to soups and stews without more work

because these liquids, unlike water, are already flavorful. Of course, you can always make soup and stew with plain water, but broth just makes them better.

CANNED CHICKEN BROTH: 2 cans (14½ ounces each)

I prefer Pritikin canned broth because it has no added salt nor fat. If you can't find the Pritikin brand, substitute another brand of low-salt chicken broth. When you use regular canned broth, use half broth and half water in the recipes to cut the salty flavor.

For folks who know that the flavor of the broth makes all the difference in the world, I feel compelled to mention the new frozen broths on the market packaged and distributed under the name Perfect Addition. They are available in 8-ounce microwavable frozen tubs. They are unsalted, flavorful, and worth the expense. This company makes chicken, beef, and fish stocks. I rely on the chicken and fish.

CLAM JUICE: 2 bottles (8 ounces each)

This is a good substitute for homemade fish stock. Because it is a bit salty, my recipes temper its flavor with water or wine.

TOMATO JUICE: 1 can (16 ounces)

For a change of pace and to add color, I sometimes substitute tomato juice for chicken broth or clam juice in soups or stews.

FISH: When I'm feeling lazy or I can't get to the fish store, I'll add canned fish to a cold salad or pasta dish. I avoid packaged frozen fish because it smells funny to me. Whenever I can, I buy canned fish packed in water to avoid the unnecessary fat.

MACKEREL (preferably packed in water): 1 can (16 ounces)

When working on a low-cholesterol cookbook, I was forced to examine the merits of canned mackerel. I am now a convert. I like it not so much

for its reputedly miraculous cholesterol-lowering properties, but because it has more taste, zip, and moisture than tuna.

SALMON (preferably packed in water and with bones in): 2 cans (3½ ounces each)

I use this in salads, sandwiches, and in some pasta sauces instead of tuna. Bones-in adds calcium.

TUNA (preferably packed in water): 2 cans (7 ounces each)

I have this on hand for a change from mackerel!

SMOKED MUSSELS OR CLAMS: 1 or 2 cans (3 to 4 ounces each)

I like some smoked fish in pasta dishes or salads; use it sparingly though, for too much overpowers the palate.

SARDINES (preferably packed in water): 2 cans (3½ ounces each)

Both my husband and I love the flavor of sardines and use them freely in a salad or sandwich to make a quick summer meal. Try to get the kind with bones in to jack up your calcium. If sardines aren't to your taste, then rely on tuna.

FROZEN FOODS

Here is the list of frozen fruits and vegetables which, in certain types of recipes, are perfectly acceptable substitutes for the fresh variety.

VEGETABLES: I buy all my frozen vegetables in 10-ounce packages because my freezer is so small. However, if you have the space, take advantage of the larger economy sizes. Once you've opened the large bags, repackage any leftovers into 2-cup portions, which equals a 10-ounce package.

You'll have to do some detective work on your own to determine if a brand-name frozen vegetable is better than the generic brand and worth the higher price.

CORN KERNELS: 1 package (10 ounces)

I love freshly picked corn on the

cob, but frozen corn kernels are just fine when used in stews, stir-fries, or even salads.

STRING BEANS, FRENCH CUT: 1 package (10 ounces)

For everyday cooking and even in salads, I rely on thawed french-cut green beans, for I find the fresh beans, once cooked, often taste bland and have a woody texture.

PETITE PEAS: 1 package (10 ounces)

If I had a garden I would grow peas and take all that trouble to shell them because, for my money, shucked peas are as sweet a treat as fresh corn. But the fresh peas available in city markets are more like starchy cannonballs, making all that work of shelling them singularly unrewarding. So I use frozen "petite" peas instead (they're more delicate) in all recipes that call for peas and use them thawed, without further cooking, in some of my salads.

LIMA BEANS: 1 package (10 ounces)

Once in my life, I ate steamed freshly picked lima beans and discovered that, like fresh peas and corn,

they were full of sweetness without a trace of starch. Alas, I don't have a garden nor access to one, so here, too, I rely on frozen limas.

CHOPPED SPINACH: 1 package (10 ounces)

Although fresh spinach tastes better than frozen spinach, it is a chore to clean it well, and I never have the energy to clean more than a half pound at a time. So for cooked soups and stews, I use chopped frozen spinach; the frozen whole leaves taste slimy.

ARTICHOKE HEARTS: 1 package (10 ounces)

As far as I'm concerned, frozen artichoke hearts are a separate species from fresh artichokes, for their tastes are completely different. The frozen hearts taste grassy; the fresh hearts, buttery. I like them both

in their own way but always keep the frozen hearts in the house for stews and salads.

❁

FRUITS:

BERRIES: 1 package (12 ounces) unsweetened strawberries, blueberries, or raspberries; 2 packages (10 ounces each) frozen raspberries in "lite" syrup

While their texture tends to be soft, thawed frozen raspberries or strawberries often have a deeper flavor than their fresh counterparts. They are especially appropriate when puréed for a dessert sauce or blended into other fresh fruits as an accent of flavor. Try to buy the unsweetened whole fruit or the fruit packed in "lite" syrup so that their tart flavor comes through.

I always have frozen raspberries packed in syrup on hand to use as a quick dessert sauce, to blend with other fresh fruit, or to spoon over store-bought pound cake. Because raspberries seem so luxurious to me, using them with more ordinary ingredients makes dessert more festive.

FROZEN DESSERTS:

ICE CREAM, TOFUTTI, OR FRO-ZEN YOGURT: 2 pints of your favorite

It is imperative that you have in the freezer at least one pint of ice cream, ice milk or sherbet, Tofutti or frozen yogurt, depending on your diet needs and taste. It's a fail-proof dessert and a spoonful or so goes a long way in soothing workday irritations.

SWEETENERS AND DESSERT FIXINGS

The prudent dessert for a work-week menu is fresh fruit. And most often, that's what I prudently choose. But who, at the end of a particularly tough day, wants to be prudent? What I need is a treat. When ice cream straight from the carton becomes too routine, I do something different and I need the fixings on hand to help. If you're like me, you will too.

SWEETENERS: There are many reasons why sweeteners are needed—to stir into a cup of coffee, to pick up the flavor of a casserole, to sweeten a bowl of berries.

SUGAR: 1 bag (5 pounds) granu-lated white and 1 box (16 ounces) light or dark brown

Ordinary granulated white sugar is an obvious choice, but I like to have brown sugar, dark or light, on hand as well because it has a more robust flavor.

CONFECTIONERS' OR SUPER-FINE SUGAR: 1 box (16 ounces)

Either one of these is handy to have for times when you need an in-stantly dissolving sugar.

LIQUID SWEETENERS: 1 jar or can honey and maple syrup (16 ounces)

Honey and real maple syrup are my liquid sweeteners of choice be-cause of their distinctive flavor.

JAMS: 1 jar (12 ounces) red cur-rant jelly and 1 jar (12 ounces) jam or jelly of your choice

Red currant, raspberry, and straw-berry jams and jellies are frequently to be found in our cupboard. But if I had room for only one, it would be red currant jelly. To my taste, it has just the right balance of sweetness and acidity—perfect between bread or as a sweetener in dessert—and jelly dissolves more easily over heat than jam.

If you're concerned about eating too much sugar, then buy only fruit- or juice-sweetened jams and jellies; the consistency is dense but the flavor intense.

❀

OTHER FIXINGS:

EXTRACTS: 1 bottle (2 ounces) vanilla and 1 bottle (1 ounce) almond

Lots of desserts taste more festive when spiked with drops of vanilla or almond extract. Other extracts taste too artificial.

EVAPORATED SKIM MILK: 2 cans (12 ounces each)

This is a product I discovered when I was experimenting with ways to make low-fat desserts taste rich. Desserts are prized at my place of work where the executives have the sweet tooth of children but the cholesterol levels of middle-aged men.

Now I always have 2 to 4 cans of evaporated milk in my pantry and add it as I would heavy cream—to a sauce or to cake and other desserts. It adds a hint of sweetness and a touch of richness without the fat and/or excessive calories.

COCOA POWDER: 1 package (8 ounces)

Since it is the cocoa powder that contains all that delicious deep chocolate flavor, a touch of cocoa powder combined with confectioners' sugar or mixed into evaporated skim milk or a touch of liqueur can bring the joy of deep chocolate flavor into our lives without cholesterol.

I recommend Droste's or Van Houtens', both imported Dutch cocoa powders. They taste more authentically chocolate than our domestic variety.

NUTS: 1 can (4 ounces) walnuts; 1 can (4 ounces) pecans; and 1 can (12 ounces) unsalted peanuts

Although somewhat high in fat, nuts add a lovely crunch to weekday desserts. I have peanuts on hand, not only for desserts, but also for savory dishes and quick snacking.

(See also Pantry on the Run on page 41 for more snacking ideas.)

PREPARED BAKED GOODS:

COOKIES: 2 packages (7 to 8 ounces each) plain butter cookies or shortbread and 1 package (7 to 8 ounces) plain chocolate cookies

How nice it would be if we had enough time to bake our own pound cake, shortbread, and simple choco-late cookies and have these on hand at all times for those emergency sweet-tooth attacks. But this never happens in my house, and I doubt it happens in yours.

In truth many commercial products nearly rival homemade goods. It ought to be easy enough for you to find an excellent-tasting commercial brand. If you have 2 or 3 of these items in your pantry, you will always be able to have a somewhat fancy dessert during the week if you want it. These simple baked goods take on myriad characters when sandwiching fruits, jellies, nuts, or whipped cream.

POUND CAKE: 1 package (1 pound; I prefer Pepperidge Farm)

I usually cut a pound cake in half and store both pieces in the freezer to pull out later when I need it.

OILS AND VINEGARS

It's amazing how a well-considered stash of oils and vinegars can be the key to adding that special touch to your daily cooking.

OILS: I rarely cook with butter. Almost all of my recipes are cooked in vegetable or olive oil. Readers can substitute butter for these oils, or, if they wish, they can add a nubbin of butter at the end of cooking time to add a smooth finish.

VEGETABLE OIL: 1 bottle (32 ounces)

A good neutral-flavor oil like canola (Puritan), safflower, or sunflower would be my first choice.

OLIVE: 1 bottle (32 ounces)

If I only had room in my pantry for one bottle of olive oil, it would have to be a medium-flavored oil that works in cooking as well as salad dressings; the taste of the dark green extra-virgin olive oil is overpowering in cooked dishes.

Of the medium-flavored golden-hued olive oils, my first choice would be a cold-pressed oil imported from Italy; my second choice would be an all-purpose Spanish olive oil. Both of these are readily available in most supermarkets.

SOLID OIL

*I*n theory, one should store oils in a pantry—provided it is a cool and dark one—so that the oil remains fresh and in its liquid state, ready to be used at any moment. My pantry consists of a couple of shelves in the kitchen cabinet of an overheated Manhattan apartment and were I to store oils on those shelves, they would turn rancid within a week.

So, I keep my opened bottles of olive and other vegetable oils in the refrigerator where they keep fresh for months. The only little problem that occurs with this storage method, however, is that olive oil will congeal when kept that cold. It might even congeal in uneven ways, with the oil forming solid little white specks on top of a more liquid oil underneath. Don't be alarmed; the flavor will remain good but the oil will be hard to pour.

You can liquefy oil in two ways. The first is the fastest. Simply run the bottle (closed) under hot water, constantly turning it so that the heat of the water liquefies the oil. As soon as the amount of oil you need for your recipe is of pouring consistency, turn off the water. Of course, if you have the time, just remove the oil from the refrigerator and let it sit about 20 minutes. By then it should be of pouring consistency.

MAYONNAISE: 1 jar (1 pint) reduced-calorie (light), low-cholesterol, or regular Hellmann's

During the week I use a reduced-calorie or reduced-cholesterol mayonnaise to cut back on fat. It's healthier but also tastes sweeter than I'd like, so on weekends I indulge myself and "bring out the Hellmann's," which I do believe is the best.

❧

VINEGARS: Fortunately these days supermarkets stock excellent imported Italian or French vinegars; for the American wine and herb vinegars are too harsh for my taste. I use lots of vinegar in my cooking, so that when I can't find a good-quality vinegar at the supermarket, I go to a health food or gourmet store to seek one out because the quality of the vinegar makes such a difference. I like to have several different vinegars on hand for a change of pace in flavor as well as color. Select at least two types:

RED WINE VINEGAR: 1 bottle (12 ounces)

Dessault Fils is my favorite brand of red wine vinegar as well as white wine and tarragon vinegars. It has good flavor and body and is not too harsh.

BALSAMIC VINEGAR: 1 bottle (12 ounces)

Balsamic vinegar is a lovely mellow wine vinegar; the best are aged and imported from Italy. It has a sweet flavor and lovely aroma that is superb in salad dressings and is so gentle that you can use more of it in a vinaigrette than you would ordinary red wine vinegar. Substitute a Spanish sherry wine vinegar or rasperry vinegar if balsamic is not available.

WHITE WINE VINEGAR: 1 bottle (12 ounces)

I use this when I want to avoid the dark color of a red wine vinegar in salads.

TARRAGON VINEGAR: 1 bottle (12 ounces)

I love this vinegar for its lovely herby aroma; it's terrific in all kinds of salads. Here again, Dessault Fils is the brand I prefer.

RICE VINEGAR: 1 bottle (12 ounces)

A mild, somewhat sweet white vinegar and good in salads, rice vinegar is available in some supermarkets, gourmet, and health food stores as well as in Korean produce markets where Oriental ingredients are sold.

CONDIMENTS

In a way, condiments are like accessories—they make or break the outfit. A good selection will give you the freedom to create hundreds of different recipes even when the focal point of your dinner—chicken cutlets, pasta, or baked potatoes—remains the same.

This condiment list is pretty basic, and I suspect you already have a number of these items in your cupboard. As with every other suggestion I make, I am assuming you will add to this list any of your favorites I have left out and omit those you don't care for.

PIMIENTOS, ROASTED RED PEPPERS, OR SWEET PEPPERS:
1 or 2 jars (4 ounces each)

I use pimientos or roasted peppers to add a touch of roasted aroma to some dish or when I want the flavor of the peppers but don't want to dice and cook fresh bell peppers. For a change of pace, I use sweet red peppers.

JALAPENO OR NACHO PEPPERS:
1 jar (12 ounces) pickled

My husband and I love very hot food, so we end up tossing hot peppers into many a dish. This is an optional ingredient. You could substitute dried red pepper flakes or Tabasco sauce.

I usually find these in the Tex-Mex section of the supermarket.

OLIVES: *1 jar (6½ ounces) cured black*

Or you could substitute a jar of black olive paste, see Supermarket Ethnic Ingredients on page 31.

TABASCO: *1 bottle (2 ounces)*

This sauce is wonderful for those times you'd like a little fire in your dish but are too lazy to dice chilies. This is in addition to or instead of jalapeños.

WORCESTERSHIRE: *1 bottle (5 ounces)*

A good American seasoning to use in uncooked dressings and sauces.

KETCHUP: *1 bottle (14 ounces)*

Believe it or not, I use ketchup often instead of tomato paste to add color and a spark of flavor to dressings and sauces.

BARBECUE SAUCE: *1 bottle (12 or 16 ounces)*

I add this in small quantities to dressings and sauces.

HORSERADISH: *1 jar (5 ounces) white*

I love this condiment in sandwiches or in sauces that go with seafood. I prefer the white kind so that I don't have to worry about the red hue messing up the color of the dressing.

MUSTARDS: *1 jar (8 ounces)* Dijon

Dijon mustard is my first choice. Sometimes I have Pommery grainy mustard on hand as well because it has a gentler flavor.

REAL LEMON AND LIME JUICE:
1 bottle (8 ounces) of each

I prefer the flavor of fresh-squeezed lemon or lime juice, but for the times when I am just too lazy to take out the juicer, the bottled juice comes in handy. It is also a boon to have on hand when you have run out of fresh lemons and your recipe cries out for that special tang of citrus.

Most of these recipes were tested with Real lemon juice. In general you can substitute equal amounts of fresh lemon juice for the juice made from concentrate, but you can add half again as much fresh juice to add even more tang. Recipes made with fresh lemon juice can just take more of its flavor without tasting sour.

CAPERS: *1 jar (3 ounces) non-pareil*

I especially like these with fish or tossed in salads or pasta dishes.

PICKLES: *1 jar (16 ounces) kosher dill*

I love these with fish and poultry salads and sometimes use them to flavor a salad dressing.

SPICES AND DRIED HERBS

By no means is this list sacred. It is merely a reflection of my likes and dislikes; your tastes and needs will guide you in your own selection.

SALT: *1 box (26 ounces) iodized*

Although many people are restricting their sodium intake, I like to add salt to all of my dishes because it picks up the flavor like nothing else. For the most part I let my readers decide how much salt and pepper to use by directing them to "season to taste with salt and pepper."

I use finely ground salt. Some people say coarse or kosher salt is tastier than regular salt, but I can't find a noticeable difference. Also kosher salt comes in a huge box and usually cakes in the humidity of our apartment long before we get to the bottom of the box.

PEPPERCORNS, WHOLE: *1 jar (about 2 ounces)*

When I gave cooking classes, I used to instruct my students to season light-colored dishes with white pepper so that they did not look as if specks of dirt had fallen into them.

If you have the room, then by all means store both black and white peppercorns. White pepper has less bite to it than black. Be sure to store them in two different pepper grinders so that you can tell one from the other. It is, however, perfectly acceptable to have only black peppercorns around.

Preground pepper, however, doesn't do the trick. The flavor just isn't there. Invest in a good pepper grinder and use freshly ground pepper in all your recipes. You'll be surprised what a difference it makes.

❀

HERBS AND SPICES: All of these spices come in bottles of about 1½ ounces each.

If you wish to prolong the shelf life of your herbs and spices, buy them in small quantities and store them away from light and heat.

Bay leaves: One leaf goes a long way. Use in soups and stews.

Caraway seeds: I like the warm bite of caraway in winter soups and stews and with anything that has peppers, mushrooms, cabbage, or potatoes in it.

Cardamom: A sweet aromatic spice used mostly in baking, cardamom is delicious when added to Indian dishes.

Cayenne pepper: Another "hot" touch I can add to my recipes.

Chili powder: This is a standby in our house—even our daughter is fond of it.

Chinese five-spice powder: An interesting spice to have around if you like Chinese-flavored food but don't want to shop for all those special ingredients you need to make a dish taste authentically Chinese.

Cinnamon, ground: A mainstay in desserts but excellent as well in many a Mexican or Indian recipe.

Cumin, ground: This slightly bitter and highly aromatic spice is my most favorite flavor in the world, so I use it quite freely.

Dried red pepper flakes: Another one of the many ways to introduce heat into food. I like this kind because you get a whole flake of hotness to bite on.

Fennel: Its lovely licorice taste is especially good in fish stews and soups.

Garlic powder: I know I go on about the virtues of fresh garlic, but I confess to sometimes cooking with the powdered kind—but only in cooked dishes; for raw garlic powder is a bit harsh. If I have simmered a dish and feel it is missing the flavor of garlic, I might add the powder and simmer it a while longer. It's also good for those times when you're too lazy to bother with chopping garlic.

Ginger: I like the sharp peppery flavor of fresh ginger, but I often resort to the ground kind because fresh ginger shrivels up and dries out easily and I often end up tossing out half of what I've bought.

Lemon peel: Stock up on this to have available an instant citrus pick-me-up without the bother of having to grate the fresh peel.

Mint: Dried mint does have flavor and can be used in cooked dishes, but fresh mint is better with fruit salads.

Nutmeg: I like to store this whole because I prefer the flavor of freshly grated nutmeg. You can, however, buy the ground kind—the flavor might not be as intense.

Orange peel: I stock this for the same reasons I do lemon peel.

Oregano: Good in many a winter dish where you want an easily recognizable Italian accent.

Rosemary: I love it with ham, potatoes, and in soups. This herb reminds me of Italy.

Tarragon: I like this in salad dressings, with cold poultry, and vegetable salad. It reminds me of summer in France.

Thyme: This powerful mintlike herb is a good all-purpose herb and used quite a bit in French cuisine.

SUPERMARKET ETHNIC INGREDIENTS

Reflecting the increased interest in ethnic cuisines of the 1980s, supermarkets now offer a selection of ethnic ingredients. A section with Mexican and Chinese ingredients is standard, and more recently Italian and Japanese ingredients have found their way into most stores as well.

My style of cooking is highly influenced by these and other cuisines. I freely add ethnic accents and seasonings to renovate the character of standard recipes and compensate for the missing richness of fat. The results are marvelous tasting but decidedly inauthentic dishes.

Note that if these items are not available in your supermarket, you'll have to hunt for them at a gourmet store.

MEXICAN: I adore the peppery taste of Mexican food and add chilies or hot peppers to a variety of dishes, hot and cold.

Green chilies, chopped: 2 cans (4 ounces each)

The selection of chilies in the Tex-Mex section of the supermarket is usually quite extensive and includes a variety of ready-made sauces and prepared foods such as refried beans or chili con carne. I have tried these on occasion but found them to be unsatisfactory versions of the real thing. They suffer from a surfeit of dehydrated vegetables and artificial colors and flavors.

JAPANESE: I was delighted to find that my supermarket stocks a whole sushi-making kit and with it an assortment of Japanese ingredients. I don't make sushi at home but draw freely from the Japanese ingredients to season my own concoctions.

MIRIN: 1 bottle (10 ounces; optional)

RICE VINEGAR: 1 bottle (12 ounces)

ORIENTAL SESAME OIL: 1 bottle (5 ounces)

SOY SAUCE: 1 bottle (5 ounces)

I like the flavor of mirin, a sweet

rice wine—it is not essential but nice to have. I also love the flavor of rice vinegar in dishes other than Oriental ones. I make many of my salad dressings with rice vinegar because I like its mild and polished flavor. Sesame oil is the most recognizable of all Oriental flavors. It is pungent and a little of it goes a long way.

CHINESE: I never cook authentic Chinese food at home. It's too much trouble to replicate what I can easily and inexpensively order out. I do find, however, that a small selection of Chinese ingredients is a terrific boon to my pantry. In addition to the soy sauce, sesame oil, and rice vinegar found also in the Japanese section, I stock:

CHILI PASTE WITH GARLIC: 1 jar (8 ounces)

This is a hot, very garlicky condiment. A teaspoon of this stuff goes a long way to liven up the simplest of dishes.

CANNED WATER CHESTNUTS: 1 can (8 ounces)

I like their crunch in salads.

HOISIN SAUCE: 1 bottle (8 ounces)

I like to add a touch of this sweet spicy paste to stir-fried vegetables or sautéed poultry.

❀

ITALIAN: The mere fact that the Italian word "pasta" has come to mean any number of noodle and macaroni dishes is an indication of how profoundly we have been influenced by Italian cuisine. This interest in pasta has extended to other Italian ingredients as well: pesto sauce, olive paste, and risotto, to name but a few. I am fortunate enough to have a nearby supermarket that carries these items. If yours doesn't, try a gourmet or specialty food shop.

ARBORIO RICE: 1 package (8 ounces; optional)

Arborio rice is a short-grain rice grown in the Po valley and is the best rice to use when making risotto. It has a wonderful creamy texture and absorbs more liquid than our American short- or medium-grain rice.

OLIVE PASTE: 1 jar (3 ounces)

Black or green olive paste, or olivada, is made of crushed pitted olives mixed with olive oil and sometimes garlic. It is delicious spread on bread, mixed into pasta sauces, or used to flavor a sauce made from pan drippings. I use it as a seasoning, somewhat as I would mustard.

PESTO: 1 jar (4 ounces)

Pesto in Italy is an incomparable pasta sauce made from fresh basil leaves, garlic, olive oil, pine nuts, and Parmesan cheese. It is cumbersome to make at home during the week, but the jarred variety never measures up to the flavor of the homemade version. Although I would never use prepared pesto as a pasta sauce, I do like a teaspoon or so of it as a seasoning accent in pasta sauces, cold salads, or sandwich spreads.

SUN-DRIED TOMATOES: 1 jar (8 ounces)

These are tomatoes that have been dried, then packed in olive oil and salt. They have a distinctive flavor, a bit acidic and sweet, and a wonderful pulpy texture. I use them in sauces and as the base for salad dressings. At times I even spread slices of them on ham sandwiches.

TOMATO PASTE: 1 tube (4½ ounces)

See page 21 for a description.

FRESH GOODS

Fresh goods is a catchall phrase I came up with to describe various fresh ingredients like meat, vegetables, fish, and so on that you'll need to create dinners and that you can buy at the supermarket.

The meats and poultry freeze beautifully so that, even on days you don't have time to shop for fresh ingredients, you'll always have something in the house for dinner.

Of course this list will vary depending on your needs and preferences, and you'll have to add such staple items as eggs, orange juice, and milk.

VEGETABLES AND FRUITS: These are the vegetables and citrus fruits with which I flavor my recipes. See also Pantry on the Run (page 41) for fresh vegetables for snacks. As I've said before, this list is personal and I suggest you add or subtract items according to your likes and dislikes.

ONIONS: 1 to 2 pounds

Be sure to have lots of these on hand as they are essential to the life of any good cook.

GARLIC: 1 head

I depend on garlic to bring life to the simplest of dishes, and I love garlic with almost everything. (I have a friend who is convinced that garlic would be terrific even with chocolate, but I'm skeptical.)

When choosing garlic, make sure the cloves feel plump and firm.

SCALLIONS: (green onions): 1 bunch

Although not as essential as onions or garlic, scallions are good to have around because they can bring the flavor of onion to a dish without having to chop and cook onions. Raw scallions are great in salads or sliced over pasta.

Look for firm, shiny bunches without brown discolorations or dried-out green tops.

CARROTS: 1 bunch

These are as essential to a good cook as are onions. Carrots add a basic mild sweet taste to any dish, and they're also good for snacking.

They also lessen guilt. If you can get your family to munch on raw carrot sticks with dinner, you won't have to worry if the meal is a bit short on cooked vegetables.

Look for firm carrots with green tops; avoid flabby carrots.

CELERY: 1 bunch

I hate celery but recognize that most people like it. Some people like the fibrous crunch of raw celery, and

others simply like it for its flavor.

Look for plump, bright green stalks of celery. Avoid those with dried-out brown edges on the tops.

BELL PEPPERS: 2 or 3, preferably red

I am married to a man who was born in Budapest, and who introduced me to the joys of snacking on raw peppers. I love the flavor of cooked peppers in soups, pasta sauces, grain dishes, and stews. I prefer the pricier red bell peppers to green because they're sweeter and more colorful.

Look for firm peppers; avoid ones with soft spots or ones that are shriveled and dried out.

LEMONS AND LIMES: 2 or 3 of each

In the supermarket list that preceded this, I suggested you buy bottled lemon and lime juice, but I want to stress here that you should use the bottled juice mostly for emergencies. The flavor of freshly squeezed citrus juice is far superior.

I use limes about as much as I do lemons, but in the recipes in this book you may substitute lemon juice when lime juice is called for.

Look for plump firm fruit.

❀

HERBS: Although I think it is perfectly all right to rely on dried herbs and spices to season your recipes, I think that a good handful of chopped fresh herbs makes a world of difference in how a dish tastes. I don't use herbs as garnish — just flavor.

FRESH HERBS: Parsley (preferably Italian, or flat leaf), coriander, dill, and basil, when in season; 1 bunch each

I always buy fresh parsley and coriander, and when I'm in the mood and when the herbs are in season, I'll buy fresh dill and basil as well.

Most people don't bother with fresh herbs because by the time they get around to using them at the end of the week, the herbs have wilted. However, if you store herbs as I do, they'll keep sparklingly fresh for a week. Store them in the refrigerator with the stems in a glass of water, as you would flowers in a vase, and cover the leaves with a plastic bag.

When you buy fresh herbs, look for bright fresh bunches. The leaves should not be droopy.

❀

DAIRY: Cooks without dietary restrictions may want to store dairy products higher in fat than the ones on this list: you may want delicious goodies like ice cream, sour cream, and regular yogurt instead of the nonfat kind.

However, even devil-may-care eaters ought to consider my sensible list for workweek cooking, for if you cut back on fats during the week, you can indulge more freely over the weekend. (Note, as I mentioned at the beginning of the chapter, this list 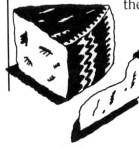 does not include milk, butter, or margarine, which I assume you have on hand, if these items are part of your daily diet.)

PLAIN NONFAT YOGURT: 1 pint

My family eats lots of spicy soups and stews, often made with complex carbohyhdrates. Stirring yogurt into these mixtures "cools" them down while jacking up the protein count.

In our house yogurt functions the way heavy cream did in "the good old days." We stir it into soups (off the heat) for a fine finish and use it as the base for salad dressings, dips, and dessert toppings. In summer we even make a light meal of it by mixing it with a salad of either diced fresh vegetables or fruit.

LOW-FAT COTTAGE CHEESE: ½ or 1 pint

Keep cheese in the house for times when you need an instant protein fix. The lower the cheese is in fat, the healthier it will be. I happen to actually enjoy low-fat cottage cheese because its neutral flavor mixes well with any number of other ingredients.

PART-SKIM RICOTTA CHEESE: 1 pint

I usually have this in the house for times when I crave a smoother texture and a richer flavor than that of cottage cheese. In the summer, we have ricotta cheese mixed with peaches and different kinds of berries for dinner. In most of my recipes, you may, if you prefer its flavor, substitute ricotta for cottage cheese.

PARMESAN: ½-pound chunk imported Parmigiano-Reggiano or ½ pound grated imported.

If you could buy just one hard cheese, it would have to be Parmesan because it is terrific in so many ways — it is wonderful stirred into grains and vegetable salads or sprinkled on pastas or in soups. When I have imported Parmesan in the house, I even eat it sliced wafer thin in tomato sandwiches.

Because I really do prefer the flavor of the imported Italian Parmigiano-Reggiano (this is not culinary pretension speaking), I refrigerate it in large chunks, wrapped several times in foil to keep it from drying out.

But because I can't always get to the special store that sells authentic Parmesan, I also store some grated Parmesan of a lesser quality but also imported. Steer clear of the grated domestic Parmesan stored on supermarket shelves; it is pretty awful.

EGGS: 1 dozen, large

I always have eggs in the house, not only for the pancakes or muffins I make for Sunday breakfast, but because I love them on occasion for a fast and nutritious dinner. A few of the recipes in the book call for eggs, but if you're not fond of them, buy only a half dozen.

❧

MEAT, POULTRY, AND FISH: If you can't get buy fresh meat and fish every day, then buy some about once a week and freeze it. It is worth investing in freezer paper because it will lengthen the "shelf life" of whatever it is you are freezing. Keep in mind that when you freeze something, you are not arresting deterioration, you are simply slowing it down.

After I have bought fish and poultry or whatever I need for the week, I cut some of it into chunks or strips and freeze it packed in individual portions no larger than 4 ounces. This gives me the flexibility I need because I can defrost just one package at a time if only one of us is eating or several packages at once if we're all having dinner together.

GROUND BEEF: 1 pound, stored in four 4-ounce patty packages

I always have some lean ground round in the house because my child likes some meat dishes or pasta dishes made with it. You also might like to have these patties at the ready for quick hamburger meals.

Ground beef can be frozen for 3 to 4 months.

SMOKED LEAN HAM: 1 pound diced or julienned and stored in four 4-ounce packages

I try to buy 95- or 96-percent fat-free ham, preferably smoked. I like to have this around for its smoky flavor; it is wonderful with bean and grain dishes, stirred into greens and hearty winter soups, and also makes for a great protein addition to vegetable, legume, and grain salads.

Frozen ham keeps for about 3 months.

❧

POULTRY: We rely on boneless chicken or turkey breasts for much of our weekly protein intake because it is lean and neutral in taste. I have at least a pound of one or the other in the freezer at all times.

CHICKEN OR TURKEY BREASTS OR CUTLETS, BONELESS: 1 pound of each, cut into strips or chunks and stored in four 4-ounce packages (cutlets can be left as is)

GROUND TURKEY: 1 pound, optional (buy if you want to substitute it for beef in ground beef recipes)

I package some chicken as individual flat cutlets, ready to be sautéed. Some of the chicken or turkey I cut into 1-inch chunks or strips about 1 by ½ inch. I find this to be the best size to toss in a stew or soup. Frozen chunks take only about 10 minutes to cook, even unthawed, and all the juices or nutrients that might leach out of the defrosting meat go right into the soup pot.

Frozen poultry in chunks or thin pieces will keep for 2 months only.

If you are on a diet very low in cholesterol and fat, then buy ground turkey to substitute in recipes, like meatballs, chili, and spaghetti sauce, that call for ground beef. Ground turkey is preferable to ground chicken because it has a chewier texture that is meatier. Be very careful though to use ground turkey within a day of purchase or freeze it because it is so perishable.

❧

FISH: We live only blocks away from one of Manhattan's most fabulous fresh fish markets where any number of common and exotic fish can be purchased on any given day. I must admit that when I feel like cooking fish I just pick it up fresh on the way home.

I realize, however, that most people aren't so lucky. They should buy a pound or two of fresh fish at a time and freeze it. Frozen fish is best in soups, casseroles, or one-pot dishes, and the best fish to freeze are the sturdier kinds like monkfish, halibut, salmon, or sea scallops. Freeze it in 6-ounce portions; it will keep 2 to 3 months.

If you're going to sauté, bake, or poach fish, try to get your hands on it fresh.

If fresh fish is too hard to come by in your neck of the woods, I have included lots of recipes that rely on canned fish like tuna.

BREADS (fresh and packaged): In our house, bread is really the staff of life. Not a meal goes by — and I mean it — that my husband does not have a couple of slices of bread, even if the main course is a starchy dish. I too love bread, but am less avid a consumer than he is. Often the bread at one of our meals takes the place of rice or potatoes and is one way we make sure we integrate "grains" in our diet. But in order to make the bread count as a wholesome nutritious food, we eat mostly freshly baked French, Italian, or sourdough white bread or freshly baked whole-wheat, rye and multi-grain breads bought at a bakery, gourmet, or health food store.

If a trip to a good bakery or health food store for fresh and wholesome bread is impossible for you to make on a regular basis, then buy several breads at once and freeze them. Also stock up on whatever other breads your family enjoys for breakfast or lunch like English muffins or cornbread for example.

MULTI-GRAIN, WHOLE-WHEAT OR RYE BREAD: 1 or 2 loaves (1 to 1½ pounds)

If you absolutely cannot find a fresh whole-grain bread, then buy a loaf of one of the packaged and sliced varieties put out by Pepperidge Farm ("sprouted wheat" is a good one, for example).

FRENCH, ITALIAN, OR SOURDOUGH: 1 loaf (about 8 to 12 ounces)

When we want to eat white bread, my husband and I prefer American sourdough or French bread. However, we always have on hand a loaf of sliced, packaged white bread because the mainstay of my daughter's lunch is a peanut butter sandwich and she prefers this type of bread.

PITA: 1 package (6 small; 12 ounces) white or whole wheat

I like pita in winter to use as the base for individual quick pizzas and in summer to stuff with salads, for you can get so much more into them than between two slices of bread.

TORTILLAS: 1 package either corn (12; 10 ounces) or flour (10; 12½ ounces)

Tortillas are usually located in the refrigerator section of the supermarket. They are wonderful for repackaging leftovers to turn them into a different kind of meal.

I store my tortillas in the freezer wrapped in packets of six.

Because frozen tortillas tend to dry out and break when you roll them around the filling, it is best to heat them to soften, rather than just letting them sit out.

TACO SHELLS: 1 box (12 tacos; 4½ ounces)

I use tacos to add crunch to soups but also to recycle leftovers the way I use tortillas. To add variety to my meals, I alternate between the flour tortillas, corn tortillas, and tacos.

GOURMET AND ETHNIC STORES

If you can't find the ethnic goods listed in "Supermarket Ethnic Ingredients" then search for them in a gourmet or ethnic food market.

In addition to those ingredients, you can find some other special ones, none of which are essential to your pantry but will definitely make your weekly meals more exciting and varied.

DRIED MUSHROOMS (*Italian porcini or French cèpes): 1 package (½ to 1 ounce)*

Porcini and cèpes are the best tasting of all the dried mushrooms. They're intensely aromatic with an earthy and robust flavor and well worth the expense because just a touch elevates the most humble of sauces, soups, or stews.

TUNA: *2 to 3 cans (4 ounces each)*

Tuna packed in olive oil and imported from Italy or France bears little resemblance to American canned tuna and is a real treat. It is gentle and sweet tasting, moist and delicious — a wonderful addition to pasta and salads and great in sandwiches.

CHESTNUTS, WHOLE: *1 can (15 ounces), preferably roasted*

As much as I love fresh chestnut desserts, I never make them because there is too much work involved in peeling them. So when I hanker for the taste of chestnuts, I buy them canned and dress them up in some outrageous way.

CHAMPAGNE OR RASPBERRY VINEGAR: *1 bottle (8 ounces)*

Every now and then I stock up on a couple of herb or fruit-flavored vinegars to diversify my salad dressings as well as other recipes made with vinegar.

HEALTH FOOD STORE

In addition to a terrific selection of grains and legumes that are usually not available at the supermarket, health food stores stock delicious cold-pressed oils without preservatives, flavored vinegars, organically grown fresh fruits and vegetables, and fabulous whole-grain breads.

They also stock a wider variety of canned and jarred beans than the supermarket; for example, I have found adzuki and Great Northern white beans. The health conscious will find an array of sodium- and sugar-free foods like chicken broth, tomato and barbecue sauces, jams, applesauce, and canned fruit.

❧

GRAINS: You can buy grains in bulk at a health food store as well as find some exotic grains the supermarket doesn't stock. The advantage of buying unpackaged grain is that you can buy in small quantities, about ½ pound of each or 2 cups worth, and if you don't like it, you're not stuck with a huge quantity.

Store all grains if possible in the fridge. If you don't have room, then store them in a tightly covered jar in a cool pantry. Keep up to 4 months.

QUINOA: 1 package (12 to 14 ounces)

Quinoa is an ancient grain, which was the staple crop of the Inca civilization. It has been rediscovered and is now widely available. It is a highly nutritious grain and a significant source of protein; its texture is wonderfully crunchy. The whiter the grain, the better it is. Check the Index for a recipe.

MILLET: 1 package (12 to 15 ounces)

You may be familiar with millet only as bird seed. It is, however, an almost-perfect grain nutritionally. Millet has a rich earthy aroma and nutty flavor. See the Index for a basic recipe.

SOBA (buckwheat noodles): 1 package (8 to 16 ounces)

This buckwheat noodle is also available in Oriental food stores. I use soba mostly in soups and one-pot dishes rather than as a pasta because the noodles are gluten-free and tend to break apart after they are cooked.

BREADS: 1 to 2 whole-grain loaves (1 to 1½ pounds each; see page 38)

❧

ETHNIC AND EXOTIC SEASONINGS:
These specialty items are to be found only in a health food store. While they aren't essential, there's no reason not to try them. They keep indefinitely and having them around will give you a wider range of flavors and seasonings to choose from.

MISO PASTE: buy the smallest amount possible

This is a paste made from fermented soybeans and grains. If you like its salty flavor, use it as a spread on sandwiches or as a seasoning in dressings. It keeps indefinitely, in the refrigerator.

TAHINI: 1 can (15 ounces)

Tahini is a paste of crushed raw sesame seeds. It is the characteristic flavor of hummus, a Middle Eastern spread of chick-peas and garlic. It is mostly used in Middle Eastern cuisine, but I love to stir it into bean purées or spread it on bread as I would peanut butter.

Once opened, the can must be refrigerated or the tahini will turn rancid. If the oil from the seeds floats to the top, simply stir it back into the sesame paste to prevent the tahini from drying out.

PREPARED SESAME AND SEAWEED SEASONING: 1 jar or package (2 to 4 ounces)

This is a fantastic Japanese seasoning. It is a mixture of unhulled white or black sesame seeds flavored with salt only or with salted and dried sea vegetables. I flavor rice and other grain dishes with it, sprinkle it on sandwiches, or add it to soups and stews.

SPIRITS

I always keep a couple of bottles of red and white wine around with which to season a sauce, stew, or dessert.

Never cook with a wine that doesn't taste good enough to drink because when you cook with wine, you only evaporate the alcohol, you don't alter the flavor. The wine you cook with need not be expensive, it just has to taste decent.

WHITE WINE: 2 bottles

I use a dry white wine in cooked and uncooked dishes because it works with almost any ingredient and its neutral color makes it infinitely usable.

RED WINE: 2 bottles

I suppose you could get away with having only white wine in the house, but it's better to have both white and red. Red wine has a more robust flavor than white and is thus better in hearty meat and bean recipes.

COGNAC OR BRANDY: 1 bottle

For a change, substitute Cognac or brandy for wine in a sauce. These are also great to season fresh fruit mixtures.

PORT OR MADEIRA: 1 bottle

If you have a bottle of one or of the other, you'll have a wider range of flavors at your disposal. Madeira or port is what I use when I want a sweet spirited accent.

PANTRY ON THE RUN

Here are some ideas for food that is worth keeping in the house to snack on when you're so starved you can't wait until dinner or when you've eaten so early that you need a substantial nibble before retiring.

LIGHT SNACKING: The best snacks if you just want to nip an edge off your hunger are fruits and vegetables because they won't fill you up and displace your hunger for dinner. The ones I prefer to stock up on are fruits and vegetables that need a minimum of preparation before I can eat them.

Fruits especially cut the appetite without filling you up because of the fructose. Dried raisins, apricots, and prunes as well as fresh apples, pears, and bananas are perfect snacking fruits—they're ready to pop into your mouth without peeling or other preparation.

Raw vegetables like bell peppers, cherry tomatoes, fennel, celery, snow peas, and green beans are also terrific snack foods because they need only a quick rinse before you can eat them.

❀

PROTEIN-RICH FOR A HEFTY HUNGER: The problem with the following snacks is that they are so delicious you can all too easily make a meal out of them unwittingly.

Polly-O makes a fresh mozzarella cheese called "fior di latte," which is packed in water and sold in either 4, 6, or 27 rounds to a 9-ounce tub. These are terrific, really nutritious, protein-rich snacks.

Spoonfuls of cottage cheese or ricotta also will surely nip the edge off your hunger.

Nuts are another protein-rich snack but high in fat and so filling.

MONDAY-TO-FRIDAY SHOPPING LIST

SUPERMARKET

DRIED GOODS

PASTA

1 lb. elbow macaroni, penne, or fusilli
1 lb. orzo or acini pepe
1 lb. linguine fini, spaghetti, or fettuccine
1 lb. capellini

GRAINS

1 to 2 lb. long-grain white rice, preferably converted
1 lb. basmati or Texmati rice, brown or white
1 lb. short-grain brown rice (optional)
2 lb. yellow cornmeal
1 box (13 oz.) kasha (roasted buckwheat kernels)
Nice but not necessary:
1 box (6 oz.) Near East wheat pilaf
1 box (5¼ oz.) Near East tabouleh
1 box (10 oz.) Near East couscous
1 box (16 oz.) pearl barley

LEGUMES

1 lb. lentils
1 lb. split green peas

DRIED FRUITS

1 box (12 oz.) raisins
1 box (10 oz.) currants
1 box (12 ounces) apricots
1 box or can (10 or 8 ounces) pitted prunes

CANS AND JARS

LEGUMES

1 or 2 cans (16 to 19 oz. each) *each* black beans, red kidney beans, chick-peas, white cannelini beans
Nice but not necessary:
Small pink and small white beans

VEGETABLES

2 or 3 cans (14½ or 16 oz. each) peeled whole tomatoes
1 can (28 oz.) Italian plum or Redpack whole tomatoes packed in purée
2 or 3 cans (14½ oz. each) stewed tomatoes
2 cans (14½ ounces) Italian-style stewed tomatoes
1 tube (4½ oz.) tomato paste
1 jar (1 pound) pickled beets or 1 can (14 ounces) sliced beets

FRUITS

1 can (8 oz.) *each* apricots or peaches, pears, and crushed pineapple (packed in water, natural juices, or "lite" syrup)

SAUCES

2 jars (1 lb.) spaghetti sauce
1 jar (16 oz.) applesauce
1 or 2 jars (4 or 6 oz. each) baby fruit purée: apple, peach, or pear

BROTH AND JUICE

2 cans (14 ½ oz. each) chicken
broth, no or low salt
2 bottles (8 oz. each) clam juice
1 can (16 oz.) tomato juice

FISH

1 can (16 oz.) mackerel, packed
in water
2 cans (3½ oz. each) salmon,
bones in and packed in water
2 cans (7 oz. each) tuna, packed
in water

1 or 2 cans (3 to 4 oz.) smoked
mussels or clams
2 cans (3½ oz. each) sardines,
smoked or packed in water

FROZEN FOOD

VEGETABLES

1 package (10 oz.) *each* corn
kernels, french-cut string
beans, petite peas, lima beans,
chopped spinach, and artichoke hearts

FRUITS

1 package (12 oz.) unsweetened
strawberries, blueberries, or
raspberries
2 packages (10 oz. each) frozen
raspberries in "lite" syrup

FROZEN DESSERTS

2 pints ice cream, Tofutti, or frozen yogurt

SWEETENERS AND DESSERT FIXINGS

SWEETENERS

1 bag (5 lb.) granulated white
sugar
1 box (16 oz.) light or dark
brown sugar
1 box (16 oz.) confectioners' or
superfine sugar
1 jar (16 oz.) honey
1 can or jar (16 oz.) maple syrup
1 jar (12 oz.) red currant jelly
1 jar (12 oz.) jam or jelly
of your choice

DESSERT FIXINGS

1 bottle (2 oz.) vanilla extract
1 bottle (1 oz.) almond extract
2 cans (12 oz. each) evaporated,
low-fat or skim milk
1 package (8 oz.) Droste's cocoa
powder
1 can (4 oz.) walnuts
1 can (4 oz.) pecans
1 can (12 oz.) unsalted
peanuts

BAKED GOODS

2 packages (7 to 8 oz. each)
plain butter cookies or shortbread
1 package (7 to 8 oz.) plain
chocolate cookies
1 package (1 lb.) pound cake

OILS AND VINEGARS

OIL

1 bottle (32 oz.) vegetable oil
1 bottle (32 oz.) olive oil
1 jar (1 pint) reduced-calorie
(light), low-cholesterol, or
regular Hellmann's mayon-
naise

VINEGAR

1 bottle (12 oz.) red wine vinegar
1 bottle (12 oz.) balsamic vinegar
1 bottle (12 oz.) white wine vinegar
1 bottle (12 oz.) tarragon vinegar
1 bottle (12 oz.) rice vinegar (may be in Oriental food section)

CONDIMENTS

1 or 2 jars (4 oz.) pimientos, roasted red peppers, or sweet peppers
1 jar (12 oz.) jalapeño, or nacho peppers
1 jar (16 oz.) cured black olives
1 bottle (2 oz.) Tabasco sauce
1 bottle (5 oz.) Worcestershire sauce
1 bottle (14 oz.) ketchup
1 bottle (12 or 16 oz.) barbecue sauce
1 jar (5 oz.) prepared white horseradish
1 jar (8 oz.) Dijon mustard
1 bottle (8 oz.) *each* Real lemon and lime juice
1 jar (3 oz.) nonpareil capers
1 jar (16 oz.) kosher dill pickles

SPICES AND DRIED HERBS

1 box (26 oz.) iodized salt
Whole black peppercorns
Bay leaves, caraway seeds, cardamom, cayenne pepper, chili powder, Chinese five-spice powder, ground cinnamon, ground cumin, dried red pepper flakes, fennel seeds, garlic powder, ground ginger, dried lemon peel, dried mint, whole or ground nutmeg, dried orange peel, dried oregano, rosemary, tarragon, and thyme

SUPERMARKET ETHNIC INGREDIENTS

Mexican:
2 cans (4 oz. each) chopped green chilies
Japanese:
1 bottle (10 oz.) mirin (optional)
1 bottle (12 oz.) rice vinegar
1 bottle (5 oz.) Oriental sesame oil
1 bottle (5 oz.) soy sauce

Chinese:
1 jar (8 oz.) chili paste with garlic or with soybean
1 can (8 oz.) water chestnuts
1 bottle (8 oz.) hoisin sauce
Italian:
1 package (8 oz.) Arborio rice (optional)
1 jar (3 oz.) olive paste (olivada)
1 jar (4 oz.) pesto
1 jar (8 oz.) sun-dried tomatoes

FRESH GOODS

VEGETABLES AND FRUITS

1 to 2 pounds onions
1 head garlic
1 bunch scallions (green onions)
1 bunch carrots
1 bunch celery
2 or 3 bell peppers, preferably red
2 or 3 *each* lemons and limes

HERBS

1 bunch parsley, preferably Italian (flat-leaf)
1 bunch coriander
Nice but not necessary:
1 bunch dill
1 bunch basil

DAIRY

1 pint plain nonfat yogurt
½ or 1 pint low-fat cottage cheese
1 pint part-skim ricotta cheese
½ lb. Parmigiana-Reggiano or grated imported Parmesan cheese
1 dozen large eggs

MEAT, POULTRY, AND FISH

1 lb. ground beef in 4-oz. patties
1 lb. smoked ham, 95 or 96% fat free
1 lb. skinless, boneless chicken or turkey breasts or cutlets
1 lb. ground turkey (optional)
1 lb. fish (buy fresh and freeze)

BREAD (fresh and packaged)

1 to 2 loaves (1 to 1½ lb.) whole-grain
1 loaf (8 to 12 oz.) French, Italian, or sourdough bread
1 package (6 small; 12 oz.) white or whole-wheat pita bread

1 package (12; 10 oz.) corn or flour (10; 12½ oz.) tortillas
1 box (12; 4½ oz.) tacos

GOURMET AND ETHNIC STORES

1 package (1 oz.) dried porcini or cèpes (mushrooms)
2 to 3 cans (6½ or 7 oz.) tuna packed in olive oil
1 can (15 oz.) whole chestnuts
1 bottle (8 oz.) Champagne or raspberry vinegar

HEALTH FOOD STORE

GRAINS

1 package (12 to 14 oz.) quinoa
1 package (12 to 15 oz.) millet
1 package (8 to 16 oz.) soba (buckwheat noodles)

EXOTIC SEASONINGS

Miso paste, smallest amount possible
1 can (15 oz.) tahini
1 jar or package (2 to 4 oz.) prepared sesame and seaweed seasoning

SPIRITS

2 bottles dry white wine
2 bottles dry red wine
1 bottle Cognac or brandy
1 bottle port or Madeira

THE MONDAY-TO-FRIDAY KITCHEN

EQUIPMENT

Now that you've got your pantry set up, it's time to make sure you've got the right equipment as well. And by right equipment, I mean the pots and pans that will make the daily task of cooking easiest for you. This doesn't mean you must rush out and buy a whole new set of skillets and whisks. On the contrary, review my list, then decide whether you really need to add anything to what you already own.

In a nutshell, a couple of pots and skillets, a chopping board, and a sharp knife are all you need for Monday-to-Friday cooking. However, my list is slightly more extensive than that because it includes the key items which, for me, have simplified the task of daily cooking. Most people probably have most if not all the items I describe below. As with the pantry suggestions, this list reflects the size of my family, my tiny kitchen, and my particular style of cooking. Your essential equipment list will look a bit different, reflecting your own particular needs. To determine what equipment you should have, first think about what dishes you especially like to eat and cook most frequently. For example, if you rely on stews and soups to feed your family, then maybe it's time to buy that enamel-lined heavy-duty pot you've been yearning for, so that those dishes will be the best they can possibly be.

CHOPPING BOARD: This is first on my list because I prefer to do most of my dicing, slicing, and mincing with a sharp chef's knife on a chopping board. Chopping by hand has always been a tension-reliever for me, and it also involves less clean-up than the food processor. One large chopping board is enough, even though I own a small one as well. It should be made of durable hard plastic that is easy to keep clean and is dishwasher safe.

KNIVES: Although you can get away with owning only one high-quality sharp chef's knife, having two or three knives is better. I recommend a 4-inch paring knife, a 6-inch all-purpose utility knife, and a 10- to 12-inch (depending on how big your hand is) chef's knife. The best knives are made from carbon steel mixed with stainless steel.

FOOD PROCESSOR: If the time is right and the dish I'm making requires more chopping or grating than I'm prepared to do by hand, a food processor comes in very handy. In addition I own a mini-chopper, which is like a miniature food processor. Even though I wouldn't say this is essential, it does a much better job than the food processor in mincing small quantities of ginger, garlic, and fresh herbs. Because it is so small, it is easy to clean, which is why I find myself using it more often than I do the food processor.

BLENDER

If you don't own a food processor, a blender is almost as handy. It doesn't chop, but it does blend and liquefy, so you can mix salad dressings and purées. A blender, a chopping board, and a sharp knife is enough for Monday-to-Friday prep.

SAUCEPANS: Please remember that this list is meant only as a guide. In other words, I want you to have an idea of what it is I mean when I refer to a "small" or "large" pot. Never skip a recipe because you think you don't own the right equipment. When in doubt, use what you have!

The ideal saucepan is made of heavy stainless steel, with an aluminum- or copper-reinforced bottom. Stainless steel is the material of choice because it doesn't react with acidic ingredients as does iron and aluminum. The reinforced bottom is essential because stainless steel is a poor heat conductor and food burns.

Try to purchase saucepans with metal handles so that, if need be, you can stick the pans in the oven without worrying about the plastic handles melting.

You should have 3 or 4 saucepans, all with tight-fitting lids: a small one (1½ or 2 quart), a medium-size one (3 to 4 quart), and a large one (6 quart). If you have the room, invest in an 8-quart one that you could use for baking casseroles as well as for boiling pasta and cooking large batches of soups or stews. The enamel-lined cast-iron ones are great because you don't have to worry about any food reacting with the pot.

The number and the size of the saucepans you own depend on the size of your family and how much food you cook at one time. It is important that whatever you cook not be crowded in the pan so that the food will cook evenly. Nor should the

pan be too wide or the edges of the pan will burn as the food cooks.

SKILLETS: Lots of my recipes are one-pot meals or two-for-one dishes. That is, two parts of a dinner are cooked in a single skillet. Therefore the skillets I rely on are at least 10 to 12 inches wide and preferably 2 inches deep. They have sloping high sides so lots of food will fit. These skillets should also be made of heavy reinforced stainless steel with metal handles so that you can stick them into the oven. They should come with tight-fitting lids. If you have the room, I also recommend purchasing 9- and 7-inch skillets for sautéeing smaller quantities.

In order to reduce your fat intake, at least one of the large skillets should be coated with a nonstick material. It will make cleaning up a lot easier, too. Be sure that you choose a heavy nonstick skillet so that the food cooks evenly without burning.

The size of the specific skillets you

purchase should reflect the size of your household and how much food you cook at once. A single person will need smaller skillets than a person who cooks for a family of six.

Be sure to choose the right size skillet for the way you cook. It should be big enough to prevent the food from crowding, but not so large that the food will burn.

OVENPROOF CASSEROLES OR BAKING PANS: If your saucepans aren't ovenproof, you'll have to invest in a couple (4 and 6 quart) of casseroles. They should also be burner proof and have tight-fitting lids.

The best of these pans are made of heavy-gauge stainless steel and have reinforced bottoms or they are enameled-lined so you can cook any ingredient without discoloration or reaction. Earthenware, although attractive, has limited use because it can only be used in the oven.

I use a 13 × 9-inch aluminum baking pan for roasting meat, but any shallow ovenproof pan that is large enough will do. Glass ones can also be used in a microwave.

PRESSURE COOKER: In the winter when I crave the taste of long-simmering dishes but time is of the essence, I make them in my pressure cooker. Pot roasts, dried beans (without presoaking), and long-simmering soups can be assembled and cooked in the pressure cooker in less than an hour.

I recommend the T-Fal pressure cooker because it requires less water than other brands; you can braise with it and you won't have to resign yourself to all of your recipes having a decidedly "boiled" taste and texture.

A 6-quart pressure cooker is adequate. If you have the room to store it, an 8-quart cooker is better; it can double up as a pasta pot or you can use it when you cook recipes in double batches.

VARIOUS AND SUNDRIES: Have on hand 2 sets of measuring spoons, 1 set of dry measuring cups, and 2 liquid measuring cups: a 1-cup and a 2-cup capacity.

ORGANIZING THE EQUIPMENT IN THE KITCHEN

I f you're like me, equipment that's not within easy reach is equipment that doesn't get used. So, once you assess what you'll really need, organize your shelves so that it is all within easy reach. This bit of reorganizing will shave minutes off your food preparation time and definitely prevent the frustration that comes with not being able to find what you're looking for.

Whatever pots and skillet you use daily should be placed, however you can manage it, within easy reach so that they are readily accessible. People with especially small kitchens might even consider keeping their most often-used pot or skillet right on the range or even in the dish drainer.

Other essentials are an assortment of mixing bowls, wooden spoons, whisks, metal spatulas for turning foods, rubber spatulas for folding, ladles, slotted and serving spoons for mixing and serving, and tongs for taking meat out of the pan. You'll also need a colander and strainers of assorted sizes for draining.

To save on clean-up, it's handy to have a couple of capacious and good-looking serving bowls made of glass or ceramic that you can also use for the assembly and mixing of salads.

If you're a big meat eater or like the idea of making roasts to have leftovers to use later in the week, buy an instant-reading thermometer to make sure your finished roast is prepared to the correct degree of doneness. These instant thermometers are inserted in the roast and immediately removed to read the meat's internal temperature; these do not stay in the meat for the duration of roasting time. The best brand to buy is Taylor.

A small rotary or four-sided hand-held grater is good if you use lots of grated cheese.

Be sure to have a supply of freezer wrap on hand so that you can freeze a week's supply of meat and make the best use of leftovers.

SMALL EQUIPMENT CHECKLIST

A couple of other invaluable items that will make your life easier:

An erasable calendar (see page 58)

A nonpermanent, washable marker to go with it

A box of gallon-size and sandwich-size Ziploc bags for space-saving freezer bags.

MICROWAVE: In this book I mention the microwave only when I feel it does something better or more efficiently than a traditional technique does. I've discovered that time gained by cooking small quantities in a microwave is lost when dealing with larger quantities.

After endless cooking failures, I have arrived at a short list of uses for the microwave—to defrost, to reheat dinners a portion at a time, to melt chocolate, and to cook fresh artichokes.

For microwave cooking I use the ovenproof glassware I have on hand for baking. The most useful sizes for me are a 13 × 9-inch baking pan, and 9-, 10-, and 12-inch pie plates.

TOASTER OVEN: I prefer a toaster oven to an old-fashioned toaster because it is great for reheating individual portions or baking small quantities of food for 1 or 2 people.

ELECTRIC MIXER: Whether hand held or stationary, an electric mixer is essential if you do any kind of baking or if you ever whip up egg whites or heavy cream. People on cholesterol-free diets especially should think of getting an electric mixer because in many a dish whipped egg whites function as a terrific alternative to whole eggs.

ONE COOK'S DICE IS ANOTHER COOK'S MINCE

In keeping with the relaxed and casual attitude I have towards everyday cooking, here is my list of loosely defined cooking terms. The explanations here are just to clarify the meaning of the terms I use in the book. But keep in mind that when I call for an ingredient to be minced, chopped, diced, or sliced, it is not to drive you crazy nor to dictate to you but to add variety and interest to the texture and look of the dish. Bear in mind, too, that if you are in a great hurry and don't feel like slicing some red peppers after you've just finished chopping the onions, then don't! Throw the lot in the food processor if this is easier for you and you don't mind washing the machine.

You should also know that a minced ingredient cooks more quickly than if it were sliced or chopped. In a sauté or stir-fry for example, you want the ingredients to be quickly cooked; the extra time spent on preparation is saved in cooking. On the other hand, in long-simmering stews and soups, how the onions are chopped matters less.

I realize, too, that I am lucky because I own both a good food processor and a mini-chopper. You may not be in that position and so the fine distinctions of a chop or mince will just be cookbook lingo. All of that is fine with me, as long as it saves you time and energy.

BOIL: When a liquid moves around furiously, sending large bubbles of air up to the surface, it is at a boil.

CHOP: To cut food into uneven pieces about ½ inch in size. (Please don't stand there with a tape measure; this is just to give you an idea!) *Finely chop* means to cut food into uneven pieces about ¼ inch in size.

DEGLAZE: After sautéing or roasting, there are coagulated juices that have leaked out of the food and stuck to the pan. They are full of flavor and should not be discarded. To loosen them, add to the pan a liquid such as broth, wine, or water. Bring the liquid to a boil while scraping up these browned particles with a whisk. The particles will dissolve in the liquid. This is known as "deglazing" the pan.

If, however, you're not in the mood for deglazing a pan, be sure to add some tap water to it after you're finished sautéing, so that the skillet will be easier to wash up later.

DEVEIN: To cut a notch down the curved back of a peeled shrimp to expose the large green and black intestine and remove it. Get them to do this when you buy the shrimp if you can; it's worth paying a little extra.

DICE: To cut food into even squares, usually ⅛ to ¼ inch in size, unless otherwise indicated. I usually take the time to dice when I make a salad for dinner, for I like the texture and look it gives to the dish. Again, if this is too precise for you, then just chop the ingredients into rough pieces, any size you like.

FOLD: This term usually refers to folding beaten egg whites into a dense base. To do so, first lighten the base by adding some egg whites to it. With a rubber spatula, incorporate the egg whites into the base with a cutting and lifting motion. Do not use a stirring motion or you will deflate the whites. Then fold the remaining egg whites into the lightened base.

GRATE: To form thin strips or shreds of a vegetable or cheese by using the grating blade of a food processor. I think it is worth using the processor for this because you'll save so much time in preparing the vegetables and cooking them afterwards.

JULIENNE: To cut food into matchstick-size or slightly larger pieces. Again, I only use this technique when I have enough time and when the look of the dish is important to me.

MINCE: To chop food into such fine pieces that it is as close to a purée as possible without being puréed — especially good for the quick cooking of garlic and ginger in stir-fries and sautés. It is also a good idea for fresh herbs but is certainly not essential when doing a whole bunch.

POACH: To cook food gently while it is submerged in a liquid that is barely moving. Bubbles should only occasionally break the surface of the liquid. This process is used to cook fragile foods like fish so they do not fall apart.

MONDAY-TO-FRIDAY TIMING

When figuring out how long it takes to complete one of these recipes, I included all the preparation time as well as the cooking time.

The timing for the cooking itself starts after the liquid has come to a boil or a simmer. Again, this has been taken into account in the approximate time given it takes to make each dish.

SAUTE: To cook food in a little fat in an uncovered skillet over medium to high heat for a short period of time.

SHRED: To cut food into thin long strips, as in shreds of cabbage.

SIMMER: To cook food gently while submerged in a liquid in which bubbles gently break the surface. This cooking is slightly more active than poaching but is still way under the boiling point.

STIR-FRY: To cook food in a little fat in an uncovered skillet or wok over high heat while moving the food around constantly.

WHIP: To beat air into food, as in whipping egg whites.

WHISK: To stir ingredients together with a wire whip in order to blend them thoroughly. (A fork makes a better substitute for a whisk than does a spoon.)

MONDAY-TO-FRIDAY CLEAN-UP

When I asked my friend Barbara for any tips she might want to share with me on how to make dinner clean-up easier, she answered "Yeah, my husband Art does it all." Not a bad idea, I thought, to get someone else in the household to do all the clean-up, especially if you've done all the cooking. Still somebody is going to be doing the washing up after dinner—it might as well be as easy as possible.

TYPES OF DISHES AND COOKING: If you choose to cook complicated dishes that involve lots of preparation and precooking, you're going to end up with lots of pots and pans to clean up as well. In planning your menus, choose meals that don't require the use of more than a couple

of pots, skillets, or baking pans and keep the cooking techniques simple.

For example, if you make a hearty soup or one-pot meal, you can afford to use another pan or pot for dessert. If you make a meat dish in one skillet, then make a two-for-one side dish in another so that you don't end up with three pans to clean.

During the week I think it always makes sense to rely on the most simple of culinary techniques and on ones, like sautéing, steaming, or stewing, which in and of themselves are relatively clean. Broiling and frying are a couple of techniques I have nearly completely eliminated from my repertoire, even on weekends, because they are extremely messy no matter how much care I take in executing them.

Whenever I spot a step in a recipe I know is mostly for the aesthetics of the dish, I skip it to save time. Peeling tomatoes, broccoli, and asparagus, for example, creates more clean-up than the difference in the eating makes it worth.

ONE VESSEL, TWO PURPOSES: If you cook two or three parts of your meal in a single pot, like in a soup, skillet supper, or one-pot stew, you'll save on pot washing. But you can also save some elbow grease if you remember to mix ingredients together in the same pan you bake them in, or if you get in the habit of mixing a salad dressing first in the bottom of the salad bowl and then add the salad ingredients.

Other tips of this sort are to store leftovers in the same pot or bowl you'll use to reheat or serve them. If you have room in your freezer, store leftover stews or soups in casseroles or pots that you will later reheat them in.

Instead of overcooking vegetables separately and then assembling them later in your pot, cook them one after another in sequence in the same pot, adding the longest-cooking vegetables first and the shortest-cooking vegetables last.

When you use canned tomatoes, add them whole to the pot and break them up against the side with a wooden spoon.

When you need to set some cooked food aside, for example, sautéed meat, so that you can make the sauce in the skillet, set that food on one of the dinner plates. Any drips on the plate can be wiped off before the final dinner is dished out.

GIVE UP ON GADGETS: You'll find that keeping the use of gadgets to a minimum will alleviate quantities of small parts and odd shapes to be washed. Even though I use my food processor when I have a lot of chopping to do, for almost all of my everyday cooking I use a chopping board and sharp chef's knife so that clean-up is a little simpler.

CLEAN AS YOU GO, THEN SOAK: Dividing the clean-up part of dinner into three small chunks of time is psychologically easier on me because it makes the whole mess seem less burdensome.

First I always "clean as I go"—that is wash up the small number of preparation utensils I've used before dinner is served. Sometimes before dinner I even have the time to soak a pot or pan. And because the dinners I make are so simple, this part of clean-up is minimal.

The second phase is after-dinner clean-up of plates and cutlery, but because there are only three of us and dinner is no more than two courses, this part is also quickly done.

The third phase could be the most burdensome—the scrubbing of pots and pans—but we avoid that mess by soaking them for two hours at least, sometimes overnight. Soaking skillets and pots reduces the time and effort it takes to scour them by at least half. Sometimes I wash out the pans right before I go to bed; other times I do them the following morning before work or even the following day when I come home from work.

MISCELLANEOUS TIPS: One of the easiest solutions to the problem of clean-up would be to rely on disposable baking pans, dishes, and utensils. However, this is ecologically irresponsible as well as expensive.

The one disposable item I do make use of is the makeshift roasting rack I fashion out of foil. However, in order to make this item ecologically sound, I only use foil that has already been used once.

Before you get down to the business of sudsing and washing, with a rubber spatula, first scrape particles of congealed food off of cutting boards and utensils, skillets, pots, and pans and dinner dishes. This will make the work of washing up a lot easier as well as keep your drain from getting clogged with stray bits of food.

Nonstick skillets and pans make fish-dinner clean-up an easy job.

THE EFFICIENT COOK

Finally, here are some tips that will save you time and help you get the most out of your culinary efforts.
- The smaller the cut or dice of an ingredient, the faster it cooks.
- To save time, you don't have to thaw frozen vegetables, like corn, peas, lima beans, and artichoke hearts, before adding them to soupy dinners like one-pot meals.

- Use high heat to make the process of sautéing or stir-frying a lot faster and efficient. Using high heat is an efficiency trick I learned working in restaurants where everything and every dish is hurried. I make sure the skillet and oil are very hot before I begin to sauté. When I am using a thick and heavy skillet like a cast-iron pan, I heat the pan dry over high heat for a few seconds to speed up the process even more. Then I add the oil, heat it for a few seconds until it is very hot, and begin the cooking procedure. Ingredients "take" to the pan and cook very quickly, saving time.

■ When you are in a super hurry, buy precut vegetables—usually carrots, celery, and peppers come this way. When you get home you just have to give these vegetables a few more whacks with your knife to get them ready for cooking. But precut vegetables are expensive and not that fresh, so save this tip for out-of-the-ordinary circumstances.

■ If you know on Tuesday night (you have your calendar tacked onto your refrigerator) that Wednesday night you won't have much time to prepare a meal, then wash, chop, dice, and mince extra of whatever ingredients you're getting ready for Tuesday's meal and refrigerate the extras in plastic bags. This works for meats and poultry and all vegetables, except for onions which tend to taste acrid and bitter when cut and left standing. Store extra minced garlic in olive oil so that it doesn't dry out.

■ Don't buy precut meat, poultry, or vegetables more than a day in advance because all food loses nutritional value once it's cut and spoils faster than when left whole.

■ Whenever you can (even with recipes not from this book), try to use whole packages of frozen vegetables and whole cans of tomatoes, so that you don't have odd bits and pieces of ingredients that eventually go to waste. For example, if a recipe (from another cookbook) calls for 1 cup frozen corn kernels, use the whole pack instead and either omit something else from the recipe or content yourself with more volume in the dish.

■ Cook in oil instead of butter or other animal fats, not only because it is healthier but also because oil doesn't congeal when at room temperature or chilled. Leftovers that were cooked in oil don't have to be reheated or recooked unless you want them to be; they can be eaten at room temperature or added to a salad.

■ Omit steps in recipes (in other cookbooks) that have you doing extra work just to make a dish look good. You'll notice that although I use lots of fresh herbs, they're always integral to the flavor of the recipe. I would never go to the trouble of mincing something just to garnish a dish (except when company is coming).

■ If how a dish looks is also important to you, then choose vividly colored vegetables with which to season your recipes and accompany main courses.

■ Although my recipes are riddled with fresh tomatoes, nary a one has been peeled before chopping. Whenever I think the texture of tomato peel would be unpleasant in a recipe, I use canned peeled tomatoes instead of fresh.

MONDAY-TO-FRIDAY STRATEGIES

COOKING FOR A NEW REALITY

Before I lay out my strategy suggestions for making weekday meals as effortless as possible, here's a word or two to explain how I came to develop my Monday-to-Friday recipes. These dishes add up to an everyday healthy cuisine that reflects the changing American food scene as much as it expresses my personal food philosophy.

In 1977 I was corporate chef at *The Institutional Investor* magazine, and the publisher had invited to lunch Rosser Reeves, dean of advertising. I was to "knock the socks off of him." Now, throughout my career as a professional chef, I've been faced with many challenges, but only twice was I given this type of nerve-racking assignment, which is simply to create an impressive, unforgettable meal for an important guest. How does one impress a man accustomed to eating at the best French restaurants? Well, in those days nouvelle cuisine was just coming into vogue and what impressed was a cuisine that combined French haute cuisine techniques with unusual ethnic ingredients.

I started the menu with a tomato and basil sorbet, followed it with a sauté of duck breast accompanied by a sauce of reduced duck stock seasoned with hoisin and star anise and finished with butter, and the dessert was a three-meringue extravaganza layered with different buttercreams.

Those were the years when home cooks spent hours in the kitchen. They had learned about good taste from Julia Child and were busily replicating pâtés en croûte, croissants, and the most complex of sauces. And as these culinary feats could only be executed with extraordinarily time-consuming techniques, this type of cuisine became weekend entertainment, a sort of cooking hobby that eventually was shelved because it was rich, time-consuming, and couldn't translate into everyday fare.

In October of 1988, again I was corporate chef, this time in a real estate firm. The chairman of the board had invited Dr. Dean Ornish, a renowned physician from California whose studies were beginning to show how dietary and lifestyle changes could stop and even reverse the effects of hardening of the arteries. My assignment was to impress him with a creative, memorable cholesterol- and fat-free meal.

For this lunch, I served a warm seviche of scallops marinated in fresh lime juice and flavored with coriander. A dish of pasta was combined with shiitake mushrooms and chickpeas and simmered in a sauce made from roasted peppers. A green salad was served with a dressing of sun-dried tomatoes, and dessert was a beautiful platter of poached pears in a caramelized sauce.

In the 1990s, as this most recent lunch reflects, Americans crave a cuisine that will give voice and direction to their growing health and dietary concerns as well as accommodate their frantic lives and complicated work and family needs. These harried schedules lead to poor eating habits —grabbing the wrong food on the run or ordering take-out food like fried chicken that is too fatty. Hence the need for a healthier new system that will replace the old one and yet still fit our frantic pace.

The dishes I cook in the corporate kitchen at work are virtually fat and cholesterol free, but the ones I prepare at home aren't as pure. That is because my work cooking is severe and ascetic, whereas my home cooking is moderate and healthy enough to balance my weekend forays into restaurant sampling and more calorie-laden indulgences.

I feel so bombarded and confused by the volume of contradictory nutritional information that proliferates on newspaper food pages that I have lost track of what it is exactly that I should and should not be eating. To make sense of this morass of do's and don'ts I reduced all of these dietary guidelines to a couple of simple precepts I know I can remember.

■ I've cut down on fats, vegetable as well as animal.

■ I eat less meat—smaller portions and less frequently.

■ I've increased my consumption of vegetables, fruits, and especially complex carbohydrates (grains and legumes).

If you keep these three principles in mind, you'll be well on your way to establishing a reasonable and healthy Monday-to-Friday diet that isn't too harsh to stick to during the week.

Cutting down on fats: The single most important principle to remember in establishing a healthy everyday diet is to cut down on fats, even if you are not trying to lose weight. Cutting down on fats includes all types of fats—vegetable as well as animal—and that means reducing the amount of fat you cook

with as well as how much fat you consume. For cholesterol cutting, you should also be watchful of the types of fat you eat and try to switch from those that are saturated, like tropical oils, butter, and lard, to ones that are monosaturated or polyunsaturated like canola, olive, and other vegetable oils.

To help reduce our daily intake of fat, I limit the oil I use in cooking to 1 to 2 tablespoons for every 4 portions. Of course, how much of that I use depends on the cooking technique and the ingredients.

You will notice, though, that I am not a fanatic about this issue, and most of my recipes, especially the sautés, require some type of fat. This is because, as professional chefs are fond of saying, "flavor is born in fat," which simply means that the taste of an ingredient is released in fat not in liquid. If you have ever tried to sauté onions in a nonstick skillet without the aid of even a smidgeon of oil, you'll have noticed that the flavor of the onions, even after they've wilted,

is raw and bitter, which it wouldn't be had the onions been first cooked in a bit of fat.

I've managed to come up with a way of sautéing that is a hybrid of traditional sautéing and complete nonfat cooking. The technique uses just enough fat to release the flavor but not so much that the dish is unhealthy.

For example, generally when I sauté onions, I cook them in about a tablespoon of oil over high heat until they begin to pick up some golden color and stick to the bottom of the pan. This means that the sugars in the onions are caramelizing and they are taking on a lovely flavor; they'll also emit a terrific aroma. When they begin to stick to the bottom of the pan, I add a tablespoon of water, wine, or chicken broth to loosen them from the pan and to make sure they don't burn. I continue to sauté them this way over fairly high heat until the onions are wilted, soft, and aromatic.

Cutting down on meat: American guidelines on nutrition urge us to limit our daily intake of meat and poultry to about 4 ounces a day. If you have no concept of how little this really is, then buy a scale, weigh 4 ounces of meat, and you'll see. For people used to a meat-centered diet, such a small portion will look awfully pathetic. To make that tiny-looking portion appear more ample, cook the meat, cut it into wafer-thin slices, and fan the slices across the plate to spread them out.

Switching from animal to vegetable proteins: Every day we learn that a healthy diet should include more vegetarian than animal protein because it is higher in fiber, minerals, and vitamins and lower in fat and cholesterol. This is easier said than done, especially in a culture such as ours which favors meat as the primary source of protein.

First of all, what are vegetarian proteins? They are ones that come from plant foods like grains (wheat, rice, corn) and legumes (dried beans, lentils, split peas). The problem with most of these proteins, except for exotic quinoa, is that in and of themselves they lack some essential amino acids that would make them complete proteins.

This sounds complicated, but it really isn't. What this means to the diner and the cook is that grains and legumes need to be eaten either with each other so that the amino acids in one complements the other, as in a rice and bean dish, or the vegetarian proteins can be eaten separately if they are accompanied by a complete protein, for example, a peanut butter sandwich (legume) accompanied by a glass of milk (complete animal protein).

To get into this healthier habit, first try a transitional phase where you substitute, once or twice a week, a complex carbohydrate vegetarian protein for an animal one. This could be a black bean soup into which you stir a spoonful of nonfat yogurt and serve with corn bread, or it could be a rice and vegetable jambalaya accompanied by a glass of low-fat milk.

Another way to ease into this way of eating is, in one-pot meals and main-course soups, to substitute ¼ cup cooked beans, lentils, or grains for a couple of ounces of meat, poultry, or fish. Gradually increase the amount of beans and grains and reduce the animal protein.

SPECIAL TOUCHES

■ *To make these new vegetarian proteins more appealing, season them with a healthy dose of chopped herbs or with your family's favorite spicing.*

■ *You will notice that when you cut out the fat, you often cut out the flavor. To compensate, use spices and fresh herbs with abandon and freely add touches of fresh citrus or vinegar for tang.*

■ *Although the best way to cut down on meat is to offer meatless dishes that are so good that meat isn't missed, die-hard meat lovers might balk and need a transition period to make the shift less traumatic. First you could switch from high-fat meats like beef and lamb to leaner ones like veal and poultry. Then, after that change takes place, serve one meatless meal a week, gradually increasing the number of days a week that are vegetarian.*

■ *Another tip to keep in mind when 4-ounce portions of meat seem skimpy is to make the side dishes ample and beautiful.*

■ *Add small touches of good-tasting fat, butter, grated cheese, or sour cream at the end of cooking time, as you would a seasoning. Adding these at the last moment introduces their flavor without saturating the dish with unnecessary calories and fat.*

■ *When fighting weight gain as well as cholesterol, use only nonstick skillets which require less fat for you to use them.*

STRATEGIC PLANNING

Armed with a full pantry, a kitchen equipped with accessible tools, and a book of Monday-to-Friday recipes, now what? A variety of dining strategies that can solve your dinner needs on a regular basis, that's what. And they begin with the five basic planning steps.

THE FIVE PLANNING STEPS

For most of us, cooking during the week is a frantic last-minute affair. We often think about dinner after coming home from work and dinner is then pulled together haphazardly with whatever is on hand. Suggestions and recipes for making those hurried "quick" dinners are found in cookbooks galore. However, coming up with a dinner night after night, week after week, that is both easy and satisfying can't always be done at the last minute and is best when planned. Rest assured that the bit of time you spend planning, shopping, and cooking ahead over the weekend or the start of the week will save you both time and effort later in the week.

1. The weekly calendar: Planning menus doesn't have to be as intimidating as scheduling a White House dinner. For most of us a week's menus simply means planning dinners for the family with few special situations—entertaining business associates, parties, potluck suppers, or other commitments—to worry about. Good planning ensures you'll have enough ingredients in the house with which to make supper and reduce the number of shopping expeditions to the supermarket.

Several years ago at Christmas I received what proved to be one of the most useful presents ever: an erasable monthly calendar. I tacked it on the refrigerator and it has been there ever since along with a nonpermanent marker. At the beginning of each month I write on the calendar obvious upcoming commitments and events that affect our lives. After that I write in each new commitment or schedule change as it comes up. On the weekends before I do my shopping, I then glance at the calendar, think about the types of meals I'm going to have to cook, then plan my shopping list accordingly.

If you can't find a monthly erasable calendar, then buy a sheet of erasable plastic (the kind you can write on with washable ink) on which you draw in either a weekly or monthly calendar. Or, if you have a computer, type out a calendar, save it on a disk, and print it out each week or month.

2. Matching meals to schedules:
Matching meals simply means that the dinners you plan should mesh with everyone's schedule. Any effort made at the planning stage is effort saved later in the week.

Let's say you take a look at your calendar and notice that on Monday everyone in the family has late-afternoon commitments and no one will be home until 8 or 9, but you're also unsure if they'll want dinner that late or will have eaten already. Tuesday you're home for dinner with the kids, but your partner won't be home until after a business meeting at some unknown hour. Wednesday night you and your kids are eating out, but your partner will be home early and on his own. Thursday night is family night and shaping up normally, but Friday the teenagers are out for the evening and you and your spouse will just want to recuperate from the hassles of the week.

Well, if you know that everyone including the chief cook will be home late on Monday, but you're not sure who will be eating, then maybe Sunday night is the time to prepare a soup that could be reheated on Monday. Another alternative would be to roast some meat or poultry for Sunday supper and to stock up on fresh vegetables so that you could turn Sunday night's cold roast into a main-course salad. Another solution would be to assemble a main-course salad on Sunday so that on Monday everyone can help themselves whenever they get home

Tuesday is easy because the schedule allows the cook time to pre-

THE MICROWAVE SOLUTION

*F*or those of you who own a microwave, heating stews and soups by the portion in a microwave is a wonderful solution to the problem of diners who come in at odd hours, after dinner has been made.

A single serving of dinner can be reheated in the microwave in just a fraction of the time it takes to reheat an entire potful of something. Also when you heat a potful of soup or stew over and over again, you risk scorching the bottom and reducing it to a thickness you won't like. Microwaving the portions of food keeps the texture and flavor of the dish intact.

pare a meal. The meal might be a stir-fry for which the raw ingredients can be prepared in advance and cooked to order if you like, or just cooked in advance and served at room temperature.

That same stir-fry can then be dressed up in a salad for Wednesday night so that it will taste different and no one will resent eating the same dish two days in a row. Thursday is another easy night because there's enough time to cook a meal and it looks as if the family will be gathered together at the same time. Thursday, though, could also be the night to use up all the leftovers, since the following night, Friday, is the end of the workweek and ideal for take-out food. And, of course, if on Friday take-out food seems too boring, on your way home from work you could pick up some fresh ingredients that can be sautéed for a fast and easy supper.

3. Divvy up tasks: Now is the time to think about what in your household needs doing every week and who can help with these tasks. If at all possible, enlist the help (even minimally) of other members of the household. My eight-year old daughter sets and clears the table at dinner-

time; my husband does a part of the weekday shopping. Although the time I save is minor, the feeling of relief is major. Here are some divvying-up ideas. Keep in mind that if your kids are home alone, after school, in addition to watching TV, they can perform some very simple tasks that will make life for the cook just a tad easier.

In general, the more a person likes doing an activity the more he or she will stay with it. I hate "wet" work but enjoy straightening up, so I stay away from washing dishes, but always put them away. If everyone in your family prefers certain tasks to others, try rotating chores so no one always gets stuck with the hated one. If possible, take turns cleaning up, planning the meals, or shopping.

If you expect your children to take some responsibility for the preparation of dinner, without your supervision, be sure you make them a list of what tasks they're expected to do and by what time they should be done doing them. Be sure that none of the tasks you assign involve any risk to

their well-being. Don't ask a child to preheat the oven, to cook something, or do any chopping, unless he or she is really old and competent enough to accomplish these tasks.

Other tasks young and older children can perform without difficulty are:
- Taking frozen items out of the freezer to defrost; lining up the pots or pans you'll need later; measuring out ingredients needed to make dinner.
- They can also assemble ingredients needed for a blender sauce right in the blender and keep them in the refrigerator until you get home.
- They can scrub potatoes and other vegetables; place meat in a roasting pan; do simple salad dressings; or fill up a pot full of water to boil for pasta and set it, off the heat, on the stove.
- They can help you get a head start by plumping up grains like bulgur and couscous so they're ready to be cooked the minute you walk in the door.

■ They can break off parsley or watercress or strawberry stems; snap off the ends of asparagus; rinse off fresh fruits; and crumble up cookies for desserts.

Basically you can always enlist the help of children for doing simple and very kitchen safe tasks, and the more they like the dish you're going to cook, the happier they'll be to help.

Even young children can help with setting and clearing the table, taking out the garbage, or drying the dishes. Small children love to feel grown up and enjoy participating in simple food preparation like peeling carrots.

Picky eaters can be urged to make their own alternative supper (a sandwich or cereal even) on nights when what you've cooked is not to their liking.

And everyone should take responsibility for the shopping list. Whoever eats the last can of tuna has to add it to the list.

4. The shopping list and filling in the pantry: Thinking about what to make for dinner every night wouldn't be nearly so dreary if it didn't also involve the prospect of endless trips to the supermarket. Who, at the end of a workday, wants to spend half an hour getting in and out of the grocery store before they can even begin to cook?

On Saturday or Sunday after you know how your week is shaping up, figure out what you are going to cook (see Sources of Inspiration on page 69). Take a look at the recipes and make a detailed shopping list. The more you plan this phase and the more detailed the list you write, the less likely you'll find yourself standing in the supermarket express line in the middle of the week. And while you're making your weekly shopping list, don't forget to check your pantry to see what needs to be restocked.

While we're on the topic of shopping lists, for those of you with a computer, it's handy to type up a list of items you always have in the house and which you usually use within a week (this could include some things on your pantry list as well). Save the list on a disk and print it out weekly.

You can tack it up on your refrigerator and just make a check next to the item when you need to replace it. At the bottom of this list jot down additional items you need that particular week.

If all of this is too complicated, then just make sure you have a piece of paper in the kitchen for jotting down the items you will need to replace at the end of the week. If you don't write them down the moment you run out of them, you'll probably forget about them when the time comes to make your shopping list.

5. Sunday Start-Up Cooking: Sunday start-up cooking is a wonderful way to get part of your weekday meals done in advance. It can be no more complicated than cooking a double batch of Sunday (or Saturday night) supper and using the leftovers during the week.

If you have the time, especially on cold dreary winter weekends, and you like to cook, Sunday start-up can also include a separate dish or two specifically made for later in the week. When I was a kid, I hated when the answer to "What's for dinner?" was "leftovers." Now that I have a family of my own, knowing that there are leftovers waiting in the refrigerator makes my day. Of course, I make sure leftovers are as exciting to the rest of the family as they are a relief for me.

Gradually, as you learn to recycle leftovers in imaginative ways, you'll get into the habit of cooking larger amounts of whatever it is you are making just to have the leftovers for a new dinner the following night.

Many recipes in this book include ideas for making use of those specific leftovers, but here are some more general notions so that you can learn to improvise and become a thrifty, clever cook.

❦

THE ART OF RECYCLING AND REPACKAGING

Eating leftovers served again in their original form is not unlike wearing the same outfit to work two days in a row—it's unimaginative and dull. What is needed is the same goods cleverly disguised in a new package.

Repackaging leftovers need not be complicated or involve a lot of work on your part. It can be as simple as adding a single new ingredient to the original dish, changing its texture, presenting it in a new package (like in tacos or phyllo dough), or

serving it at a different temperature.

The more simply the food has been cooked, the easier it will be to recycle it, to find it a new identity, and to camouflage its original incarnation.

RESTAURANT LEFTOVERS

Always take home any substantial remains from a restaurant dinner. Chinese, Mexican, and Indian food is the easiest kind to recycle. Many dishes can be reheated and bits of leftovers can be stirred into a freshly made bowl of rice, pasta, or grains.

Leftover restaurant meats can be recycled as you would a homemade roast. Fish remains are the only kind I leave on my plate because fish spoils readily and travels neither well nor far.

SPECIFIC IDEAS FOR SPECIFIC LEFTOVERS

Soups, stews, and other "mixed-up" dishes can change in flavor by thinning the leftovers with a liquid different from the original liquid—

like clam juice instead of tomato juice, for example. Or the dish can be bolstered by the addition of one fresh ingredient and a new herb, or it can be puréed so that its texture is transformed from a chunky soup into a smooth one.

Casseroles like rice pilafs or baked bean dishes on can be thinned with liquid, have an additional ingredient tossed in, and served as a hot soup the second day.

Stir-fries are a snap to recycle: They can be stir-fried a second time along with a new ingredient for variety; dolled up with mayonnaise or vinaigrette and eaten chilled or at room temperature, or minced, thinned with a sauce, and tossed over a bowl of pasta, lentils, or grains.

Poultry, veal, pork, and fish—the leaner flesh—are best not reheated so that they don't dry out. Small amounts of leftovers can be chopped and reheated in juicy soups, stews, or pasta dishes where the dry texture won't be noticed. Leftovers from these meats are also terrific tossed in salads, used as sandwich stuffers, or minced in a tortilla, taco, or phyllo dough filling.

Be sure to use any leftover seafood within a day.

Red meats like beef and lamb, especially when cooked plain, are a bit easier to reheat because they are fattier and thus juicier. Reheating doesn't dry them out as much as it does the leaner meats. They can be chunked and reheated in soups, stews, casseroles, and stir-fried dishes. They can be used in salads and sandwiches—both hot and cold—or minced into taco, tortilla, or omelet fillings.

Plain boiled pasta can be reheated in just about anything and alongside just about everything. Pasta is good reheated or served cold. The only way I won't reheat pasta is to stir-fry it because it hardens.

GOOD TO THE LAST DROP

*S*midgeons of anything should always be saved and recycled. Leftover shreds of cheese, spoonfuls of plain yogurt, or traces of ratatouille can be used in fillings for tacos, phyllo dough, tortillas, and omelets or even in sandwiches, salads, and dressings.

Don't even throw out that last bit of pesto, olive paste, or chutney. Instead add some oil and vinegar or lemon juice right to the bottle, shake the ingredients together, and you've created an original dressing at the same time you've almost eliminated the job of washing out the jar.

Leftover salad dressing can be used to marinate boneless, skinless chicken breasts or fish overnight. Whereas I would never go to the trouble of making a marinade, I use leftover bits of dressing in this way; it does give more flavor to baked fish and chicken.

Single ingredients—meats, fish, grains, legumes, and vegetables cooked alone and plainly—are ideal leftovers. Because they are cooked singly and plainly, that is not in the company of other ingredients nor with many seasonings, they can be added as is to soups, pasta dishes, one-pot meals, sandwiches, and salads and can even be recycled more than once.

For example, a side dish of plainly steamed carrots or simmered black beans can be reused the following night as one of many ingredients in a hearty soup and, if there is still more left, can be added to a cold salad on the third night.

Dressed greens and salads look wrinkled the second day, but don't throw any of it out. Dressed salads taste good even if they don't look good. Camouflage their appearance, while you make the most of their flavor, by stuffing them into pita bread sandwiches or by burying them in chunky, brightly colored main-course salads.

❧

PLANNING FOR THE WEEK AHEAD

Not all Monday-to-Fridays are the same. On winter weekends you might enjoy spending some time in the kitchen cooking a hefty three-course supper that will yield the makings of a couple of more dinners later in the week. Summer Sundays, though, are more likely to be spent outdoors, leaving you little or no time in the kitchen. Some weeks you can anticipate everyone's schedule; other weeks you'll have to deal with the unexpected.

In this section you'll find a strategy for whatever comes your way.

THE IDEAL WEEK INCLUDING A SUNDAY START-UP

In the best of all possible worlds, this is how you would proceed to ensure an easygoing Monday-to-Friday week filled with good meals.

First, during the weekend you would go over the family's commitments and plans for the week to come. Since this week is ideal, you know when family members will be coming home to dinner, and you can

count on them sticking to their schedules. You also know when you'll be going out and when you'll be staying in and who will be doing the cooking.

Figuring out the week's meals comes next (see Sources of Inspiration on page 69 for help) and what advance cooking you can do over the weekend. You'd make your shopping list, which would include items you needed to restock your pantry, and get your shopping done. At this point it is also a good idea to note on your calendar what fresh ingredients you need to pick up during the week. For example, if you intend to cook swordfish on Wednesday, jot down on your calendar that on the way home on Wednesday you must pick up some fresh fish. If you don't make note of it at the time you plan your menus, you might forget it later.

Once your shopping is done, prepare whatever ingredients you can. If you know that on Tuesday you are going to serve a main-course soup (based on Sunday night's supper) with chunks of fresh chicken, you could get the cutting of the poultry done right after you buy the chicken. The chicken can then be frozen and cooked right in the soup without thawing it first.

And finally you'd do some start-up cooking on Sunday, which is nothing more than making clever use of Sunday's supper. Sunday start-ups at our house, especially on cold winter weekends, usually consist of my making a hefty Sunday supper from which I get lots of goodies done for the week to come. I might start out with a soup of some sort as a first course. I make enough so that in the middle of the week I can revise that soup with fresh ingredients and serve it as a main course.

After my Sunday soup, I might serve one of the two chickens I roasted with baked or steamed vegetables. With the other bird, I can make a salad, a stuffing for omelets, or a stir-fry along with some fresh vegetables on Monday or Tuesday night.

I also make a double batch of a vegetable dish or bake some extra potatoes, again to use in later in the week.

Spending extra time and thought on my Sunday meal yields the makings of at least two weekday dinners. With this accomplished, cooking for the rest of the week seems almost done and the prospect of cooking once or twice at the end of the week seems less onerous than if I had to start from scratch every night. On the weeknight or two for which I have not cooked in advance, I make a change-of-pace dinner. On those nights, I usually make a quick sauté of fish or meat or make a meal of an omelet followed by some wonderful dessert.

THE IDEAL WEEK WITH NO SUNDAY START-UP

In this type of week, more typical of hot summer months, you may not want to spend any time cooking over the weekend, but you still want to ensure a pretty easy workweek to follow.

Since this plan is also for an ideal week, I have assumed that the pantry is full and you've had time, even if it

is Sunday evening, to go over your calendar for the week and think about your meals to come. In this type of week, you've also done your shopping. What is different is that you've had no time to cook anything in advance, so basically Monday becomes your start-up cooking day.

The first meal you cook at the beginning of the week (a Monday or Tuesday) should be like your Sunday start-up, only simpler because you'll have less time. That first night would be a good time to make a hearty stew — in double batches, of course,

so that Wednesday or Thursday night is taken care of too. Or, if you're short on time Monday night, do a large stir-fry of some sort that can be turned into a salad supper Tuesday or Wednesday.

The second time you get around to cooking should also yield leftovers for the end of the week. By cooking twice in this week, you can count on four meals. Then you only have to think about one more night, which can easily be taken care of by making sandwiches, an omelet, or plainly baked fish served with a steamed vegetable.

A CRAZY WEEK WITH NO PLANNING TIME BUT A FULL PANTRY

In this third type of week, I have assumed that you haven't had time to plan your menus or do your shopping, but your pantry is full. Also, this week doesn't include a Sunday start-up, and in looking ahead, you see that you'll be coming home at odd hours almost every evening, and you can't count on anyone having any spare time.

Fear not, if your pantry is full, on a couple of nights you can resort to pantry meals (see the Pure Pantry Chapter on page 77), making a soup from canned ingredients on one night and a pasta dish on another. This is the week, too, that on the night or two you do have enough time to cook, you should again be making double batches of whatever it is you are cooking. Make dishes that can be easily reheated or served at room temperature.

If you have time on a given night to do any shopping, be sure to pick up the makings of at least two meals. Even if you end up not using those ingredients, you can freeze them or cook them up over the weekend in some hearty stew. The fresh ingredients that you do buy should be able to stay fresh in the refrigerator for a day or so at least. This way if the unexpected happens and you don't get to cook them when anticipated, they won't spoil.

If you do get around to marketing but are not sure what you want to cook, shop with the following guidelines in mind: Stock up on a protein of some sort (meat, dairy, eggs, or vegetarian), get two kinds of vegetables (fresh or frozen), and maybe a starch, even if it is only bread. Also

pick up salad ingredients. The first chance you get, you can cook up the fresh ingredients in a standard meal, then use the remains the next night in whatever salad you have also shopped for.

WORST CASE SCENARIO: THE MOTHER HUBBARD SYNDROME

In other words a bare cupboard and no planning, shopping, or start-up time. Even on those evenings or weeks when you don't know who will be eating when and you haven't had time to plan, shop, or cook in advance, and your pantry is bare to boot, don't despair! Here are the strategies for those nights.

During these weeks, the obvious solution is carry-out cuisine or to serve breakfast as supper. An omelet or some other egg dish, or even a bowlful of hot cereal will do in a pinch and doesn't require much in the way of fresh or even pantry ingredients. In the summer, cottage cheese mixed with fruit or vegetables frequently turns up on our table on nights like these.

But you don't have to rely on these obvious solutions. You can be more inventive with a minimum of ingredients. At some point someone in the family can pick up some readily available food. Recently I investigated the tiny little Spanish "bodegas" which abound in my neighborhood. Where I live, these local grocery stores are the closest thing I could find to the "convenience" stores that dot the American landscape. You know the type of store I'm referring to: it sells newspapers, it might have a gasoline pump outside; it carries lots of potato chips, cookies, soda and beer, but also has other canned goods from which, believe it or not, you can rustle up a decent meal.

Although my local convenience stores stock an amazing array of intriguing Spanish ingredients, like fresh jalapeño peppers, special corn flour from which to make tortillas, and the most extensive collection of canned beans I have ever found anywhere, they also carry what I believe to be countrywide standard food items.

In each of these stores I found noodles, rice, and often (in the breakfast cereal section) cornmeal from which to make cornmeal purée. All had little delis at which I could buy chunks of smoked ham or turkey and Cheddar cheese. The small refrigerated case stocked eggs, milk, grated Parmesan, cottage cheese, yogurt, bacon, and some type of breakfast sausage. If there was a frozen foods case, it stored ice cream and bags of ice mainly but also, on occasion, packages of frozen corn kernels, chopped spinach, and green beans.

If there were no frozen goods, there were lots of staple canned goods on the shelves including some type of beans (even if it was only barbecued beans) corn, soups, tomato juice, spaghetti sauce or stewed tomatoes, tuna, and salmon. And to spice things up I could always find barbecue sauce and ketchup, green olives, pimientoes, mustard, oil, vinegar, and pickles. So, armed with those widely available goods, stocked in the smallest of grocery stores, you can come up with slightly more inventive fare than you thought possible.

■ Thin a can of chicken broth with 2 cups of water or tomato juice or stewed tomatoes. Add about ¼ cup raw rice and a package of frozen corn kernels, and bring the liquid to a boil. Dice in some smoked ham or turkey and you've created a meal-in-a-soup. Instead of the ham or turkey, you could stir grated Cheddar or Parmesan cheese into the soup.

■ Heat a package of frozen chopped spinach in canned broth. Add a couple of beaten eggs and cook until the eggs solidify into strands. Sprinkle with grated Parmesan and add lots of freshly ground black pepper.

■ Enrich and stretch a commercially prepared spaghetti sauce. Sauté some garlic in olive oil (if you don't have fresh garlic, sauté a bit of garlic powder and a pinch of dried oregano), add a package of thawed frozen chopped spinach, and sauté for a few minutes until hot. Add a can or two of drained tuna or salmon and 2 cups of prepared spaghetti sauce. Simmer and pour over cooked noodles, cornmeal purée, rice, or even toasted bread.

■ Dress up a can or two of drained red beans or prepared baked beans (if that is all you can find) with prepared barbecue sauce, thawed frozen peas or corn, and smoked ham cubes. Bake until hot; serve over cooked rice or cornmeal purée or just serve with bread.

■ Cook up some breakfast sausage or bacon along with chopped garlic and crushed pepper flakes. Drain, then slice or crumble the mixture over cooked noodles. If you have any parsley on hand, chop it and toss it with the noodles and bacon. Or instead of the parsley, add some minced green olives.

■ Purée cottage cheese with dried herbs and pimentoes or sweet peppers and toss it with prepared spaghetti sauce in which you heated frozen corn kernels; serve over rice or cooked noodles.

With a little imagination and ingenuity, no more Mother Hubbard Syndrome.

MONDAY-TO-FRIDAY MENUS

One way of simplifying Monday-to-Friday planning is to think of the menu in terms of two courses only. The menu might end up being made up of three courses, especially if dessert consists of ice cream or some other store-bought goodies, but you should only think in terms of cooking two of the courses.

THE TWO-COURSE MEAL

First decide if the smaller course surrounding the main one is to be an appetizer or dessert. Obviously on weeks you are cooking every night of the week, one of the ways to vary your meals is to serve an appetizer one night and a dessert on another.

Now why bother with courses at all? Because it's an easy way to add variety to your weekly meals. It's a way of stretching out the relaxing time dinner ought to be. It's a way of adding texture and contrast to your dinners because Monday-to-Friday meals should be pleasurable and nourishing as well as easy and uncomplicated.

Once you've thought of your main course (which can be dictated by circumstances or inspired by mood), what precedes or follows can be determined in a variety of ways. One way I use is to contrast the hot and cold courses. If you serve a hearty main-course soup, follow it with a chilled fresh dessert or precede it with a salad or even a plateful of room-temperature steamed vegetables.

Another trick is to contrast the time spent on one course with how much time is spent on the other. If the main course takes little time to prepare, then it's worth spending some time making a lovely dessert. Sandwiches, egg, and salad courses lend themselves to fanciful desserts, and making dessert is a touch appreciated even by the most picky and hard-to-please eaters.

Another way of making up courses is to break up the three-dish main course into separate courses. For example, you might want to serve a dish of veal scaloppine as a main course as well as a quick-cooking vegetable. Instead of trying to cook both at the same time, you could serve the vegetable separately as a first or second course preceding or following the meat.

A casserole that bakes in the oven is lovely followed by a vegetable or green salad or preceded by steamed asparagus or by chilled avocado. Or, if you make a casserole that cooks by itself in the oven, you will have lots of time to prepare a dessert to follow.

SOURCES OF INSPIRATION

Why with the quantities of cookbooks on every conceivable international, national, and regional cuisine do people still, every day of the week, wonder what to make for dinner? How come the average cook resorts to preparing the same meal night after night when entire sections of the newspaper are devoted to food alone?

The answer is that, in spite of the proliferation of written recipes, the average American still doesn't know how to plan an everyday menu. TV shows, cookbooks, and magazines have shown us how to make puff pastry and homemade pasta, but they haven't taught us how to improvise and create basic good everyday meals.

Because so many cooks have learned from written recipes and not from family members for whom cooking was as comfortable a skill as reading and writing, they're at a loss as to how to cook without a recipe in front of them. Knowing how to follow a series of recipe steps is not the same as knowing how to cook and how to plan a menu.

How then can you come up with spontaneous and fresh menus without relying on recipes? By using a "hook" or focus that will inspire your meal. Once inspired, then turn to a specific recipe if you must to find out how to cook whatever it is you wish to prepare. To help you get started, sample menus appear in the Appendix.

The single focus: One idea that has guided me through the perils of daily dinner planning was given to me by my good friend Rolly Woodyatt, who learned it from her father, the family chef. Philip Woodyatt, a wonderful cook I am told, thought of just one thing he wanted to eat for dinner and the rest of the meal followed from that. In the fall this one dish might have been a slice of homemade apple pie with a slice of Cheddar cheese, or

in the spring a bunch of asparagus sauced with hollandaise and accompanied by a slice of crusty Italian bread. On occasion he was known to make just chocolate cake for dinner that he, his wife, and two daughters would consume at a sitting.

My dinners are not quite as eccentric as that, but the tale did lead me to set aside the classic trio of protein, starch, and vegetable in favor of more eclectic meals. I now simply think of one ingredient or one type of dish I want to make and the accompaniments follow naturally.

How then do you decide on the single focus that will inspire your menu? There are several ways. Focus on one favorite food, on a seasonal ingredient, on the weather, or your mood. Or a menu can be focused by who it is you'll be feeding, what their dietary needs and schedules are like, how easy the clean-up will be, or simply by thinking of what you've had the night before and don't want to eat again.

Focusing on favorite foods: The favorite food notion works especially well in tandem with thinking about the seasons. Although Americans can buy imported fruits and vegetables out of season, these ingredients are not as tasty as when they've been grown locally and in season nor are they as affordable.

Do the strawberries look especially juicy and ripe? Then they become the centerpiece of the meal, accompanied by a portion of ricotta or cottage cheese. Are the asparagus so thin you just have to devour them night after night until they grow fat and woody? Then asparagus for dinner it is, with a slice of smoked ham and whole-wheat bread. If the season for a particular food is especially short, then indulge your fancy and have your favorite dish every day of the week or until you tire of it. Remember that dinner will always be more pleasurable to prepare if you love what you're about to eat.

Focusing on seasons and weather: Not only do the seasons bring different foods to the market but the weather also inspires different types of dishes and culinary techniques.

On a sticky summer night, dinner can be made from what is on hand or from what can be eaten raw. Spring and summer are times when the lighter flesh of poultry and fish take center stage and the heftier meat dishes recede into the background.

Fall nights call for the in-between seasons feel of substantial sautés accompanied by a light vegetable dish or a tomato salad, whereas cold dreary winter nights call for lusty stews, juicy roasted meat, and hearty starch and winter vegetable dishes that can restore sagging spirits.

Focusing on health concerns: If you or someone you're cooking for is hoping to lose weight, emphasize menus composed mostly of vegetable and fruit dishes. It's also best to eat less meat and more lower-in-fat fish and poultry.

Even if you're not trying to actually lose weight, you might still want to use health as an occasional inspiration for a couple of days after you've indulged in menus rich in creamy foods. These healthy menus should be light, emphasize vegetables, and use protein that is low in both fat and cholesterol.

Focusing on who you're cooking for: In thinking about what to eat for dinner, always keep in mind who besides yourself you'll be feeding and what they like to eat. Will your kids, partner, or roommate be home? If yes, the menu will have to accommodate their likes and dislikes as well as your own.

If you have a family, you're going to have to come up with menus that will please everyone to some extent. Rather than force your kids to eat foods that they don't like, always include at least one dish you can depend on them eating.

Focusing on schedules: A major factor that determines what appears on the nightly dinner table is the cook's schedule—when is the cook coming home and how much time does he or she have to spend on making dinner.

The type of meal you make might be inspired by whether or not the family will eat together or in sequence or by each individual's schedule and hunger pangs. If eating in sequence is in order, then one-pot meals that can be easily reheated in single portions might be the solution for that night, as would individual pizzas or taco or tortilla suppers.

Focusing on types of cuisine and dishes: Types of cuisine can be another source of inspiration. On days when you have more time to think about what you are cooking, the character of a particular cuisine can become an inspirational hook as can a counterpoint between types of dishes.

One night can feature Italian-style dishes, followed the next night by a dish with an Oriental flare. My Monday-to-Friday dinners are not culinarily and ethnically correct, but thinking along ethnic lines gets me out of a rut and leads me along a new path of seasoning.

Or for variety follow a hearty one-pot meal with a light salad the next night. Keep alive the notion that dinner can be full of surprise, counterpoint, and enjoyment. If you try to balance one night against the next, you will automatically introduce variety into your weekly menus.

Focusing on an easy clean-up: If you've got work to do after dinner or if you're just plain tuckered out and need to put your feet up, you'll want to make a dinner that's as simple as possible to clean up. The easiest meals to assemble on those nights are salads followed by soups, stews, and skillet suppers.

Focusing on a balanced diet: The boredom of everyday meals stems from the endless repetitiveness of serving up the same dish night after night. When we're in a hurry or tired, as most of us are after a workday, we're not exactly in the right frame of mind to begin experimenting with new recipes and different foods.

One way to break out of the routine without a lot of effort is to plan menus that make the centerpiece of each meal different from what it was the night before. If you've had a pasta

or grain main-course on Monday night, try for fish or chicken on Tuesday. If salad is dinner on Wednesday, then Thursday is a night for a hot meal.

Or let your menus be inspired by the old-fashioned notion we learned in grade school of a balanced diet. If one night you eat meat, have fish the night after and perhaps a meal of vegetables, rice, and beans the night after that.

If you've made a large roast from which you will have leftovers for a second meal, try not to serve these two meals two days in a row. Skip a day in between to introduce variety and balance in your diet.

Focusing on comfort foods: Food should give sustenance and comfort. If you're really tired, you'll want to make the simplest of meals. If you're feeling blue or put out, you might want to feed on comfort foods that soothe like pasta, starches, and puddings.

If you're feeling energetic and

plan to go out after dinner, keep your supper light so you're not weighed down.

HOW TO TURN A FOCUS INTO A REAL MEAL

Once you've grabbed hold of the one idea that will be the dinner focus, then round it out so that you get a more complete meal.

Here's where the old-fashioned notion of the balanced diet comes into play again. But remember dinner doesn't have to be a slice of meat, a side of vegetable, and one of starch every night of the week.

If the focus of your menu is a favorite food like a baked potato, then top it with a protein like Cheddar or cottage cheese and serve a green on the side to make the meal complete. Or at the end of summer if dinner consists of a rich salad of ripe tomatoes served with whole-grain bread, you might want to precede it with a light protein soup so that you feel more fully nourished.

Also remember that the elements of the meal don't have to be cooked separately, nor is there any rule that every meal must always have a protein, vegetable, and starch. Ameri-cans on the average consume a lot more protein than they need. So don't feel guilty if for a few days the focus of your meals is vegetable and starch. Conversely if for a couple of days running your meals are mostly protein, don't beat yourself up about it—just make sure that you get a balanced diet spread over the week.

THE MONDAY-TO-FRIDAY DINNER PARTY

Although this hardly ever happens in my house, I do know people who, for reasons that are completely mysterious to me, invite guests over for dinner during the week. Now even though I don't play hostess on a work night, I do think there are some simple solutions for those people who choose to or, perhaps through no choice of their own, have to entertain guests during the week.

■ The key to a successful during-the-week dinner party is to cook a meal much like any other weeknight dinner and gussy it up to make it look grand. Be sure to decorate the table to add to the festivity.

■ Plan and cook as much as you can in advance. The entire procedure probably will take a couple of days. Two days before the party, plan the menu and shop for the ingredients. The night before the party, cook and prep as much as possible. Even if you're comfortable handling last-minute cooking on the evening of the party, don't burden yourself with more than one last-minute dish. Everything else should be made in advance.

■ Choose dishes that involve a minimum of clean-up. Rule out messy roasts unless you use disposable baking pans. (Ordinarily I don't recommend disposable pans because they're not easily recyclable. However, it's okay to make an exception for that rare midweek dinner party.)

■ Set the table the night before. Use good dishes and flatware so that the emphasis is on how the table looks and how the meal is presented. This will contribute to a special feel without your having to do more cooking.

■ Try to create a centerpiece to make the table look festive. Flowers are the obvious choice, but if you don't have

time to buy flowers nor want to spend the money, create a gorgeous centerpiece with a bowl of brightly colored fruits or vegetables. Contrasting red and yellow peppers makes an unusual centerpiece; as does a bouquet of purple broccoli. After the party is over, you get to eat the centerpiece.

■ Even if you are planning a menu much like one you would serve to your family, stretch it into three courses. Salad or a separately cooked vegetable makes a fine starter. Then serve the main course and end with dessert. If the main course is skimpy, you could insert a cheese course in between it and dessert to give more substance to the menu. This strategic spacing of the courses contributes to the weight and look of the meal but doesn't require more cooking.

■ Only when you are entertaining during the week, would I recommend you mince fresh herbs to garnish a dish to make it more attractive. Minced parsley turns plain steamed potatoes into a more elegant dish, and chopped chives give a finished look to a big bowl of hearty soup.

■ Introduce a note of surprise whenever you can. This will contribute to a party atmosphere without more work on your part. Buy an unusual walnut or olive bread for example, or serve an exotic imported beer, which are so in fashion at the moment.

READY TO GO

Now that your pantry is full, your kitchen is set up conveniently, and your strategies are in place, you're practically home free as a Monday-to-Friday cook. The recipes that follow will take you the rest of the way.

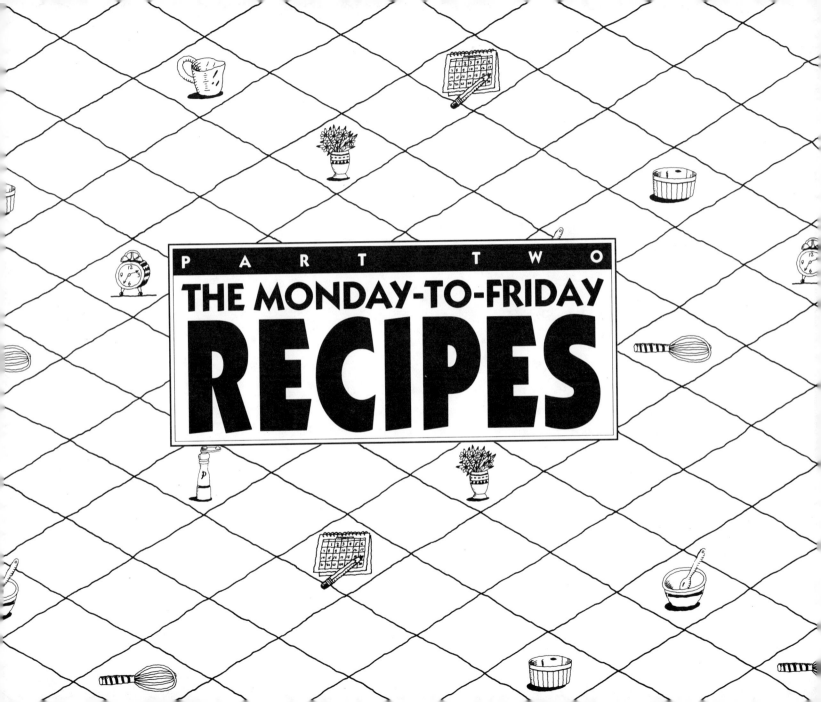

PART TWO

THE MONDAY-TO-FRIDAY
RECIPES

PURE PANTRY

These recipes show how you can still get dinner on the table when you have only dried, frozen, or canned ingredients on hand. Once you get the hang of it, you'll always be able to make dinner even when you haven't had time to shop for a single fresh ingredient.

But these recipes aren't just for pantry ingredients. They can be embellished with fresh ingredients, leftover vegetables, or other bits of leftovers in the refrigerator as well.

Dinners made entirely from prepared ingredients need not be boring: Pair two unusual ingredients together like extravagant dried mushrooms with humble chick-peas; substitute an unusual grain, like quinoa (KEEN-wah) when common rice comes to mind; combine opposite tastes, like sweet with sour, hot with mild, or spicy with tame.

And remember, recipes aren't written in stone. They are just one person's version of a particular dish, and there's always room for improvisation to accommodate another person's taste and needs.

Keep in mind, though, that the first rule of improvisation is that less is more. Don't think that by layering taste after taste, you're going to come up with a distinctive and original dish. You'll end up with a murky mélange if you mix too many ingredients and too many spices and herbs: They'll camouflage, not enhance, the primary taste you're trying to highlight. Remember, the main ingredients star in the dish, and the spices and herbs and other flavors should merely accent and highlight them.

If you've never improvised a dish before, start by making only one change or addition to an already familiar recipe. For example, a little crunchy cucumber or fennel is welcome in a soft couscous dish. And contrasting vibrant colors always adds to the satisfying feel. Once you become comfortable with just the one change, then expand your horizons by making more. Remember that when you begin to cook without following a recipe to the letter, you'll probably create some dishes you won't be especially proud of. Don't be discouraged: The only way to become comfortable with creating your own dishes is to try a change at a time and to taste and taste and taste some more.

STEWED TOMATOES

I always have at least one can of Italian-style stewed tomatoes on hand for nights when I really have no time at all to chop and cook. In addition to the tomato flavor, this variety of canned tomatoes also has onions and peppers, so that you don't have to go to the trouble of preparing these vegetables separately in order to get their flavor into the dish you're cooking. Stewed tomatoes work best in soups or soupy stews where lots of flavors come together in a pleasing whole.

NO-WORK SALMON CHOWDER

MAKES 4 SERVINGS
TIME: 30 MINUTES

Essentially this is a no-work no-clean-up meal — in other words, the ideal Monday-to-Friday recipe. Canned salmon, with its pretty pink color and gentle flavor, is a wonderful and unexpected addition to this soup.

If making the soup for only 1 or 2 eaters, cut the amounts in half, except for the corn of which all should be added so that you aren't left with half a package of vegetables.

> 1 can (15½ ounces) salmon or 2
>   cans (7 ounces each) tuna
>   packed in water
> 1 package (10 ounces) frozen corn
>   kernels, thawed
> 2 cans (14½ ounces each) Italian-
>   style stewed or stewed tomatoes
> 2 bottles (8 ounces each) clam juice
> ½ cup long-grain white rice
> ½ teaspoon garlic powder
> Salt
> 2 to 3 drops Tabasco sauce

1. Drain the salmon. Combine all the ingredients except for the salt and Tabasco in a medium-size saucepan and bring the liquid to a boil over medium heat.

2. Reduce the heat to low and simmer covered until the rice is very tender and the flavors blend together, about 20 minutes. Season to taste with salt and Tabasco.

FESTIVE MACKEREL SALAD

MAKES 4 TO 6 SERVINGS
TIME: 10 MINUTES WORK
1 HOUR NO-WORK CHILLING TIME

High in protein, rich in texture, and full of contrasting flavors, this dish is a tasty and quick pick-me-up, perfect for dog-day summer nights. It keeps for 2 days only, after that the acid of the citrus juice turns the fish to mush.

For dessert serve a Fresh Fruit Salad or Melon with Rum, Lime, and Ginger Sauce (see Index for recipes).

1/4 cup olive oil or mayonnaise
1/4 cup lemon or lime juice
2 cans (15 ounces each) mackerel or
    4 cans (7 ounces each) tuna
    packed in water
2 packages (10 ounces each) frozen
    corn kernels or lima beans,
    thawed
2 pickled whole jalapeño peppers
1/2 cup bottled sweet red or roasted
    peppers
1/2 cup fresh parsley or coriander
    leaves (optional)
Salt and freshly ground black
    pepper

1. Whisk the oil or mayonnaise with the lemon or lime juice in the bottom of a serving bowl.

2. Drain the mackerel, pat it dry, and flake it into the bowl. Drain the corn well, pat dry, and add it to the bowl. Mince the jalapeños and peppers and add them to the bowl. Rinse and mince the fresh herb, if using, and add it to the bowl.

3. Toss the ingredients together well and season to taste with salt and pepper. If you have the time, cover the salad and chill for an hour before serving.

CHICK-PEAS, PIMIENTOS, AND SMOKED OYSTERS

MAKES 4 SERVINGS
TIME: 15 MINUTES

Here's a summer meal in an instant. If you have any of the suggested fresh salad ingredients, by all means add them. But, your dinner won't suffer if your salad crisper is bare.

1 jar (3 ounces) pimientos or
    roasted peppers
1 package (10 ounces) frozen petite
    peas, thawed
2 cans (3 1/2 ounces each) smoked
    oysters
2 cans (16 ounces each) chick-peas,
    rinsed and drained
2 tablespoons balsamic vinegar
Salt and freshly ground black
    pepper
1/2 cup fresh herbs such as parsley
    or dill (optional)
Lettuce greens (optional)
2 bell peppers (optional)
Tomatoes (optional)

1. Chop the pimientos. You should have 1/2 cup.

UNDERSTANDING MONDAY-TO-FRIDAY COOKING TIMES

When a recipe notes only one time, for example 35 to 40 minutes, that means that from the moment you begin to prepare it until the time you serve the dish it will take 35 minutes. Although you may not be busy every one of those minutes, there really won't be much free time, either.

On the other hand, when a recipe notes 10 minutes of work and 1 hour of no-work cooking time, that means the recipe involves 10 minutes of work, whether it is in the preparation steps or in attended cooking time, and another hour of cooking time that doesn't involve the cook at all: no basting, no stirring, no other steps. While the food cooks, relax and read the paper!

SECOND TIME AROUND

TANGY BEET SALAD: Leftovers are great layered with mayonnaise and sliced tomatoes and stuffed in warm pita pockets.

2. In a serving bowl, combine the peas, smoked oysters with their oil, pimientos, chick-peas, and vinegar. Season to taste with salt and pepper.

3. If you have the fresh ingredients on hand, rinse, stem and mince the herbs, and toss them with the salad. Serve over rinsed, dried greens, sliced peppers, or tomato wedges.

TANGY BEET SALAD WITH SMOKED SARDINES

MAKES 4 SERVINGS
TIME: 10 TO 15 MINUTES, NOT INCLUDING CHILLING TIME

It's the unusual combination of flavors that makes the ingredients in this recipe taste so good together. The bite of the pickled onions and the sweetness of the beets are wonderful contrasts to the richness of the smoked sardines.

¼ cup olive oil
1 teaspoon Dijon mustard
4 cans (3½ ounces each) skinless, boneless smoked sardines packed in water
1 can (16 ounces) sliced beets
1 jar (about 3 ounces) cocktail onions
1 medium-size sour pickle
¼ cup fresh parsley or dill leaves (optional)

1. Whisk the oil with the mustard in the bottom of a serving bowl.

2. Drain the sardines and add them to the bowl. Break them up into pieces with a fork.

3. Drain and chop the beets, then add them to the sardines. Drain and halve the cocktail onions; add them to the bowl. Finely chop the pickle; add it to the bowl. Combine the ingredients thoroughly.

4. Rinse and mince the fresh herb if using, and toss it with the sardines and beets. Serve the salad immediately or cover and chill up to 4 hours before serving.

SWEET-AND-SOUR HAM CASSEROLE

**MAKES 4 SERVINGS
TIME: 10 MINUTES WORK
30 MINUTES NO-WORK COOKING
TIME**

Think of how much clean-up time you save by mixing this casserole right it its baking dish!

In this recipe the prunes soften the tang of the sauerkraut and harmonize with the ham; the nuts and allspice add contrast. If this is not one of your totally desperate days and you have time to shop, consider making Maple and Cinnamon Acorn Squash or Baked Butternut Squash as a second dish—it doesn't take any work, just time to cook (see Index for page numbers).

1 pound sauerkraut
½ pound pitted prunes
¼ pound walnuts or pecans
1 pound ham, boiled or smoked, preferably 95% or more fat free
¼ teaspoon ground allspice
½ cup chicken broth or water
Freshly ground black pepper

1. Preheat the oven to 375°F.

2. To remove some of its saltiness, rinse the sauerkraut in cold water and drain in a sieve. Rinse and drain again, then squeeze dry. Strew the sauerkraut in a small casserole dish.

3. Dice the prunes and nuts and add them to the casserole. Trim all the fat from the ham and cut the meat into ½-inch cubes. Add it to the casserole. Add the allspice, broth, and pepper to taste, and combine the ingredients right in the casserole.

4. Cover and bake until heated through, about 30 minutes.

CORN PLUS CORN

**MAKES 4 TO 6 SERVINGS
TIME: 30 MINUTES**

This is a favorite meal of mine because of the delicious double dose of corn both in the kernels and in the cornmeal. Some days my family is satisfied with a bowlful of this for dinner; other days I amplify the meal by serving it with another dish, like Sweet-and-Sour Red Beans or Emergency Barbecued Chicken (see Index for page numbers).

SECOND TIME AROUND

HAM CASSEROLE: Leftovers can be wrapped in phyllo dough and baked at 400°F until heated through, about 30 minutes. See Strudel Your Way (check the Index) for how to do this. If there's leftover squash to boot, dice and mix it into the sauerkraut and ham leftovers before you wrap them in the phyllo.

SECOND TIME AROUND

CORN PLUS CORN: To get a second meal out of the leftovers, sauté some julienned ham in 1 to 2 tablespoons olive oil over medium heat until hot, then add the leftover double-corn purée and sauté until hot. Remove from the heat and sprinkle with some grated Parmesan or Cheddar cheese.

1 medium-size onion
¼ cup corn, vegetable, or olive oil
1 package (10 ounces) frozen corn kernels, thawed
1 cup cornmeal
4 cups chicken broth or water
Salt and freshly ground black pepper
2 tablespoons butter (optional)

1. Mince the onion. Heat the oil in a medium saucepan over medium heat. Add the onion and sauté until tender, about 5 minutes.

2. Add the corn kernels and sauté for another minute just to heat them up.

3. Add the cornmeal and stir constantly over low heat, until the cornmeal begins to smell a little toasty, about 1 minute.

4. Add the broth and whisk the ingredients together. Stirring continuously so that the cornmeal doesn't lump up, bring the liquid to a boil over medium heat. Season to taste with salt and pepper. Cover the saucepan and simmer until the cornmeal is thick, about 15 minutes.

5. Remove the saucepan from the heat, adjust the seasoning, and whisk in the butter for enrichment if you wish.

MEDITERRANEAN SKILLET DINNER

MAKES 4 SERVINGS
TIME: 45 TO 50 MINUTES

The cracked wheat, seasoned with pesto and sun-dried tomatoes, is a delicious foil for chick-peas or small pink beans.

6 sun-dried tomatoes packed in oil
1 tablespoon vegetable oil
1 cup cracked wheat or bulgur wheat or 1 box (5¼ ounces) Near East tabouleh (save seasoning packet for another use)
1 or 1½ cups chicken broth or water
2 tablespoons prepared pesto
Salt and freshly ground black pepper
1 can (16 ounces) chick-peas or small pink beans

1. Finely chop the sun-dried tomatoes and set aside.

2. Heat the oil in a large skillet over medium heat. Add the cracked or bulgur wheat or tabouleh and sauté until toasty brown, 2 to 3 minutes. Add the broth or water (1½ cups for cracked wheat, 1 cup for bulgur or tabouleh).

3. Cover the skillet and cook until the wheat is tender, 10 minutes for bulgur or tabouleh; 20 minutes for the cracked wheat. If the wheat is tender but has not absorbed all of the water, remove the cover and cook for another few minutes, stirring occasionally until the excess moisture has evaporated.

4. Add the sun-dried tomatoes and pesto to the wheat and season to taste with salt and pepper. Spread the chick-peas over the wheat; cover and cook, stirring the mixture once, until the chick-peas are heated through, about 10 minutes.

BULGUR AND RED BEAN CHILI

MAKES 4 SERVINGS
TIME: 5 MINUTES WORK
1 HOUR NO-WORK COOKING TIME

This is a good standard dish worth having in your repertoire, for it takes no time at all to prepare and can be eaten as a main course or served as a side dish. Shreds of remaining roasted meat or poultry can be tossed in and reheated during the last moments of cooking.

Some complementary side dishes include Orange-Juice-Steamed Carrots, Lemon Green Beans, Cauliflower with Red Pepper Ribbons, or Tri-Color Peppers (see Index for page numbers).

1 cup bulgur wheat or 1 box (6
ounces) Near East wheat pilaf
(save seasoning packet for
another use)
1¾ cups chicken broth or water
2 cans (16 ounces each) red kidney
beans
½ cup prepared chili sauce
1 can (4 ounces) chopped green
chilies
3 to 4 drops Tabasco sauce
Salt

1. Preheat the oven to 375°F.
2. Place the bulgur in a mixing bowl and pour in enough broth to cover. Let stand until tender and moist, about 30 minutes.
3. Rinse and drain the kidney beans and combine them with the chile sauce, chopped green chilies, Tabasco, and salt to taste in a medium baking pan.
4. When the bulgur is soft, drain it in a sieve and press out any excess liquid with your hands. Add the bulgur to the baking pan and mix well. Cover the pan with aluminum foil and bake until very hot, about 30 minutes.

SECOND TIME AROUND

MEDITERRANEAN SKILLET DINNER: Reheat leftovers as is in a microwave or in a 350°F oven for 15 minutes; don't reheat this on top of the stove or the bottom will burn.

■ *Smarten up leftovers by adding diced fresh tomatoes, lots of minced parsley, and a lemon vinaigrette. Serve cold.*

NEAR-EAST SEASONING PACKETS

Although it is preferable to buy cracked wheat and bulgur in bulk, I realize many people can only purchase it in boxes marketed under the brand name "Near East." Also included in these boxes are seasoning packets. My ecologically thrifty heart tells me that it is wrong just to toss the seasoning packets aside because each one contains about 3 tablespoons of spices for which the consumer has paid dearly.

However, I don't use the seasoning packet as recommended on the box because I find that the sheer quantity of spices overwhelms the flavor of the grains. You could empty the seasoning into a jar and save it to use in other recipes. Because the seasoning in the packets is heady, composed I think mostly of dried garlic and mint, reserve it for robustly flavored dishes. To these recipes, add ⅛ to ¼ teaspoon or substitute it for the quantity of spices and herbs recommended in the recipes. I think such an addition or substitution would work best in this book with (see Index for page numbers):

- No-Work Salmon Chowder
- Curried Fish with Rice
- A Winter Dish of Chick-Peas and Wild Mushrooms
- Tomato and Garlic-Flavored Chick-Peas
- Michele's Foundation Soup
- Chunky Peasant Vegetable Soup
- Barley-Vegetable Chowder
- Bean Minestrone
- A Good Basic Meat Sauce
- Chicken Breasts a l'Italienne
- Chicken Stew à la Bouillabaisse
- Roasted Game Hens with Tarragon-Cheese Stuffing
- Herbed Lamb Chops
- Protean Ratatouille
- Monday-to-Friday Gumbo
- Multi-Colored Bulgur
- Cracked Wheat à la Jambalaya
- Three Bean Stew with Vegetables
- Middle-Eastern Barley, Lentil, and Rice Casserole
- Chick-peas with Fennel and Roasted Peppers
- Aromatic Rice with Vegetables
- Minted Cherry Tomatoes

SUNNY COUSCOUS

MAKES 4 SERVINGS
TIME: 30 MINUTES SERVED COLD
45 MINUTES SERVED HOT

You might want to assemble this meal on a night when you're not sure of the hour anyone is eating, because the mix tastes equally good served hot, at room temperature, or even chilled.

1 box (10 ounces) or scant 2 cups
   couscous
2½ cups hot tap water
2 tablespoons Oriental sesame oil
2 tablespoons vegetable oil
6 tablespoons rice vinegar
1 tablespoon soy sauce
½ teaspoon chili paste with soy
   beans (optional)
1 can (5 ounces) sliced bamboo
   shoots
1 can (8 ounces) sliced water
   chestnuts
1 can (15½ ounces) salmon,
   preferably packed in water
1 package (10 ounces) petite peas,
   thawed
Salt and freshly ground black
   pepper

1. Steep the couscous in the hot water until plumped and tender, about 30 minutes.

2. Meanwhile combine the oils, vinegar, soy sauce, and chili paste in a serving bowl.

3. Drain the bamboo shoots, water chestnuts, and salmon. Add them to the bowl along with the peas and combine well.

4. When the couscous has softened, drain it in a sieve to remove any excess water. Break up any clumps with a fork or your fingers. Add the couscous to the bowl and combine with the other ingredients. Season to taste with salt and pepper.

5. Serve immediately or cover and chill until serving time. This will keep refrigerated for 2 days. If you choose to serve this hot, cover and heat in a 350°F oven for 15 minutes.

CURRIED FISH WITH RICE

MAKES 4 SERVINGS
TIME: 35 MINUTES

An amalgam of hot and mellow spices transforms a plain mix of dry rice, frozen spinach, and canned sal-

DOUBLING UP

SUNNY COUSCOUS: You can make a double batch, making half with the salmon and serving it hot. Reserve the other half for sometime later in the week. To it add canned tuna or leftover cold cuts or cooked meat or poultry instead of salmon.

mon into an exotic supper. If you have enough time to shop for the fresh ingredients, serve it with a sliced red pepper and scallion salad.

> 2 packages (10 ounces each) frozen
>   chopped spinach, thawed
> 3 to 4 cans (6½ or 7 ounces each)
>   canned salmon, preferably
>   packed in water
> 2 tablespoons vegetable oil
> 1 teaspoon curry powder
> 1 teaspoon ground cumin
> 1 teaspoon ground cinnamon
> ½ teaspoon ground cardamom
> ½ teaspoon ground coriander
> ¼ teaspoon cayenne pepper
> 2 cups long-grain white rice
> 4½ cups bottled clam juice or water
> Salt and freshly ground black
>   pepper

1. Drain the spinach and the salmon separately.

2. Heat the oil in a large saucepan over medium heat. Add the spices and stir-fry for a few seconds to release their aroma. Add the spinach and stir-fry just to heat it up, about 1 minute.

3. Add the rice and clam juice and stir to combine. Bring the liquid to a simmer. Cover the pan and simmer over low heat until the rice is just done, about 20 minutes.

Check on the rice about halfway through cooking to make sure the liquid is not evaporating too quickly; if you think it is, add a few more tablespoons of liquid and reduce the heat.

4. Stir in the salmon, cover, and simmer until heated through, about 5 minutes longer. Season to taste with salt and pepper.

VARIATION

You also can make this dish in a casserole and bake it in the oven. The advantage is that it cooks more evenly without risk of scorching the bottom; the disadvantage is that it takes longer.

Prepare the dish in an ovenproof saucepan as directed. In step 3, after you have brought the liquid to a simmer, cover the saucepan and bake in a 350°F oven until the rice is tender, about 30 minutes. Stir in the salmon and bake until the salmon is hot, 5 to 10 minutes longer.

ESPECIALLY GOOD FOR CHILDREN

CURRIED FISH: If you have a kid (or kids) who doesn't like salmon, toss half of the curried rice with some shredded or chunked leftover chicken instead. For the adults, toss the remaining curried rice with the salmon, adjusting the amount to your own taste.

SOOTHING CREAMY RICE

MAKES 4 SERVINGS
TIME: 35 MINUTES

This simple meal of rice, cheese, and peas is terrific for families with young children because you can omit the fiery spicing until after you've served the kids. The peas add a sweet touch that is popular with smaller children.

1 cup long-grain white or brown
  rice
2 or 2¼ cups chicken broth or
  water
2 to 3 ounces Cheddar or Parmesan
  cheese (¾ cup grated)
1 package (10 ounces) frozen petite
  peas or lima beans, thawed
1 teaspoon Worcestershire sauce
⅛ teaspoon cayenne pepper or 2 to
  3 drops Tabasco sauce
Salt and freshly ground black
  pepper

1. In a medium-size saucepan, combine the rice with the broth (the larger amount of liquid is for the brown rice). Bring the liquid to a boil over medium heat, cover, and simmer until the rice is almost tender, about 15 minutes for white rice and 25 minutes for brown rice.

2. While the rice is cooking, grate the cheese.

3. When the rice is tender, stir in the peas and simmer covered 5 minutes more.

4. At this point you can serve half of this to the kids or stir in some cheese and then serve. If you're making this for grown-ups only, stir in the Worcestershire, cayenne, and the grated cheese. Remove the pan from the heat and continue to stir until the cheese is entirely melted. Season to taste with salt and pepper and serve immediately before the dish gets gummy.

FIERY TUBETTI WITH TUNA AND BLACK OLIVES

MAKES 4 SERVINGS
TIME: 20 MINUTES

While everyone is familiar with tuna as a quick protein fix in salads or between the bread, few think of it as a terrific fresh fish alternative in cooked dishes. You'll discover in this dish how super and sophisticated tuna

SECOND TIME AROUND

SOOTHING CREAMY RICE: *The cheese and rice turn somewhat hard when refrigerated overnight, so the best way to reheat leftovers is to layer them in a baking pan and top with some tomato sauce. Cover the baking pan and bake in a microwave or a toaster oven or regular oven preheated to 350°F for as long as it takes to get very hot.*

SECOND TIME AROUND

FIERY TUBETTI: Leftovers are delicious served as a salad with a mustard mayonnaise dressing or a vinaigrette. Chopped fresh tomatoes are a nice addition.

can taste dressed up with black olives and red pepper flakes.

The other attractive feature of this recipe is that there's hardly any work involved in making it. You assemble the sauce ingredients in a bowl, boil and drain the pasta, and then toss the two together. The warmth of the pasta heats the sauce enough so that you're spared the clean-up of a second pan.

Salt
1 pound tubetti, tubettini, or elbow
    macaroni
2 cans (7 ounces each) tuna packed
    in water
1 package (10 ounces) frozen petite
    peas, thawed
¼ cup olive oil
¼ cup lemon juice
2 tablespoons black olive paste or
    pesto
½ teaspoon dried red pepper flakes,
    or more to taste

1. Bring a large pot of salted water to a boil over high heat. Add the pasta and cook until tender but still firm to the bite, about 10 minutes.

2. Meanwhile, drain the tuna and peas. Place the olive oil, tuna, peas, lemon juice,

olive paste, and pepper flakes in a mixing bowl. Mix well with a fork.

3. When the pasta is cooked, drain it thoroughly and return it to the pot, off the heat. Add the tuna mixture to the pot and toss to combine. Cover the pot and let the mixture sit for a minute or so to heat through. Season to taste with salt and more pepper flakes, if desired.

LEMONY PASTA WITH SMOKED FISH AND CAPERS

MAKES 2 SERVINGS
TIME: 20 MINUTES

Nubbins of tubettini—squat, ¼-inch hollow noodles—take on a somewhat Sicilian identity when combined with an amalgam of smoked oysters, sardines, capers, and lemon juice. If you have a fat bunch of fresh parsley on hand, you can mince the leaves and add them at the end to make the recipe taste even better.

I've made this recipe for just 2 because the taste is quite exotic and you should make it in a small batch first to see if you like it. If you do, next time double the ingredients to serve 4.

Salt
1⅓ cups tubettini or orzo
Leaves from 1 big fat bunch fresh
    parsley (optional but preferable)
1 can (3 to 4 ounces) smoked
    oysters, mussels, or clams
    packed in oil
1 can (2½ ounces) smoked sardines
    packed in oil
2 tablespoons lemon juice
1 tablespoon capers
Freshly ground black pepper

1. Bring a large saucepan of salted water to a boil over high heat. Add the pasta and cook until the pasta is tender but still firm to the bite, about 10 minutes.

2. Meanwhile, rinse and stem the parsley. Coarsely chop the parsley in a food processor. Add the oysters and sardines with their oil, the lemon juice, and capers; process briefly just until coarsely chopped. (You can also chop by hand, but this is easier.)

3. Drain the pasta and return it to the pot, off the heat. Add the smoked fish mixture and toss the ingredients until well combined. Season to taste with salt and pepper. Serve immediately, before the ingredients cool too much.

VARIATION

Smoked Fish Pasta with Raisins—an even more authentic Sicilian combination: Steep ¼ cup raisins, preferably golden, in 2 tablespoons lemon juice. Use 2 cans smoked sardines and omit the other smoked shellfish and lemon juice.

Toss the lemon-steeped raisins and sardine mixture with the cooked pasta.

ACINI PEPE WITH ARTICHOKE HEARTS AND SALMON

MAKES 4 SERVINGS
TIME: 20 MINUTES

The beady texture of the acini pepe complements the flakiness of the salmon. If you omit the artichoke hearts or corn, you can serve either a vegetable or salad with this.

SECOND TIME AROUND

LEMONY PASTA: Leftovers make the basis of a terrific salad. Add a diced red or green bell pepper for crunch and a dressing of ¼ cup mayonnaise blended with 1 tablespoon lemon juice. Give the salad a toss and serve on a bed of greens with an additional sprinkling of parsley over all.

Salt
2 cups acini pepe, orzo, or elbow
    macaroni
2 packages (10 ounces each) frozen
    artichoke hearts or corn kernels,
    thawed (optional)
4 cans (6½ ounces each) salmon or
    tuna packed in water
3 tablespoons lime or lemon juice
¾ cup spaghetti sauce, homemade
    (see Index) or prepared
½ cup bottled clam juice or chicken
    broth
Salt and freshly ground black
    pepper

1. Bring a large pot of salted water to a boil over high heat. When the water comes to a boil, add the pasta and cook until tender but still firm to the bite, about 10 minutes. If you're using the artichokes or corn, add them to the boiling water for the last minute of cooking.

2. Meanwhile drain the salmon and place it in a mixing bowl. Add the lime juice, spaghetti sauce, and clam juice, and stir to combine.

3. Drain the pasta and vegetables and return them to the pot. Off the heat, add the salmon mixture and toss until well combined. Season to taste with salt and pepper. Serve immediately.

SECOND TIME AROUND

ACINI PEPE: Serve leftovers chilled and dressed with an herb vinaigrette. Add more fish or some chopped fresh vegetables, such as bell peppers, mushrooms, or tomatoes, if desired.

CREAMY LENTIL CASSEROLE WITH DRIED APRICOTS

MAKES 4 TO 6 SERVINGS
TIME: 40 MINUTES

When you combine humble lentils with exotic millet and infuse them with the fiery heat of curry and the subtle sweetness of apricots, you'll have turned a few pantry ingredients into exciting fare.

If you've got some smoked ham in the freezer or leftover meat in the fridge, cube and reheat it in the casserole along with the apricots at the end of the cooking time. A dollop of plain yogurt finishes this dish nicely.

1 tablespoon olive oil
1½ teaspoons curry or chili powder
1 cup millet or brown rice
1 cup dried lentils
4 cups chicken broth or water
Salt and freshly ground black
    pepper
1 cup dried apricots
Plain low-fat yogurt or sour cream
    (optional)

1. Preheat the oven to 375°F.

2. Heat the oil in a 4-quart ovenproof pan or casserole over medium heat. Add the curry powder and millet and sauté, stirring occasionally, until the millet begins to smell toasty, about 1 minute.

3. Add the lentils and broth. Bring the liquid to a boil and season to taste with salt and pepper. Cover and bake until the grain and lentils are almost completely tender, about 25 minutes.

4. Meanwhile, cut the apricots into halves.

5. Stir the apricots into the casserole, cover, and bake until all the ingredients are cooked through and hot, about another 10 minutes. Adjust the seasoning and serve with a dollop of yogurt if you like.

BARBECUED BLACK BEANS AND RICE

MAKES 4 SERVINGS
TIME: 25 MINUTES

Even on nights when you're so tired you find yourself wishing for a live-in cook, you'll have enough energy left to whip up this delicious supper because it is virtually work free.

Although this alone is filling enough for dinner, if you crave a fresh vegetable, broccoli or cauliflower goes well and is nice and easy to prepare. Simpler still is a package of frozen vegetables heated as you cook the black beans.

1 cup long-grain white rice
2 cups water
2 cans (16 ounces each) black beans
1 can (14½ ounces) Italian-style stewed tomatoes
1 can (4 ounces) chopped green chilies
1 package (10 ounces) frozen corn or other vegetable of your choice, thawed (optional)
2 tablespoons barbecue sauce, or more to taste
¾ teaspoon ground cumin
Salt and freshly ground black pepper

1. Bring the rice and water to a boil in a medium-size saucepan. Reduce the heat, cover the pan, and simmer until the rice is just tender, about 18 minutes.

2. Meanwhile rinse and drain the beans and combine with the tomatoes, chilies, corn if using, barbecue sauce, and cumin in another medium-size saucepan.

ESPECIALLY GOOD FOR CHILDREN

BARBECUED BLACK BEANS: Omit the cumin and green chilies. When the barbecued beans are cooked, set aside 1 portion to remain mild. Stir ½ teaspoon cumin into the remaining beans and simmer a minute or so more to integrate the flavor of the spice.

SECOND TIME AROUND

BARBECUED BLACK BEANS: Leftovers can be thinned with broth or water, heated, and served as a soup on the second night.

DRIED MUSHROOMS

Dried wild mushrooms infuse food with a deep woodsy flavor unmatched by that of fresh mushrooms. Added to a long simmering soup or casserole, they make everyday fare taste festive.

During the week, though, it's hard to make use of these tasty nuggets because most recipes instruct one to presoak the dried mushrooms for at least 1 hour before using. On ordinary work nights, who has time to presoak an ingredient before getting down to the business of cooking? I discovered, quite by accident, that if the dried mushrooms are cooked in a dish that has plenty of liquid like a soup or stew, for at least 45 minutes, the mushrooms soften as well as if you had presoaked them.

Simmer the beans gently over low heat until the rice is cooked, about 10 minutes. Season to taste with salt and pepper.

3. If the rice has not absorbed all of the liquid, drain it off. Season the rice to taste with salt and pepper. Ladle the rice into deep bowls, then ladle the black beans with sauce over the top.

A WINTER DISH OF CHICK-PEAS AND WILD MUSHROOMS

MAKES 4 TO 6 SERVINGS
TIME: 5 MINUTES WORK
45 MINUTES NO-WORK COOKING TIME

The most ordinary of ingredients takes on a special character with the addition of dried mushrooms. I discovered that you don't need to presoak dried mushrooms if you simmer them in enough liquid long enough.

Serve this over cooked pasta or grains.

2 cans (16 ounces each) chick-peas
½ ounce dried wild mushrooms, preferably imported
1 can (14½ ounces) stewed tomatoes, or Italian plum tomatoes, coarsely chopped, with juices
Pinch of garlic powder
Salt and freshly ground black pepper

1. Drain and rinse the chick-peas. Break the dried mushrooms into small pieces and combine them with the chick-peas, tomatoes, and garlic powder in a medium-size saucepan.

2. Bring the liquid to a simmer over medium heat, while pressing the tomatoes against the side of the pan to break them up. Cover the saucepan and cook until the mushrooms are tender, about 45 minutes. Season to taste with salt and pepper.

VARIATION

If you have fresh mushrooms on hand, thinly slice ½ pound mushrooms and sauté them in 1 tablespoon olive oil in a medium-size saucepan until hot. Add 2 tablespoons water, cover the saucepan, and simmer over medium heat until softened, about 5 minutes. Add the dried mushrooms and proceed with the recipe as directed.

EXOTIC MILLET AND RAISIN CASSEROLE

MAKES 4 SERVINGS
TIME: 35 MINUTES

The beauty of this recipe is that it requires a minimum of work and yet tastes special because it makes use of the unusual grain millet. Those cooks who are more at ease with familiar foods can substitute rice. Serve with crusty bread and fruit for dessert.

1 cup hulled millet, quinoa, or long-
   grain white rice
1 can (14½ ounces) stewed
   tomatoes
½ cup raisins
½ teaspoon dried lemon peel
1½ cups chicken broth or water,
   plus more if needed
Salt and freshly ground black
   pepper to taste
1 package (10 ounces) frozen
   chopped spinach, thawed
½ cup walnuts

1. Combine all the ingredients except for the spinach and walnuts in a medium-size saucepan. (If using quinoa, rinse it first under cold running water to rid it of any saponin residue.)

2. Slowly bring the liquid to a boil over low heat. Cover and simmer until the grain is tender and has absorbed all of the liquid, 20 to 25 minutes. Be sure to check after 15 minutes of cooking; if too much liquid has evaporated, add more broth or water.

3. Meanwhile squeeze the spinach dry and coarsely chop the walnuts.

4. When the grain is tender, stir in the spinach, cover, and simmer 5 minutes longer. Stir in the walnuts and adjust the seasoning. Serve hot.

TOMATO AND GARLIC-FLAVORED CHICK-PEAS

MAKES 4 TO 6 SERVINGS
TIME: 5 MINUTES WORK
25 MINUTES NO-WORK COOKING
TIME

Some time back, I developed recipes for a low-cholesterol cookbook. The foods that actively help to reduce choles-

SECOND TIME AROUND

EXOTIC MILLET: This casserole is another example of a dish that works well as a second-time-around soup. Add enough chicken broth or water to the leftovers to thin the casserole to a hearty soup consistency. Sprinkle the top with plenty of fresh parsley.

terol are mostly legumes, grain brans, and fish high in omega-3 fatty acids. At that time I came up with this uncommon combination of chick-peas and sardines; it proved to be as felicitous in flavor as it is purportedly beneficial to one's health. It is also remarkably easy to prepare—a delightful bonus to the repertoire of any Monday-to-Friday cook.

2 cans (16 ounces each) chick-peas
3 cans (3½ ounces each) smoked
   sardines packed in water
1 cup spaghetti sauce, homemade
   (see Index) or prepared
2 tablespoons grated Parmesan
   cheese, or more to taste
¼ teaspoon garlic powder
Freshly ground black pepper to taste

1. Preheat the oven to 350°F.

2. Rinse and drain the chick-peas. Drain the sardines separately. Combine all the ingredients thoroughly in a 13 × 9-inch baking pan. Cover the pan with aluminum foil and bake until heated through, 20 to 25 minutes.

SOUPS

Soups, like stews, are perfect weeknight fare. In a single pot the foundations of a nutritious dinner—protein, vegetable, and starch—are combined and carried in a tasty broth. Soups are appropriate any time of the year, the range of flavor possibilities is infinite, and they make use of all sorts of ingredients—both fresh and leftover. I can't think of an easier way to make dinner, which is what these soups are—the main course not just the starter.

If it's soup for dinner during the week, it can't take longer than an hour to prepare and cook. And, it has to include protein: meat, poultry, fish, eggs, or some complementary protein combination, like beans and grains. Once I've decided on the main protein, I build my soup around it. The soup will also include a foundation of seasoning vegetables, a liquid of some sort, the herbs and spices that will give it a distinctive identity, additional vegetables for color and nutrition, and perhaps a starch for body.

THE FOUNDATION FLAVORS

First I create a bed of taste by stewing flavorful vegetables that work best with the basic protein and the other surrounding ingredients.

Onions or other members of the onion family, carrots, and celery are sure-fire neutral flavors that work with everything. Bell peppers, tomatoes, and mushrooms form the second tier of seasoning vegetables.

They're more aromatic and distinctive than onions and carrots and dominate other tastes; use them only if you like their unique flavors.

I consider the vegetables listed above "foundation flavors" because they add character to soup, work well with a huge variety of other tastes, can be cooked in advance, and their flavors remain constant even with reheating.

Never add to the foundation of a soup members of the cabbage family: Brussels sprouts, broccoli, cabbage, kohlrabi, or cauliflower because with reheating, their texture turns mushy and their flavor turns acrid.

Once I've chosen one or a number of these seasoning vegetables, I stew them tenderly in some oil just until soft. I then add the liquid and whatever protein I've settled on.

THE LIQUID

If the ingredients that make up the soup are hearty and flavorful enough, the liquid need not be more complex than water. Broths and stocks add flavor of course, and on occasion, I'll use either canned chicken broth or clam juice. Tomato juice, vegetable juice, and canned tomatoes are other liquid alternatives.

THE SEASONINGS

Dried herbs and spices are added along with the liquid and further contribute to the identity of the soup. The character of each soup is determined by what I like and what's in season, but I find that my taste memories guide me in determining how the recipe develops.

For example, I associate beans with Tex-Mex flavors, so that the seasonings in my bean soups will include oregano, cumin, or chili powder. If lamb is the star protein, then curry flavors like cumin and turmeric or Middle Eastern seasonings, like cardamom and mint, find their way into the pot. My idiosyncrasy is to make seafood soups based on French dishes—thyme, tarragon, saffron, and white wine come to mind. Cornmeal soup reminds me of polenta, so then Italian seasonings play a crucial role. Seasoning possibilities are endless and should be playfully orchestrated according to palate and creativity.

THE VEGETABLES AND STARCH

Additional vegetables add flavor, color, as well as nutrition. They should be added to the soup in sequence according to how long it takes for them to cook. Your choice in vegetables will be guided by seasonal availability and your own tastes, of course.

Add starch when you want hearty filling soup, especially in winter. Diced potatoes or yams, pasta

beads, crumbled dried bread, pieces of corn chips, tortilla strips, as well as an assortment of grains or beans all add weight, thickness, and flavor.

FINISHING TOUCHES

A cheerful scattering of chopped fresh herbs, a sprinkling of grated hard cheese, a scoop of yogurt or sour cream, or a dash of a condiment such as pesto or black olive paste adds the final layer of flavor as well as a lovely finish.

MAKING AND STORING SOUP

Because I'm so fond of soup, I always make a double batch of the base and freeze the foundation in portions of two. Then whenever I want soup, I can heat the frozen base, add a frozen or fresh vegetable, a protein and starch, and almost instantly I've created a substantial and flavorful dinner.

Refrigerated soups last 3 to 4 days; frozen soups will keep up to 6 months.

MICHELE'S FOUNDATION SOUP: NEW ENGLAND CHOWDER

MAKES 4 SERVINGS
TIME: FOUNDATION SOUP: 30 MINUTES
30 MINUTES MORE FOR ADDITIONAL INGREDIENTS

I named this chowder "foundation" soup because it is the perfect example of a hearty basic soup that can change character throughout the week to please your family's individual tastes and needs. It is both simple and full of American down-home goodness.

If you double or triple the base and freeze it in 2-cup portions, you can then thaw the frozen portions any night of the week and finish it with potatoes and seafood.

To make this soup in larger or smaller quantities, figure on for each portion: ½ onion, ½ rib celery, 1 medium potato, 1 to 2 carrots, 4 to 6 ounces fish, and 1 to 2 cups broth or other liquid.

To round out the meal, either first serve Watercress Salad with Ricotta Pecorina, A Basic Vegetable Salad, or A Monday-to-Friday Green Salad, or follow this soup with Broiled Bananas or Brown-Sugar-Glazed Pineapple (see Index for page numbers).

2 large onions
2 ribs celery (optional)
2 tablespoons vegetable or olive oil
4 to 6 carrots
1 can (14 ounces) Italian plum
    tomatoes
⅓ cup dry white wine
2 cups fish stock or water or 2
    bottles (8 ounces each) clam
    juice
4 medium-size boiling potatoes
Salt
½ teaspoon dried herb, such as
    thyme, marjoram, or oregano
2 to 3 drops Tabasco sauce
1 to 1½ pounds fish fillets, such as
    monkfish, halibut, fresh tuna, or
    cod
½ cup fresh herb leaves such as
    parsley or dill (optional)

1. Finely chop the onions and celery.
2. Heat the oil in a medium-size saucepan over medium heat. Add the onions and celery and sauté for about 1 minute, just to get them sizzling. Cover the pan, reduce the

TOMATO TIME-SAVER

Chopping canned tomatoes is a messy job whether you do it on a cutting board or in a food processor. To save yourself a preparation step and clean-up, add the whole tomatoes to the pot whenever a recipe instructs you to add chopped canned tomatoes. Break them up by smashing them against the side of the pot with a wooden spoon.

heat, and simmer gently, stirring on occasion, until the onions are translucent, about 5 minutes.

3. Meanwhile peel and slice the carrots ½ inch thick.

4. Add the tomatoes with their juices to the pan and break them up against the side of the pan with a wooden spoon. Add the carrots, wine, and broth. Cover the pan and simmer gently for 10 minutes, or for however long it takes to peel the potatoes. (Foundation soup can be made up to this point then frozen. The potatoes should be cooked fresh because they don't freeze well.)

5. Peel the potatoes, cut them into 1-inch chunks, and add them to the pan. Season to taste with salt, the dried herb, and Tabasco. Cover and simmer until all the ingredients are tender, about 30 minutes.

6. Meanwhile cut the fish into small pieces. Rinse and mince the fresh herb, if using. About 5 minutes before serving, add the fish and fresh herb, if using, and simmer just until the fish is cooked through. Adjust the seasoning.

VARIATIONS

■ Add 1 package (10 ounces) frozen corn kernels or chopped spinach when you add the potatoes.

■ **Chicken Chowder:** For the fish stock and fish, substitute chicken broth and 1 pound boneless, skinless chicken or turkey breasts, cut into small pieces.

■ **Vegetarian Chowder:** For the fish stock and fish, substitute vegetable broth and 4 firm bean curd cakes, cut into small pieces.

BEEF AND NOODLE SOUP A LA VIETNAMESE

MAKES 4 SERVINGS
TIME: 1 HOUR

Chunks of beef, soothing noodles, and crisp bean sprouts come together in a hot and spicy broth, making this soup a best bet for cold nights. Intriguingly flavored, it is based on a Vietnamese dish, and although hardly an authentic rendition, the contrast of hot with sour and the abundance of coriander is typical of the tastes of Southeast Asia.

I usually precede this with a green salad and serve ice cream for dessert.

1 pound boneless beef round
2 cloves garlic
1 piece (1 to 2 inches) ginger
1 piece (2 inches) cinnamon
2 quarts water, plus more as needed
1 large bunch fresh coriander or
     Italian (flat-leaf) parsley
¼ pound vermicelli, capellini, or
     Chinese or buckwheat (soba)
     noodles
Salt
2 tablespoons lime or lemon juice
2 cups fresh bean sprouts
½ teaspoon dried red pepper flakes

1. Cut the meat into ¾-inch cubes. Peel the garlic. Combine the beef, ginger, garlic, and cinnamon in a soup pot. Add the water and bring it to a boil over medium heat, skimming off the scum that floats to the surface. Reduce the heat to low and very gently simmer the soup until the meat is tender, about 45 minutes. Continue to remove the scum that rises to the top. As the liquid evaporates, replenish it with fresh water.

2. Meanwhile rinse, stem, and mince the coriander and measure out the remaining ingredients.

3. When the meat is tender, add the noodles and simmer until they're tender, 5 to 10 minutes. Season the soup to taste with salt.

4. Remove the soup from the heat and stir in the lime juice, bean sprouts, pepper flakes, and coriander. Remove the garlic, ginger, and cinnamon stick. Adjust the seasoning and serve piping hot.

VARIATION

To make this soup using roast beef, substitute 2 cups of cubed or julienned leftover roast beef for the fresh beef. In step 2, simmer for 10 minutes only, then proceed with the rest of the recipe.

CHICKEN SOUP WITH RICE

MAKES 4 SERVINGS
TIME: 25 MINUTES

Even though I originally made this soup to warm us up on a winter night, I agree with Maurice Sendak who says, "All seasons of the year are nice for eating chicken soup with rice."

While this surely will appeal to kids and adults alike, with a few changes you could turn this into a sophisticated seafood soup for grown-ups only.

CHICKEN BROTH

Whenever I poach chicken breasts or any other chicken parts, I always freeze in ice cube trays any remaining cooking liquid. Even if the flavor isn't strong enough to serve as is, the liquid makes a flavorful base for other dishes I might be planning during the week.

Following the soup, serve a hearty salad like Spinach, Orange, and Ricotta Cheese Salad or Watercress Salad with Ricotta Pecorina or a substantial dessert like Sautéed Chestnuts and Pineapple or Port-Soused Fruit with Yogurt (see Index for page numbers).

2 cups chicken broth
3 cups water
1 tablespoon lemon juice
1 clove garlic
½ cup long-grain white rice
1 pound boneless, skinless chicken
  breasts
1 cup fresh parsley leaves (optional)
Salt and freshly ground black
  pepper

1. Combine the chicken broth, water, and lemon juice in a medium-size saucepan. Peel the garlic clove and drop it in. Cover the pan and bring the liquid to a boil over high heat.

2. Add the rice, cover, and simmer over medium heat until the rice is soft, about 15 minutes.

3. Meanwhile cut the chicken into thin shreds. Rinse and mince the parsley.

4. When the rice is tender, add the chicken. Cover and continue to simmer until the chicken is just cooked through, about

5 minutes. Fish out the garlic clove and season the soup to taste with salt and pepper. Serve immediately. Grown-ups can sprinkle parsley over the top of their bowls if they wish.

VARIATION

Seafood and Rice Soup: In step 1 increase the lemon juice to 2 tablespoons and add a 1-inch piece of fresh ginger.

Substitute 1 pound seafood, such as squid cut into 1-inch-thick slices, crabmeat, or sea scallops for the chicken and fresh coriander for the parsley.

In step 4, simmer the seafood until it just turns opaque, then stir in the coriander. Fish out the ginger with the garlic.

GINGERY CHICKEN AND SPINACH SOUP

MAKES 4 SERVINGS
TIME: 30 TO 35 MINUTES

You've just come home from an after-work cocktail party and you need to eat something quickly, both light and substantial. Ginger infuses this soup with just the right amount of bite, the chicken gives it substance, the spinach makes it healthy, and the noodles provide some comfort. Comforting, too, is that clean-up is kept to a minimum because dinner is cooked in a single pot.

1 onion
1 piece (½ inch) fresh ginger or ¾
*   teaspoon ground*
1 tablespoon Oriental sesame or
*   vegetable oil*
6 cups chicken broth or water
1 package (10 ounces) frozen
*   chopped spinach*
1 pound boneless, skinless chicken
*   or turkey breasts*
½ bunch scallions (green onions),
*   or 1 small bunch fresh coriander*
2 cups vermicelli, fine egg noodles,
*   orzo, or pastina*
3 to 4 tablespoons lemon
*   juice*
Salt and freshly ground
*   black pepper*
Sesame seeds (optional)

1. Finely chop the onion. Peel and mince the ginger.

2. Heat the oil in a soup pot over medium heat. Add the onion and ginger, in-crease the heat to high, and sauté for a few seconds to release their aroma. Add the broth and spinach. Cover the pot and bring the liquid to a boil. Reduce the heat and simmer until the spinach is thawed, about 10 minutes.

3. Meanwhile cut the chicken into thin shreds or ¾-inch chunks. Slice the scallions including about 4 inches of the green tops, or rinse, stem, and mince the coriander leaves.

4. When the spinach has thawed, stir the soup, then add the chicken and noodles. Cover and simmer until the noodles and chicken are cooked, about 5 minutes. Add the scallions or coriander and the lemon juice. Season to taste with salt and pepper.

Serve immediately, passing the sesame seeds for sprinkling over each portion.

CHUNKY VEGETABLE-CHICKEN SOUP

MAKES 4 TO 6 SERVINGS
TIME: 35 TO 40 MINUTES

Not unlike the ginger chicken soup that precedes, this soup is lighter

TO THAW OR NOT TO THAW

Save yourself some time by adding frozen vege-tables directly to a soup or stew. They'll thaw right in the pot as they cook. The dish might take a few more moments to cook, but the overall timing won't change much.

MUSHROOM STEMS

Although mushroom stems don't make attractive eating, I often save both domestic and shiitake stems to use in flavoring stocks. Domestic stems get soft and if the soup is a thick one, you can certainly leave them in, hidden among other ingredients. On the other hand, shiitake stems remain rubbery and should be removed.

and more appropriate for spring. It is so easy and quick that I never double the recipe.

Follow the soup with a seriously rich dessert like Unbelievable Chocolate-Chestnut Purée, or Chocolate-Walnut Pudding or Sauté of Summer Fruit (see Index for page numbers).

By the way, this is also a terrific soup to make use of leftover bits of roast chicken, turkey, or game hens.

4 carrots
12 fresh mushrooms, preferably shiitake
2 quarts chicken broth or water or combination of both
½ small head bok choy, Chinese cabbage, or romaine lettuce (enough for 2 cups shredded)
4 radishes
1 pound boneless, skinless chicken breasts or 2 cups cubed leftover poultry
2 bean curd cakes, preferably soft
1 bunch watercress
2 scallions (green onions)
2 tablespoons lemon juice
1 tablespoon soy sauce
Salt and freshly ground black pepper

1. Peel and thinly slice the carrots. Stem, rinse, and thinly slice the mushroom caps (save the stems to flavor a bean stew).

2. Place the carrots, mushrooms, and chicken broth in a medium-size saucepan. Bring the liquid to a boil over medium heat. Reduce the heat and simmer covered for about 10 minutes.

3. Cut the bok choy into thin shreds. Thinly slice the radishes. Cut the chicken into thin strips or ¾-inch chunks.

4. Add the bok choy, radishes, and chicken to the pan, and simmer until the chicken is cooked through, about 5 minutes.

5. Meanwhile cut the bean curd into ½-inch dice. Rinse and stem the watercress. Thinly slice the scallions including about 4 inches of the green tops. Add these to the soup along with the lemon juice and soy sauce; simmer just until the greens are wilted. Remove from the heat, season to taste with salt and pepper, and serve.

CHUNKY PEASANT VEGETABLE SOUP

MAKES 6 TO 8 SERVINGS
TIME: 30 MINUTES WORK
30 MINUTES NO-WORK COOKING
TIME

Naming this soup "peasant vegetable" means you can toss into the pot just about anything you want. What matters is that the soup be rich and have enough chunky vegetables in it to call it dinner.

2 onions
4 cloves garlic
½ head green cabbage
2 carrots or parsnips
2 white turnips or boiling potatoes
2 fresh beets or 1 can (16 ounces)
    sliced beets
2 tablespoons olive oil
2 quarts chicken broth or water
1 ham hock (optional)
½ cup pearl barley or cracked wheat
½ teaspoon dried marjoram
1 can (16 to 19 ounces) white
    cannellini beans or chick-peas
1 to 2 tablespoons lemon juice
Salt and freshly ground black pepper

1. Finely chop the onions and mince the garlic. Core the cabbage and cut it into thin shreds. Peel and slice the carrots ½ inch thick. Peel and dice the turnips and fresh beets (just dice canned beets).

2. Heat the oil in a soup pot over medium heat. Add the onions and sauté, stirring on occasion, until they begin to wilt, 3 to 4 minutes. Add the garlic and cabbage and sauté 1 minute.

3. Add the broth to the pot along with the ham hock if using, barley, marjoram, carrots, turnips, and fresh beets (if using canned beets, add them later). Bring the liquid to a boil, cover the pot, and simmer over medium heat until the barley is tender, about 30 minutes.

4. Add the white beans with their liquid and the canned beets if using. Simmer for 10 minutes more. Add the lemon juice and salt and pepper to taste. If you've added a ham hock, remove it from the soup, cut off the meat, return the meat to the soup, and simmer until hot, about 2 minutes.

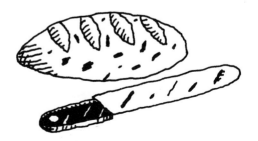

SECOND TIME AROUND

CHUNKY PEASANT VEGE-TABLE SOUP: I've made this in a large quantity so that you can get two meals out of it. If you're going to freeze this, make it with turnips, not potatoes which get waterlogged when frozen.

DOUBLING UP

OODSY MUSHROOM
AND SCALLOP

*SOUP: This is a perfect
soup base to make in dou-
ble or even triple batches
and freeze in 2-cup por-
tions for a rainy day. The
base works as well with
poultry, grains, or pasta as
it does with fish. However,
to make the base neutral
enough to use with these
other ingredients, use
chicken broth or water
instead of the clam juice.*

WOODSY MUSHROOM AND SCALLOP SOUP

**MAKES 4 SERVINGS
TIME: 40 TO 50 MINUTES**

This refreshing fish soup is perfect summer fare. To round out the dinner, accompany it with slices of a robust whole-grain bread and follow it with a lovely fruit dessert such as Cherry Clafouti or Rhubarb-Strawberry Dessert (see Index for recipes).

*1 clove garlic
³⁄₄ pound fresh domestic mushrooms
¹⁄₄ pound fresh shiitake mushrooms
2 bell peppers, preferably red
1 tablespoon vegetable or olive oil
¹⁄₄ cup water, or more if needed
1 can (14¹⁄₂ ounces) stewed
    tomatoes
1 bottle (8 ounces) clam juice
¹⁄₂ teaspoon dried oregano
1¹⁄₂ pounds sea scallops or boneless,
    skinless monkfish or fresh tuna
Salt and freshly ground black
    pepper*

1. Finely mince the garlic. Stem, rinse, and pat dry the mushrooms (reserve the mushroom stems for another soup), then thinly slice the caps. Core, seed, and thinly slice the bell peppers.

2. Heat the oil in a soup pot over medium heat. Add the garlic and sauté for a few seconds just to release the aroma. Add the mushrooms and peppers and sauté for a minute to get them cooking.

3. Add the water, cover the pot, and simmer over low heat until the mushrooms and peppers are tender, about 10 minutes. Check on them every now and then to make sure they're not scorching. If the water has evaporated, add a few more tablespoons and continue to simmer.

4. Add the stewed tomatoes, clam juice, and oregano to the pot. Bring the liquid to a boil, cover, and simmer gently over low heat for another 10 minutes, while you prepare the scallops. (This soup base is now ready for you to add whatever you wish to turn it into dinner. See Doubling Up.)

5. Remove the tough, rubbery appendage from the side of each scallop and halve them if they are large (or cut the fish into 1-inch chunks). Add the scallops to the soup and simmer uncovered until just cooked through, 2 to 3 minutes. Season to taste with salt and lots of pepper.

SOUP WITH TUNA AND SUMMER VEGETABLES

MAKES 2 SERVINGS
TIME: 30 TO 35 MINUTES

This soup is lovely on nights when you need to sup on something light yet filling and when you feel like spending even less time on cooking than you ordinarily do. If I'm still hungry after this, I usually dig into a sandwich or whip up a salad.

1 bunch scallions (green onions)
1 medium-size cucumber
4 small tomatoes
6 radishes
2 cans (7 ounces each) tuna packed
    in water
½ cup fresh coriander or parsley
    leaves
1 bottle (8 ounces) clam juice
2 cups water
3 tablespoons lemon juice
1 tablespoon capers
1 teaspoon black olive paste
    (optional)
Salt and freshly ground black
    pepper

1. Thinly slice the scallions including most of the green tops. Peel, halve, seed, and finely chop the cucumber. Quarter, seed, and chop the tomatoes. Thinly slice the radishes. Drain the tuna. Rinse and mince the coriander.

2. In a medium-size saucepan, combine the scallions, cucumber, tomatoes, radishes, tuna, clam juice, and water. Cover the pan and bring the liquid to a simmer over medium heat. Simmer gently until the radishes are tender, about 10 minutes.

3. Stir in the lemon juice, capers, coriander, and olive paste if using. Simmer until all the ingredients are hot, about 1 minute longer. Season to taste with salt and pepper.

POLENTA SOUP

MAKES 4 SERVINGS
TIME: 45 MINUTES

This colorful combination of tomatoes, corn, and green chilies is thickened with cornmeal into a robust polentalike porridge. Make a meal of it by accompanying it with ham sandwiches and a watercress salad.

SECOND TIME AROUND

SOUP WITH TUNA: *Leftovers should be eaten hot the next day, for they won't keep any longer than that. If there isn't enough for a second dinner, add more clam juice to the soup along with more tuna to stretch the protein content. In addition you could add cooked rice or another light grain.*

SECOND TIME AROUND

POLENTA SOUP: To reheat the soup, you must first thin it with some broth or water or it will scorch as you heat it and have a gummy texture. You can enrich the soup on the second day by adding some cubed ham or leftover pork roast.

1 medium-size onion
2 cloves garlic
2 large tomatoes or 1 can (14½ ounces) Italian plum tomatoes
1 to 2 tablespoons corn or vegetable oil
6 cups chicken broth or water
1 package (10 ounces) frozen corn kernels
1 can (4 ounces) chopped green chilies
¼ cup fresh coriander or parsley leaves
½ cup yellow cornmeal
Salt and freshly ground black pepper
1 tablespoon lemon or lime juice
½ cup shredded Cheddar cheese (optional)

1. Chop the onion and mince the garlic. Core and finely chop the tomatoes, reserving the juices.

2. Heat the oil in a medium-size saucepan over medium heat. Add the onion and sauté 2 to 3 minutes.

3. Add the garlic, tomatoes, broth, corn, and chiles. Bring the liquid to a simmer, then cover the pan and cook gently over low heat for 15 minutes. Meanwhile rinse and mince the coriander.

4. While whisking constantly, slowly drizzle the cornmeal into the simmering soup. Simmer gently uncovered until thickened, about 10 minutes. Stir the bottom on occasion to make sure the cornmeal isn't sticking.

5. Season the soup to taste with salt and pepper. Right before serving, stir in the lemon juice, Cheddar cheese if using, and coriander. Adjust the seasoning and serve immediately.

BARLEY-VEGETABLE CHOWDER

MAKES 4 TO 6 SERVINGS
TIME: 20 MINUTES WORK
45 MINUTES NO-WORK COOKING TIME

Cook a batch of this soup on a winter night when you are in need of sustenance but barely have the energy to boil water.

The barley with beans is both nutritious and satisfying. A portion of this robust soup is enough dinner for me, but if you think it won't be enough, follow it with a vegetable salad or with a dessert like Broiled Bananas or Brown Betty Peaches (see Index for recipes).

This is not a soup to make in double batches and save for future use. Potatoes, barley, and beans just don't take well to freezing. Leftovers, though, can be refrigerated and eaten a couple of days later.

6 cups chicken broth or water
½ cup pearl barley, short-grain
    white rice, or orzo
1 medium-size boiling potato
1 medium-size white turnip
1 rib celery
2 to 3 carrots
6 scallions (green onions)
1 bunch escarole or romaine lettuce
1 can (16 to 19 ounces) white
    cannellini beans
Salt and freshly ground black
    pepper
Grated Parmesan cheese (optional)

1. Combine the broth and barley in a soup pot and bring the liquid to a simmer over medium heat.

2. Add each vegetable to the pot as you prepare it: Peel the potato and turnip and cut them into ¾-inch chunks. Dice the celery. Peel the carrots and slice ¾ inch thick.

3. Bring the liquid to a boil, then cover the pot, reduce the heat, and simmer gently for 30 minutes.

4. Meanwhile thinly slice the scallions including 4 inches of the green tops. Rinse and coarsely chop the escarole.

5. Add the white beans with their liquid to the soup. Season to taste with salt and pepper. Simmer covered 15 minutes longer. Add the escarole and scallions and simmer until wilted, about 2 minutes. Adjust the seasoning. Serve very hot with grated Parmesan on the side.

VARIATIONS

If you omit the barley and the beans, you've got a light vegetable soup, a reliable first course for any night of the week. You can add sliced chicken or turkey to this starter soup for a main course that is lighter than the original barley and bean combo.

SECOND TIME AROUND

BARLEY-VEGETABLE CHOWDER: Barley is as absorbent as a Bounty paper towel (or so we've been led to believe), so that you'll have to thin any leftover soup with broth or water the next day. After you've brought it to a simmer, you can stretch the leftovers with chopped fresh greens and slivers of fresh chicken.

SAVORY THICK GREENS SOUP

MAKES 4 TO 6 SERVINGS
TIME: 35 MINUTES

This thick and hearty soup, replete with beans and greens, is so filling that I doubt you'd want to eat anything more for dinner.

2 bunches scallions (green onions)
2 large tomatoes or 1 can (14½ ounces) Italian plum tomatoes
2 tablespoons olive oil
2 cans (16 ounces each) red or white kidney beans
1 cup long-grain brown or white rice
2 quarts chicken broth or water
Salt and freshly ground black pepper
1 pound fresh greens, such as kale, spinach, turnip, or mustard greens, or 1 package (10 ounces) frozen chopped greens, thawed

1. Thinly slice the scallions, including most of the green tops. Puree the tomatoes (fresh or canned, with seeds and skin) in a food processor or blender until smooth.

2. Heat the olive oil in a soup pot over medium heat. Add the scallions and sauté until just beginning to wilt, about 1 minute.

3. Add the tomatoes, beans with their liquid, rice, and broth. Bring the liquid to a boil and season to taste with salt and pepper. Cover the pot and cook gently over low heat until the rice is tender, about 25 minutes for brown rice, 20 minutes for white rice.

4. Meanwhile trim and rinse the greens, then coarsely chop. If you're using frozen greens, add them to the soup pot and simmer 10 minutes more. If you're using fresh greens, add them to the pot and simmer just until wilted, 3 to 4 minutes. Adjust the seasoning and serve hot.

EGG RIBBON SOUP

MAKES 4 SERVINGS
TIME: 15 TO 30 MINUTES

When you want something quick and light as well as nourishing, this tasty soup is just the ticket.

6 cups chicken broth
4 eggs or 8 egg whites
½ pound fresh spinach or 1 bunch
    watercress or 8 leaves escarole
    or romaine lettuce or 1 package
    (10 ounces) frozen chopped
    spinach, thawed
Salt and freshly ground black
    pepper
¼ cup grated Parmesan cheese
    (optional)

1. Bring the broth to a boil in a medium-size saucepan over medium heat.

2. Meanwhile, lightly beat the eggs in a mixing bowl. Rinse, stem, and chop the fresh greens, or drain the frozen spinach well.

3. Add the greens to the broth and bring the liquid back to a simmer.

4. Whisking constantly, pour the beaten eggs into the soup. The eggs will curdle into ribbon-shaped strands. Season to taste with salt and pepper and remove the pan from the heat. Ladle the hot soup into bowls and sprinkle Parmesan over each portion, if you desire.

VARIATIONS

Shreds of leftover roasted chicken, smoked ham, or chopped and fresh peeled shrimp can be added in step 2 along with the greens.

CORN, TORTILLA, AND SPLIT PEA SOUP

MAKES 4 SERVINGS
TIME: 50 MINUTES

To give even more substance to this already hearty dish, add diced smoked ham or cooked sliced chorizo.

When this soup is not enough for dinner, I follow it with a cucumber salad or Watercress, Water Chestnut, and Red Pepper Salad or with Cranberry-Pear Mousse instead (see Index for page numbers).

2 quarts chicken broth or water
1 cup or ½ pound split green peas
4 medium-size boiling potatoes
1 cup fresh coriander leaves
1 bunch scallions (green onions)
4 corn tortillas
1 package (10 ounces) frozen corn kernels
1 can (4 ounces) chopped green chilies
1 teaspoon dried oregano
½ teaspoon ground cumin
Salt
3 to 4 drops Tabasco sauce, or more
    to taste
2 to 3 tablespoons lime juice

DOUBLING UP
•

CORN, TORTILLA, AND SPLIT PEA SOUP: You can make the split pea base in a double batch and freeze half for another day, but if you do, you should omit the potatoes.

SECOND TIME AROUND

CORN, TORTILLA, AND SPLIT PEA SOUP: To get a radically different second meal out of leftovers, mince 1 clove garlic and chop 2 red bell peppers; sauté in 2 tablespoons oil in a large skillet until tender. Add 2 cups diced ham and the leftover soup and simmer until hot. Add more liquid if the soup is too thick. Off the heat, stir in ½ bunch fresh parsley, stemmed and minced.

1. Combine the broth and peas in a large soup pot. Slowly bring the liquid to a boil over low heat. Meanwhile peel the potatoes and cut them into 1-inch chunks. Add the potatoes to the broth as you peel and cut them. When the liquid comes to a boil, reduce the heat to low and simmer, partially covered, until the potatoes and split peas are tender, about 30 minutes. (This is the split pea base. See Doubling Up, page 109.)

2. While the split peas are cooking, rinse and mince the coriander. Thinly slice the scallions including 4 inches of the green tops. Toast the tortillas for a few minutes in a 350°F oven or toaster oven until somewhat dry and crisp. (If you don't have the energy, then don't bother. The tortillas won't taste as good but will still be okay.) Break the tortillas into 1-inch pieces.

3. When the split peas and potatoes are tender, add the corn, green chilies, oregano, and cumin. Simmer for 10 minutes. Season to taste with salt and Tabasco.

4. Add the tortillas, coriander, scallions, and lime juice. Simmer until the tortillas soften, 2 to 3 minutes more. Adjust the seasoning and serve hot.

SPLIT PEA SOUP WITH CAULIFLOWER AND SAUSAGE

MAKES 4 SERVINGS
TIME: 1 HOUR

Make this soup when a rainy day has got you down and you need something that is hearty to eat yet easy to make to soothe your spirits and warm your soul.

The type of sausage you choose depends on your diet, but it should be of high quality because it greatly affects the flavor of the soup.

This dish is so rich, I don't serve anything else for dinner.

½ pound fresh or frozen sausage links, preferably not too spicy
3 cloves garlic
1 cup or ½ pound split green peas
2 quarts chicken broth or water
½ teaspoon dried herb, such as rosemary, thyme, or marjoram
Salt and freshly ground black pepper
1 small head cauliflower
1 cup fresh herb leaves, such as parsley or dill

1. Slice the fresh sausage ½ inch thick and sauté in a large soup pot over medium heat just until cooked through, 5 to 10 minutes. If you're using frozen sausage links, cook them according to package directions, then slice ½ inch thick. Remove the sausages to a plate.

2. Mince the garlic. Add the garlic, split peas, broth, and dried herb to the pan. Bring the liquid to a boil over medium heat. Reduce the heat to low, cover, and simmer until the split peas are tender, about 35 minutes. Season lightly with salt and pepper (the sausage will add more seasoning later).

3. While the split peas are cooking, separate the cauliflower into small florets. Rinse and mince the fresh herb.

4. When the split peas are cooked, stir them vigorously with a whisk to slightly purée them. Add the cauliflower and simmer covered until tender, about 10 minutes. Add the sliced sausages and heat for a minute or so longer to heat them through.

5. Remove the pot from the heat and adjust the seasoning. Stir in the parsley and serve hot.

VARIATION

For vegetarians, omit the sausages and add instead 2 cups more liquid and ½ ounce dried mushrooms with the split peas. Add ½ cup long-grain rice or other grain or 1 cup

orzo or acini pepe with the cauliflower and cook until tender.

BEAN MINESTRONE

MAKES 4 TO 6 SERVINGS
TIME: 1 HOUR

Keep this stick-to-the-ribs bean dish in mind for frigid winter nights. You can keep the soup simple for kids by making it with just vegetables and pasta or make it heartier for adults by adding the beans. The Parmesan adds a world of flavor, so please don't omit it unless your diet so dictates.

To complete the meal, I serve either Cabbage and Pepper Slaw or Basic Vegetable Salad. When kids are around, I skip the salad and serve dessert instead. We like Sliced Oranges and Vanilla.

SECOND TIME AROUND

BEAN MINESTONE: If you anticipate having leftovers, don't stir in the Parmesan because it doesn't reheat well; serve it on the side instead.

Leftovers should be thinned the next day with broth, water, or tomato juice because the soup thickens quite a bit with standing. Also chopping and adding a big bunch of fresh parsley or dill will brighten the soup's flavor the second night.

ESPECIALLY GOOD FOR CHILDREN

BEAN MINESTRONE: Omit the fennel or celery, lima beans, and canned beans if you think it's necessary. You can simply add pasta after step 2 and simmer for 10 minutes. Serve Parmesan on the side.

If grown-ups are to partake of this, you can add the beans and fresh spinach after all the kids are served and simmer another 10 minutes to heat up the beans. The pasta will be mushy but the soup still tastes yummy.

1 clove garlic
1 bulb fennel or 2 ribs celery
2 carrots
2 tablespoons olive oil
3 cups water
1 can (28 ounces) Italian plum
   tomatoes
1 package (10 ounces) frozen lima
   beans or corn kernels
1 can (16 ounces) red or white
   kidney beans
1/2 teaspoon dried marjoram
Salt and freshly ground black pepper
1 pound fresh spinach or 1 package
   (10 ounces) frozen chopped
   spinach, thawed
1 cup elbow macaroni or orzo
1/2 cup freshly grated imported
   Parmesan cheese

1. Mince the garlic. Trim the feathery tops from the fennel and cut the bulb lengthwise in half; cut out the core and coarsely chop the fennel into 1-inch pieces (coarsely chop the celery). Peel and slice the carrots 1/2 inch thick.

2. Heat the olive oil in a soup pot over medium heat. Add the garlic, fennel, and carrots and sauté until the vegetables are hot and sizzling, 3 to 4 minutes. Add the water, cover, and simmer over low heat until the vegetables are barely tender, about 5 minutes.

3. Add the tomatoes with their juices and break them up against the side of the pot with a wooden spoon. Add the lima beans; rinse and drain the red beans and add them too. Bring the liquid to a boil over medium heat. Add the marjoram and salt and pepper to taste. Reduce the heat to low and simmer, covered, until the flavors come together, about 30 minutes.

4. Meanwhile rinse, stem, and coarsely chop the fresh spinach if using.

5. Stir the macaroni and frozen spinach, if you are not using fresh, into the soup and simmer until the pasta is tender, about 10 minutes more.

6. Add the fresh spinach if using and simmer just until wilted. Remove the soup from the heat, stir in the Parmesan, and adjust the seasoning. Serve hot.

SPICED PEANUT AND SWEET POTATO SOUP

MAKES 4 TO 6 SERVINGS
TIME: 55 MINUTES

I sometimes omit the beans in this soup to create a lighter version of it, which I then follow with a substantial main-course salad like Smoked Seafood Salad or Salad of Smoked Turkey and Bulgur (see Index for page numbers).

1 medium-size onion
1 clove garlic
2 medium-size sweet potatoes
2 tablespoons vegetable oil
½ teaspoon ground cumin
½ teaspoon chili powder
½ teaspoon ground cinnamon
¼ teaspoon cayenne pepper
2 tablespoons tomato sauce
    or ketchup
¼ cup peanut butter, preferably
    "natural"
4 cups chicken broth or water
2 cans (16 ounces each) white beans
Salt and freshly ground black
    pepper

1. Finely chop the onion and mince the garlic. Peel the sweet potatoes and cut them into 1-inch cubes.

2. Heat the oil in a medium-size saucepan over medium heat. Add the onion and sauté, stirring on occasion, until the onion begins to wilt, about 5 minutes.

3. Add the sweet potatoes, garlic, spices, tomato sauce, peanut butter, broth, and beans with their liquid. Bring to a boil. Reduce the heat to medium-low and simmer, covered, until the sweet potatoes are very tender, about 35 minutes. Season to taste with salt and pepper and serve hot.

GAZPACHO

MAKES 4 SERVINGS
TIME: 20 MINUTES

Basically this soup is simply a mess of fresh crisp vegetables puréed with tomato juice. A heaping bowl of gazpacho accompanied by a Picnic Loaf (see Index), or sandwiches of ham, cheese, or chick-pea purée makes a most satisfying summer supper. Leftovers keep for 3 to 4 days.

 **ESPECIALLY GOOD FOR CHILDREN**

SPICED PEANUT SOUP: The following changes make this an appealing soup for kids. (Well, my kid liked it.) Reduce the ground spices to ¼ teaspoon each and omit the cayenne and white beans. Purée the soup in a blender before serving and top with sour cream.

SECOND TIME AROUND

GAZPACHO: Strips of fresh mozzarella cheese and crumbled hard-boiled egg are lovely additions that turn the soup into a more substantial next day meal.

4 scallions (green onions)
4 bell peppers, preferably red
4 small cucumbers
1 clove garlic
4 cups tomato juice
¼ cup fresh herb leaves, such as
*   parsley or basil (optional)*
1 to 2 tablespoons olive oil
1 to 2 tablespoons red wine vinegar
Salt and cayenne pepper
1 cup cubed day-old French or
*   Italian bread (optional)*

1. Trim the scallions and cut them into large pieces. Core, seed, and quarter the peppers. Peel and seed the cucumbers, then coarsely chop. Peel the garlic.

2. Purée the above ingredients with the tomato juice, herb, and olive oil in a blender or food processor. The mixture should be chunky. Add vinegar, salt, and cayenne to taste.

3. If you find the mixture too soupy, add cubed dried bread and purée again until it is thick enough for your taste. Cover and refrigerate, at least 1 hour or until serving time.

PASTA

Pasta, in all its assorted shapes and sizes, sauced in infinite ways, served hot or cold, is the mainstay of our meals at least twice a week, every week, all year long. Pasta provides the perfect solution for hurried weekday meals: the noodles are done in 10 minutes and the sauce can be as quick as a splash of olive oil and a sprinkling of grated cheese.

Pasta is also a great Monday-to-Friday solution for what to do with yesterday's roast and leftover cooked vegetables, or cupfuls of last week's stew, smidgeons of grated cheese, or remnants of condiments.

The choices of pasta are endless. They come in all kinds of shapes and thicknesses, and they can be either fresh and soft like noodles made from white flour and egg, or dry and pre-shaped like the packaged noodles made from hard durum wheat.

Saucing the pasta affords you even more variety than the type of pasta. A sauce can be made from any-thing that will at once moisten, season, and bind the noodles together in some harmonious and delicious-tasting whole: A smooth purée of cheese or a heap of chopped fresh tomatoes bound with fragrant olive oil and seasoned with parsley. Or the sauce can be a meal in itself, such as ground meat and minced vegetables bathed in tomato sauce.

What pasta shape you cook is really up to you. If you've stocked your pantry well, you will have a variety to choose from. Do keep in mind the following:

- It's easier to envelop long strands of noodles with smooth sauces that cling to them. A thin coating of olive oil, a dab of butter with a drizzle of herbs, or a sauce of smoothly puréed ingredients adhere to these slippery noodles, while chunky sauces, with bits and pieces of ingredients, simply bounce off them.
- The coarse and robust sauces combine better with the twists and turns of shaped pasta or hollowed-out tubes that were designed to snag and ensnare the toothsome chunks of ingredients.
- Snippets of tubettini, grains of orzo, and beads of acini pepe, served as side dishes, are best left plain—dressed at most with a toss of oil or butter, and a sprinkling of salt, pepper, and maybe fresh herbs.

SPICY SPAGHETTINI

—

**MAKES 4 SERVINGS
TIME: 25 MINUTES**

This is a fresh and light pasta dish, perfect for people on a diet and for sticky summer nights. The juices of the fish and zucchini make for a natural, light sauce.

Salt
2 cloves garlic
1 pound zucchini, yellow squash, or
　　pattypan squash
1 pound monkfish, sea scallops, or
　　fresh crabmeat
1 pound spaghettini or linguine fini
¼ cup olive oil
1 teaspoon dried red pepper flakes,
　　or more to taste
2 tablespoons lemon juice

1. Bring a large pot of salted water to a boil for the pasta.
2. Meanwhile mince the garlic. Rinse the zucchini and cut into ½-inch dice. Cut the fish or seafood into ½-inch pieces.
3. When the water comes to a boil, add the pasta and cook until tender but still firm to the bite, about 10 minutes.
4. Meanwhile heat the olive oil in a large skillet over medium-high heat. Add the garlic and sauté for a few seconds until you can catch its aroma. Add the pepper flakes, lemon juice, zucchini, and fish. Season to taste with salt. Cover the skillet, reduce the heat, and simmer gently until the seafood is cooked through, 6 to 8 minutes.
5. Drain the pasta and portion it out into wide bowls. Ladle the sauce over the top and serve immediately.

VARIATION

Substitute about 3 cups finely diced leftover roast chicken or 1 pound finely cubed fresh poultry for the fish.

ORZO WITH SALMON AND ASPARAGUS

—

**MAKES 6 TO 8 SERVINGS
TIME: 40 TO 45 MINUTES**

This looks gorgeous, tastes wonderful, and is a good example of how to turn pasta into a one-pot meal—simply cook the ingredients in sequence and save on clean-up. This is purposely made in a large batch so you have enough leftovers to serve for the next day or so.

> 1½ pounds salmon fillets or tuna fillets or fresh shrimp, peeled and deveined
> 36 medium asparagus spears
> 2 cups fish stock or bottled clam juice and 4 cups water, or 6 cups water
> Salt
> 1 box (16 ounces) orzo or acini pepe
> 1 small bunch fresh dill or basil
> 6 small or 4 medium-size tomatoes
> 2 to 4 tablespoons olive oil
> 2 tablespoons white wine vinegar
> ¼ teaspoon dried red pepper flakes
> Freshly ground black pepper

1. With tweezers or small pliers, pluck any stray bones from the salmon. Cut the fillets into 1-inch cubes. Break the tough (silvery) ends from the asparagus and cut the spears into ½-inch lengths.

2. Bring the stock and/or water to a boil in a large saucepan over medium-high heat. Add salt to taste and orzo, stir a couple of times, and cook partially covered for 4 minutes.

3. Add the asparagus, cover, and cook until the asparagus is tender, another 4 minutes. Add the fish, cover, and cook until it is just cooked through, 3 to 4 minutes more.

Drain in a sieve and return to the pot, off the heat.

4. While all of this is going on, rinse and stem the dill and put the leaves in a food processor. Quarter the tomatoes and add them along with the oil, vinegar, and pepper flakes. Process until puréed.

5. Stir the tomato sauce into the pasta and season to taste with salt and pepper. Serve immediately in deep dishes.

BUCKWHEAT NOODLE RAGOUT

MAKES 4 SERVINGS
TIME: 35 TO 40 MINUTES

Buckwheat noodles, vegetables, and seafood cooked in a light broth is a terrific meal to make when you're unsure of the hour you'll be dining. The broth and cooked vegetables can be held off the heat up to a couple of hours if need be. When you're ready to eat, just pop the fish into the noodles and dinner's done in a flash.

A Watercress, Water Chestnut, and

SECOND TIME AROUND

***ORZO WITH SALMON:** Leftovers are best served chilled and additionally dressed with chopped fresh bell pepper and more of the tomato vinaigrette described in step 4 or with Basic Vinaigrette (see Index). Because of the fish, don't keep leftovers longer than a day.*

SECOND TIME AROUND

BUCKWHEAT NOODLE RAGOUT: Because the noodles will swell and absorb all of the liquid when they stand in the broth overnight, before you reheat the dish, add more water or water mixed with clam juice to make the consistency soupy once again. You can stretch the leftovers into a second meal by adding more seafood, such as smoked mussels, and a thawed frozen vegetable, such as petite peas or corn kernels.

Red Pepper Salad (see Index) makes a fine course to precede or follow this meal.

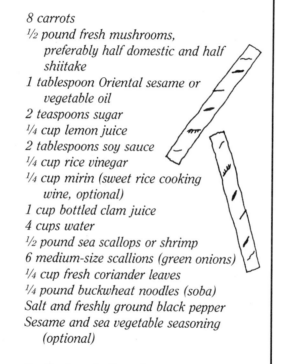

> 8 carrots
> ½ pound fresh mushrooms, preferably half domestic and half shiitake
> 1 tablespoon Oriental sesame or vegetable oil
> 2 teaspoons sugar
> ¼ cup lemon juice
> 2 tablespoons soy sauce
> ¼ cup rice vinegar
> ¼ cup mirin (sweet rice cooking wine, optional)
> 1 cup bottled clam juice
> 4 cups water
> ½ pound sea scallops or shrimp
> 6 medium-size scallions (green onions)
> ¼ cup fresh coriander leaves
> ¼ pound buckwheat noodles (soba)
> Salt and freshly ground black pepper
> Sesame and sea vegetable seasoning (optional)

1. Peel and slice the carrots ¼ inch thick. Stem the mushrooms (reserve the stems for soup), rinse, and thinly slice the caps.

2. Heat the oil in a deep large skillet or large saucepan over medium-high heat. Add the carrots and mushrooms and sauté about 1 minute. Stir in the sugar, then add the lemon juice, soy sauce, rice vinegar, mirin if using, clam juice, and water. Bring the liquid to a simmer over medium heat; cover and simmer 5 to 10 minutes.

3. Meanwhile trim the tough, rubbery appendage from the side of each scallop and halve them, or peel, devein, and halve the shrimp. Trim the scallions and thinly slice. Rinse and finely chop the coriander. (If you are going to hold the broth until much later, refrigerate these prepared ingredients until ready to use.)

4. About 5 minutes before serving, add the noodles to the broth and bring the liquid back to a simmer. Cover the pan and simmer until the noodles are almost tender, about 5 minutes.

5. Stir the scallops or shrimp into the noodles and simmer covered until the seafood is just cooked through, 2 to 3 minutes more. Remove the skillet from the heat and stir in the scallions and coriander. Season to taste with salt and pepper. Serve in deep dishes, and sprinkle with sesame seasoning if you wish.

VARIATIONS

Thin capellini or vermicelli noodles can be substituted for the buckwheat noodles but should be cooked for only 2 to 3 minutes.

Strict vegetarians can substitute ½ pound firm tofu, diced, for the seafood.

ELBOWS WITH TUNA AND SUN-DRIED TOMATOES

MAKES 4 SERVINGS
TIME: 35 TO 40 MINUTES

Here's a terrific dish to make when you know you won't have time to cook the following night; it tastes wonderful served hot on the first night and served chilled, as a pasta salad, on the second night.

This is as much a cinch to make as it is a pleasure to eat. The tuna and carrots take on a special character when combined with the sunny taste of black olives and sun-dried tomatoes. This is also perfect for families with split tastes: grown-ups can enjoy the sophisticated flavor of the sauce and the kids can have the macaroni simply dressed with olive oil and cheese.

For dessert I serve fresh fruit, ice cream, or, when I have the time, Raspberry Mousse (see Index).

Salt
1 large onion
4 medium-size carrots
¼ cup sun-dried tomatoes packed in oil
1 cup (tightly packed) fresh parsley leaves, preferably Italian (flat-leaf)
1 pound (4 cups) elbow macaroni, penne, or fusilli
½ cup olive oil
2 cans (7 ounces each) tuna packed in water
2 tablespoons black olive paste
1 teaspoon dried red pepper flakes
Freshly ground black pepper

1. Bring a large pot of salted water to a boil for the pasta.

2. Thinly slice the onion. Peel and slice the carrots ¼ inch thick. Finely julienne the sun-dried tomatoes. Rinse and mince the parsley.

3. Add the pasta to the boiling water before cooking the sauce.

4. Heat the olive oil in a large skillet over medium heat. Add the onion and carrots and sauté until somewhat softened, 5 minutes. Add the sun-dried tomatoes, lower the heat, cover, and simmer until the carrots and onions are completely tender, 7 to 10 minutes more.

SECOND TIME AROUND

ELBOWS WITH TUNA: Make the entire recipe in a double batch so that you can serve half of it as a pasta salad the next night if you won't have time to cook or if you're coming home late and want dinner waiting in the fridge. On the second night, add (to a full recipe) ½ cup Basic Vinaigrette (see Index), freshen up the color by adding more chopped fresh parsley, and bolster the protein content by adding more tuna if it needs it.

5. Add the tuna to the skillet along with the black olive paste and pepper flakes; sauté a few minutes longer just to heat the tuna through. Remove the skillet from the heat.

6. When the pasta is tender but still firm to the bite, drain it well. Stir the parsley into the sauce and season to taste with salt and pepper. To serve, dish some pasta into each bowl and ladle the sauce over top.

AROMATIC EGGPLANT AND CHICKEN WITH PASTA SHELLS

MAKES 4 TO 6 SERVINGS
TIME: 1¼ HOURS

This spicy combination of eggplant and carrots is amazingly versatile as a base in which to stew anything from cubes of chicken to leftover roast lamb. Vegetarians can make a meal of it, too, by mixing in cooked black beans or by topping it with ricotta cheese.

SECOND TIME AROUND

AROMATIC EGGPLANT: Reheating this dish will cause the chicken to toughen, but you can eat it at room temperature or chilled, stuffed into pita bread, tossed with some greens, or mixed into cool plain yogurt.

1 large eggplant (about 1¼ pounds)
Salt
2 medium onions
2 green bell peppers
4 medium-size carrots
4 medium-size cloves garlic
2 tablespoons vegetable oil
½ teaspoon ground cardamom
½ teaspoon cayenne pepper
½ teaspoon ground coriander
½ teaspoon ground cumin
½ teaspoon ground ginger
¼ teaspoon ground cloves
¼ teaspoon paprika or ground turmeric, for color
2 cans (14½ ounces each) Italian plum or stewed tomatoes
1 pound pasta shells, fusilli, or penne
1 pound boneless, skinless chicken breasts

1. Cut the eggplant into 1-inch cubes and toss them with 1 teaspoon salt in a mixing bowl; let stand about 20 minutes while you prepare the other ingredients.

2. Chop the onions. Core, seed, and chop the peppers. Peel and thinly slice the carrots. Mince the garlic.

3. Bring a large pot of salted water to a boil for the pasta.

4. Heat the oil in a large saucepan over medium heat. Add the onions and peppers and cook covered over low heat until tender, about 5 minutes. Add the garlic and spices; sauté for a few seconds until you can smell the aroma. Add the carrots, then the eggplant, squeezing out as much moisture as you can before tossing it into the pot. Add the tomatoes and break them up against the side of the pan with a wooden spoon. Cover, and cook over medium heat until the vegetables are tender, about 20 minutes.

5. Meanwhile add the pasta to the boiling water, cook until tender but still firm to the bite, about 10 minutes, and drain. Cut the chicken into 1-inch cubes.

6. About 5 minutes before the vegetables are done, add the chicken and simmer until cooked through. Season the sauce to taste with salt and ladle over the drained pasta shells.

PASTA FAGIOLI WITH VEGETABLES

MAKES 4 SERVINGS
TIME: 1 HOUR

On a dreary, cold winter night when you're tired and in need of solace, make this heartwarming dish of beans and pasta. You'll derive comfort both from its soothing flavor and from the fact that it requires a minimum of preparation and very little clean-up.

My version of pasta fagioli, an Italian comfort dish par excellence, is inauthentic, but it's loaded with restorative vegetables, rich in homemade goodness.

1 onion
2 green bell peppers
4 carrots
2 tablespoons olive oil
1 can (28 ounces) imported Italian
    plum tomatoes
2 cloves garlic
2 cups water
1 teaspoon dried rosemary
1 can (19 ounces) chick-peas
½ pound (2 cups) elbow macaroni
Salt and freshly ground black
    pepper

SECOND TIME AROUND

PASTA FAGIOLI: Beans and pasta act like sponges, so that the dish will be very thick the following day. Thin with water or broth and simmer until heated through. To change the character of the dish on the second night, stir in ½ cup grated Cheddar cheese or Parmesan after you've reheated it.

THE LAYERED VEGETABLE COOKING TECHNIQUE

If you'd rather not make a favorite recipe because it requires you to cook lots of vegetables separately and then combine them later, try this method: You can save on time and pot washing if you sauté or simmer the vegetables in sequence, beginning with those that take the longest to cook and ending with those that are quick to cook.

The ones that take longest to cook are carrots, cauliflower, broccoli, peppers, onions, and root vegetables. Mushrooms can be cooked for a long or short time. Vegetables that are quickly cooked are summer squashes, snow peas, and fresh greens. Thawed frozen vegetables shouldn't be cooked for more than a couple of minutes.

1. Finely chop the onion. Core, seed, and finely chop the peppers. Peel and thinly slice the carrots.

2. Heat the olive oil in a medium-size saucepan over medium heat. Add the onions, peppers, and carrots; cook covered over low heat until tender, about 10 minutes.

3. Add the tomatoes with their juices to the pan and break them up against the side of the pan with a wooden spoon. Peel the garlic and drop the cloves into the pan. Add the water and rosemary. Simmer covered over low heat until all the vegetables are soft, about 15 minutes.

4. Rinse and drain the chick-peas and add them to the pan. Simmer until the chick-peas are heated through and the flavors are well blended, about 10 minutes more.

5. Add the pasta to the pan, cover, and cook over medium heat until the pasta is tender, about 10 minutes.

6. Fish out the garlic cloves if you can find them (or warn your diners about their presence if you can't). Season to taste with salt and pepper and serve very hot.

VARIATIONS

■ To finish the flavor, sometimes I stir in an additional 2 tablespoons olive oil or butter at the end of the cooking time.

■ To sharpen the bite, I add a few drops of Tabasco sauce when seasoning the dish.

■ To add an intriguing taste, I might add 2 cups shredded escarole or radicchio leaves at the end and simmer just until wilted.

PASTA (OR GRAINS) PRIMAVERA

MAKES 4 SERVINGS
TIME: 45 MINUTES

Restaurant recipes for pasta primavera assume the cook has at his or her flank an army of sous-chefs who are dicing, chopping, blanching, and precooking an array of spring vegetables before she or he even begins to assemble the dish.

My version is designed for the ordinary home cook and achieves the same taste as restaurant versions. Instead of cooking each vegetable separately and then assembling the lot with the pasta, I cook them in a single skillet, beginning with the ones that take longest to cook.

Traditionally this spring vegetable sauce is served over pasta, but it tastes as good with rice, baked fish, or plain sautéed chicken.

Because Pasta Primavera is filling

and satisfying enough for a dinner, at most I serve some bread alongside it.

Salt
1 package (10 ounces) frozen petite peas
1 large onion
1 large bell pepper, preferably red
1/2 pound fresh mushrooms, shiitake
     or domestic
6 carrots
12 asparagus spears
2 fresh large tomatoes
1/2 cup packed fresh basil leaves
1 pound pasta, such as fusilli, elbow
     macaroni, orzo, or penne
1/4 cup olive oil
1/2 cup chicken broth or dry white wine
Freshly ground black pepper
Grated Parmesan cheese (optional)
Ricotta cheese (optional)

1. Bring a large pot of salted water to a boil for the pasta. Remove the peas from the freezer to thaw.

2. Finely chop the onion. Core, seed, and cut the pepper into thin strips. Stem, rinse, and thinly slice the mushrooms (reserve the stems for soup). Peel and slice the carrots 1/4 inch thick. Snap off the tough ends of the asparagus stems (about 1 inch from the bottom) and cut the spears into 1/2-inch lengths. Cut the tomatoes into quarters, remove the seeds with a spoon, and dice. Rinse and mince the basil.

3. Add the pasta to the boiling water, then begin the sauce.

4. Heat the olive oil in a large pot or skillet over medium heat. Add the onion and bell pepper and sauté for 1 minute to release their aroma. Cover the pan, reduce the heat, and simmer until tender, 5 minutes.

5. Add the mushrooms and broth to the pot; cover and simmer for another 5 minutes. Add the carrots and asparagus to the pot; cover and simmer until the vegetables are just tender, about 5 minutes more. Add the peas and simmer 1 minute to heat them through. Season to taste with salt and pepper.

6. Meanwhile drain the pasta the moment it is cooked but still firm to the bite. Return the drained pasta to the cooking pot and leave it, off heat, until the sauce is done.

7. You can finish and serve the dish two ways: Serve a portion of pasta to each person, then ladle the sautéed vegetables and tomatoes on each portion. Sprinkle with basil, and serve. The advantage here is that leftovers of either pasta or vegetables can be put to better use when kept separate than when combined. Or, mix the vegetables, tomatoes, and basil into the pasta right in the pot and toss well off heat. Season to taste with salt and pepper and ladle into deep plates. Either way, serve grated Parmesan and/or ricotta on the side if you wish.

TO MIX OR NOT TO MIX

Because I'm always hurried during the week, I let my husband and daughter (and anyone else eating with us) tackle the joy of mixing and combining the pasta with its sauce right in their own bowls. I settle a nest of noodles into each person's bowl, then just ladle the sauce on top. However, if you think a thorough premixing of noodles and sauce is crucial to the flavor of the meal, then combine the two, off heat, right in the pot you cooked the noodles and then dish it out.

VARIATIONS

■ **With cauliflower or broccoli:** Omit the asparagus, tomatoes, and basil. Mince 1 clove garlic and separate 1 head cauliflower or 1 bunch broccoli into florets.

Sauté the garlic a few seconds before you add the mushrooms. Increase the chicken broth to 1 cup. Add the cauliflower or broccoli with the carrots.

■ **With corn:** Substitute 1 package (10 ounces) frozen corn kernels for the peas. Increase the mushrooms to 1 pound. Substitute fresh mint or parsley for the basil. Mince 1 clove garlic and sauté it a few seconds before you add the mushrooms. Add the corn with the carrots.

■ **With squash and green beans:** Omit the peas and asparagus. Substitute mint for the parsley. Cut ½ pound fresh green beans into 1-inch lengths. Finely dice 2 medium yellow squash. Add the green beans and squash with the carrots.

PAPA PRIMAVERA

*O*ne of the all-time fabulous dishes I had in Florence was **papa pomodoro,** *a thick, aromatic soup made from stale Tuscan bread which is softened and simmered with fresh tomatoes, olive oil, and garlic.*

I love the flavor of this dish and adore the concept of bread as the mainstay of my dinner, but I don't like the pasty texture that results from stirring the bread in liquid over heat. Instead, I have come up with this compromise — "papa primavera" — a dish conceived and executed by me and nowhere to be found, I wager, in any classic Italian repertoire.

In the center of deep soup plates, I break up into small pieces dried (stale or dried in the oven) country whole-wheat Italian bread. I blanket the bread in each bowl with about ½ cup diced fresh tomatoes and 1 tablespoon chopped basil, drizzle 1 tablespoon olive oil over all, and let the bread soften while I make the vegetable mix for Pasta Primavera. I bring the hot vegetables and juices to a boil and ladle them over the bread and tomatoes. I let the dish set for about 5 minutes until the bread is soft enough to dig in.

CAPELLINI WITH HERBED COTTAGE CHEESE

MAKES 2 SERVINGS
TIME: 20 MINUTES

Puréeing cottage cheese with olive oil creates a richly flavored sauce without the calories or the saturated fat of heavy cream. This luscious concoction, flavored with tarragon and lemon and ready in 2 minutes, is an altogether appealing combination with thin noodles.

The sauce is enough for ½ pound of pasta, or for 2 portions. Simply double the proportions when serving 4. Serve broccoli or asparagus as a side dish.

Salt
1 shallot or 2 scallions (green onions)
¼ cup olive oil
¼ cup fresh parsley leaves
2 teaspoons dried tarragon
1 tablespoon lemon juice
½ teaspoon dried lemon peel
1 cup low-fat cottage cheese
Freshly ground black pepper
½ pound capellini, linguine fini, or spaghettini

1. Bring a large pot of salted water to a boil for the pasta.

2. Peel and halve the shallot (or trim the scallions and cut them into 2-inch pieces) and drop it into a food processor. Add the oil, parsley, tarragon, lemon juice, lemon peel, and cottage cheese. Purée until the mixture is smooth. Season to taste with salt and pepper.

3. Add the pasta to the boiling water and cook until tender but still firm to the bite, 5 to 10 minutes (depending upon how thick the pasta is). Drain the pasta and return it to the pot, off the heat. Add the cheese mixture and toss thoroughly. Serve immediately.

VARIATIONS

■ **For a richer version,** substitute ricotta cheese or ½ cup each soft fresh goat cheese and cottage cheese or ricotta for the cottage cheese.

■ **For an even richer version,** use ½ cup each of mascarpone and soft fresh goat cheese.

MID-WEEK MIRACLES

Often by Wednesday, my Monday-to-Friday momentum runs low and I'm stuck mid-week with no leftovers and no meal in mind. That's when I'm particularly pleased to have a quick and easy selection of pasta dishes in my repertoire. Capellini with Herbed Cottage Cheese is a favorite—creamy and comforting yet calorie efficient, it's a family pleaser that helps me over the Wednesday hurdle.

ESPECIALLY GOOD FOR CHILDREN

NEW-FASHIONED MAC-ARONI: Use the smaller amount of cheese and omit the Worcestershire and Tabasco. Grown-ups can drizzle these seasonings over their portions.

SECOND TIME AROUND

NEW-FASHIONED MAC-ARONI: To reheat the left-overs, top them with bread crumbs and bake in a toaster oven if you're reheating a small quantity or regular oven preheated to 350°F until hot, about 15 minutes.

NEW-FASHIONED MACARONI AND CHEESE

MAKES 4 SERVINGS
TIME: 25 MINUTES

I love macaroni and cheese, but during the week, I never make it the classic way because I don't have time to first make a white sauce, then cook the macaroni, assemble the dish, and finally put it in the oven to bake.

So I've come up with a technique that eases the work and speeds up the process. Choose the larger amount of cheese if you prefer a more powerful flavor.

¼ to ½ pound sharp Cheddar
  cheese, or half Cheddar and half
  Parmesan cheese
Salt
2 cups milk, whole or skim
2 tablespoons cornstarch
½ pound (2 cups) elbow macaroni
2 teaspoons Worcestershire sauce
Freshly ground black pepper
2 to 3 drops Tabasco sauce, or more
  to taste

1. Grate the cheese, or if you're feeling too lazy to take out the grater (as I always am), cut the cheese into paper-thin slices or into cubes no larger than ½ inch. Bring a large pot of salted water to a boil for the pasta.

2. Whisk the milk and cornstarch together in a medium-size saucepan (not aluminum or iron) and set aside.

3. Add the macaroni to the boiling water and cook until tender, about 10 minutes.

4. At the same time, slowly bring the milk and cornstarch to a simmer, whisking constantly, over medium heat. As the milk comes to a simmer, it will thicken. Stir three-quarters of the cheese into the sauce and reduce the heat to very low. Cook, stirring constantly, until the cheese melts. Add the remaining cheese, remove the pan from the heat, and let the remaining cheese melt. Add the Worcestershire sauce and season to taste with salt, pepper, and Tabasco.

5. Drain the elbows thoroughly and toss them with the sauce before serving or simply ladle the sauce over the pasta. Serve immediately.

VARIATION

To turn this into a complete meal, thaw 2 packages (10 ounces each) chopped spinach. Place the thawed spinach in a strainer and squeeze out as much moisture as you can with your hands. After the milk thickens, stir in the spinach before you add the cheese and proceed as directed.

FETTUCCINE WITH ARTICHOKES, FETA, AND TOMATOES

MAKES 4 SERVINGS
TIME: 35 MINUTES

The feta cheese adds protein, flavor, and body to this dish of fettuccine, which is otherwise sparingly dressed with artichokes and chopped fresh tomatoes.

This is light and easy to digest. On days when you're in need of something more to eat, follow it with a fish course like poached salmon baked under herbs.

Salt
1 can (14 ounces) artichoke hearts or 1 package (10 ounces) frozen artichoke hearts, thawed
4 tomatoes
¼ cup black olives or 1 tablespoon black olive paste
1 pound fresh or dried fettuccine, linguine fini, or spaghettini
4 to 6 ounces feta, goat, or Cheddar cheese
Freshly ground black pepper

1. Bring a large pot of salted water to a boil for the pasta.

2. Drain the artichokes and finely chop. Quarter the tomatoes, remove the seeds with a spoon, and finely chop. (The artichokes and tomatoes can be chopped together in a food processor.) If you're using whole olives, pit and then mince them.

3. Add the pasta to the boiling water and cook until tender but still firm to the bite, 2 to 3 minutes for fresh pasta or 10 minutes for dried.

4. Meanwhile bring the artichokes, tomatoes, and olives to a simmer in a large skillet. When the pasta is done, drain it and put a portion in each person's bowl.

5. Crumble the feta or goat cheese or grate the Cheddar into the sauce, then season to taste with salt and pepper. Ladle the sauce over the pasta and serve immediately.

SECOND TIME AROUND

FETTUCCINE WITH ARTICHOKES: Leftovers are delicious served the next day in a spinach salad with or without leftover fish.

CREAMY PENNE WITH WHITE CABBAGE AND BEANS

MAKES 4 SERVINGS
TIME: 45 MINUTES

Serve this sauce with pasta that can catch the mellow chunks of cabbage and bean. The grape juice softens the cabbage and the ricotta adds a creamy flavor and boosts nutrition.

A salad or a steamed vegetable, like a plateful of greens or steamed cauliflower, is all you need to make the meal complete.

Salt
1 large onion
½ head green cabbage
1 tablespoon olive oil
½ teaspoon anise or fennel seeds
1 cup white grape juice
2 cans (16 ounces each) white
*   cannellini beans*
1 pound penne, tubetti, elbows, or
*   fusilli*
Salt and freshly ground black pepper
1 cup ricotta cheese, whole or part-
*   skim (optional)*

1. Bring a large pot of salted water to a boil for the pasta.

2. Finely chop the onion. Core and cut the cabbage into thin shreds.

3. Heat the olive oil in a large saucepan over medium heat. Add the onion and sauté until tender, about 5 minutes. Add the cabbage, anise, and grape juice. Bring the liquid to a boil, cover, and simmer over low heat until the cabbage is nearly tender, about 10 minutes.

4. Rinse and drain the beans and add them to the cabbage. Cover and simmer about 10 minutes more.

5. Meanwhile add the pasta to the boiling water and cook until tender but still firm to the bite, about 10 minutes. Drain the pasta and return to its cooking pot, off heat. Season the cabbage and bean sauce with salt and pepper to taste. Add it to the pasta and toss well. Serve immediately, topped with ricotta if you wish.

PENNE A LA HUMMUS

MAKES 4 TO 5 SERVINGS
TIME: 40 TO 45 MINUTES

Here's a pasta dish for those who love the earthy Middle Eastern fla-

SECOND TIME AROUND

PENNE A LA HUMMUS: *Leftovers are delicious served over fresh salad greens and dressed with a vinaigrette. Adding tuna gives the hummus an even fresher face.*

vors of hummus: chick-peas, garlic, lemon, and tahini. The addition of watercress and fresh coriander picks up the color.

Make this on a day when you have no idea when everyone is going to eat, for this dish works at all temperatures: warm, room temperature, and chilled, dressed with additional lemon juice.

This is so satisfying, you'll want only a light fruit salad to complete the meal.

4 cloves garlic
1 jar (7 ounces) roasted red peppers
2 cans (16 ounces each) chick-peas
2 to 3 tablespoons tahini
6 tablespoons lemon juice
1 tablespoon olive oil
4 cups chicken broth or water
2 cups penne or elbow macaroni
2 bunches watercress
1 large bunch fresh coriander
Salt and freshly ground black
    pepper

1. Mince the garlic. Drain and chop the peppers. Drain the chick-peas and rinse. Thoroughly blend the tahini and lemon juice and set aside.

2. Heat the olive oil in a large saucepan over medium heat. Stir in the garlic and peppers and sauté for a few seconds until you can smell the garlic. Add the chick-peas, broth, and macaroni. Bring the liquid to a boil, then cover and simmer gently until the pasta is tender, about 15 minutes.

3. Meanwhile rinse the watercress and coriander and cut off their stems about ¼ inch below the bulk of the leaves. Chop the watercress and coriander leaves together.

4. When the pasta is tender, stir in the watercress and coriander and simmer a few seconds just until the leaves are wilted. Remove the pan from the heat and stir in the tahini mixture. Season to taste with salt and pepper. Cover the pan and let stand 10 minutes before serving; it tastes better served warm, not hot.

TUBETTINI WITH MINTED SPINACH AND RICOTTA

**MAKES 2 SERVINGS
TIME: 30 TO 35 MINUTES**

I much prefer the flavor of fresh spinach to frozen, but I recoil from the tedious job of ridding these greens of sand and grit. Every now and then, though, when I'm making dinner for just the two of us

ADDING TAHINI

Remember, when using tahini in hot dishes such as Penne à la Hummus, add it off the heat because heating the sesame paste alters its flavor and turns the taste bitter.

and when washing the spinach is the only demanding job involved in getting dinner on the table, I indulge my love of these fresh emerald leaves.

In this recipe, once the spinach is cleaned and chopped, it demands no further work, for it's gently wilted by the heat of the cooked pasta.

This is lovely served with Chicken Breast with Citrus or with Roasted Hens Flavored with Lemon, Garlic, and Raisins (see Index for page numbers).

To feed 4, simply double the recipe.

1 pound fresh leaf spinach
Salt
2 scallions (green onions)
½ cup part-skim ricotta cheese
1 tablespoon olive oil
1 tablespoon lemon juice
1 tablespoon fresh mint leaves or
  1 teaspoon dried
Freshly ground black pepper
½ pound tubettini or elbow
  macaroni

1. Stem the spinach and rinse the leaves thoroughly. Drain the spinach, then coarsely chop.

2. Bring a large pot of salted water to a boil for the pasta.

3. Trim the scallions and cut into pieces. Place the scallions, ricotta, olive oil, lemon juice, and mint in a blender or food processor; purée until smooth. Season to taste with salt and pepper.

4. When the water comes to a boil, add the pasta and cook until tender but still firm to the bite, 7 to 8 minutes. Drain the pasta and return it to the pot, off the heat. Add the chopped spinach and ricotta mixture; toss until well combined and the spinach is barely wilted. Serve immediately or the dish will turn gummy.

SPAGHETTI A LA LASAGNE

MAKES 4 SERVINGS
TIME: 20 TO 25 MINUTES

I adore a good lasagne but hate the work and time involved in precooking the noodles, making the sauce, layering the dish, and baking it for an hour. This is more than I can handle on a weekday.

When I crave lasagne during the week, I make this simple spaghetti dish instead. All the elements of a good lasagne are here, but they are combined in a simpler way: Spaghetti tossed with tomato sauce is topped with ricotta cheese mixed with Parmesan, olive oil, and fresh parsley.

> Salt
> 3 cups spaghetti sauce, homemade (see Index) or prepared
> 1 pound spaghetti or spaghettini
> ½ cup (tightly packed) fresh parsley leaves
> ¼ cup olive oil
> 1 pound ricotta cheese, whole or part-skim
> ¼ cup grated Parmesan cheese
> Freshly ground black pepper

1. Bring a large pot of salted water to a boil for the pasta. Heat the spaghetti sauce in a small saucepan.

2. Add the pasta to the boiling water and cook until tender but still firm to the bite, 8 to 10 minutes.

3. Meanwhile rinse and mince the parsley. Combine the olive oil, ricotta, Parmesan, and parsley in a small mixing bowl; season to taste with salt and pepper.

4. When the pasta is done, drain it and return it to the pot, off heat. Add the spaghetti sauce and toss well.

5. Ladle the pasta with sauce into deep bowls and top each portion with the ricotta mixture. Serve immediately.

VARIATIONS

There are two ways you can amplify the sauce:

■ **To add beans,** heat 1 can (16 to 19 ounces) red, black, or white beans with their juices in a large skillet, mashing the beans as you heat them. Stir in spaghetti sauce, bring the sauce to a simmer, and proceed as directed.

■ **To add meat,** crumble ½ pound ground veal or beef in a large skillet and sauté, stirring constantly, over medium heat until the meat is no longer pink. Stir in the spaghetti sauce, bring the sauce to a simmer, and proceed as directed.

HOMEMADE SPAGHETTI SAUCE

**MAKES ABOUT 1 QUART
TIME: 30 MINUTES WORK
2 HOURS NO-WORK COOKING TIME**

Because so many of my recipes call for a good spaghetti sauce, I want to include a recipe for a good basic one. Obvi-

WHAT TO DO WITH OVERCOOKED PASTA

Toss pasta that has gotten too mushy for plain saucing with some olive oil, ricotta cheese, fresh herbs, and a vegetable (petite peas work nicely), and top with bread crumbs. Bake at 375°F until hot and the bread crumbs are toasty, about 20 minutes.

WHAT TO DO WITH CLUMPY PASTA

f your leftover pasta has settled into an undissectable clump, dice it and toss it into soups to soften and cook further. It makes a nice change from rice.

ously this sauce can't be made during the week, but it makes for a good weekend project.

This recipe yields 1 quart but it can be doubled. It is most practical to freeze this in 1-cup portions.

The carrots sweeten the sauce and add an orange tint, but they can be omitted if you prefer a more acidic sauce.

> 2 carrots
> 1 onion
> 2 ribs celery
> 2 cloves garlic
> 6 pounds fresh tomatoes or 2 cans (28 ounces) Italian plum tomatoes
> 1 bay leaf
> 8 sprigs fresh parsley
> 1 teaspoon dried thyme
> ¼ cup olive oil
> ¼ cup (tightly packed) fresh basil leaves or 1 tablespoon prepared pesto
> Salt and freshly ground black pepper

1. Peel the carrots and mince. Also mince the onion, celery, and garlic. (You can do all of this in a food processor if you first cut the vegetables into large pieces.)

2. If using fresh tomatoes, drop the tomatoes into a large pot of boiling water for 30 seconds. Remove them and let cool for a few seconds, then slip off their skins and discard. Halve the tomatoes and scoop out the seeds with a spoon; chop the pulp. If using canned tomatoes, drain and coarsely chop them. Wrap the bay leaf, parsley, and thyme in a small piece of cheesecloth.

3. Heat the olive oil in a noncorrosive large saucepan over high heat for a few seconds. Add the minced vegetables and garlic, reduce the heat to low, and cook gently until the vegetables are tender but not browned, 5 to 7 minutes.

4. Stir in the tomatoes and herb bag. Cover the pan and simmer over low heat for 1 hour, stirring every now and then.

5. Uncover the pan and simmer 1 hour longer to thicken the sauce. Meanwhile rinse and chop the basil. Add the basil for the last 20 minutes of cooking time.

6. Remove the herb bag from the sauce. Press the sauce through a sieve and discard the solids. Season the sauce to taste with salt and pepper. Let cool to room temperature, then ladle it into 1-cup freezer containers and freeze for up to 1 year.

WHITE AND GREEN SEAFOOD PASTA SAUCE

MAKES 4 SERVINGS
TIME: 35 MINUTES

This delicately seasoned sauce of seafood, parsley, capers, and cucumbers is quick to make and as pretty to look at as it is good to eat. Serve it over short fat pasta or baked potatoes. Don't make more sauce than you need because it does not keep well.

2 cloves garlic
4 medium-size cucumbers
½ cup fresh parsley leaves
1 pound seafood, such as squid,
    scallops, fresh crabmeat or
    peeled and deveined shrimp
¼ cup olive oil
¼ cup drained capers
Salt and freshly ground black
    pepper

1. Mince the garlic. Peel the cucumbers and cut them lengthwise in half. With a small spoon, scoop out the seeds and discard. Dice the cucumbers into small cubes. Rinse and mince the parsley. Cut the seafood into small chunks: thin rings for squid, halves for sea scallops, or small chunks for crab or shrimp.

2. Heat the olive oil in a deep large skillet over high heat. Reduce the heat to medium, add the garlic and seafood, and stir-fry for a couple of minutes.

3. Add the cucumbers and capers. Cover the skillet and simmer over low heat until the seafood is cooked through, about 5 minutes.

4. Remove the skillet from the heat and add the parsley. Taste before seasoning with salt and pepper as the capers will have already added a bit of saltiness. Serve hot.

A GOOD BASIC MEAT SAUCE

MAKES 4 CUPS OR ENOUGH FOR 4 SERVINGS
TIME: 50 MINUTES

A meat sauce serves many uses: it's a way to get protein on your pasta, a way to use up cooked meat, and a way to bring together bits and pieces of leftover ingredients.

EMERGENCY "INSTANT" MEAT SAUCE

Sauté 1 pound lean ground veal or ground beef round in a medium-size skillet over medium heat until the meat is no longer pink. Add 2 cups prepared spaghetti sauce and simmer 10 minutes. Season to taste with salt and pepper.

ESPECIALLY GOOD FOR CHILDREN

A GOOD BASIC MEAT SAUCE: Whereas adults appreciate the chunkiness of this sauce, I've found that children prefer it puréed. A quick spin in the blender of the children's portions will help to make this dish a family favorite.

The meat can be either ground veal or beef, chopped fresh pork, poultry, or ham, or whatever else you have on hand or feel like eating. Enriched with corn, peas, or another cooked vegetable, the meat sauce becomes a Monday-to-Friday meal.

1 medium-size onion
2 bell peppers, preferably red, or 2
    carrots
1 to 2 tablespoons olive oil
1 pound lean ground meat, such as
    veal or beef round, or boneless
    fresh pork or poultry or ham
1 can (28 ounces) Italian plum
    tomatoes, whole tomatoes
    with tomato puree, or
    stewed tomatoes
1 teaspoon dried oregano
Salt and freshly ground black
    pepper

1. Finely chop the onion. Core, seed, and finely chop the peppers or peel and finely chop the carrots. If using fresh pork or poultry or ham, cut into ½-inch cubes.

2. Heat the olive oil in a deep large skillet over high heat. Reduce the heat to medium, add the onion and peppers or carrots and sauté, stirring on occasion, until the vegetables soften a bit, about 5 minutes.

3. Add the meat and sauté, stirring constantly, until the meat is cooked through, about 5 minutes. Add the tomatoes with their juices and break them up against the side of the skillet with a wooden spoon.

4. Add the oregano, cover the skillet, and simmer over low heat 20 to 30 minutes or as long as it takes to boil the water and cook your pasta or grain. Stir the sauce every now and then to make sure it's not sticking to the bottom of the pan. When the sauce is done, season it to taste with salt and pepper. If you wish, purée it in a food processor for a smooth texture.)

VARIATIONS

In step 3, substitute 3 cups chopped cooked meat, poultry, or beans for the fresh meat. In step 4, simmer for only 10 minutes.

BLACK BEAN AND PARSLEY SAUCE

MAKES 4 SERVINGS
TIME: 35 MINUTES

The fresh tomatoes add tang and moisture to the beans to make this sauce both juicy and flavorful. Serve it over short hollow shapes such as fusilli, penne, or elbows. But don't limit this to pasta only; it's also great over polenta, with plainly cooked exotic grain dishes like millet or quinoa, or just as a terrific side dish to serve with meat or poultry. Make a double batch of the recipe and freeze half for another day.

> 2 cloves garlic
> 4 fresh tomatoes or 1 can (14½ ounces) Italian-style stewed tomatoes
> 1 can (16 ounces) black beans
> 2 tablespoons olive oil
> ½ teaspoon dried lemon peel
> Salt and freshly ground black pepper
> 1 cup (tightly packed) fresh parsley leaves

1. Mince the garlic. If using fresh tomatoes, quarter them, remove the seeds with a spoon, and chop the pulp. Rinse and drain the black beans.

2. Heat the olive oil in a deep large skillet over medium heat. Add the garlic and tomatoes and sauté, stirring with a spoon, until you can smell the garlic and the tomatoes begin to wilt, about 2 minutes.

3. Add the beans and lemon peel. Season to taste with salt and pepper. Reduce the heat to low, cover the skillet, and simmer for 20 minutes (which is plenty of time to cook the pasta or grain). While the sauce is cooking, rinse and mince the parsley.

4. When you are ready to eat, remove the sauce from the heat and stir in the parsley. Adjust the seasoning and serve hot.

LUSTY VEGETABLE-BEAN SAUCE

MAKES 4 SERVINGS
TIME: 45 MINUTES

This hearty sauce, full of chunky bits of vegetables and rich chick-peas, turns any potful of pasta or grains into a complete meal. A nice substitute for the chick-peas are small pink or red kidney beans. Black beans, however, spoil the color of the sauce.

If possible make a double batch of this sauce and freeze half for another day—to use either as a sauce or as the base for a hearty soup or stew.

1 medium-size onion
2 bell peppers, preferably red
4 fresh tomatoes or about 4 cups
   canned tomatoes
½ pound fresh mushrooms, shiitake
   or domestic
2 cans (16 ounces each) chick-peas
2 tablespoons olive oil
1 package (10 ounces) frozen corn
   kernels
Salt and freshly ground black
   pepper
¼ cup fresh basil or parsley leaves
   (optional)
1 to 2 tablespoons olive oil or butter
   (optional)

1. Finely chop the onion. Core, seed, and finely chop the peppers. Coarsely chop the fresh tomatoes if using, seeds and all. Stem, rinse, and thinly slice the mushrooms (reserve the stems for soup). Rinse and drain the chick-peas.

2. Heat 2 tablespoons olive oil in a deep large skillet over medium heat. Add the onion and peppers and sauté until the onion begins to turn translucent, about 2 minutes.

3. Add the tomatoes, mushrooms, chick-peas, and corn to the skillet. If using canned tomatoes, add them with their juices and break them up against the side of the skillet with a wooden spoon. Stir the sauce to break up the corn kernels and to make sure the sauce is not sticking to the bottom of the skillet. Season to taste with salt and pepper.

4. Cover the skillet and simmer the sauce over low heat 20 to 25 minutes (enough time to boil the water and cook your pasta or grain). While the sauce is cooking, mince the fresh herb, if using.

5. To enrich and smooth the sauce, you could whisk in 1 to 2 tablespoons olive oil or butter just before serving. Stir in the fresh herb and serve hot.

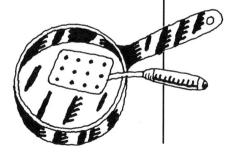

SEAFOOD

Of all the foods to cook during the week, fish is right up there in the perfect category. It's light, fast, and easy to prepare; it's low in calories, fat, and cholesterol; and best of all it tastes wonderful.

But, fresh fish can be a difficult choice. I know because I am the mother of a fish hater as well as the partner of a fish lover. So, I've figured out how to make stew and soup foundations that marry as happily with poultry as they do with fish. This way I have to cook only one dish that accommodates both my husband's and my daughter's divergent tastes.

WHAT FISH TO BUY MONDAY TO FRIDAY

Buy fish that is ready to be cooked immediately: boneless fillets or steaks can be quickly baked or sautéed; scallops can be stir-fried; meaty monkfish can be chunked and dropped into soup. If a fillet of fish, like bluefish for example, is too big for a single portion, try to cajole the fishmonger into slicing it into individual portions so that you don't have to mess with it at home. I don't recommend buying clams or mussels in the shell during the week because they are so cumbersome and time-consuming to wash and prepare for cooking.

Make sure also that you always have in the freezer a portion or two of sea scallops or cubed monkfish for emergencies. You can pop a single or several portions into a stew or soup without having to thaw them first.

BUYING FRESH FISH

In a perfect world, you'd have time to shop for ingredients daily, you'd only cook fresh fish, and you'd buy fish only from the finest fishmonger.

In the real world some days I have time to buy fresh fish, but most days I don't. My solution is to load up on fresh fish on any given day I have time, then go home, divide the fish into individual portions, and freeze them for another day.

If at all possible, purchase fish from a fish market—it's always fresher than fish from a supermarket, and the fresher the fish, the better it tastes. But even if you find such a market nearby, you've got to apply the "freshness" test to make sure the fish you're buying is the best quality possible. All fish shops should smell clean, sweet, and fresh. Steer clear of "fishy" smelling stores.

Some supermarkets have a fish section where the fish is portioned and packaged daily. If so, it is probably pretty fresh. If you must buy pre-packaged fish, make sure it smells fresh and that the fish looks shiny and moist without any dried-out edges or great gashes in the flesh.

BUYING FROZEN FISH

If you live inland where fresh fish is hard to come by, your best bet is to buy frozen fish that has been properly handled. Look for fish flesh that is solidly frozen and looks glossy without dried-out corners or discoloration on the flesh (freezer burn). The wrapping should be in direct contact with the frozen fish, and avoid packages that have "snow" at the bottom because this means the fish was frozen and thawed several times.

If possible buy "glazed fish," which is fresh fish that has been frozen solid soon after the catch so that a thick even coat of ice forms over the entire surface of the fish to protect it from drying out.

To use frozen fish, thaw whole fish, fillets, or steaks overnight in the refrigerator. Save small pieces of frozen fish for soups and stews where their somewhat watery texture doesn't matter.

BEST WAYS TO STORE

When buying fresh fish, don't hold it in the refrigerator for more than a day. If you can't get to it within 24 hours, freeze it.

To freeze fresh fish, place the unwrapped fish in individual portions on a baking pan or baking sheet and freeze until solid. Then wrap each portion, preferably in freezer paper, label, and keep frozen.

Lean species like sole, snapper, bass, and salmon will keep up to 4 months in the freezer; oily species like bluefish, only up to 2 months.

Cooked fish can be refrigerated for one day only and is best flaked into salads or reheated in soups. It also can be frozen up to 2 months, but then it should be used in soups to camouflage the texture.

WHY YOU SHOULDN'T BROIL FISH

Most people broil fish because they believe it's the least complicated and caloric method. And while I love the crusty moist broiled fish produced in restaurants, I hate the dried-out smelly kind made at home.

Restaurants achieve their delicious broiled fish with intense-heat-generating professional broilers and grills. At home, all you may have is a rather weak unadjustable source of heat. In addition, after the broiling is done, you're left with a messy broiler pan to clean up.

So if it's low-cal fish you're after, turn to the simple recipes for fish sautéed in nonstick skillets or fish that is steamed, poached, or baked.

THINK ABOUT BAKING INSTEAD: When pressed for time and looking for a dinner that requires a minimum of work, just pop some fish in the oven and bake until done. Baking is the least complicated method of cooking fish, is suitable for almost all types of fish, and works for either single or half dozen portions at a time.

Somewhat oily fish, like bluefish, mackerel, fresh tuna, and swordfish, can be baked plain. Leaner fish, like snapper, flounder, halibut, and sole, should be baked under a blanket of herbs, a drizzle of oil, or covered on a moist bed of diced vegetables so that it won't dry out.

MOIST POACHED SALMON

MAKES 4 SERVINGS
TIME: 25 MINUTES NO-WORK COOKING TIME

Ironically enough, my way of poaching fish is not only the lazy cook's method but also the one that produces the moistest and most tender flesh imaginable. And even though I use this method mostly for salmon, you should know that it works equally well with other tender-fleshed fish like bass, snapper, and halibut.

All you need to do is set the fish in a skillet large enough to accommodate it in a single layer, then cover it with water (or a mixture of water and white wine or clam juice and some spices). Slowly bring the liquid to a simmer, cook for a minute or so, and then turn off the heat. Voilà—it's done.

The fish can be kept warm in the pan until ready to serve; or, if you're going to serve the fish at room temperature or chilled, it should cool to room temperature right in the poaching liquid so that its moistness is preserved.

Hot poached salmon is terrific served with boiled corn, steamed asparagus, or Herbed New Potatoes; chilled poached salmon is terrific with chilled asparagus, artichokes, and Cucumber Salad or Parslied Rice and Pepper Salad (see Index for page numbers).

4 salmon steaks or fillets (6 to 8 ounces each)
Salt and freshly ground black pepper
4 cups water or combination of water and dry white wine or bottled clam juice
½ teaspoon dried dill, whole coriander seeds, or peppercorns (optional)
2 tablespoons unsalted butter
2 tablespoons minced fresh chives or dill leaves (optional)
Lemon wedges for serving

1. Arrange the salmon steaks in a single layer in a shallow skillet wide enough to accommodate them without crowding. Season with salt and pepper. Add enough water to completely cover the salmon. Add the dried herbs and/or peppercorns if using.

2. Slowly bring the liquid barely to a simmer over medium-low heat. Reduce the heat to low, cover the skillet, and simmer until the top of salmon looks opaque, 2 to 3 minutes. Turn off the heat and let stand cov-

DOUBLING UP

POACHED SALMON: When I poach salmon, I invariably get two meals out of it by cooking 8 steaks at a time and saving half of them for the next day.

When cooking this many steaks, I find it easier to poach them in the oven: Preheat the oven to 350°F, place the salmon steaks or fillets in a single layer in a large baking pan, cover the fish with whatever poaching liquid you like, seal the baking pan with aluminum foil, and bake 30 to 45 minutes. Cooking the fish this way takes a lot longer, but it never gets overdone.

Serve half the steaks hot that night and the remaining steaks chilled the next day (no longer).

SECOND TIME AROUND

POACHED SALMON: If you haven't got enough salmon left to turn into a full meal, remove the skin and bones and flake the remaining fish into a soup or a pasta dish or mix it with mayonnaise for a sandwich spread.

ered for 10 minutes or until the other parts of your meal are completely cooked or the table is set.

3. Remove the salmon from the poaching liquid with a spatula and blot both sides of the fish with paper towels to remove the excess water. Set each salmon steak on a dinner plate and top with a pat of butter and a sprinkling of herb if using. Serve with lemon wedges on the side.

VARIATION

For chilled cold poached salmon, let it cool to room temperature in the poaching liquid, then remove it, blot it dry, and refrigerate until cold; this will help preserve its moistness. Serve chilled salmon with dill mayonnaise or tangy vinaigrette.

BAKED SALMON ON A BED OF SWEET PEAS

MAKES 4 TO 6 SERVINGS
TIME: 40 MINUTES

The sweet peas and tangy tomatoes are an excellent foil for salmon as well as a slew of other fish.

This dish is best baked in the oven — the fish will cook evenly and the peas and tomatoes won't scorch.

If you wish to serve a side dish, try Quick and Easy Couscous or Herbed New Potatoes (see Index for page numbers).

1 onion
1 clove garlic
2 tomatoes
2 tablespoons olive oil
2 packages (10 ounces each) frozen
    petite peas, thawed
1/4 cup lime juice
1 teaspoon sugar
Salt
1 to 2 drops Tabasco sauce, or more
    to taste
4 to 6 salmon or halibut steaks
    (about 6 ounces each) or 1 1/2
    pounds tuna or bluefish fillets

1. Preheat the oven to 375°F.
2. Finely chop the onion; mince the garlic; core and cut the tomatoes into 3/4-inch chunks.
3. Heat the olive oil in a large ovenproof skillet over medium heat. Add the onion and sauté until tender, about 5 minutes.
4. Add the garlic and tomatoes; sauté for another minute or so. Add the peas and

lime juice and bring the liquid to a simmer. Season to taste with sugar, salt, and Tabasco.

5. Set the fish steaks over the vegetables. Cover and bake until the fish is cooked through, 20 to 25 minutes. Serve hot.

MEDITERRANEAN TUNA

MAKES 4 SERVINGS
TIME: 45 TO 50 MINUTES

In this recipe, fresh tuna steaks are steamed over a heavenly mixture of fennel braised in a sauce of tomatoes, white wine, and olive paste. The fennel base is delicious and works well with some meats like cubes of smoked ham or as a sauce in which to reheat slices of leftover roast lamb.

Serve with another vegetable, a potato dish, a grain, or pasta.

2 cloves garlic
1 onion
2 bulbs fresh fennel, 4 ribs celery, or 1 package (10 ounces) frozen artichoke hearts, thawed
2 tablespoons olive oil
1 can (14½ ounces) stewed tomatoes
¼ cup dry white wine
1 teaspoon dried oregano or fennel seeds
Salt and freshly ground black pepper
1 tablespoon black olive paste or pesto
4 tuna, swordfish, or halibut steaks (about 6 ounces each)

1. Finely mince the garlic and chop the onion. Remove the feathery tops from the fennel, then core and cut the bulb into ¾-inch slices (or cut the celery into ½-inch pieces or coarsely chop the artichokes).

2. Heat the olive oil in a deep large skillet over medium heat. Add the garlic and onion and sauté, stirring on occasion, until the onion is translucent, about 5 minutes.

3. Add the fennel, tomatoes, white wine, and oregano. Bring the liquid to a simmer and season to taste with salt and pepper. Cook the mixture, covered, over very low heat until the fennel is tender, about 15 minutes.

4. Stir the olive paste into the fennel mixture and set the tuna steaks on top.

FISH-COOKING CLEAN-UP

There's almost zero clean-up when you sauté, poach, or bake fish in nonstick cookware. The special nonstick material is especially effective in repelling sticky fish skin that hangs on mercilessly to ordinary pots and pans. You'll never have to soak nonstick pans to get them clean.

Cover the skillet and simmer until the fish is cooked, 5 to 10 minutes longer.

VARIATION

To turn this into a one-pot meal, scrub 4 medium boiling potatoes and very thinly slice. Increase the oil in step 2 to ¼ cup. In step 3 add the potatoes after you add the fennel and increase the wine to ½ cup. Simmer until the potatoes are tender, about 45 minutes (instead of 15). During this time, stir the potatoes every 10 minutes or so to make sure they don't stick to the bottom of the skillet. (It's all right even if some do stick to the pan as they'll form lovely crunchy bits that taste wonderful; but be sure to incorporate these crunchy bits into the potatoes every time you stir.) Proceed with step 4 as directed.

FRESH TUNA STEAKS OVER PIQUANT KALE

MAKES 4 SERVINGS
TIME: 55 MINUTES TO 1 HOUR

This splendid mix of kale, pickles, capers, and tomatoes is a wonderful foil for fresh tuna. This is uncomplicated to make as well as delicious and healthy to eat. Serve with Baked Beets, Herbed New Potatoes, Kasha and Onions, or Millet with Parmesan (see Index for page numbers).

1 onion
2 tomatoes
1½ pounds kale or 1 package (10 ounces) frozen chopped spinach, thawed
1 cup fresh parsley leaves
8 tiny cornichons or ¼ cup chopped nonsweet pickles
2 tablespoons olive oil
¼ cup dry white wine
1 tablespoon capers
Salt and freshly ground black pepper
1½ pounds fresh tuna, swordfish, or halibut steaks

1. Preheat the oven to 375°F.
2. Finely chop the onion. Quarter the tomatoes, remove the seeds with a small spoon, and cut the pulp into ½-inch chunks. Stem, rinse, and chop the kale. Rinse and mince the parsley. Thinly slice or chop the cornichons.
3. Heat the olive oil in a large oven-proof skillet over medium heat. Add the onion and sauté until tender, about 5 minutes.

4. Add the white wine and simmer 2 to 3 minutes. Stir in the tomatoes, pickles, capers, and kale. Cover and simmer over low heat until the kale is tender, about 15 minutes. Uncover the skillet and season the vegetables to taste with salt and pepper.

5. Set the tuna over the vegetables. Cover and bake until the tuna is nearly cooked through with traces of red or pink in the center, 10 to 15 minutes. (If the tuna is cooked all the way through, it will be too dry.) Serve hot.

HOT SWORDFISH WITH CHILLED PARSLEY VINAIGRETTE

MAKES 4 TO 6 SERVINGS
TIME: 25 MINUTES

To embellish a stark piece of baked fish, top it with a lively vinaigrette such as this parsley and scallion mix. The cool dressing against the warm fish makes for an inspired contrast.

Other fish that take as nicely to this treatment are mackerel fillets and tuna or shark steaks.

Serve this with Baked Potatoes, Maple-Cinnamon Acorn Squash, or Baked Beets (see Index for page numbers).

*4 to 6 swordfish steaks (about 6
    ounces each)*
2 tablespoons olive oil
1 tablespoon lemon juice
Salt
2 scallions (green onions)
*½ cup fresh parsley or coriander
    leaves*
2 tablespoons red wine vinegar
*1 tablespoon black olive paste,
    pesto, or 2 sun-dried tomatoes
    packed in oil, minced (optional)*
Freshly ground black pepper

1. Preheat the oven to 350°F for 10 minutes.

2. Set the swordfish steaks in a baking pan and lightly rub them on both sides with 1 tablespoon each oil and lemon juice. Season with salt.

3. Bake the fish until just cooked through, 10 to 15 minutes. (The rule of thumb is 10 minutes per inch of thickness.)

4. While the fish is baking, trim and cut the scallions into large pieces. Rinse the parsley. Purée the scallions, parsley, vinegar, remaining 1 tablespoon oil, and the olive paste in a blender or food processor. Season

HOW MUCH IS A PORTION?

When buying fish, figure on 6 ounces per person for boneless fillet or shelled seafood or 8 ounces per person for bone-in steaks, whole fish, or shell-on seafood.

FISH REDUX

P lainly cooked fish can be reheated in a soup or stew, but mixed dishes (fish cooked with other ingredients) should be eaten the next day chilled in a salad and dressed with a vinaigrette. Don't keep fish leftovers longer than a day.

Here are some recipes in which leftover fish substitutes beautifully (see Index for page numbers):

Soups
- *Michele's Foundation Soup*
- *Woodsy Mushroom and Scallop Soup*
- *Seafood and Rice Soup*

Salads
- *My Salad Nicoise*
- *Spicy Cabbage Salad with Mackerel*

One-Pot Meals
- *Protein Ratatouille*
- *Winter Seafood Stew*

to taste with salt and pepper. When the fish is done, transfer it to dinner plates and spoon the parsley vinaigrette over each portion.

BAKED BLUEFISH ON A BED OF FENNEL

MAKES 4 SERVINGS
TIME: 50 MINUTES TO 1 HOUR

This is unfussy and uncomplicated, yet very tasty. A good side to serve with it is Perfect Rice, Grated Beets, or Brussels Sprouts Rounds (see Index for page numbers).

2 cloves garlic
2 bulbs fresh fennel
2 tablespoons olive oil
½ cup dry white wine
½ teaspoon dried orange peel
½ teaspoon fennel or anise seeds
1 cup spaghetti sauce, homemade (see Index) or prepared
Salt and freshly ground black pepper
4 bluefish, halibut, salmon, or yellowtail snapper fillets (about 6 ounces each)

1. Preheat the oven to 375°F.
2. Finely mince the garlic. Trim and discard the feathery tops from the fennel, then core the bulb and slice ¾ inch thick.
3. Heat the olive oil in a large oven-proof skillet over medium heat. Add the garlic and fennel and sauté about 1 minute just to release their aroma. Add the white wine, orange peel, and fennel seeds. Bring the liquid to a simmer, then cover and continue to simmer until the fennel is tender, 15 to 20 minutes.
4. Add the spaghetti sauce and season to taste with salt and pepper. Set the fish, skin side down, on top of the fennel mixture. Cover and bake until the fish is cooked through, 20 to 25 minutes.

SALSA-BAKED BLUEFISH

MAKES 4 TO 6 SERVINGS
TIME: 30 MINUTES

The green chilies and tomato sauce both suffuse the fish with tangy zest and keep it moist while baking. Accompany the dish with Herbed New Potatoes or Aromatic Rice with Vegetables (see Index for page numbers).

1 can (14½ ounces) Italian plum
   tomatoes
4 scallions (green onions)
1 jalapeño pepper, fresh or pickled
1 can (4 ounces) chopped green
   chilies
2 tablespoons olive oil (optional)
2 tablespoons lemon juice
Salt and freshly ground black
   pepper
4 to 6 bluefish or mackerel fillets, or
   tuna or swordfish steaks (about
   6 ounces each)

1. Preheat the oven to 400°F.

2. Drain the tomatoes. Trim and cut the scallions into large pieces. Seed the jalapeño, if desired. Purée the tomatoes, scallions, chilies, jalapeño, olive oil, and lemon juice in a blender or food processor. Season to taste with salt and pepper.

3. Pour half the salsa in a baking pan large enough to hold the fish in a single layer. Set the fish fillets, skin side down, on top and pour the remaining salsa over them. Bake uncovered until the fish is cooked through, about 20 minutes. Serve hot.

FISH IN AN HERB BLANKET

MAKES 4 SERVINGS
TIME: 35 MINUTES

My editor, Suzanne, suggested I try cooking fish under a blanket of herbs. I did and it was wonderful. It's a recipe that works well with firm fish that is cut thick, like tuna, swordfish, halibut, or salmon.

All you do is blanket the fish with lots of herbs and bake until done. When the fish comes out of the oven, it is suffused with a faint yet distinctive fragrance. The thicker the fish, the longer it must cook under the herbs and the more flavorful it will be. Keep this recipe in mind for dieters.

1 large bunch fresh parsley
1 large bunch fresh dill or basil
1 bunch fresh thyme (optional)
2 pounds halibut, salmon, or
   swordfish steaks or bluefish,
   tuna, or mackerel fillets
1 to 2 tablespoons rice vinegar
Salt and freshly ground black
   pepper

SECOND TIME AROUND

*SALSA-BAKED BLUEFISH:
Leftovers are terrific, either chilled or at room temperature, because the salsa marinates the cooked fish and keeps it from spoiling. Serve a salad of grains or potatoes to round out the second meal.*

Don't keep the leftovers more than a day because even with the marination, the fish won't taste good after that.

SECOND TIME AROUND

FISH IN AN HERB BLAN-KET: Because this is so plainly cooked, leftovers are wonderful tossed with mayonnaise or vinaigrette dressing and used in a salad or as a sandwich stuffer.

1. Preheat the oven to 400°F for 15 minutes.

2. Rinse the herbs and chop off their stems. Rub the fish with the vinegar and season with salt and pepper.

3. Set the fish in a baking pan and cover with the herbs. Bake until the fish is cooked through, 15 to 20 minutes. (It takes a little longer because of all the herbs.)

4. When the fish is done, discard the herbs and serve the fish hot.

BAKED FISH WITH VEGETABLES

MAKES 4 SERVINGS
TIME: 45 MINUTES

Baking is the easiest way to prepare fish, and almost all types of fish, lean and fatty, can be cooked this way. This is my overall first choice for cooking fish because it does not dry out the flesh nor does it result in a difficult-to-clean broiler pan.

If you're willing to go to a little more trouble, sauté some vegetables, then set the fish on top of them and bake. This way you flavor and moisten the fish and get the additional bonus of having two parts of your dinner cook at the same time.

In this recipe, minced peppers and mushrooms seasoned with chili paste make a lovely bed of flavors for bluefish, tuna, swordfish, or halibut. See Variations following the recipe for other flavor beds that go well with other types of fish.

Serve baked fish with a plain starch such as steamed potatoes, pasta, couscous, rice, or another grain, or with another vegetable like grated beets or root vegetables.

1 piece (½ inch) fresh ginger
2 bell peppers, preferably red
4 carrots
½ pound fresh mushrooms,
*　domestic or shiitake*
2 tablespoons Oriental sesame oil
1 teaspoon chili paste with soy
*　beans*
2 tablespoons rice vinegar
2 pounds halibut or swordfish steaks
*　or bluefish or mackerel fillets*
Salt

1. Preheat the oven to 375°F.
2. Peel the ginger. Core and seed the

peppers. Peel the carrots. Mince these ingredients in a food processor or by hand. Stem and rinse the mushrooms, then thinly slice the caps (reserve the stems for soup).

3. Heat the oil in a large ovenproof skillet over medium heat. Add the minced ingredients and sauté for a minute just to get them cooking. Add the mushrooms, chili paste, and rice vinegar. Cover the skillet and cook over low heat until the vegetables are soft, about 10 minutes.

4. Set the fish on top of the vegetables. Sprinkle with salt and bake until the fish is just cooked through, 20 to 25 minutes.

VARIATIONS

■ If you're into simplicity, place the fish in a baking pan, spread some oil or butter over the top, and sprinkle on herbs; bake for about 10 minutes per inch of thickness.

■ For a lovely bed for 1 pound of sole fillets (or 2 small whole bass, 1½ pounds each), use 1 chopped onion and 1 pound thinly sliced carrots for the vegetables and sauté in vegetable or olive oil. Season with 1 teaspoon dried tarragon and 2 tablespoons lemon juice.

■ For cod or fresh tuna, use 4 chopped tomatoes for the vegetables and sauté in olive oil. Season with 1 teaspoon dried thyme and 2 tablespoons dry white wine. This is lovely with 1½ pounds cod or fresh tuna fillets.

CRACKLING FISH FILLETS

MAKES 2 SERVINGS
TIME: 12 TO 15 MINUTES

This is a modern, Monday-to-Friday, healthy and updated version of *sole meunière*, that wonderful haute cuisine fish fried in clarified butter and sauced with more butter seasoned with lemon and parsley. Here the fish is sautéed in a nonstick pan to create the required crusty exterior without all that fat. The pan is then deglazed with water and lemon juice to create a light sauce. A single tablespoon of butter and some minced parsley is stirred into the sauce to add finish and flavor.

I find it easier to sauté fish for 2 people only. If you wish to make this dish for 4, double all ingredients and use two skillets.

Make an easy side dish to go with this: either serve a Monday-to-Friday Salad first and serve some bread with the fish or make a two-in-one dish of Aromatic Rice with Vegetables (see Index for recipe page numbers).

MICHELE'S IDIOSYNCRATIC THOUGHTS ABOUT COOKING FISH

Stir-frying and sautéing are the two techniques I rely on when I want to make an incredibly speedy fish dinner. Stir-frying speeds things up because you cook using high heat and small pieces. Plus when I stir-fry the fish along with a selection of vegetables, I can get two parts of the dinner done at the same time. Sautéing also uses high heat and is fast. It is the method I use when I crave a crispy coating around the fish, but don't want to deep-fry.

Although deep frying is America's best-loved way of cooking fish, it isn't mine. Not only doesn't it do justice to the delicate flesh and aroma of fish, it is complicated and messy and I steer clear of it.

SAUTÉED FISH

f I had to choose just one way of cooking sole it would be to dip it lightly in flour and sauté it quickly in butter. The whole procedure takes but a few minutes and produces a wonderful pearly white flesh enrobed in a brittle butter coating. You can serve it as is—with a dash of lemon or lime juice—or deglaze the pan and make a quick sauce.

For people on diets, I suggest sautéing the fish in a nonstick skillet, using just a film of oil in the pan to make sure the fish does not stick.

Because the whole procedure only takes just a few minutes, prepare whatever side dish you're serving before you cook the fish.

This procedure also works well with snapper, salmon, monkfish, and even scallops.

¼ cup fresh parsley leaves
¾ pound sole fillets
1 to 2 tablespoons olive oil
2 tablespoons all-purpose flour
¼ cup water
2 tablespoons lemon juice
1 tablespoon butter
Salt and freshly ground black pepper

1. Rinse and mince the parsley. Cut the fish into 4 manageable pieces. Brush a large nonstick skillet with olive oil. Dip the pieces of fish in flour and shake off the excess.

2. Heat the skillet over medium heat until very hot, about 2 minutes. Add the floured fish and sauté, without moving the fish around, until it just sets and turns a bit golden, 1 to 2 minutes. With a spatula, flip the fish over to the other side and cook until the fish is firm and cooked through, about 2 minutes longer. Remove the fish to dinner plates.

3. Add the water and lemon juice to the skillet and increase the heat to medium-high. Using a wooden spoon or spatula, scrape up any browned bits on the bottom of the pan and boil until syrupy, about 2 minutes. Remove the skillet from the heat and swirl in the butter and parsley. Season with salt and pepper and pour the sauce over the fish.

SPINACH-STUFFED SOLE

MAKES 4 SERVINGS
TIME: 35 TO 40 MINUTES

Quinoa is delicious with this, as is cracked wheat and rice. This dish is light enough so that you can guiltlessly indulge in dessert.

2 red bell peppers
1 to 2 tablespoons olive oil
¼ cup dry white wine
½ teaspoon dried tarragon
Salt and freshly ground black pepper
¼ pound fresh spinach
1½ pounds sole fillets

1. Core, seed, and cut the peppers into long, thin slices.

2. Heat the olive oil in a deep large skillet over medium heat. Add the peppers and sauté, stirring on occasion, until somewhat tender, about 5 minutes.

3. Add the white wine and tarragon to the peppers and season to taste with salt and pepper. Bring the wine to a simmer, cover, and cook gently until the peppers are soft, about 5 minutes.

4. Meanwhile stem and rinse the

spinach. Cut each sole fillet lengthwise in half along the vertical bone line. If the fillets are still large, cut them crosswise in half again. Place a few spinach leaves on each piece of sole. Roll up each fillet around the spinach and secure each roll with a couple of toothpicks.

5. Set the sole rolls on top of the peppers. Cover the skillet and continue to cook over low heat until the fish is just cooked through and the spinach has wilted, 15 to 20 minutes. Remove the toothpicks from the rolls and serve hot.

CORIANDER-FLAVORED MONKFISH CURRY

MAKES 4 SERVINGS
TIME: 40 MINUTES

The appeal of this curry is that it tastes as good hot served over grains as it does at room temperature along with a vegetable salad.

Serve with a basic grain dish like quinoa, cracked wheat, millet, or rice or as a fish sauce over pasta.

2 onions
2 cloves garlic
1 piece (½ inch) fresh ginger
2 large or 4 small tomatoes
1½ pounds monkfish or sea scallops
½ cup fresh coriander leaves
2 tablespoons olive oil
1 teaspoon ground cinnamon
1 teaspoon curry powder
2 tablespoons lime or lemon juice
Salt and freshly ground black pepper

1. Finely chop the onions; mince the garlic; peel and mince the ginger. Quarter the tomatoes, scoop out the seeds with a spoon, and chop the pulp. Cut the monkfish into 1-inch pieces or remove the tough, rubbery appendage from the side of each scallop. Rinse and mince the coriander.

2. Heat the olive oil in a large skillet over medium heat. Add the onions and sauté, stirring frequently, until softened, 3 to 4 minutes. Add the garlic, ginger, and tomatoes; sauté about 2 minutes. Add the cinnamon and curry powder and sauté for a minute longer. Stir in the monkfish and lime juice; cook, stirring, until the fish is cooked through, 5 to 7 minutes. Remove the skillet from the heat, stir in the coriander, and season to taste with salt and pepper.

VARIATION

For a vegetarian curry, substitute 2 cans (16

SECOND TIME AROUND

MONKFISH CURRY: This dish is excellent the next day chilled and served as a salad with diced bell peppers mixed in for textural contrast and dressed with an Herb Vinaigrette (see Index).

MIRIN

As I mentioned in the Pantry section of this book, I like to keep mirin, the Japanese cooking wine, on hand. I find that its sweet flavor marries beautifully with many dishes, and I am especially fond of it in fish preparations.

ounces each) chick-peas, drained, for the monkfish.

MONKFISH IN MISO SAUCE

MAKES 4 SERVINGS
TIME: 25 TO 30 MINUTES

Make sure you have all your ingredients prepared before you begin because the fish takes just a few minutes to cook. Round out the meal with a starch; a bowl of plainly boiled short-grain brown rice is my favorite. Also, if you're only cooking for two, halve the recipe because it does not take well to reheating.

> 1 piece (½ inch) fresh ginger
> 1 pound snow peas or mushrooms
> 1 bunch scallions (green onions)
> 1 pound monkfish or bluefish fillets, peeled and deveined shrimp, or cleaned squid
> 1 tablespoon Oriental sesame oil
> 1 tablespoon sugar
> 2 tablespoons mirin (sweet rice cooking wine) or rice vinegar
> 2 tablespoons miso paste
> Freshly ground black pepper

1. Peel and mince the ginger; you should have a generous tablespoon. Trim and string the snow peas, or stem, rinse, and thinly slice the mushrooms (reserve the stems for soup). Thinly slice the scallions including 4 inches of the green tops. Cut the fish into ¾-inch chunks or the squid into ½-inch-thick rings.

2. Heat the oil in a large skillet over medium heat. Add the ginger and stir-fry for a few seconds until you can smell it.

3. Add the sugar, snow peas or mushrooms, and fish or shellfish; stir-fry for a minute or so. Add the mirin, cover the skillet, and simmer over low heat until the vegetables and seafood are just tender, 3 to 5 minutes.

4. Remove the skillet from the heat and add the miso. To dissolve the miso, work it back and forth in a circular motion with a wooden spoon until it loosens up and becomes pasty. Mix all the ingredients well, add the scallions, and season to taste with pepper. If dinner is delayed, serve this dish at room temperature, because the miso and snow peas do not take kindly to reheating.

RED SNAPPER FILLETS WITH CITRUS

MAKES 4 SERVINGS
TIME: 35 TO 40 MINUTES

If you're in a real hurry, steam the fish in the skillet on top of the stove. Or if you are baking a grain dish or other side dish in the oven, cook the fish alongside it and figure on just 15 short minutes for the fish to be done.

2 shallots
¼ cup fresh parsley leaves
½ pound fresh mushrooms
1 tablespoon olive oil
½ cup orange juice
½ cup bottled clam juice
Salt and freshly ground black pepper
1 pound red snapper, perch, or
    turbot fillets (or sole if there is
    nothing else)

1. Mince the shallots. Rinse and mince the parsley. Stem the mushrooms, rinse, and thinly slice the caps (reserve the stems for soup).

2. Heat the oil in a large skillet over medium heat. Add the shallots and sauté for about a minute. Add the mushrooms and sauté a moment more just to get them somewhat soft. Add the orange juice and clam juice and bring the liquid to a boil.

3. Cover the skillet and simmer gently until the mushrooms are completely tender, 5 to 7 minutes. Uncover the skillet and boil the juices over high heat until somewhat thickened, about 5 minutes. Season to taste with salt and pepper. (The recipe can be made ahead up to this point 1 hour in advance.)

4. Fifteen minutes before you're ready to sit down to dinner, reheat the mushrooms in the skillet over medium heat. Set the fish fillets on top of the mushrooms and season with salt and pepper. Cover the skillet and steam the fillets until just cooked through, 6 to 8 minutes (or bake covered at 350°F for 15 minutes). Sprinkle the fish with the parsley and serve immediately.

FISH STEAMED IN THE MANNER OF EN PAPILLOTE

MAKES 4 SERVINGS
TIME: 40 TO 45 MINUTES

This is my Monday-to-Friday way of achieving the flavor of a fish cooked

CITRUS CHOICES

Some ingredients go together so naturally that you never think to give others a chance. So it is with fish and lemon juice. But there are other citrus choices, and they, too, suffuse fish with a tangy, fresh flavor of their own. Next time it's fish for dinner at your house, perk it up with orange juice or lime juice for a change.

HOW TO TURN A COMPLICATED RECIPE INTO A MONDAY-TO-FRIDAY DISH

This example of how I turned a cumbersome fish en papillote recipe into a simple casserole, without sacrificing flavor, might encourage you to develop your own alternative approaches to recipes you'd like to prepare but avoid because of the bother involved.

Prepared the classic way, fish en papillote involves dicing and blanching a number of vegetables, searing the fish, then assembling the two together in parchment. The parchment package must be wrapped carefully and correctly or steam escapes and the purpose of all the work is lost. The result is truly spectacular when it is successfully prepared: The parchment balloons in the oven entrapping all of the fish and vegetable juices. The diner then opens the package letting a burst of intoxicatingly aromatic steam escape under his or her nose.

My adaptation is less dramatic but equally successful in terms of taste. During the week I have no energy or time to precook and blanch ingredients before I begin the real job of cooking. So, in this recipe, I cook all of the aromatic vegetables in a single pot, adding one after the other, in sequence, until they're all cooked to the right consistency.

Another problem with the original is that the vegetables are used only as aromatic seasonings. This means cooking a side dish of vegetables to complete the meal. In my version, I increased the amount of vegetables so that they're an integral part of dinner as well as seasoning for the fish. And, instead of searing the fish first, I simply lay it on top of the vegetables. To hermetically seal in the juices, I cover the pot with foil before placing a lid on top of it.

In the end, I haven't sacrificed flavor, although I have lost the drama of opening the packages at the table to release that wonderful whiff of steam. If you really miss that trick, gather your diners in the kitchen to witness the unwrapping of your casserole!

en papillote without all the work and bother of the classic dish.

Here the fish and vegetables are hermetically sealed in an airtight casserole so they steam in their own aromatic juices.

4 carrots
½ pound fresh mushrooms
1 medium-size yellow squash
1 medium-size zucchini
2 tablespoons vegetable oil or
    butter
¼ cup dry white wine
Salt and freshly ground black
    pepper
4 firm-fleshed fish fillets or steaks,
    such as turbot, striped bass,
    perch, or salmon (about 6
    ounces each)
4 scallions (green onions)

1. Preheat the oven to 375°F.
2. Peel and slice the carrots ¼ inch thick. Trim the ends of the mushrooms, rinse, and thinly slice. Rinse the squash and zucchini and cut into ½-inch dice.
3. Heat the oil in a large ovenproof skillet over medium heat. Add the carrots and mushrooms and sauté for a couple of minutes to release their aroma. Add the wine and reduce the heat to low. Cover and simmer until the carrots are slightly tender,

about 3 minutes. Add the squash and zucchini, cover, and simmer until the vegetables are cooked through but still somewhat crisp, about 2 minutes more. Season to taste with salt and pepper. Remove from the heat.
4. Set the fish on top of the vegetables and season with salt and pepper. After the skillet has cooled somewhat, cover it tightly with aluminum foil, making sure the foil hugs the sides and edges of the skillet so that no steam can escape. Place the lid over the foil.
5. Bake 15 minutes so that the fish is just cooked through. While the fish is cooking, thinly slice the scallions including about 3 inches of the green tops.
6. Remove the lid and foil from the skillet, sprinkle the scallions over the fish, and serve with the vegetables and their juices.

HALIBUT STEAMED OVER APPLES

**MAKES 4 SERVINGS
TIME: 30 MINUTES**

Fish with apples is an unexpected but utterly delightful combination. Serve with a side dish such as Snappy Snow Peas, Cracked Wheat, or Pan-Steamed Yellow Squash (see Index for page numbers).

1 clove garlic
4 Granny Smith apples
1 tablespoon vegetable oil
¼ cup dry white wine
Salt and freshly ground black pepper
½ cup fresh parsley leaves
½ cup plain nonfat yogurt
2 teaspoons prepared white horseradish
4 fish steaks, such as halibut, salmon, mako, or swordfish (about 6 ounces each)

1. Mince the garlic. Peel and core the apples, then cut them into ½-inch dice.

2. Heat the oil in a deep large skillet over medium heat. Add the garlic and apples; stir-fry for a few seconds to combine. Add the wine and season to taste with salt and pepper. Cover the skillet and simmer over low heat until the apples are tender, 5 to 7 minutes.

3. Rinse and mince the parsley, then stir it into the yogurt.

4. When the apples are tender, stir in the horseradish. (The recipe can be made up to this point 1 hour in advance and reheated.)

5. Set the halibut steaks over the apples, cover, and simmer over medium heat until the fish is just cooked through, about 10 minutes. Serve each person a portion of fish and apples and top with a dollop of parslied yogurt.

VARIATION

For a meal-in-a-pot, peel and cut 4 medium-size boiling potatoes into ½-inch cubes; add the potatoes to the skillet with the apples. Cover and simmer until the potatoes are tender, about 20 minutes. Check the skillet every now and then to make sure the potatoes are not scorching; if they begin to stick to the bottom of the pan, add a few tablespoons water and continue to simmer. You can make the dish in advance up to this point; the longer the potatoes and apples simmer together, the more mellow their flavor and the more tender their texture.

COD SIMMERED IN RED WINE

MAKES 4 SERVINGS
TIME: 50 MINUTES

The red wine and caper base can be made hours, even days, in advance.

Just toss the fish in at the end and simmer for a few moments. Cod gives off lots of liquid so plan to serve this with a starch such as bread, potatoes, or a grain to sop up the delicious juices.

If you can afford the calories and cholesterol, do add the butter at the end, for it adds a lovely finish to the sauce

2 onions
1 cloves garlic
2 tablespoons olive oil
2 tablespoons all-purpose flour
1 cup dry red wine
1 cup bottled clam juice
2 tablespoons capers
¼ teaspoon dried thyme
¼ teaspoon dried oregano
Salt and freshly ground black pepper
1 cup fresh parsley leaves
1 pound cod, orange roughy, or
    scrod fillets, or sea scallops
1 to 2 tablespoons unsalted butter
    (optional)

1. Mince the onions and the garlic.

2. Heat the olive oil in a large skillet over medium heat. Add the onions and garlic and sauté until they begin to soften, 2 to 3 minutes. Reduce the heat to low, and simmer

until the onions are tender, about 5 minutes. If the onions begin to stick to the skillet, add a couple of tablespoons of water.

3. Add the flour to the skillet and cook, stirring constantly, for a minute or so. Add the red wine, clam juice, capers, thyme, and oregano. Bring the liquid to a boil over medium-high heat, stirring occasionally with a whisk; boil, stirring vigorously, until thickened. Reduce the heat to low and simmer gently uncovered for 15 minutes. Season to taste with salt and pepper.

4. Meanwhile rinse and mince the parsley. Cut the cod into 1-inch chunks.

5. Five to ten minutes before you plan to eat, bring the sauce back to a simmer and add the fish. Cover and cook over very low heat until the fish is just cooked through, about 5 minutes.

6. Cut the butter, if using, into 6 pieces, add it to the fish, and stir it around. The cod will tend to break apart at this point, but it won't matter when you spoon this over potatoes or grains. Remove the skillet from the heat, adjust the seasoning, stir in the parsley, and serve immediately.

VARIATION

This is wonderful when made with chicken instead of cod. Just substitute chicken broth for the clam juice and 1 pound boneless, skinless chicken or turkey breasts for the cod.

USING LEFTOVER WINE

Unless the occasion and therefore the meal is really special, I never open a bottle of wine only for the purpose of adding a cup of it to a dish I am preparing. On the other hand, after a meal at which I do serve wine, I never toss any that is leftover down the drain. This is the wine I use to make splendid midweek meals like the cod dish on this page. Even if I only have a half cup, the flavor it adds is luscious, and I can easily make up the additional half cup of liquid with clam juice or broth.

RAINBOW STIR-FRY

MAKES 4 SERVINGS
TIME: 20 MINUTES

A visually pleasing dish that marries well with Snappy Snow Peas and Minted Cherry Tomatoes (see Index for page numbers), and looks great with white rice.

> 1 pound bay or sea scallops, fresh
> crabmeat, peeled and deveined
> shrimp, or tuna fillet
> 2 bell peppers, preferably red or
> yellow
> 1 clove garlic or shallot
> 2 bunches watercress or 1 pound
> fresh spinach
> 2 tablespoons vegetable or olive oil
> 1 tablespoon lemon juice
> Salt
> ⅛ teaspoon dried red pepper flakes,
> or more to taste

1. Remove the tough, rubbery appendage from the side of each sea scallop or dice the tuna. Core, seed, and chop the pepper. Mince the garlic or shallot. Stem and rinse the watercress or spinach; chop the spinach if using but leave the watercress leaves whole.

2. Heat the oil in a large skillet over medium heat. Add the peppers, reduce the heat, and cook until somewhat tender, 3 to 4 minutes.

3. Add the garlic, seafood, and lemon juice to the peppers and sauté over medium heat, stirring on occasion, just until the seafood is cooked through, about 5 minutes.

4. Add the watercress or spinach and sauté until wilted. Season to taste with salt and red pepper, and serve immediately.

CHINESE CHILI SCALLOPS

MAKES 4 SERVINGS
TIME: 10 MINUTES

One day at work right before serving lunch, I opened a package of what I thought were chicken breasts defrosting in the refrigerator. Guess at my surprise when I found I had sea scallops instead. For reasons I can't remember, the ingredients for the chicken wouldn't work with scallops, so in a flash I came up with this recipe—devised with condiments I always have on hand.

Serve this with either steamed asparagus or a Stir-Fry of Summer Salad Vegetables (see Index) or plainly boiled acini pepe or orzo. If you don't have chili paste, use barbecue sauce instead but then omit the soy sauce.

1 pound bay or sea scallops
1 tablespoon chili paste with garlic
1 tablespoon rice vinegar
2 teaspoons soy sauce
1 teaspoon Chinese five-spice
   powder (optional)
1 to 2 tablespoons vegetable or
   Oriental sesame oil
Salt and freshly ground black
   pepper

1. Remove the tough, rubbery appendage from the side of each sea scallop. In a bowl, combine the scallops, chili paste, rice vinegar, soy sauce, and five spice powder.

2. Heat the oil in a large skillet, preferably nonstick, over medium-high heat. Add the scallops with the seasonings and any juices. Sauté, stirring constantly, over high heat until the scallops are just cooked through, 2 to 3 minutes for bay scallops; 3 to 4 minutes for sea scallops. Season to taste with salt and pepper if needed.

3. Spoon the scallops and their juice directly from the skillet onto a plate and serve.

THE BEST AND EASIEST SOFT-SHELL CRABS

MAKES 2 SERVINGS
TIME: 10 TO 12 MINUTES

Soft-shell crabs frequently are the focus of quick and simple meals during the spring and early summer. Because cooking the crabs is messy and speedy, I don't bother fussing with a side dish and always serve these as a separate course. To round out the meal, sometimes I precede this with a pasta dish or follow it with a salad of steamed spring vegetables.

This is the type of meal I usually

SECOND TIME AROUND

CHINESE CHILI SCALLOPS: Leftovers are best eaten cold as a salad or sandwich stuffer, and they're good tossed with some mayonnaise mixed with lemon juice or more rice vinegar.

cook for just the two of us because sautéing crabs for several people is a job that requires too many skillets.

Be really careful when you sauté the crabs. A friend of mine has taken to wearing rubber gloves when she makes these because the crabs sputter, pop, and spatter wildly when they hit the hot skillet. Avert your face as you're cooking and be sure to turn them gingerly, using a spatula or long-handled tongs.

½ cup all-purpose flour
Salt and freshly ground black
    pepper
4 to 6 medium-size soft-shell crabs,
    cleaned
2 tablespoons vegetable oil
2 tablespoons unsalted butter
½ cup water
Lemon wedges for serving

1. Season the flour with salt and pepper. Coat the crabs with the seasoned flour and shake off any excess.

2. Heat the oil in a large skillet over medium-high heat for a few seconds until hot. When the oil is hot, add the butter and melt. Add the crabs to the skillet and sauté until golden, 3 to 4 minutes per side. Remove the crabs to dinner plates.

3. Add the water to the skillet and increase the heat to high. Using a wooden spoon or spatula, scrape up any browned bits on the bottom of the pan and boil until the liquid is reduced to ¼ cup, 2 minutes. Season the pan juices with salt and pepper and pour them over the crabs. Serve immediately with lemon wedges.

POULTRY

Like fish, chicken and other poultry are ideal for Monday-to-Friday dinners. Poultry's neutral flavor blends with myriad vegetables, seasonings, herbs, condiments, and spices so that the cook can create an infinite number of dishes. Its firm yet delicate texture is always tender, it appeals to most children, and, depending on how it's prepared, it can be low in fat and cholesterol.

Chicken especially is available and ready to cook in enough forms — whole, quartered, in parts, either on the bone or off — so that the cook won't tire of making it the dinner entrée more than once in a week.

BUYING CHICKEN

Although chicken comes in a variety of forms, I find there are three that are easiest for weekday meals. On the weekends I often roast a whole bird (or two) so that I have leftovers to quickly turn into dinner during the work week. Boneless chicken breasts are super fast to cook during the week and can be dressed up in endless ways. Chicken parts come in handy when I want the taste of chicken on the bone but don't have the two hours it takes to cook a whole chicken.

CHICKEN BREASTS

If I were only allowed to buy chicken in one form, it would have to be a boneless, skinless chicken breast. Nothing else offers such an endless variety of quick and painless dinner possibilities.

When I do my weekly shopping I automatically pick up a pound of boneless chicken breasts because I know that if I don't get around to cooking them within a day of purchasing, I'll chunk them up and freeze them in individual portions for another day.

In an emergency, when I've forgotten to defrost anything for dinner, I add however many portions I need at the time to a hearty soup or stew without thawing the chicken first. Whatever moisture is lost by thawing the chicken this way is retrieved in the juices of the soup or stew.

I don't advise buying boneless chicken breasts already cut into strips; they're more expensive and they've been handled more than I think is sanitary.

CHICKEN PIECES

During the week, when I want chicken on the bone but don't have the time to roast a whole chicken, I bake chicken pieces.

Chicken parts are a cinch to cook. Flavor them first by dipping them in olive oil or leftover salad dressing and then, to keep them moist and give them texture, coat them with plain bread crumbs or bread crumbs mixed with cheese, nuts, or herbs. All you need to do then is bake until done.

Chicken breasts on the bone are great to bake because you can use the little pocket between the skin and the meat to stuff with bits of cooked vegetable stews, like ratatouille. This helps get rid of odd leftover bits and pieces you have in the fridge while flavoring the breast meat and keeping it moist at the same time.

When making stews or casseroles with chicken on the bone, I prefer to use the dark meat because it tastes better and stays juicier than the white meat. Before adding chicken to a stew, I always remove the skin and fat because I hate the flabby texture of stewed chicken skin.

ROASTS

Just like with meats, I turn to roasted poultry when I want to create leftovers from which I'll get another meal or two.

Sunday evenings at our house often involve the roasting of a couple of chickens. The first one is for Sunday dinner, and the second one is saved for dinners later in the week. Some leftovers go into sandwiches for school lunches, and others I save to make a main-course salad supper on a night I know I won't have time to cook.

To keep the leftover chicken, I remove the meat from the bone, take off the skin, then wrap the meat well, and refrigerate it for up to 2 days. If it's going to be longer until I get to use it, I can always freeze the chicken and add it when I'm ready to a soup, stew, or pasta sauce.

GAME HENS

I like to roast these little birds when I want the flavor and texture of roasted chicken but don't have the time it takes to make one. Game hens cook in about half the time of a 3- to 4-pound bird.

TURKEY

Until fairly recently, turkeys were only available whole, and even then, only at holiday times. When you bought one, unless you were feeding a hoard, you had to make a month-long commitment to leftovers—or so it seemed. Now, turkey parts are available, and I use them to add variety to my weekly poultry diet. Even though the taste of turkey is akin to chicken, it has a distinctive texture and flavor of its own. I substitute boneless turkey breast for boneless chicken breasts in some stews or casseroles, and when I'm feeling thrifty, I'll substitute turkey cutlets in a recipe for veal scallopine.

For people who are watching their weight or their cholesterol intake, ground turkey in an ideal substitute for ground beef, because it is low in fat, yet has enough chew to make it acceptable.

POULTRY COOKING TO AVOID

Broiling is one of the most popular ways Americans cook poultry (and fish) because they think it is easy and healthy. Most people plop the chicken in a broiling pan, let it burn on one side, turn it over, burn it on the second side, and end up with a dinner that is charred on the outside and either raw or desiccated on the inside.

To broil chicken properly, one must carefully baste the chicken every few minutes to make sure it does not burn and dry out. Well, let's face it, this careful tending is not what any of us looks forward to at the end of a workday, so we broil in a lazy way and end up with a bad-tasting dinner.

If you resort to broiling because you think it's healthy and easy, think again. If you're concerned with diet, turn to other recipes that feature boneless chicken stir-fried in a non-stick pan or chicken that is added to lean soups. Another fast and fat-free way to make chicken during the week is to bake the whole parts with the skin on and then remove the skin before serving. Leaving the skin on while the chicken bakes protects the flesh and keeps it moist. To flavor the flesh underneath, drizzle it with lemon juice and sprinkle with lots of minced fresh herbs.

TO WASH OR NOT TO WASH CHICKENS

I know it is a common practice in most households to rinse a chicken before cooking it in order to rid it of bacteria, and I think this is a wise idea. Just be sure you pat it dry, inside and out with paper towels before proceeding with the recipe. The extra time this takes will be worth the effort.

Of course if, after you unwrap it, the chicken smells funny, then throw it out — no amount of washing will rid it of that smell which indicates it is spoiled.

BEST WAYS TO STORE POULTRY

You can't keep fresh poultry in the refrigerator for longer than 2 days. Until then you can store it in its original wrapping, but after that you should rewrap and freeze it.

To freeze, divide the chicken into portions that make sense for your family. I don't wrap more than two portions together in a single package because our family is small and a double portion is enough for us for one dinner. You can freeze poultry for up to 6 months.

When freezing chicken parts, I always separate the white meat and dark meat pieces. When freezing a whole chicken, remove the giblets first and freeze them separately if you want to keep them. Giblets are more perishable than the bird itself; they keep frozen for 2 months only.

If you have a microwave, defrosting a chicken is a snap. If you don't have one, thaw chicken in the refrigerator. Chicken parts will thaw in half a day so you can remove them from the freezer in the morning and they'll be ready to cook at night. A whole chicken, on the other hand, takes a day to defrost and should be set in the refrigerator the night before you plan to cook it.

In an emergency you can place the frozen chicken in a bowl filled with cold tap water and thaw it, still wrapped, at room temperature, changing the water frequently.

**MONDAY-TO-FRIDAY
M · E · N · U**

See The Monday-to-
Friday Menu Sampler
in the Appendix for a week-
long meal plan using
Roasted Chicken as a
Sunday Start-Up dish.

ROASTED CHICKEN

**MAKES 4 SERVINGS PER CHICKEN
TIME: 5 MINUTES WORK
1¼ to 1½ HOURS NO-WORK
COOKING TIME**

It is hard to imagine that a chicken roasted in this cavalier way is really delicious, but, I assure you, it is. Usually I throw in some baking potatoes alongside the chicken and complete our Sunday dinner with steamed broccoli. The real beauty of this recipe is that it requires no work. Sometimes I use the rendered juices and fat in the baking pan as seasoning for the potatoes and sauce for the meat. Other times, I peel the skin from the chicken and blanket the potatoes with plain yogurt and fresh pepper.

When I want lots of leftovers for dinners during the week, I roast two chickens at once.

*1 or 2 whole chickens, about 3½
pounds each
Salt*

1. Preheat the oven to 425°F for 15 minutes.

2. Remove the giblet package and any excess pieces of fat from the chicken. Pat the chicken dry.

3. Set the chicken breast side up in a baking pan. Season inside and out with salt. Bake for 1¼ to 1½ hours, depending on how brown you like the skin to be. Timing is not crucial here; the white meat gets a little dry, that's all! Remove the chicken from the oven and let it set for 10 minutes before carving.

ONE-PAN CHICKEN AND VEGETABLE DINNER

**MAKES 4 SERVINGS
TIME: 10 MINUTES WORK
2¼ HOURS NO-WORK COOKING
TIME**

This isn't a speedy recipe, but you can't beat it for ease. Although it won't become your classic weekday chicken dish, it is so good, it's worth preparing when you have the time. Simply stick a whole chicken, sweet potatoes, acorn squash, beets, and a head of garlic in the oven for about 2 hours, then, during this time, take a nap, catch up on your correspondence, read the newspaper, or watch TV because dinner is cooking by itself.

Once done, simply cool slightly, peel the vegetables, and serve.

*4 medium-size beets, about 2½
    inches in diameter
2 sweet potatoes or white baking
    potatoes, about 1 pound each
2 acorn squash, about ½ pound each
1 whole head garlic
1 whole chicken, about 3½ pounds
1 tablespoon lemon juice
Salt and freshly ground black pepper
½ teaspoon dried thyme*

1. Preheat the oven to 425°F for 15 minutes.

2. Scrub the vegetables. Trim the stems and roots from the beets, potatoes, and squash with a sharp knife and place all the vegetables on a baking sheet. Remove as much of the papery skin from the garlic as possible but leave the head whole. Add the garlic to the vegetables and bake the whole lot, without opening the oven door, for 30 minutes.

3. Remove the giblets bag and excess pieces of fat from the chicken. Pat the chicken dry. Set the chicken breast side up in a baking pan just big enough to accommodate it and rub the skin with the lemon juice. Season with salt, pepper, and thyme. After baking the vegetables for 30 minutes, add the chicken to the oven and continue to bake, without opening the door, for 1¼ to 1½ hours.

4. Remove the chicken and vegetables from the oven and let rest for 10 minutes. Set out 4 dinner plates.

5. Cut the acorn squash in half, scoop out the seeds, and set a squash half on each plate. Cut the potatoes in half and serve a half to each diner. Peel the beets, cut in half, and add to each plate. Divide the garlic cloves into 4 portions and cut up the chicken. Help each diner to some chicken, spoon juices from the roasting pan over the vegetables and chicken, and serve. You can mash the garlic into the potatoes or eat it with the beets and chicken.

GARLIC- AND MUSTARD-CRUMBED CHICKEN

**MAKES 4 SERVINGS
TIME: 15 MINUTES WORK
1 HOUR NO-WORK COOKING TIME**

In this scrumptious baked chicken dish, chicken legs are brushed with a paste

ROASTED GARLIC

Roasted whole garlic cloves are a wonderful seasoning for roasted meats and poultry. What's remarkable is that all you need to do is stick the whole head of garlic in a 350° to 450°F oven and bake it alongside any other dish you are roasting at the time. Cook at least an hour until the cloves are very tender.

Remove the garlic from the oven and let the head cool for 10 minutes. Flatten the head with your hand so that the cloves separate; they'll slip easily out of their skins. The soft garlic can be mashed onto slices of roasted meats or spread on crusty bread that has been sprinkled with olive oil.

You can also reserve the cooked garlic, covered with oil, in the refrigerator for another day.

BREAD CRUMBS

When I go to the trouble to make fresh bread crumbs, I always crumb the entire loaf of bread and save the leftovers, packed in 2-cup portions, in the freezer.

If you don't have freezer space, place any crumbs you don't use at this time on a baking sheet in a thin layer and bake alongside the chicken for 15 to 25 minutes. Stir the bread crumbs every 5 minutes until they're golden brown and completely dried out. You can then store them in a covered jar in the pantry and they won't get moldy.

If you're not sure they are dry enough after you've baked them, let the crumbs stand, uncovered, overnight before you store them—this will certainly remove any residual moisture.

of mustard, parsley, and garlic, encased in fresh bread crumbs, and baked until done. It is terrific to make on a night when you know your partner will be coming home long after everyone else has eaten because the chicken tastes delicious at room temperature. Served with a vegetable salad and slices of whole-grain bread, it makes for a fine late-night supper.

> 2 cups fresh bread crumbs, or 1/3 loaf or 1/3 pound firm white bread
> 1/4 cup olive oil
> 1/4 cup wine vinegar or lemon juice
> 1/2 cup (tightly packed) fresh parsley leaves
> 1/4 cup Dijon mustard
> 1 or 2 cloves garlic
> Salt and freshly ground black pepper
> 4 whole chicken legs or 8 chicken thighs or drumsticks

1. Preheat the oven to 400°F.
2. If you don't have bread crumbs on hand, make them by whirring the sliced bread in the food processor.
3. For the dressing, wipe out any bread crumbs from the processor, add the oil, vinegar, parsley, mustard, and garlic, and process until well mixed. Season to taste with salt and pepper.

4. Place the chicken pieces in a baking pan. Pour some of the dressing mixture over the chicken and rub it in. Turn the chicken over, pour on more of the dressing, and rub it in. (If there is any dressing left over, store it in a covered jar and use it as a salad dressing later in the week).
5. Pat a thick coating of fresh bread crumbs over one side of the chicken, then turn the chicken over and do the same on the other side.
6. Bake uncovered until the juices run clear when the chicken is pricked with a fork, about 1 hour.
7. Remove the chicken from the oven. The top crumbs will be crusty and the bottom crumbs wonderfully mushy, sort of like a bread stuffing; just spoon some on the side of each person's portion. You can eat the chicken immediately or you can serve it later at room temperature. If you plan to eat it later, remove it from the baking pan so that the pan juices don't congeal onto the chicken.

VARIATIONS

■ **To flavor the bread crumbs**: For 2 cups crumbs add: 1/4 cup grated Parmesan cheese; 1/4 cup finely chopped walnuts, almonds, or pecans; slightly less than 1/4 cup sesame seeds; 1/4 teaspoon dried herbs such as rosemary, marjoram, thyme, or sage.

■ **Vary the flavor of the dressing**: Substitute any of the following for the parsley: ¼ cup (packed) fresh shredded basil, chopped dill, or sliced scallions (green onions); ¼ cup sun-dried tomatoes or chopped roasted bell peppers.

■ **For the parsley or mustard or both**: Add 1 tablespoon pesto or black olive paste.

■ **Baked Chicken for Dieters**: Omit the oil and increase the vinegar or lemon juice to ⅓ cup. Remove all the skin and fat from the chicken and proceed as directed. Check to see if the chicken is cooked through after 50 minutes; it cooks faster than chicken with skin on.

■ **Baked Chicken Breasts**: Substitute 2 whole chicken breasts, halved and on the bone, with or without skin as you wish, for the chicken legs. If you're baking them with the skin, you can stuff the space between the skin and the flesh with a dab of prepared pesto or black olive paste, or 3 to 4 tablespoons of any cooked moist leftovers you might want to use up, such as ratatouille, stir-fried greens, cooked peppers or mushrooms, or even chick-pea purée.

Pat the bread crumbs on the meat side only; the other side hardly has any flesh over which to settle the coating. Bake chicken breasts with skin for 50 minutes and breasts without skin for 40 minutes.

CHICKEN BREASTS ITALIAN STYLE

MAKES 4 SERVINGS
TIME: 20 TO 25 MINUTES

Use this as a working model for the preceding blueprint for sautéed chicken breasts. All the variations that follow it are based on 1 pound of boneless, skinless chicken breasts.

1 pound or 2 whole boneless,
    skinless chicken breasts
1 clove garlic
½ cup fresh parsley leaves
2 tablespoons olive oil
¼ cup dry white wine
½ teaspoon dried oregano
½ cup spaghetti sauce
Salt and freshly ground
    black pepper

1. Separate the tenderloins from the breasts. If the chicken breasts are whole, cut them in half.

2. Mince the garlic. Rinse and chop the parsley.

3. Heat the olive oil in a large skillet over high heat until shimmering. Add the chicken breasts and tenderloins and reduce

---

CRUMBING CLEAN-UP TIP

In any recipe that calls for crumbing or coating, do the procedure right in the baking pan to save yourself the clean-up of extra dishes.

TIME-SAVING
CLEAN-UP TIP

*B*efore washing any pot, skillet, or casserole, wipe it out first with paper towels or used paper dinner napkins to remove as much fat and bits of food as possible. This makes after-dinner pot-scrubbing less burdensome and helps prevent the clogging of your sink's pipes.

the heat to medium-high. Sauté the chicken without disturbing the pieces for 3 to 4 minutes. You'll know to turn the chicken over when the top looks opaque (tenderloins may take only 2 to 3 minutes per side).

4. With tongs, flip the chicken over to the other side. Sauté, undisturbed again, until the chicken is cooked through, 3 to 4 minutes longer. You can tell by poking the center with the tip of a knife; it should look white with only a hint of pink. Remove the chicken to a plate (that you'll reuse for dinner) and set aside.

5. Reduce the heat to medium, add the minced garlic to the skillet, and stir-fry for about 15 seconds until you get a whiff of its aroma. Add the wine and oregano and simmer until the wine has evaporated some, about 10 seconds. Add the spaghetti sauce and simmer until slightly thickened, 1 to 2 minutes. Swish in the minced parsley and season to taste with salt and pepper.

6. Reduce the heat to low and return the chicken breasts to the skillet. Turn them over a couple of times to coat them with the sauce, then remove the chicken to dinner plates and spoon some sauce over top.

VARIATIONS

■ **For variations on the Italian theme**, substitute dried rosemary or marjoram for the oregano and substitute ½ cup stewed tomatoes for the spaghetti sauce.

Or add 1 tablespoon capers or black olive paste with the spaghetti sauce.

Or substitute ¼ cup basil fresh leaves for the parsley and omit the oregano.

■ **Chicken Breasts à la Mexicaine:**
Substitute ½ cup fresh coriander leaves for the parsley.

Omit the white wine and spaghetti sauce. Deglaze the pan with 2 tablespoons red wine vinegar, 1 teaspoon chili powder, and ½ cup chicken broth and add 1 can (4 ounces) chopped green chilies. Boil until reduced by half; about 3 minutes. Remove the pan from the heat and swirl in 2 tablespoons butter and the chopped coriander.

The butter is important here or else the sauce will be too harsh.

■ **Chicken Breasts Middle Eastern Style:**
Substitute ½ medium-size onion, minced, for the garlic and ½ cup fresh mint leaves for the parsley. Add the onion to the pan after the chicken is removed and cook until softened, about 3 minutes.

Omit the white wine, oregano, and spaghetti sauce. Deglaze the pan with ½ teaspoon cumin powder, ½ cup chicken

BLUEPRINT RECIPE FOR SAUTEED CHICKEN BREASTS

With a full pantry, you can go on to create a different recipe for sautéed chicken breasts for each week of the year. This is what you'll need:

1. The chicken: *The 1- to 1½-pound package of boneless, skinless chicken breasts I buy at the supermarket usually contains 5 pieces of chicken, each about ¾ inch thick. Many a recipe book instructs the cook to pound the chicken breasts first to even their thickness, but I simply use the chicken straight from the package—it comes out just fine. The only work I do is to remove the tenderloins, because they come off anyway in the pan and removing them helps make each chicken breast more or less even throughout. If the chicken breast is still whole, I cut it in half. If there is any remaining fat or cartilage, I remove it too.*

2. The fat: *You'll need 1 to 2 tablespoons of fat, either vegetable or olive oil or butter. I prefer oil because it's healthier, but some people prefer the flavor of butter. You could also use half of each to get the benefits of both fats.*

3. The flour: *It's not essential, but some cooks like to lightly dip the chicken in flour before sautéing to help brown the outside of the chicken and thicken the sauce. If you do use flour, save yourself the clean-up of another dish by placing the flour on a piece of waxed paper instead. You'll need about ¼ cup all-purpose flour.*

4. The liquid to make the sauce: *After you've sautéed the chicken, you'll need ½ to 1 cup liquid to deglaze the skillet and establish the base for a pan sauce. You have any number of choices for liquid: 2 to 4 tablespoons red wine, tarragon, or balsamic vinegar with ½ cup chicken broth, or ½ cup each white wine and spaghetti sauce, or maybe red wine and broth.*

5. The seasonings that lend character to the sauce: *A spice or an herb, sliced mushrooms or scallions, some chopped pimientos or chilies, a few raisins or olives are the ingredients that give each sauce its distinctive character.*

For a sauce to serve 4 people, count on either ½ to 1 teaspoon dried herbs or spices (depending upon their strength and your taste), or 2 tablespoons to ½ cup of other chopped ingredients or both.

6. Finishing touches for the sauce: *To round out the flavor of the sauce, blend in ¼ to ½ cup chopped fresh herbs at the end or, if your waistline permits, whisk in 1 to 2 tablespoons softened butter, heavy cream, or sour cream.*

MINCING FRESH HERBS

A friend of mine who loves to cook asked me an interesting question: When mincing parsley must one tear off each and every leaf from the stem before chopping? I guess if you are training to run a three-star restaurant, this would be in order, but at home you need not be so fastidious. Chop off the stems by making a single knife cut ¼ inch below the point where most of the leaves begin. You'll end up with some minced stem by doing it this way, but don't worry, it just adds flavor and a wee bit of crunch.

Dill and basil are another story. The stems are thick and shouldn't be chopped into a dish. Pinch off the leaves of basil or feathery dill and include as little of the stem as possible in your mincing.

broth, and ¼ cup currants; simmer until reduced by half, about 2 minutes.

Remove the pan from the heat and whisk in ½ cup plain yogurt and the chopped fresh mint.

■ **Chicken Breasts Spanish Style:**

Substitute ¼ cup pimientos, chopped, for the parsley.

Omit the spaghetti sauce and oregano. Deglaze the pan with the minced garlic, white wine, ½ cup chicken broth, the pimientos, ⅛ teaspoon saffron, and 1 tablespoon black olive paste. Cook over medium-high heat until the sauce is reduced by half, about 4 minutes.

Remove the pan from the heat and swirl in 2 tablespoons butter to smooth out the flavor.

■ **Chicken Breasts with Citrus:**

Lightly flour the chicken breasts and substitute 1 tablespoon each butter and vegetable oil for the olive oil.

Omit the white wine, oregano and spaghetti sauce. Deglaze the pan with ¼ cup water, ¼ cup lemon, lime, or orange juice,

and ¼ teaspoon grated citrus zest. Simmer over medium heat until slightly thickened, 1 minute.

Stir in the parsley, remove the pan from the heat, and whisk in 2 tablespoons butter.

■ **Chicken Breasts Japanese Style:**

Substitute 4 scallions (green onions), thinly sliced, for the garlic and parsley.

Lightly flour the chicken and substitute 1 tablespoon each Oriental sesame oil and vegetable oil for the olive oil.

Omit the white wine, oregano, and spaghetti sauce. Deglaze the pan with ¼ cup lemon juice and 1 cup chicken broth. Simmer over medium heat until the sauce is reduced by half, 4 to 5 minutes.

Remove the pan from the heat and swish in the scallions and 2 tablespoons butter. Pour the sauce over the chicken and sprinkle with 1 tablespoon sesame seeds.

■ **Chicken Breasts Orientale:**

Omit the garlic and parsley. Substitute Oriental sesame oil for the olive oil.

Omit the white wine, oregano, and spaghetti sauce. Deglaze the pan with 1 tablespoon soy sauce, ¼ cup rice vinegar, ½ cup chicken broth, ½ teaspoon chili paste, and 1 tablespoon hoisin sauce. Simmer over medium heat until the sauce is reduced by half, 3 to 4 minutes.

Remove the pan from the heat and swirl in 1 tablespoon butter if you wish.

■ Chicken Breasts with Mushrooms:

Substitute 1 shallot, minced, or 2 scallions (green onions), thinly sliced, and ¼ pound fresh mushrooms, thinly sliced, for the garlic and parsley. Substitute vegetable oil for the olive oil.

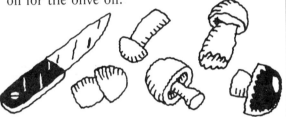

Omit the spaghetti sauce and oregano. Add the shallot or scallions and mushrooms to the pan after the chicken is removed and sauté for a minute or so to soften. Add ½ cup white wine, 1 teaspoon dried tarragon, and ¼ cup heavy or whipping cream. Simmer over low heat until slightly thickened, 2 to 3 minutes.

■ Chicken Breasts with Vegetables:

Substitute ¼ cup fresh dill leaves for the parsley. Omit the garlic. Thaw ½ cup frozen petite peas or corn kernels.

Omit the spaghetti sauce. Deglaze the pan with ½ cup white wine, ½ cup chicken broth, and the thawed vegetables. Add the oregano or another herb of your choice and simmer over medium heat until the sauce is reduced by half, 3 to 4 minutes.

Remove the skillet from the heat and swish in the minced dill and 1 to 2 tablespoons butter if you wish.

■ Chicken Breasts New York Style:

Substitute ¼ cup fresh basil leaves for the parsley and chop enough sun-dried tomatoes (packed in oil) to measure ¼ cup.

Omit the white wine, oregano, and spaghetti sauce. Deglaze the pan with ¼ cup balsamic vinegar, ½ cup chicken broth, and the sun-dried tomatoes. Simmer over medium heat until slightly thickened, about 2 minutes.

Remove the skillet from the heat and swish in the basil and 1 tablespoon butter if you wish.

■ The Utterly Lazy Cook's Sauté of Chicken Breasts:

Omit the garlic, parsley, oregano, and spaghetti sauce. Deglaze the pan with ¼ cup white wine and ½ cup water. Simmer over medium heat until the liquid has almost entirely evaporated, 4 to 5 minutes.

Remove the pan from the heat and swish in 1 to 2 tablespoons black olive paste or pesto and 1 tablespoon butter.

■ Chicken Breasts for Children Only:

Omit the garlic, parsley, white wine,

HOW TO REHEAT SAUTEED CHICKEN

If you've made the chicken and sauce but have to eat later than anticipated, cut the cooked chicken into 1-inch cubes and reheat them in the sauce over medium-low heat.

oregano, and spaghetti sauce. Deglaze the pan with ¼ cup water and ¼ cup ketchup. Simmer until very thick, about 1 minute.

Remove the pan from the heat and swirl in 2 tablespoons butter. (Believe me — some kids really love this.)

CHICKEN NUGGETS

MAKES 4 SERVINGS
TIME: 25 TO 30 MINUTES

This is a handy recipe for families where the kids have less sophisticated tastes than the adults. Without doing more work or cooking something different, you can please everyone.

Because this recipe is quick but requires tending to, be sure to finish whatever side dish you're serving first. I like this with plain cracked wheat or rice, or steamed potatoes or broccoli.

> *2 cups fresh bread crumbs, or ⅓ loaf or ⅓ pound firm white bread*
> *1 teaspoon dried herbs, such as thyme, tarragon, rosemary, and/or marjoram (optional)*
> *Salt and freshly ground black pepper*
> *1 pound boneless, skinless chicken breasts*
> *¼ cup leftover Basic Vinaigrette (see Index), or the dressing for Garlic- and Mustard-Crumbed Chicken (see page 163) or 2 tablespoons prepared pesto or black olive paste*
> *2 to 3 tablespoons olive or vegetable oil*

1. If you don't have bread crumbs on hand (premade, frozen, then thawed), make them by whirring the fresh bread in the food processor. Season with the herbs, if using, and salt and pepper to taste.

2. Place the chicken breasts on a cutting board, and, with your fingers, pull out the little fillet on the underside of each breast. Cut the chicken into strips about 2 inches long and ½ inch wide.

3. Drizzle the vinaigrette over the chicken pieces on the cutting board and rub

ESPECIALLY GOOD FOR CHILDREN

CHICKEN NUGGETS: Season a portion of the crumbs with salt and pepper only and coat the chicken with a little olive oil instead of vinaigrette to make the bread crumbs stick.

it into the chicken with your hands to make the crumbs stick to the chicken. Sprinkle the seasoned bread crumbs over the pieces and toss to coat. The coating won't be evenly distributed but it really doesn't matter.

4. Heat 2 tablespoons oil in a large skillet over medium heat until shimmering. Add the strips and sauté, without moving them, until the crumbs look golden, about 1 minute. With tongs, turn the pieces over and sauté the second side until golden, about 3 minutes. Reduce the heat to low and continue to sauté, turning the pieces frequently, until the chicken is cooked through, about 10 minutes longer.

VARIATIONS

■ Look at the variations for Garlic- and Mustard Crumbed Chicken (page 163) for ideas on how to vary the flavor of the coating or the breading.

■ The lazier way to make these nuggets is to sauté them briefly in an ovenproof skillet in 1 to 2 tablespoons oil, just to give them color, then bake at 375°F until cooked through, about 15 minutes. The chicken will taste delicious but the pieces won't be as crisp.

■ **For dieters**, coat the chicken with lemon or lime juice, vinegar, or mustard instead of vinaigrette and sauté the chicken without any oil in a nonstick skillet.

CHICKEN, RICE, AND GRAPE PILAF

MAKES 6 SERVINGS
TIME: 20 MINUTES WORK
1 HOUR NO-WORK COOKING TIME

This savory-sweet pilaf is like a stew in that it is good to make on a night when you can assemble and start the cooking of dinner early on, and then get some work done while dinner cooks. This is good, too, to serve on a night when your partner comes home late because it takes a while to cook and it will remain hot enough to eat for about 45 minutes after you've removed it from the oven.

Complete the meal with a plainly cooked vegetable like the Herbed Zucchini Sauté (see Index) or Lemon Green Beans.

CHICKEN PILAF FOR DIETERS

*C*heck the ingredients on the next page. Omit the oil. Substitute 1 pound boneless, skinless chicken breasts for the thighs.

Bring the onion, garlic, cinnamon, sugar, wine, rice, and chicken broth to a boil in a medium-size saucepan. Simmer covered over medium heat until the rice is tender, about 20 minutes. Meanwhile cut the chicken into 1-inch chunks, rinse and stem the grapes, and mince the parsley.

When the rice is tender, stir in the chicken, grapes, and parsley and simmer covered until the chicken is cooked through, 5 to 10 minutes longer.

1 medium-size onion
1 clove garlic
8 chicken thighs
2 tablespoons vegetable oil
½ teaspoon ground cinnamon
½ teaspoon sugar
1 cup long-grain white rice
½ cup dry white wine
1½ cups chicken broth or water
*Salt and freshly ground black
    pepper*
*1 pound seedless grapes, preferably
    red*
½ cup fresh parsley leaves

1. Preheat the oven to 375°F.

2. Thinly slice the onion and mince the garlic. Remove the skin and fat from the chicken thighs.

3. Heat the oil in a large casserole over medium heat. Add the chicken and sauté until somewhat brown, about 2 to 3 minutes on each side. Transfer the chicken to a plate.

4. Add the onion to the pan and sauté, stirring frequently, until softened, about 5 minutes. If the onion begins to stick to the bottom of the pan, add a tablespoonful or so of water and continue to sauté.

5. Add the cinnamon, sugar, and garlic to the pan and sauté for a few seconds until you begin to smell the aroma of the garlic. Add the rice, white wine, and chicken broth. Season well with salt and pepper.

6. Add the chicken to the pan and give the ingredients a stir. Bring the liquid to a simmer, cover the pan, and bake for 1 hour.

7. Meanwhile rinse and stem the grapes and mince the parsley.

8. After 1 hour, add the grapes to the pan and bake covered for another 10 minutes. Let stand for 15 minutes before serving, then stir in the parsley and adjust the seasoning.

CHICKEN STEW A LA BOUILLABAISSE

**MAKES 4 SERVINGS
TIME: 30 MINUTES WORK
1 HOUR NO-WORK COOKING TIME**

When you're done cooking this dish, you won't have to make anything else for dinner, for this stew, a perfect Sunday start-up meal, is richly flavored, hearty, and complete. The tomato and wine broth, infused with garlic and saffron, bathes the chicken, carrots, and potatoes with a taste reminiscent of a

DOUBLING UP

CHICKEN STEW: If you want to make this in double batches and freeze half for another day, omit the potatoes because they don't freeze well. After you thaw the leftovers, you can add ½ cup long-grain rice to the stew as you reheat it to add starch and thickening.

seafood bouillabaisse. The saffron colors the potatoes yellow, a jolly contrast to the red of the tomato and the orange of the carrots.

Before adding the chicken to the pot, I remove all the skin and fat because I hate the flabby texture of stewed chicken skin.

1 onion
4 medium-size boiling potatoes
6 carrots
4 each chicken thighs and
   drumsticks or 8 chicken thighs
1 to 2 tablespoons olive oil
1 can (14½ ounces) Italian-style
   stewed tomatoes
2 cups chicken broth or water
¼ cup dry white wine (optional)
2 cloves garlic
½ teaspoon dried thyme
¼ teaspoon fennel seeds
½ teaspoon dried orange peel
1 bay leaf
⅛ teaspoon saffron threads
Salt and freshly ground black pepper

1. Finely chop the onion. Peel the potatoes and cut each one into 8 pieces. Scrub or peel the carrots and slice ¾ inch thick. Remove the skin and as much fat as possible from each chicken piece.

2. Heat the olive oil in a large sauce-pan over medium-high heat until shimmering. Add the onions and sauté, stirring frequently, until softened, about 5 minutes.

3. Add the stewed tomatoes, chicken broth, and wine, if using. Stir in the potatoes, carrots, unpeeled garlic, thyme, fennel, orange peel, bay leaf, saffron, and chicken.

4. Bring the liquid to a boil over high heat and season to taste with salt and pepper. Reduce the heat to low, cover the pan, and simmer until the chicken is cooked through, about 1 hour. Adjust the seasoning and ladle some vegetables, chicken, and broth into each person's soup plate.

EMERGENCY BARBECUED CHICKEN

MAKES 4 SERVINGS
TIME: 10 MINUTES WORK
50 MINUTES TO 1 HOUR NO-WORK
COOKING TIME

For those nights when you have house-hold chores to do and need to get supper on the table with a minimum of work, here's the perfect recipe.

Serve this with Cracked Wheat with

CHICKEN STEW FOR DIETERS

Reduce the oil to 1 tablespoon. Substitute 1 pound boneless, skinless chicken or turkey breasts for the chicken legs. Cut the breasts into 1-inch chunks. Simmer all the ingredients except the chicken until the vegetables are tender, about 30 minutes. Add the chicken to the stew and simmer until just cooked through, about 5 minutes.

Carrots, Porcini-Flavored Lentils, Carrot Threads with Tarragon Limas, or Braised Peas and Lettuce (see Index for page numbers).

1 bunch fresh parsley or scallions
* (green onions)*
½ cup barbecue sauce
2 to 3 drops Tabasco sauce, or more
* to taste*
1 tablespoon Dijon mustard
4 chicken breast halves on the bone
* or 4 whole legs or 8 chicken*
* thighs*

1. Preheat the oven to 375°F.

2. Chop the parsley or thinly slice the scallions including most of the green tops. Mix the parsley or scallions with the barbecue sauce, Tabasco, and mustard.

3. Spread half the barbecue sauce all over the chicken and rub it into the skin. Place the chicken in a single layer in a baking pan. Cover the pan with aluminum foil and bake 35 minutes for chicken breasts or 50 minutes for legs or thighs.

4. Increase the heat to 450°F. Uncover the pan, spread the remaining barbecue sauce over the chicken, and bake uncovered until crusty and somewhat brown on top, about 10 minutes more for breasts or 15 minutes more for legs. Serve immediately or at room temperature.

SECOND TIME AROUND

BARBECUED CHICKEN: *Leftovers are best served cut off the bone and stuffed into sandwiches or added to a vegetable and grain salad. If you want to serve the chicken hot, remove the flesh from the bone before you store it, then reheat the remains in a dish of cooked grains, beans, or lentils.*

ROASTED GAME HENS WITH TARRAGON-CHEESE STUFFING

MAKES 4 SERVINGS
TIME: 15 MINUTES WORK
1 HOUR NO-WORK COOKING TIME

The stuffing keeps the hens moist while infusing them with an extra flavor. Bake beets or russet potatoes alongside the little birds so that all of your dinner cooks at once.

2 game hens, about 1½ pounds
* each*
½ cup low-fat cottage cheese, dry
* goat cheese, or cream cheese*
¼ teaspoon dried lemon or orange
* peel*
½ teaspoon dried tarragon
⅛ teaspoon garlic powder
Salt and freshly ground black pepper
1 tablespoon olive oil

1. Preheat the oven to 400°F.

2. With heavy kitchen shears cut each bird open along one side of the backbone. Cut away as much fat as possible, then rinse and pat dry. Insert your fingers under the skin covering the breast and loosen as much of the skin as you can; this pocket between the skin and the flesh is where you'll insert the stuffing. (This is easier to do than it is to describe.)

3. In a small bowl mix the cottage cheese, lemon peel, tarragon, garlic powder, salt and pepper to taste. Stuff the stuffing under the skin of the birds and place them spread open and skin side up, in a baking pan. Rub the oil over the skin of the birds and sprinkle with salt and pepper.

4. Bake until the juices run clear, not rosy, when the thigh is pricked with a fork, about 1 hour. Let stand 5 minutes before serving.

ROASTED GAME HENS FLAVORED WITH LEMON, GARLIC, AND RAISINS

MAKES 4 SERVINGS
TIME: 20 MINUTES WORK
1 HOUR NO-WORK COOKING TIME

An exotic blend of peppers, garlic, lemon, and raisins makes the most of the neutral flavor of these small birds. Plainly boiled cauliflower or pasta or grains will complete the meal nicely.

2 game hens, about 1½ pounds each
½ teaspoon dried lemon peel
½ teaspoon garlic powder
1 teaspoon dried thyme
Salt and freshly ground black pepper
4 bell peppers, preferably red
1 tablespoon olive oil
2 tablespoons lemon juice
2 cloves garlic
½ cup raisins or currants

1. Preheat the oven to 375°F.

2. With heavy kitchen shears, cut out the backbone of each bird, then cut them in half above the breastbone. Cut away as much fat as possible, then rinse and pat dry.

3. In a small bowl combine the lemon peel, garlic powder, thyme, and salt and pepper to taste. Sprinkle the spice mixture over the birds and rub it in well. Core, seed, and cut the peppers into very thin strips.

4. Heat the oil in a large ovenproof skillet over medium heat. Add the peppers, cover the skillet, and cook until they're tender, about 5 minutes. Add the lemon juice, unpeeled garlic, and raisins. Simmer covered for 10 minutes more.

5. Set the birds, skin side up, on top of the peppers and place the skillet in the oven.

SECOND TIME AROUND

ROASTED GAME HENS (either recipe): Remove the flesh from the bones and dice it. Reheat by sautéing the meat in a tablespoon of oil or butter.

Bake until the juices run clear, not rosy, when the thigh is pricked with a fork, about 1 hour. Let sit for 5 minutes, then transfer the hens to dinner plates and spoon the peppers and pan juices over them.

MINTED MUSHROOM TURKEY RAGOUT

MAKES 4 SERVINGS
TIME: 45 MINUTES

An abundance of mint is the kicker in this everyday stew of turkey and mushrooms. Be sure to use two bunches of fresh mint and don't overcook the stew or you'll end up with tough, dried-out turkey.

1 onion
½ pound fresh mushrooms,
*   domestic or shiitake*
1 pound boneless turkey breast,
*   fresh, smoked, or roasted*
2 bunches fresh mint
1 to 2 tablespoons olive oil
Salt and freshly ground black pepper

1. Chop the onion. Rinse, trim, and thinly slice the mushrooms (if using shiitakes, discard the stems). Cut the turkey into ½-inch cubes. Stem the mint and coarsely chop the leaves.

2. Heat the oil in a medium-size saucepan over medium heat. Add the onion and sauté, stirring frequently, until tender, about 5 minutes.

3. Add the mushrooms, cover the pan, and simmer over low heat, stirring every now and then, until the mushrooms are tender, about 3 more minutes.

4. Add the turkey and simmer covered until just cooked or heated through, about 3 to 5 minutes. Add the fresh mint, remove the pan from the heat, and let stand covered until the mint is barely wilted, about 1 minute. Give the stew a stir and season to taste with salt and pepper.

VARIATION

It's the abundance of fresh herbs that makes the difference in this stew. If you can't find mint, substitute 1 large bunch fresh parsley or 2 bunches fresh dill.

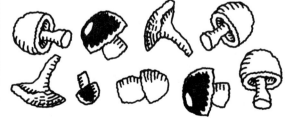

SECOND TIME AROUND

TURKEY RAGOUT: *1 can (16 ounces) white beans and 1 can (13¾ ounces) chicken broth mixed with the leftovers of this stew would make a very fine soup indeed.*

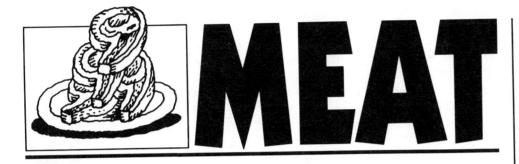

MEAT

During the week I'm usually in a hurry because I've come home late from work or because my child is starving or because I've loads of work to finish in the evening hours and I need to get dinner over with as quickly as possible. On these hectic nights I rely on quick-cooking meats and on quick-cooking techniques.

On occasion though, dinner doesn't have to be on the table as early or as quickly. On those nights I cook either large roasts or longer-simmering stews and soups because, once assembled and cooking, they require no tending to. In the time they take to cook, I catch up on chores, help my daughter with a project, or just put up my feet and read the newspaper. An added bonus I reap from these dishes is that they yield wonderful leftovers I can recycle later in the week or even freeze for another month.

MEAT IN A HURRY

Quick-cooking meats and quick-cooking methods: On hurried evenings, I get dinner on the table by relying on an arsenal of basic, uncomplicated recipes that make the best use of quick-cooking methods and quick-cooking meats. These are the times when I serve the tender cuts of meat like pork chops, lamb steaks, and ground beef that can be cooked the speediest ways I know how: stir-frying and sautéing, or baking when I'm

also trying to avoid fat. (I rarely broil because it's too messy and involves tiresome clean-up.)

Two-for-one dishes — sautés, stir-fries, and pasta sauces: Another Monday-to-Friday trick, and one that saves me clean-up, is to cook the dinner vegetable or starch (or both) in the same pan with the meat. This is the speedier alternative to stew, where all parts of the meal are simmered together in one dish.

First I brown the chops or steaks in a skillet for a few minutes on each side and remove them to a plate (that I'll reuse for dinner). If necessary I add more oil to the skillet and sauté some onions or garlic for flavor. Then I add the vegetable or starch I plan to serve with the meat and cook it briefly. Sometimes it's peppers with leftover potatoes, sometimes it's a stir-fry of greens with corn, and sometimes just a hodgepodge of steamed vegetables I've saved in the refrigerator.

Then I set the browned meat on top of the cooked vegetables, cover the skillet, and cook until tender. The dish can be finished on top of the stove or in the oven if I'm baking something else.

An even speedier single-skillet dinner is meat strips stir-fried with a mess of chopped vegetables. Or, in more extreme situations, meat sauce served over a bowlful of pasta; or a plateful of grains with ground meat, prepared spaghetti sauce, some spices, and thawed frozen vegetables.

LOOKING AHEAD— PLANNING LEFTOVERS

On Sundays when I'm feeling less rushed, I plan something that might take 2 hours to cook but isn't necessarily complicated to make and doesn't involve a lot of work. Then, I might roast a whole leg of lamb or make a potful of beef stew. Making dishes in larger quantities doesn't take a lot more time than making them in smaller ones, and it has the distinct advantage of yielding leftovers, which, during the week, become the fixings of another dinner or maybe even two.

Roasted meats: Roasted meat takes longer to cook than a steak but needs less tending to than a sauté. A large roast doesn't demand much work, and the meat left over can be used in myriad ways.

A pork roast, for example, can be eaten hot the first night and then reheated the second night in a stir-fry with snow peas or tossed into a rice and green pea casserole. The third night I can cube the cold pork into a salad or slice it into a sandwich.

Any remaining pork gets diced and frozen, and then reheated the following week in a hearty bean soup or filling pasta sauce.

Stews, casseroles, and main-course soups: When I have the time and especially when I'm feeling frugal, I make a large pot of stew, a casserole, or a main-course meat soup to serve both for dinner that night and to freeze in small portions for some future day. These long-simmering dishes make excellent use of the less expensive and less tender cuts of meat like the leg and shoulder cuts.

Stews, casseroles, and soups may take a while to cook but, once assembled and cooking on the back burner, or in the oven, they need no care. And the longer they cook, the better they taste.

Take a look at the chapter on One-Pot Meals for more ideas on the endless reheating and recycling possibilities of soups, stews, and casseroles.

TRICKING YOUR STOMACH

If you're limiting your meat intake to 4 ounces per day, you've probably noticed that cooked chops or steaks that size look awfully small on the dinner plate. But you can make a little look like a lot if you thinly slice the cooked meat across the grain and fan the slices on the plate.

SHOPPING FOR MEAT— WHAT TO BUY

When I have to do some marketing during the week, I never

have time as well to stop at a butcher shop to buy my meat or to make use of the in-house butcher in a supermarket. Instead I rely on the prepackaged meats readily available in every supermarket.

Because I know the cuts and how to cook them, I can make good use of these prepackaged meats. To make your life easier, I've made a list of the most frequently available cuts of meat and how best to cook them.

This list is not exhaustive, however. I've omitted some meats that, although readily available, don't make sense to cook during the week because they're either too cumbersome or too time-consuming to prepare.

BEEF

Beef cuts are classified into two categories: the most tender and the less tender. The most tender cuts come from the least exercised parts of the animal, which are the loin and rib areas. These cuts can be sautéed, pan-broiled, broiled, grilled, baked, or roasted.

The less tender cuts come from the most exercised parts of the animal, which are the shoulder and leg. These cuts need the gentle coddling of stewing or braising to break down the meat fibers and become tender. Cuts from the shoulder, also known as "chuck," become more tender when cooked with moist heat because they have more connective tissue and fat than do cuts that come from the leg.

Cuts from the leg, also known as "round," are leaner and thus better for people on low-fat diets even though, after cooking, they're drier and more fibrous than shoulder cuts.

Steaks to sauté, broil, grill, or pan-broil: Rib-eye steaks, also known as "Delmonico steaks," are cut from the rib end.

Shell, porterhouse, and sirloin steaks are cut from the loin end.

Steaks to braise: Chuck steaks are cut from the shoulder, round steaks from the leg.

Flank, skirt, and minute steaks: Flank and skirt steaks are delicious, inexpensive steaks which come from less tender parts of the animal. They taste wonderful and have great character provided you know what to do with them: Sear them for a few minutes on each side just until rare, then thinly slice the steak across the grain. When cooked too long, these steaks become tough and stringy.

Minute steaks are thin slices of meat, cut from the round part of the leg, that are then pounded to tenderize them. Cut the steaks into thin strips for stir-fry or sear them briefly on both sides and use in sandwiches. Cook only until rare.

SHOPPING TIP

Don't be fooled by the word "chop" or "steak" on a package of meat. If you broil or sauté a chop or steak cut from a less tender part of the animal, like the shoulder or leg, it will be tough, gristly, and inedible. Reserve these cuts for stews and braises.

Roasts to roast (dry heat): Fillet, also known as tenderloin, is cut from the loin. This roast is the most expensive but also the most tender. It has less waste and cooks faster than other roasts.

Rib-eye roast is cut from the rib.

Sirloin is cut from the loin close to the rump. It is expensive, tender, and good.

Top round roast is cut from the top part of the leg. It is leaner than the above roasts but still tender enough to roast if you don't cook it beyond rare; otherwise it will be dry and tough.

Roasts to braise, not roast: Chuck roast, cut from the shoulder, is best braised or cubed for stews.

Bottom round roast, cut from the leg, should be braised.

Boneless cubes: Chuck, cut from the shoulder, is best for stews—moist and tender.

Round, cut from the leg, is lean and dry when stewed.

Boneless stew meat should be avoided unless the package also states what part of the animal the cubes were cut from. Usually they are taken from different parts and for that reason they'll cook unevenly. This is how supermarkets make the most of their waste and why this cut is so inexpensive.

Stir-fry strips: These thin strips of meat are cut perfectly for stir-frying. Sometimes the supermarket identifies the part of the animal the strips come from; sometimes they don't. If the pieces are not identified, avoid them for they'll probably cook unevenly. It's best to cook all "stir-fry" pieces just until rare.

HOW MUCH MEAT TO BUY

When you're without a recipe to direct you, it's handy to know, more or less, how much meat to buy per person. Figure on:

4 to 5 ounces per person: boneless cuts

8 ounces per person: bone-in cuts like chops or roasts

10 ounces per person: mostly bone cuts like shanks.

Ground beef: Chuck has the most fat of all the ground meats as well as the most taste. It makes a good hamburger.

Sirloin is leaner, more expensive, and of better quality than chuck or round. The meat is moist and best for hamburgers cooked rare.

Round is the leanest of all the beef. It is best for people on low-fat or fat-free diets. Cook only until rare or it will be dry and crumbly. It is also good for meat sauces.

VEAL

Veal is the meat of a young calf. Because veal comes from a young and lean animal, all parts of the animals are leaner than beef and will tend to be drier, even the expensive quick-cooking chops.

Chops to sauté, bake, or broil: Loin chops are the most tender.

Rib chops are also good.

Chops to braise or cube for stew: Shoulder "blade" chops

Scaloppine to sauté or stir-fry: Scaloppine is the name given to thin pieces of boneless veal that can be cut from any part of the animal but are usually cut from the leg. However, the consumer has no way of knowing.

Shoulder roasts to braise: Veal roast cut from the shoulder is the only kind I've seen in supermarkets. It should be braised, not dry roasted.

Shanks to braise or stew: This is the lower leg of the calf. It is sometimes available whole but is usually cut into thick slices and labeled "osso buco" meat. Shanks should be stewed or braised in a pressure cooker if you own one.

PORK

Contrary to popular belief, hogs are now being bred to be leaner and lower in cholesterol and calories. Consequently pork should be cooked more like veal: slowly, with some moisture, and over low heat.

Chops to sauté or bake: Center-cut chops are cut from the loin end and can be bone in or out, thick or thin

---

HOW LONG TO KEEP MEAT

Fresh roasts, chops, steaks, and stew meat keep 2 to 4 days in the refrigerator.

Frozen beef, veal, and lamb keep from 6 to 9 months.

Frozen pork keeps 3 to 6 months.

Frozen ground meat keeps 3 to 4 months.

Frozen leftover cooked meat keeps 2 to 3 months.

---

cut. Since most of these chops are lean, they should never be broiled. Rib chops are cut from the rib end and are more fatty as well as more tender.

Roasts to roast: Center-cut loin roast is usually available boneless and tied.

Butt-end roast is cut from the loin close to the shoulder, so that it is fatty but juicy.

HAM

Cooked hams, whole, halved, or sliced in steaks are available both baked and smoked. For weekday dinners look for hams that are at least 95% fat free.

LAMB

Lamb is usually small and young when butchered so that most of the meat is tender enough to be cooked in any number of ways.

Chops to sauté, broil, or pan-broil: Rib chops are cut from the rib end, loin chops from the loin end.

Chops to stew: Blade chops are cut from the shoulder and are very fatty. If, however, you trim the fat and cube the meat, they are good for stewing.

Steaks to broil, pan-broil or sauté: Lamb steak is cut from the leg but is tender enough for broiling, pan-broiling, or sautéing.

Roasts to roast: Leg of lamb can be purchased whole with the bone in or out; or halved, either shank or butt end.

Rack of lamb is cut from the ribs. This roast is expensive and tender but rarely available in supermarkets.

NO-WORK ROAST BEEF: A SUNDAY START-UP DISH

MAKES 8 TO 12 SERVINGS
TIME: SEE BOX

When I prepare a roast, I like to prepare a big one so that I get lots of leftovers. Also the bigger the roast, the better the taste.

1 boneless rib roast or rib-eye roast (4 to 6 pounds), rolled and tied, or 1 filet or tenderloin (about 3½ pounds)
Salt and freshly ground black pepper

1. Preheat the oven to 450°F for 15 minutes.

2. Set the meat on a rack (rolled coils of aluminum foil are fine) in a roasting pan and place the pan in the oven. Roast until cooked to desired doneness.

3. Remove the roast from the oven and let it rest for 10 minutes. Then slice and season each slice with salt and pepper to taste.

MONDAY-TO-FRIDAY M · E · N · U

See The Monday-to-Friday Menu Sampler in the Appendix for a week long meal plan using Roast Beef as a Sunday Start-Up dish.

ABOUT ROASTING BEEF

Sunday dinners at our house invariably, except in the hot summer months, have a roast at the heart of the meal, whether of poultry, beef, pork, or lamb. Not only do I get an easy Sunday dinner out of the roast, I also provide myself with plenty of leftovers for the week which are then recycled cold in sandwiches or salads, reheated briefly in stews, casseroles, soups, and sautés, or used to stretch pasta sauces.

I'm always interested in simplifying my life and for that reason I buy a boneless beef roast because it is easier to slice and easier to deal with leftovers. I also always buy an expensive cut so that I'm guaranteed juicy, tender meat, and I always roast at high heat because it's faster.

The three beef roasts I rely on are boneless filet of beef (also known as tenderloin), which is very expensive but quick to cook; boned, rolled rib roast; and rib-eye or "Delmonico roast." The rib and rib-eye roasts are also expensive but slightly tastier than filet.

Because these cuts are well marbled, they should be cooked at high heat and, in my opinion, they taste best cooked to the rare stage.

Depending on how long it takes to cook the

roast, I also serve vegetables that can be baked alongside the meat and take about the same time to cook. See Roasted Chicken and One-Pan Chicken and Vegetable Dinner for examples. (see Index for page numbers).

ROAST BEEF COOKING TIMES

Cooking times for roast beef varies depending on the type of beef and the amount. The following are all approximately no-work cooking times. In order to be sure you've cooked your meat correctly, it is best to use a meat thermometer.

Rolled rib and rib-eye: *about 10 to 12 minutes per pound for rare (125 to 130°F on a meat thermometer) and 12 to 15 minutes per pound for medium-rare (140° to 145°F).*

For filet or tenderloin *(no matter what the weight): 18 to 20 minutes for very rare, 20 to 25 minutes for rare, and 25 to 30 minutes for medium-rare.*

MEAT THERMOMETERS

Is your oven calibrated and does it keep a consistent temperature? Was the roast chilled or at room temperature when you started to cook it? How long will it take per pound to roast a chunk of beef 3 inches thick and 12 inches long or 6 inches thick and 8 inches long? These are but some of the variables that make it so difficult to predict how long it will take to cook a roast. However, if you know the internal temperature of the roasted meat, then you will be able to tell if it is rare, medium-rare or well done. For these reasons I suggest that you rely on an "instant reading" thermometer that will tell you immediately what the internal temperature of your roast is. The Equipment list (see Index) will help you decide which one to buy.

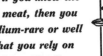

BEEF ROASTING TIPS

If you have taken the beef out of the refrigerator a couple of hours before roasting, the overall time will be less. A bigger roast will take proportionately less time to cook than a smaller roast.

The thickness of the roast affects the cooking time as well. For example, a whole filet of beef is about the same thickness throughout whether short or long so that any piece of filet, no matter what the weight, will cook in the same amount of time.

When figuring out roasting times, keep in mind individual preferences—what is rare for one person can be raw for another and slightly overdone for a third. Use an "instant" thermometer and remove the roast a couple of degrees below the temperature you desire. The temperature will continue to rise a degree or two more after you remove the roast from the oven.

PAN-BROILING STEAKS

Pan-broiling—cooking over high heat in a skillet with no fat added—calls for cuts like tender rib, loin, or sirloin steaks, or the less tender but ingeniously sliced flank or skirt steaks. These cuts are easier to cook in a skillet than bone-in tender steaks like Porterhouse or T-bone; save these for summer outdoor cooking. No matter what the supermarket package says, don't pan-broil or sauté any cut of beef from the shoulder (chuck), rump, or leg (round); these cuts should be braised.

■ *Choose a heavy, preferably a cast-iron, skillet in which to cook the steaks.*
■ *Choose steaks that are no thicker than 1 inch or they'll take too long to cook and your house will fill up with smoke. (Be sure to keep your window open when pan-broiling. A kitchen can get smoky pretty quickly.)*
■ *1-inch-thick rib, loin, and sirloin steaks take 2 to 3 minutes per side for very rare, 3 to 4 minutes per side for rare, and 4 to 5 minutes per side for medium. Don't cook the steaks beyond this stage or they'll get tough and you'll have wasted your money.*

■ *Flank and skirt steaks are thinner, about ½ inch thick, and should be cooked rare or medium-rare at most. This will take 3 minutes per side, tops.*
■ *If you're not sure whether the steak is cooked the way you like it, you can tell how rare it is without having to cut into the meat. Press the steak, as you cook it, with your finger; the flabbier it feels, the rarer it is. If you're not an expert presser, remove the steak to a plate, cut into it at its thickest point and take a peek.*
■ *Despite the dramatic haze surrounding this procedure, clean-up is easy. After cooking the meat, douse the hot skillet, off the heat, with a cup of water, making sure to avert your face when you add the liquid so you don't get a steam burn. Any charred pieces loosen up this way and the pan is a snap to clean later on.*

PAN-BROILED STEAK

MAKES 2 SERVINGS
TIME: 20 MINUTES

I make this skillet dinner only when there are the two of us, because I don't have a pan large enough to cook steaks for four and I don't like to use two pans. When I want to make rare beef for more than two people, I prepare a roast. Serve flank steak with a favorite condiment, salsa, or Herbed Vinaigrette (see Index).

1 package (10 ounces) frozen corn kernels
1 bell pepper, red or green
½ pound fresh mushrooms
1 bunch scallions (green onions)
Salt
10 ounces flank steak
Freshly ground black pepper
¼ cup water

1. Place the corn in a bowl, separating the kernels so they thaw. Core, seed, and thinly slice the bell peppers. Rinse and stem the mushrooms; trim the scallions. Thinly slice the mushroom caps (reserve the stems for soup) and scallions.

2. Sprinkle some salt on the bottom of a medium-size heavy skillet. Heat the dry skillet over high heat until you can see smoke rising up from it, about 1 minute.

3. Add the steak and cook over high heat 2 minutes per side for rare and 3 minutes per side for medium-rare. Don't cook it any longer than this because it will become tough and chewy.

4. Remove the steak from the skillet and season it lightly with salt and pepper. Set aside and keep warm.

5. Off the heat, add the water to the pan (it will sizzle and spatter wildly). Add the peppers and mushrooms and set the skillet over medium heat. Cover and cook for about 3 minutes, stirring occasionally. Add the corn and scallions and cook covered until the ingredients are tender and hot throughout, 2 to 3 minutes more. Season to taste with salt and pepper and remove the skillet from the heat.

6. Thinly slice the meat across the grain. Spoon the vegetables on the center of two dinner plates and lay the slices of steak across the top.

SLICING FLANK STEAK

In order to get the most attractive, tender slices out of your flank steak, you must remember to slice it across the grain, with your knife positioned at a 45 degree angle to the top of the meat. Flank steak is a relatively thin piece of meat and unless you angle the slices, you'll wind up with meager looking strips of beef.

SECOND TIME AROUND

CHILI: Just as with more sophisticated versions, this chili gets better the longer it simmers and the more you reheat it, so make it in double batches and freeze half to use another week.

Recycled chili is great reheated in tacos, in flour tortillas, in quick pita/pizza bread, or thinned with spaghetti sauce and tossed over pasta.

TEN-MINUTE CHILI

MAKES 4 SERVINGS
TIME: 10 to 15 MINUTES

Like many dishes in our house, this one was born of necessity. My daughter, 6 years old at the time, was not only a picky eater whose intake of food was limited to 10 items—chili among them—but also the kind of kid who might not feel hungry at 6:00 but two minutes later was ravenous. And so I came up with this incredibly easy recipe.

Serve with boiled white rice, couscous, or pasta.

*1 can (16 ounces) pink or small red
    kidney beans*
1 tablespoon vegetable or olive oil
½ pound ground lean beef round
*1 to 2 tablespoons chili powder, or
    to taste*
*½ to 1 tablespoon ground
    cumin, or to taste*
½ cup spaghetti sauce
Salt and freshly ground black pepper
*Garnishes (optional): sliced scallions
    (green onions) and sour cream,
    plain nonfat yogurt, or shredded
    Cheddar cheese*

1. Drain and rinse the beans. Heat the oil in a large skillet over medium heat. Crumble the meat into the skillet and sauté until the meat is somewhat brown, about 3 minutes.

2. Add the chili powder and cumin and cook, stirring frequently, about 1 minute, then stir in the beans and spaghetti sauce. Cover and simmer until heated through, about 5 minutes. Season to taste with salt and pepper.

3. Ladle the chili into bowls and top with scallions and a dollop of sour cream.

VARIATIONS

■ **All-Meat Chili:** Increase the meat to 1 pound and omit the beans. You can successfully substitute ground veal or turkey for the beef in this chili. Or sauté 1 pound cubed, skinless, boneless chicken breasts instead of the ground meat.

■ **Vegetarian Chili:** Omit the meat and add another 16-ounce can of beans, drained and rinsed; increase the spaghetti sauce to 1 cup.

■ **A More Authentic Chili** (if you're not so pressed for time): Sauté 1 chopped onion, 2 minced garlic cloves, and 1 chopped bell pepper until soft, 5 to 10 minutes, before adding the meat and spices. For an additional fiery touch, sauté 1 seeded and minced green or red chili with the other vegetables.

SLOPPY MIKES

MAKES 4 SERVINGS
TIME: 20 to 25 minutes

Friends often ask me how I invent recipes. It goes a little like this: I take a recipe I know, Sloppy Joes, for example. I add a new ingredient, like corn and sort of name it after someone (my husband) who likes to eat it.

Make a meal of this recipe by serving it over grains or pasta instead of bread or simply serve it as a quick meat dish alongside a steamed potato and another vegetable.

1 package (10 ounces) frozen corn
  kernels
1 onion
1 clove garlic
2 medium bell peppers, preferably red
1 tablespoon vegetable or olive oil
1 pound lean ground veal or
  ground beef round or sirloin
2 teaspoons chili powder, or more to
  taste
2 cups spaghetti sauce
4 hamburger rolls or English
  muffins, split
Salt and freshly ground black pepper

1. Place the corn in a bowl, separating the kernels so they thaw. Chop the onion. Mince the garlic. Core, seed, and chop the bell peppers.

2. Heat the oil in a large skillet over medium heat. Add the onion, garlic, and peppers and sauté, stirring occasionally, until the onions and peppers are softened, 3 to 4 minutes. If the vegetables begin to stick to the bottom of the skillet, add a tablespoonful or so of water and continue to sauté.

3. Crumble the meat into the skillet and sauté until it turns somewhat brown, about 3 minutes. Stir in the chili powder, then the corn and spaghetti sauce. Cover and simmer over low heat until all the ingredients are hot, about 5 minutes.

4. Meanwhile toast the hamburger buns or English muffins.

5. Season the meat mixture with salt and pepper to taste. To serve, set the toasted muffins or hamburger buns on plates and spoon the meat over the top.

VARIATION

Vegetarians can substitute 2 cans (16 ounces each) chick-peas or black beans for the meat.

SECOND TIME AROUND

SLOPPY MIKES: *Leftovers are perfect reheated with leftover potatoes, rolled in tortillas, or stuffed into tacos.*

CONTINUED FACING PAGE

ANATOMY OF A STIR-FRY

What we call "stir-fry" in our house is a dinner which makes use of odd bits and pieces of leftovers, quickly sautéed in a skillet. The following recipe should be thought of as a model only.

When creating your own recipe, count on 4 ounces meat and 1 to 2 cups vegetables per person. Then dice, slice, or mince the ingredients. The smaller they're chopped, the quicker they cook.

Use oil for stir-frying because the heat must be high to keep the food from steaming. Only oil can take that kind of heat.

Always begin by stir-frying those ingredients that take longest to cook, for example, raw vegetables. Add other ingredients, in sequence, ending with

STIR-FRIED BEEF WITH SCALLIONS

MAKES 4 SERVINGS
TIME: 20 MINUTES

Every now and then I crave beef, and in keeping with a healthy diet, I allow only 4 ounces meat per portion. Given that a 4-ounce steak looks meager on the dinner plate, I stretch it by slicing it thin and stir-frying it with a bunch of scallions and a handful of bean sprouts.

*1 pound beef sirloin or flank steak
   or 2 cups leftover pork, lamb, or
   beef roast cut in strips (see step 1)
1 clove garlic
1 bunch scallions (green onions)
4 cups mung bean sprouts, 1 head
   shredded romaine lettuce or
   escarole (4 cups), or 2 cups
   leftover steamed vegetables
1 tablespoon Oriental sesame or
   vegetable oil
1 teaspoon sugar
¼ teaspoon dried lemon peel
1 tablespoon soy sauce
2 tablespoons rice vinegar
Salt and freshly ground black pepper*

1. Cut the steak into strips about 2 inches long and ¼ inch wide. Mince the garlic. Thinly slice the scallions including most of the green tops. Shred the lettuce if using.

2. Heat the oil in a large skillet over medium-high heat. When the oil is hot, add the beef (either fresh or leftover), and stir-fry for 1 minute. Add the garlic, sugar, lemon peel, soy sauce, and vinegar and stir-fry 30 seconds longer. Stir in the bean sprouts or lettuce and the scallions and stir-fry until the beef is barely cooked and the vegetables have just wilted, about 10 seconds more. Remove the skillet from the heat and season to taste with salt and pepper.

VARIATIONS

Omit the garlic. Substitute a fat bunch of fresh coriander or parsley, minced, for the scallions.

To make the dish taste less Chinese, substitute ½ to 1 teaspoon of a prepared condiment such as pesto, black olive paste, chutney, or chili paste for the sugar, lemon peel, soy sauce, and vinegar in step 2.

GLAZED VEAL CHOPS

MAKES 4 SERVINGS
TIME: 20 TO 25 MINUTES

I like a sautéed veal chop when I want a speedy fix of veal that has a nice bone to chew on. You can flavor the chops with any number of quick little pan sauces, much like you can sautéed chicken breasts.

For a side dish, serve Brussels Sprout Rounds, Orange-Juice-Steamed Carrots, or Aromatic Rice with Vegetables (see Index for page numbers) and you're done with making dinner.

> 1 tablespoon olive oil
> 4 veal loin or rib chops, 1 inch thick
> 1/3 cup dry white wine or chicken broth
> 4 teaspoons prepared pesto or black olive paste
> Salt and freshly ground black pepper

1. Heat the olive oil in a large skillet over high heat. Add the veal chops and sauté until golden brown, about 3 minutes per side. Reduce the heat to low and continue to cook, turning the veal chops frequently, until they're brown on the outside and cooked through, about 10 minutes more. Remove the veal chops to dinner plates and keep warm.

2. Add the white wine and pesto to the skillet. Boil the liquid over high heat until only a syrupy glaze remains, about 1 minute. Season to taste with salt and pepper, spoon the glaze over the chops, and serve immediately.

VARIATIONS

■ You can also finish the veal chops in the oven after you've browned them on both sides. Just pop them into an ovenproof skillet and bake uncovered at 350°F until cooked through, about 20 minutes. When the chops are done, remove them from the skillet and make the sauce.

■ Substitute lemon juice for the white wine and 2 tablespoons minced sun-dried tomatoes for the pesto.

■ Substitute 2 tablespoons rice vinegar and 2 tablespoons soy sauce for the white wine and 1/4 cup sliced scallions (green onions) for the pesto. Sprinkle sesame seeds on top if you wish to complete the Oriental feel of the sauce.

■ Substitute 1/4 cup chicken broth

STIR-FRY, CONTINUED

those which are fastest to cook. Garlic should go in toward the end, after the meat is almost done, because it burns and turns acrid over high heat.

Next add the raw meat. Beef and lamb are done in a few minutes and can be served on the rare side, whereas pork takes longer because it must be cooked through.

When the meat is almost cooked, add whatever precooked or thawed frozen vegetables you are using. If you're reheating leftover cooked meat in a stir-fry, then the meat and these vegetables should be added at the same time.

The last touch should be a seasoning fillip of some sort, like soy sauce and rice vinegar or a teaspoon of a prepared condiment. Minced herbs should be stirred in, off the heat, at the last minute to preserve their fresh spark.

SECOND TIME AROUND

GLAZED VEAL CHOPS:
Because veal is dry, I never reheat any leftovers. Instead I cut the meat off the bone and slice it into a vegetable or watercress salad.

and ¼ cup heavy or whipping cream for the white wine and 1 teaspoon dried tarragon for the pesto.

VEAL SCALOPPINE

MAKES 4 SERVINGS
TIME: 10 MINUTES

Veal prepared for scaloppine that you buy at a supermarket might not be as rosy pink or as evenly cut as it should be or even sliced from the same part of the animal; but because this cut of meat is so quick to cook, supermarket scaloppine proves to be perfectly acceptable during the week and is even a boon on hectic nights.

The sauce in this recipe is robust and enlivens the bland flavor of inexpensive supermarket veal. However, if the veal scaloppine you've bought is delicate and of very

high quality, make one of the more subtly seasoned sauces suggested in the Variations that follow.

Serve with Citrus-Flavored Vegetables, Tri-Colored Peppers, broccoli, Brussels Sprout Rounds, or a grain dish of some sort (see Index for page numbers).

*1 pound veal scaloppine, sliced
    about ¼ inch thick
2 tablespoons lemon juice
1 to 2 tablespoons olive oil
½ cup chicken broth or water
¼ cup spaghetti sauce
1 tablespoon black olive paste or
    minced black olives
Salt and freshly ground black
    pepper
1 tablespoon butter (optional)*

1. Rub the veal all over with the lemon juice. (You can do this hours in advance of cooking the veal. Simply refrigerate until dinner time.) The lemon juice will perk up the flavor of the meat.

2. Heat the oil in a large nonstick skillet over medium-high heat. Add the veal and sauté until golden brown, about 1 minute per side.

3. Transfer the veal to dinner plates and keep warm. Add the broth and spaghetti sauce to the skillet and scrape up any browned bits that are stuck to the bottom of the skillet. Simmer until heated through, about 1 minute. Add the olive paste and season with salt and pepper to taste.

If desired, swirl the butter into the sauce off the heat. Spoon some sauce over the meat and serve.

Note: If preparing this dish in advance, don't add the butter to the sauce. Cut the cooked veal into thin strips and add them to the sauce, off the heat. Refrigerate if you are holding the dish longer than 30 minutes. When it's time to eat, gently reheat the strips of veal in the sauce over low heat. Swirl in the butter, off the heat, adjust the seasoning, and serve.

VARIATIONS

■ **Veal Scaloppine in Wine Sauce:** Dust the veal scaloppine with flour and shake off the excess (this will help thicken sauce later). Mince ½ cup fresh parsley leaves or ¼ cup fresh chives. Substitute ¾ cup dry white wine or Marsala for the broth, spaghetti sauce, and olive paste. Boil the liquid over high heat for a minute or two until somewhat thickened. Off the heat, swirl in the butter and minced parsley or chives.

■ **Veal Scaloppine in Citrus Sauce:** Dust the veal scaloppine with flour and shake off the excess. Mince ¼ cup fresh parsley or basil leaves. Substitute ½ cup chicken broth, ¼ cup lemon or orange juice, and ¼ teaspoon dried lemon or orange peel for the broth, spaghetti sauce, and olive paste. Boil the liquid over high heat for a minute or two until somewhat thickened. Off the heat, swirl in the butter and parsley or basil.

BRAISED VEAL: A SUNDAY START-UP DISH

MAKES 6 TO 8 SERVINGS
TIME: 5 MINUTES WORK
2¼ HOURS NO-WORK
COOKING TIME

Sunday is always my stay-at-home night to roast a leg of lamb or braise a shoulder of veal so that I have some terrific leftovers to use later in the week.

Ignore all instructions on the supermarket package that direct you to roast veal shoulder; it must be cooked with some moisture to break down the connective fibers.

Bake some potatoes, yams, acorn squash, or beets to serve with the veal and serve a salad either before or after.

MONDAY-TO-FRIDAY
M · E · N · U

See The Monday-to-Friday Menu Sampler in the Appendix for a week long meal plan using Braised Veal as a Sunday Start-Up dish.

SECOND TIME AROUND

BRAISED VEAL: When the roast is cool, slice off as much of the fat as possible, wrap the meat well and refrigerate for 3 to 4 days.

Cut the leftover veal roast into ¾-inch cubes and reheat it in Mexican Corn and Sweet Potato Sauté, or White Beans Provençale.

You could julienne or cube the chilled leftover veal and add it to Salad of Pickled Beets and Onions instead of sardines, to New York Chef's Salad, or Summer Borscht Salad.

On the third night, bits and pieces of the veal can be finely diced and reheated in a soup like Chunky Peasant Vegetable Soup or Barley-Vegetable Chowder. (See Index for all recipe page numbers.)

Veal shoulder roast, 2½ to 3½ pounds
½ cup dry white wine, chicken broth, or lemon juice
Salt and freshly ground black pepper

1. Preheat the oven to 450°F for 15 minutes.

2. Set the roast, fat side up, in a roasting pan and pour the liquid around it. Cover with aluminum foil and set the pan in the oven.

3. Immediately reduce the heat to 375°F and cook until the roast feels tender when pierced with a fork, 1¾ to 2 hours.

4. Remove the roast from the oven and let it rest for 15 minutes before serving. Thinly slice the veal. Season the slices with salt and pepper and moisten with spoonfuls of the pan juices if they're not too fatty.

VARIATION

If you have some Protean Ratatouille (see Index), you can braise the veal over that instead of using the liquid suggested above.

ROAST LEG OF LAMB: A SUNDAY START-UP DISH

**MAKES 6 TO 8 SERVINGS
TIME: 5 MINUTES WORK
1½ TO 2 HOURS NO-WORK
COOKING AND REST TIME**

This is perfect for when you have the time but not the energy to put into your cooking and when you need to create the makings of a second meal.

For the sake of research, I attempted twice to cook thawed frozen New Zealand roast of lamb packaged in plastic: both times it was ghastly. Be sure the lamb you buy is fresh and not thawed frozen. If your supermarket has an in-house butcher, then the meat should be okay.

I simply stick the leg of lamb in a hot oven and let it cook all by itself. You don't even have to season the outside layer, which is fat, because you'll remove it anyway before serving.

The 1½ hours it takes to cook the lamb is put to good use if you bake alongside it accompaniments that take the same time to cook.

Don't bother starting the lamb at one temperature and finishing it at another, for it cooks nicely at an even 400°F, but do let it rest for 15 minutes or so before slicing to give the meat juices a chance to retreat back into the muscle fibers.

Since most of the juices left in the pan are rendered fat, I discard them and serve a salsa to go along with it like Green Chili and Jalapeño Salsa or Corn and Two-Pepper Relish (see Index for page numbers).

1 bone-in leg of lamb, about 5
pounds

1. Preheat the oven to 400°F for 15 minutes.

2. Set a rack (or coils of aluminum foil) in a roasting pan and set the lamb, fat side up, on top. Roast uncovered for 1 hour 10 minutes for rare, 1½ hours for medium-rare, and 1¾ hours for medium-well done. (Obviously the meat close to the bone will be a lot less done than the outside.)

3. Remove the roast from the oven and let it sit for 15 minutes before slicing. With a sharp knife, remove and discard the outside layer of skin and fat. (If making Variation below, leave the oven on.) Thinly slice the meat as best you can. Before storing leftovers, trim away as much fat as possible and remove all meat from the bone.

VARIATION

Remove the fat from the roasting pan and deglaze the pan on top of the stove with ½ cup dry white wine. Boil, stirring continually, for 2 minutes. Add 2 cans (16 to 19 ounces each) drained and rinsed cannellini beans, 1 can (14½ ounces) stewed tomatoes, and 1 teaspoon dried tarragon. Bake for the 15 minutes it takes for the lamb to rest and, if you wish, while you slice it.

HERBED LAMB CHOPS

MAKES 2 SERVINGS
TIME: 15 TO 20 MINUTES
20 TO 25 MINUTES WITH
VARIATIONS

During the work week when I hanker for the tenderness and sweet flavor of roasted rack of lamb I make rib chops

SECOND TIME AROUND

ROAST LEG OF LAMB: *Cubed leftover lamb can be reheated in a soup like Bean Minestrone or Chunky Peasant Vegetable Soup or in a stew like Protean Ratatouille or A Good Basic Meat Sauce (see Index for page numbers).*

Or you can eat the leftover lamb chilled, accompanied by a mustard or anchovy mayonnaise and a green or basic vegetable salad. To make the mayonnaise, blend 1 cup of mayonnaise with a can of flat anchovies, 1 to 2 tablespoons lemon juice and 1 teaspoon capers. Season well with pepper.

instead. It's a lot cheaper and faster to cook chops than it is to roast an entire rack of lamb, and, since the rib chops are cut from the rack, the two cuts of meat are virtually identical.

If rib chops aren't available, I settle on equally succulent loin chops. I can always find one of these cuts at the supermarket, whereas a rack of lamb is almost impossible to find outside of a fancy butcher shop.

Whatever you do, never substitute shoulder or blade chops or lamb steaks for the chops in this recipe. These shoulder or leg cuts are very fatty and from parts of the animal that are more suitable for moist stews and braises.

The quickest, easiest, and leanest way to cook the chops is to pan-broil them, and the most delicious way to eat them is to cook them rare or pink. Please don't cook these longer than the recommended time, or they'll toughen and you'll have thrown your money away.

Lamb chops are delicious served with Sautéed Chestnuts and Pears, Braised Fennel, or Grated Beets and Apple (see Index for page numbers).

When doubling the recipe to feed four people, use two skillets.

MONDAY-TO-FRIDAY
M · E · N · U

See The Monday-to-Friday Menu Sampler in the Appendix for a week long meal plan using Leg of Lamb as a Sunday Start-Up dish.

4 to 6 rib or loin chops (2 or 3 per person), ¾ to 1 inch thick
Olive oil
3 tablespoons dry red wine
1 teaspoon Dijon mustard
¼ teaspoon dried thyme
¼ teaspoon dried rosemary
Salt and freshly ground black pepper
1 tablespoon butter (optional)

1. With a sharp knife, trim away all the outer fat from the chops.

2. Spread about 1 teaspoon olive oil in a large nonstick skillet. Heat the oil over high heat until very hot. Add the lamb chops and cook 3 minutes per side for rare lamb or 4 to 5 minutes per side for medium-rare. Remove the lamb chops to a dinner plate and keep warm.

3. Discard any fat in the pan. Off the heat, add the red wine, mustard, and herbs to the pan. Return the skillet to medium heat and, with a wooden spoon, scrape up any brown bits stuck to the bottom of the skillet. Simmer until the sauce is somewhat syrupy, 10 to 15 seconds. Season with salt and pepper, swirl the butter into the sauce off the heat, and spoon the sauce over the chops.

VARIATIONS

■ Substitute 2 tablespoons minced chopped pickles, 1 tablespoon capers, and 2 tablespoons minced fresh herb, such as parsley, for the dried herbs and mustard.

■ Substitute white wine for the red, omit the dried herbs, and finish with 1 tablespoonful minced fresh mint or tarragon.

■ Substitute lemon juice for the wine, omit the dried herbs and mustard, and add 2 teaspoons capers.

■ Substitute chicken broth for the wine and 2 teaspoons prepared black olive paste and 2 tablespoons minced fresh parsley for the dried herbs and mustard.

GINGERED LAMB STEW

MAKES 4 TO 6 SERVINGS
TIME: 15 MINUTES WORK
45 MINUTES TO 1 HOUR NO-WORK
COOKING TIME

The flavor of this stew is hot and spicy; the addition of raw chopped peppers and scallions add a striking visual note and lovely textural contrast. Plainly cooked lentils, kasha, brown rice, or quinoa would be a grand complement.

If you can't find boneless lamb stew meat, just pick up some shoulder lamb chops at your supermarket and voilà—you're set.

4 shoulder lamb chops, round bone in, or 1 pound lamb stew meat
2 cloves garlic
1 piece (½ inch) fresh ginger or 2 teaspoons ground
2 tablespoons vegetable oil
1 teaspoon sugar
1 tablespoon soy sauce
2 tablespoons rice vinegar
1 teaspoon dried mint
1 cup chicken broth or water
Salt and freshly ground black pepper
1 fresh hot red chili (optional)
1 bell pepper, red or yellow
2 scallions (green onions)

1. Trim the chops of all fat and bone and cut the meat into ¾- to 1-inch chunks. Mince the garlic and the ginger.

2. Heat the oil in a medium-size saucepan over medium heat. Add the garlic, ginger, and sugar and cook for a few seconds until you can smell their aroma.

3. Add the soy sauce, rice vinegar, mint, lamb, and chicken broth. Bring the liquid to a boil and season to taste with salt

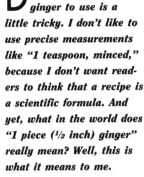

A PIECE OF GINGER

Describing how much ginger to use is a little tricky. I don't like to use precise measurements like "1 teaspoon, minced," because I don't want readers to think that a recipe is a scientific formula. And yet, what in the world does "1 piece (½ inch) ginger" really mean? Well, this is what it means to me.

Fresh ginger looks a bit like a miniature gnarled tree. Usually it has a couple of branches that emerge from a thicker stem. What I mean by a ¼-, ½-, or 1-inch piece is that size chunk of one of those little branches. Usually the branch is ½ to ¾ inch thick.

Fresh ginger tastes hot and tingly. If you like that flavor, use a lot of ginger; if you don't, use less or none at all.

SECOND TIME AROUND

ROAST PORK: After dinner I set aside some of the remaining roast for sandwiches the following day. I love roast pork sandwiches with a barbecue sauce mixed with mayonnaise.

Sometimes I cut part of the leftover roast into thin strips and dress it immediately with a fresh coriander vinaigrette so that I have the beginnings of a meat salad for the next day. Other condiments I like to season a pork salad with are mustard, pickles, salsa, horseradish, and Indian chutneys or pickles.

Sometimes I cut the leftover pork into very thin, skinny strips and freeze them. These I might reheat in a pasta sauce, in a bean dish, in a stir-fry, or in a soup like Beef and Noodle Soup à la Vietnamese (see Index), where I omit the beef and substitute the pork instead.

and pepper. If you like your stew hot, add the chili, seeded and minced. Cover the pan and simmer gently until the lamb is tender, 45 to 60 minutes.

4. Meanwhile core, seed, and finely chop the bell pepper. Thinly slice the scallions, including most of the green tops. When the stew is done, sprinkle with the bell peppers and scallions and serve hot.

ROAST LOIN OF PORK: A SUNDAY START-UP DISH

MAKES 8 TO 10 SERVINGS
TIME: 2 TO 2¼ HOURS NO-WORK COOKING AND REST TIME

Just as with beef, there are plenty of cuts of pork that are suitable for roasting, but I usually buy the one or two cuts that are the easiest to find and the fastest to prepare.

My most favorite pork roast is center-cut boneless loin. It is very lean, easy to slice, and relatively quick to prepare. The average cooking time is be-tween 1¾ and 2 hours. A juicier, but fatter, roast is the butt or blade end boneless loin, which means it is cut from the shoulder end of the loin.

Pork is bred so lean these days that roasting it is like roasting veal. The meat has little inner marbling and most of the fat is on the outside of the roast. This means that it is better roasted at 325°F to preserve some juiciness and moistness in the meat. As with all roasts, the larger the cut, the juicier the meat.

Side dishes I like to bake alongside a pork roast are sweet potatoes, white potatoes, beets, and winter and spaghetti squashes. A dish of either Glazed Root Vegetables with Ginger and Garlic or Stir-Fried Cabbage and Greens completes this meal. On occasion I'll also serve a sweet dish like Sautéed Chestnuts and Pineapple (see Index for page numbers).

1 boneless pork loin roast, center cut or butt end, 3 to 4 pounds, rolled and tied
Salt and freshly ground black pepper

1. Preheat the oven to 325°F for 15 minutes.

2. Set the meat, fat side up, on a rack (rolled coils of foil are fine) in a roasting pan. Roast uncovered until a meat thermometer inserted in the middle of the roast reads 165°F, 1¾ to 2 hours.

3. Remove the roast from the oven and let it sit for 15 minutes before carving. Then slice and season each slice with salt and pepper.

CUMIN-SCENTED BUTTERFLIED PORK

MAKES 6 SERVINGS
TIME: 30 MINUTES
15 MINUTES RESTING TIME

I adore roasted pork loin, but when I don't have the 2 hours it takes to cook it, I butterfly and broil it, and with hardly any effort, my main course is done.

I know I have made statements, right and left, about never broiling anything, especially during the week, but this is the exception that proves the rule.

"Gourmandise" sometimes wins out over laziness. This is delicious served at room temperature.

1 cup fresh coriander or parsley
*   leaves*
¼ cup olive oil
Juice of 3 limes or ⅓ cup lemon
*   juice*
1 small onion
½ teaspoon ground cumin
1 boneless pork loin, about 1½
*   pounds, trimmed of all fat*
*   and butterflied*
Salt and freshly ground black
*   pepper*

1. Preheat the broiler.

2. In a food processor or blender process the coriander, olive oil, lime juice, onion, and cumin until smooth.

3. With a sharp knife, make many shallow slashes across both surfaces of the pork. Place the pork on a broiler pan and sprinkle with salt and pepper. Pour half the coriander mixture over the pork, spreading it evenly over the meat and working it into the slashes. Flip the pork over and repeat the procedure on the other side.

4. Broil the pork 3 inches from the heat for 10 minutes. Flip the meat over and broil until cooked through, about 10 minutes more.

HOW TO BUTTERFLY A LOIN OF PORK

I *usually get a butcher to butterfly a loin of pork for me, but if you can't, this is how to do it. The pork, well boned, is rolled and tied, so untie it. Trim off all the outer fat and lay the meat out as flat as possible. It will be about 1½ inches thick. Starting from one long side, carefully split the meat in two through its thickness, stopping ¾ inch from the opposite edge. Open the meat as you would a book. Flatten it with a meat pounder or your hands to make it as even as possible. You now have a larger but thinner piece of meat, ready to dress and broil in no time flat.*

5. Remove the pork from the oven and let it rest for 15 minutes. Thinly slice the meat across the grain and serve with the pan juices.

HERBED PORK CHOPS

MAKES 4 SERVINGS
TIME: 20 TO 25 MINUTES

You can make pork chops two ways: Either sauté them over high heat just for a minute on each side to give them color and then cook them slowly and turn them frequently until done. Or sauté them over high heat to give them color and then bake them in the oven for 20 minutes until done. The latter method makes the most sense if you're cooking something else in the oven as well.

You can make a pan sauce just as you would for sautéed chicken or veal and serve the chops with just one other side dish.

1 tablespoon vegetable oil
4 pork loin or rib chops, 1 inch
    thick
2 tablespoons lemon juice
2 tablespoons water
½ teaspoon dried herb, such as
    thyme or rosemary
Salt and freshly ground black
    pepper

1. Heat the oil in a large skillet over medium-high heat. Add the pork chops and sauté until golden brown, about 1 minute per side. Reduce the heat to low and continue to cook for another 10 to 12 minutes, turning the chops frequently. They should be nice and brown on the outside and cooked through but not dry on the inside.

2. Remove the pork chops to dinner plates and keep warm.

3. Add the lemon juice, water, and herb to the skillet. Boil the liquid over high heat until syrupy, about 1 minute. Season to taste with salt and pepper, spoon the glaze over the chops, and serve immediately.

VARIATIONS

■ Substitute white wine for the lemon juice and water and proceed with the recipe.
■ Substitute ¼ cup each chicken broth and heavy or whipping cream for the lemon juice and water and 1 teaspoon dried tarragon for the thyme or rosemary.

SECOND TIME AROUND

HERBED PORK CHOPS: Pork, like veal, is dry, so the leftovers should not be reheated. Instead cut the meat off the bone, dice or slice it, and serve it in a salad or use in sandwiches.

PORK CHOPS BAKED IN A PEAR SAUERKRAUT

MAKES 4 SERVINGS
TIME: 45 TO 50 MINUTES

This is a wonderful and quick winter dish that tastes terrific with baked potatoes, acorn squash, or sweet potatoes.

1 pound sauerkraut (preferably
 bagged not canned)
1 jar (6 ounces) baby-food apple or
 pear purée
½ teaspoon caraway seeds
Salt and freshly ground black
 pepper
1 tablespoon oil
4 boneless center-cut pork chops,
 about 4 ounces each and ½ inch
 thick

1. Preheat the oven to 375°F.
2. Drain the sauerkraut, rinse well under cold running water, and squeeze dry with your hands. In a mixing bowl combine the sauerkraut, fruit purée, and caraway seeds; season to taste with salt and pepper.
3. Heat the oil in a medium-size oven-proof skillet over medium heat. Add the pork chops and sauté until somewhat browned,

about 2 minutes per side. Transfer the chops to a dinner plate.
4. Off the heat, stir the sauerkraut mixture into the pan juices in the skillet. When this is well mixed, place the seared pork chops on top and place the skillet in the oven. Bake uncovered until the pork is cooked through, about 30 minutes.

VARIATION

Substitute 1 tablespoon brown sugar, ½ cup milk or heavy or whipping cream, and 2 teaspoons Dijon mustard for the fruit purée and caraway. Proceed as directed.

HONEY-BAKED HAM

MAKES 10 TO 12 SERVINGS
TIME: 1 TO 1¼ HOURS NO-WORK
COOKING AND REST TIME

During the week it only makes sense to bake a ready-to-eat ham, whether smoked or not. I prefer boneless ham so that both carving and storing leftovers is easier. And, there should be plenty left over.

A SAFETY TIP FOR THE OVENPROOF SKILLET

When you cook something in a skillet in the oven, make sure, once you remove the skillet and place it on top of the stove, to put a towel or potholder on the handle and keep it there until the handle is completely cool.

This will remind you that the handle is scorching hot and keep you from grabbing the handle and getting badly burned.

SECOND TIME AROUND

HONEY-BAKED HAM: Ham makes terrific leftovers. You can cube it, slice it, or cut it into strips and use it in just about any recipe in this book. Ham works wonderfully well in soups, stews, casseroles, pasta sauces, salads, and in sandwiches, hot or cold.

You should follow the cooking directions on the package if there are any. If there aren't, bake as directed in this recipe and serve.

Side dishes I like to serve with ham are too numerous to mention; I think just about any flavor works with this meat. I especially like Silky Cornmeal, all types of legumes, especially black beans, and greens, root vegetables, and cabbage dishes. Figure on 1 pound to serve 3 people.

*1 boneless ready-to-eat ham, 3 to 4
   pounds
2 tablespoons honey or apricot jam
2 tablespoons Dijon mustard
Salt and freshly ground black pepper*

1. Preheat the oven to 325°F for 15 minutes.

2. Set the ham on a rack (rolled coils of foil are fine) in a roasting pan. Roast uncovered until a meat thermometer inserted in the middle of the roast reads 130°F, 45 to 60 minutes.

3. Meanwhile mix the honey and mustard. Fifteen minutes before the ham is due to come out of the oven, brush the glaze over the ham and continue to bake until done.

4. Remove the ham from the oven and let it rest for 15 minutes before carving. Season each slice with salt and pepper.

ONE-POT MEALS

During the week, making dinner is less of a hassle if clean-up is kept to a minimum, and one of the ways to save time on washing up is to make dinner in a single pot. This dinner can be a stew, a casserole, or a skillet supper.

The one-pot meal contains the main parts of dinner—the protein, the vegetables, and, on occasion, the starch as well. Just what this one-pot meal is depends on my schedule. If I'm home early enough, I prepare a stew or casserole that requires some initial work but then cooks slowly by itself without needing further attention.

If, however, my family is eating late or I don't know when my spouse will be home, I might prepare the ingredients for a skillet supper ahead of time and then, when we're all assembled, stir-fry the ingredients and have dinner on the table in minutes.

One-pot meals also offer endless reheating and recycling possibilities. They are the perfect solution for those weeks when you have time to cook on one night and know that later in the week you won't have an extra minute.

STEWS AND CASSEROLES

Stews and casseroles are homey combinations of protein, vegetables, and sometimes starch slowly cooked together in liquid. What I call stews are mixtures that can cook on top of the stove because they have enough liquid to keep the ingredients from sticking to the bottom of the pot and scorching.

What I call casseroles are grain dishes mostly that I cook in the oven because they don't have enough liquid in them to keep them from burning over direct heat.

Stews, like soups, are dishes I make in large quantities and freeze in small portions so that I always have a prepared dinner on hand that I can quickly reheat. It can be reheated as is, without change or addition, up to three days after it's made, and it will taste even better. Stews (and casseroles) can also be altered and expanded by adding more broth or a new ingredient to change its original character. If you freeze a stew in individual portions, older kids can easily reheat it in a microwave or on the stove and make dinner for themselves.

Traditionally stewing, braising,

and other slow-cooking methods were reserved for those ingredients, like dried beans or tough meats, which need a long time to become tender. However, from Monday to Friday I don't have that much time. So with some ingenuity, I've developed methods to speed things up.

For example, I'll make a classic braised chicken dish with chicken breasts instead of a quartered chicken to reduce the cooking time to minutes. While this shortcut sacrifices some of the depth of flavor, I can compensate for it by adding more vegetables and by seasoning more generously with spices or fresh herbs.

On those nights when I crave the depth of flavor and tender texture of slow-cooked dishes, I pull out my pressure cooker.

SKILLET SUPPERS OR STIR-FRIES

A skillet supper is like a stew in that it has all the makings of dinner in a single pot. What distinguishes this type of dish from a stew or casserole is that it requires almost no liquid and the taste and texture are quite different.

I make these kinds of one-pot meals either if I'm not sure when we'll be eating or if I need to make dinner in a hurry. The time saver is that any type of ingredient cut into small pieces (which can be done hours ahead of time) cooks much more quickly than if left in large pieces.

But not only are skillet suppers a boon for nights when dinner is needed in a hurry, they are also another way of quickly reheating diced leftover meat and poultry and of making good use of a cupful of parboiled vegetables.

PRESSURE COOKING

I've included a few pressure-cooker recipes at the end of this one-pot chapter, because I've rediscovered the value of this remarkable gadget. This great time-saving pot regains the flavor of slow cooking that is lost in some recipes when I cook in my unorthodox and time-saving manner, and it does so in a fraction of the time it takes to slowly simmer a stew.

EATING "SERIATIMLY"

Throughout my book, you'll notice I frequently refer to the hypothetical (but realistic) situation when partners and children eat at different times in the evening. From my experience, the notion that the old-fashioned, family-style, home-cooked meal is coming back into vogue is a lot of malarkey.

In my family, my daughter is hungry at 5:30 or 6:00—an hour too early for me to eat—and my husband often comes home later than he had planned. As a result, we eat "seriatim," because I don't believe in forcing people to eat at some predetermined dinner hour that rarely coincides with an individual's hunger pangs.

But eating in this cavalier fashion doesn't prevent us from enjoying each other's company, the most important point, I think, of the family dinner. I always keep my family company when they eat, even if I'm not sharing in the meal.

HAM, HOMINY, AND GREEN CHILI STEW

MAKES 4 SERVINGS
TIME: 45 MINUTES

Although a portion of this heady stew is enough dinner for us, those with heartier appetites should couple it with a heaping plateful of white rice.

2 onions
2 green bell peppers
1 pound lean smoked or baked ham
    or smoked poultry preferably
    95% or more fat free
2 tablespoons olive oil
1 can (16 to 19 ounces) hominy or
    2 packages (10 ounces each)
    frozen corn kernels, thawed
2 cans (4 ounces each)
    chopped green chilies
1 teaspoon dried oregano
1 tablespoon red wine vinegar
Salt and freshly ground black pepper
1 cup fresh parsley leaves

1. Finely chop the onions. Core, seed, and chop or thinly slice the peppers. Cut the ham into small cubes.
2. Heat the oil in a medium-size casserole or a deep, large skillet over medium heat. Add the onions, reduce the heat to medium, and sauté until translucent, about 5 minutes.
3. Add the peppers, cover, and simmer gently until the peppers are somewhat tender, about 5 minutes more. Add all the remaining ingredients except for the parsley and season to taste with salt and pepper. Cook covered over low heat until the ingredients are tender and hot, 10 to 15 minutes.
4. Meanwhile chop the parsley. When the stew is done, stir in the parsley, adjust the seasoning, and serve.

COMFORT STEW

MAKES 4 TO 6 SERVINGS
TIME: 30 MINUTES WORK
1 HOUR 10 MINUTES NO-WORK
COOKING TIME

This is a good example of how easily you can create a great tasting stew without much fuss. What you do need, though, is time; so plan to make this on an evening when you have about an hour and a half before dinner to give the stew time to gently cook. The dish abounds in

SECOND TIME AROUND

HAM, HOMINY, AND GREEN CHILI STEW: A second meal can be made of this by using it as a stuffing in tacos and tortillas. Chop up fresh tomatoes and onions, and shred some lettuce to use as toppings, if you wish.

SECOND TIME AROUND

COMFORT STEW: If you wish, make a double batch up through step 5. Freeze the stew in portions for one or two or however many you have to feed at once. Because this is the foundation of a complete meal but takes a while to cook, it's great to have it handy in the freezer to complete at a later date.

Leftovers are good just reheated with additional liquid so the pasta doesn't burn on the bottom.

vegetables and pasta and will satisfy the hungriest of souls.

Those short on time but still in need of stew should take a look at the pressure-cooker recipes at the end of this chapter.

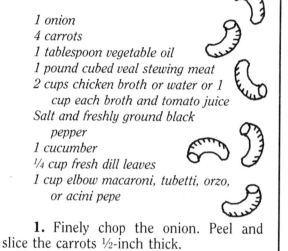

1 onion
4 carrots
1 tablespoon vegetable oil
1 pound cubed veal stewing meat
2 cups chicken broth or water or 1
    cup each broth and tomato juice
Salt and freshly ground black
    pepper
1 cucumber
¼ cup fresh dill leaves
1 cup elbow macaroni, tubetti, orzo,
    or acini pepe

1. Finely chop the onion. Peel and slice the carrots ½-inch thick.

2. Heat the oil in a large saucepan over medium heat. Add the onion and sauté, stirring frequently, until translucent, about 5 minutes.

3. Add the veal, increase the heat to high, and sauté until the veal begins to brown, about 10 minutes. The veal will throw off lots of water, but don't be alarmed.

4. Add the chicken broth and bring it to a boil over medium heat. Cover and simmer gently for 10 minutes. With a spoon,

remove any scum that has risen to the surface.

5. Add the carrots to the veal and season to taste with salt and pepper. Cover and simmer over low heat until the veal is tender, about 40 minutes more.

6. Meanwhile peel, seed, and cut the cucumber into ½-inch cubes. Mince the dill.

7. When the veal is done, stir in the pasta and simmer covered until the pasta is tender, about 10 minutes more.

8. Add the cucumber and dill and let the stew stand, off the heat and covered, for 10 minutes to warm the cucumber without cooking it through. Adjust the seasoning and serve hot in deep bowls.

MONDAY-TO-FRIDAY GUMBO

MAKES 4 TO 6 SERVINGS
TIME: 20 MINUTES WORK
20 TO 45 MINUTES NO-WORK
COOKING TIME (see step 3)

This fiery number ought to wake up your taste buds on even the dullest of days. Make the gumbo in a double batch because it is so easy to do and so delicious to eat. As with all stews, it tastes even better the next day.

3 scallions (green onions)
1 small onion
1 rib celery
½ bell pepper, preferably red
2 cans (about 16 ounces each) small
    red kidney or pink beans
2 tablespoons vegetable oil
1 teaspoon garlic powder
¼ teaspoon cayenne pepper, or
    more to taste
1 teaspoon dried thyme
1 can (13¾ ounces) chicken broth
1 package (10 ounces) frozen
    chopped spinach, thawed
1 pound boneless, skinless chicken
    or turkey breasts
½ cup fresh parsley leaves
Salt

1. Trim and thinly slice the scallions. Finely chop the onion and the celery. Core, seed, and finely chop the pepper. Rinse and drain the beans.

2. Heat the oil in a large saucepan over high heat until almost smoking. Add the scallions, onion, bell pepper, and celery; reduce the heat to medium and stir the vegetables around with a wooden spoon until tender, about 3 minutes.

3. Add the garlic powder, cayenne, and thyme and stir-fry for a few seconds. Add the broth and mix it in with a whisk. Bring the liquid to a boil, then add the beans and spinach. Cover the pan and simmer over low heat at least 20 minutes to bring the flavors together. You can simmer this up to 1 hour; the longer the stew cooks, the more the flavors meld.

4. Meanwhile cut the poultry into ½-inch cubes and mince the parsley.

5. Right before serving, stir in the chicken and parsley; simmer until the poultry is cooked through, about 5 minutes more. Season to taste with salt and serve hot.

VARIATIONS

■ This becomes a spicy seafood stew by substituting 1 pound crabmeat, sea scallops, or cubed monkfish for the chicken.
■ Turn the gumbo into a spicy complementary protein dish by omitting the chicken and adding another can of beans. Serve over rice, millet, or quinoa, or pasta.
■ Add a cup or two of vegetables, such as chopped carrots or corn kernels, with the beans and spinach, and simmer along with the other ingredients.
■ Omit the frozen spinach in step 3 and add ½ pound rinsed and chopped fresh greens, such as Swiss chard, beet greens, or kale, before adding the poultry. Simmer along with the chicken.

SIMMERING STEWS

Nothing tastes quite like a stew that has been left to simmer just the right amount of time, then left to rest just the right amount of time. The texture of the ingredients are perfect and their flavors have all melded together in a wonderful potion. But, never fear. Monday-to-Friday stew recipes take into account a cook's lack of endless simmering time. If you have extra time, great, simmer your stew a little longer. If you don't, don't worry. All the flavors and textures will still be perfect.

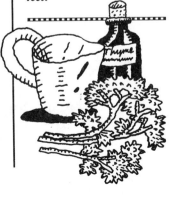

HOW DO YOU KNOW WHEN THE OIL IS HOT?

When you're heating up oil to sauté, test it first to see if it is hot enough. To do that, either splash a drop of water into the oil or toss in a piece of onion or vegetable. When the oil is hot enough, the water or vegetable will make a loud sizzling sound.

WINTER SEAFOOD STEW

MAKES 4 SERVINGS
TIME: 45 MINUTES

This is a quick and light dinner, suffused with the sturdy flavor of fresh sage and potatoes. See the variation that follows on how to turn this into a summertime stew.

1 small onion
1 red bell pepper
2 tablespoons olive oil
1/2 pound fresh mushrooms
1 bottle (8 ounces) clam juice
     or 2 cups water or chicken
     broth
1/2 cup dry white wine
2 cans (14 1/2 ounces each) Italian-
     style stewed tomatoes
1 teaspoon grated lemon zest or 1/2
     teaspoon dried lemon peel
3 or 4 fresh sage leaves or 1/2
     teaspoon dried
1 pound new potatoes
1 pound monkfish or sea scallops or
     combination of the two
Salt and freshly ground black
     pepper

1. Finely chop the onion. Core, seed, and chop the pepper.

2. Heat the oil in a large saucepan or deep, large skillet over medium heat. Add the onion and bell pepper and stir-fry for a moment until you hear them sizzle. Reduce the heat to low, cover the pan, and simmer until tender, about 10 minutes.

3. Meanwhile rinse, stem, and thinly slice the mushroom caps (save the stems for soup).

4. Add the mushrooms, clam juice, white wine, tomatoes, lemon zest, and sage to the pan. Using a wooden spoon, gently break the tomatoes into pieces right in the skillet. Simmer covered for a few minutes while you prepare the potatoes.

5. Scrub the potatoes and cut into 3/4-inch cubes. Add them to the skillet and simmer covered until tender, about 30 minutes.

6. Meanwhile cut the monkfish into 1-inch pieces or remove the tough, rubbery appendage from each scallop and slice them in half if they're big.

7. When the potatoes are tender, stir in the seafood; simmer covered until just cooked through, about 3 minutes more. Season to taste with salt and lots of pepper.

VARIATION

Summer Seafood Stew: Substitute 1/4 cup minced fresh basil for the sage. Substitute 2 cups of diced fresh vegetables, such as zuc-chini, yellow squash, or asparagus for the potatoes and simmer 3 to 5 minutes in step 5. In step 7 add ¼ pound snow peas along with the seafood.

ASIAN LENTILS WITH POTATOES AND CHICKEN

MAKES 4 TO 6 SERVINGS
TIME: 20 MINUTES WORK
1 HOUR NO-WORK COOKING TIME

The Asian touches of rice vinegar, soy sauce, chili paste, and water chestnuts transform a plebeian combination of lentils and potatoes into an intriguing mix. When you're bored with chicken, use turkey or leftover pork or ham instead.

This dish is filling; at most I would serve it with a green salad on the side.

1 small onion
4 medium-size boiling potatoes
1 to 2 tablespoons Oriental sesame or vegetable oil
6 cups chicken broth or water
1 cup brown lentils
1 bunch scallions (green onions)
1 cup fresh coriander or parsley leaves
1 pound boneless, skinless chicken breasts or turkey fillets
1 can (4 ounces) sliced water chestnuts
1 tablespoon rice vinegar
1 tablespoon soy sauce
1½ teaspoons chili paste, or to taste
Salt

1. Mince the onion. Peel the potatoes and cut them into ¾-inch cubes.

2. Heat the oil in a large saucepan over medium heat. Add the onion and sauté until it begins to get tender, 2 to 3 minutes.

3. Add the broth, lentils, and potatoes. Bring the liquid to a boil, then reduce the heat to low and simmer covered until the lentils are tender, about 45 minutes.

4. Meanwhile trim and thinly slice the scallions and mince the coriander. Cut the chicken into ½-inch cubes or strips. Drain the water chestnuts.

5. When the lentils are tender, stir in

CLEVER CONDIMENTS

By using prepared condiments like olive or chili paste, pesto, hoisin sauce, and chutney, you can enhance and embellish the taste of ordinary ingredients. And by changing the condiments in a recipe, you can get a number of different-flavored dishes out of one formula.

I don't recommend using large doses of these intriguing ingredients nor do I use them "solo" as a finished sauce; rather I think of them as accents that accessorize and transform the taste of common foods. Also remember not to use too many together. For example, you can accent a dish with ½ teaspoon curry powder and 1 tablespoon Indian chutney or Indian relish. However, don't use both chutney and relish, or, say, olive paste with hoisin sauce.

the chicken, water chestnuts, vinegar, and soy sauce. Cover the pot and simmer until the chicken is cooked through, 5 to 10 minutes more. Stir in the scallions, coriander, and chili paste. Season to taste with salt and serve hot.

MEATY CHILI WITHOUT THE MEAT

MAKES 4 SERVINGS
TIME: 20 MINUTES WORK
20 TO 40 MINUTES NO-WORK
COOKING TIME

The deep meaty flavor of this chili comes not from beef but loads of fresh mushrooms; the more shiitakes you can afford, the meatier this will taste.

Although the recipe was developed for 4, it can be expanded in almost infinite ways, which makes it a fine candidate for doubling up and freezing half for a rainy day. To double or triple the recipe, figure on a generous ¼ pound mushrooms and ½ can beans per person.

Although this is delicious served over a bowl of rice, it is better yet over polenta. Include as many of the condiments as you have on hand or have time to prepare.

> 1 to 2 pounds fresh mushrooms, combination domestic and shiitake
> 2 hot chilies, green or red, fresh or pickled
> 2 tablespoons olive oil
> 2 tablespoons ground cumin
> 3 tablespoons ground chili powder
> 2 cans (16 ounces each) beans, black, red kidney, or pink
> ½ cup spaghetti sauce, homemade (see Index) or prepared
> Salt
> 1 cup long-grain white rice
> Condiments (optional): Chopped fresh coriander leaves, lime wedges, chopped fresh tomatoes, plain yogurt or sour cream, and shredded Cheddar cheese

1. Stem, rinse, and coarsely chop the mushrooms (reserve the stems for soup). Seed and mince the chilies.

2. Heat the oil in a medium-size saucepan over medium heat. Add the mushrooms, reduce the heat to low, and simmer covered, stirring occasionally, until the mushrooms are tender, about 10 minutes.

SECOND TIME AROUND

MEATY CHILI: The leftovers can be served the second time as a topping for an open-faced sandwich on a hamburger bun or for a pita pizza. Obviously leftovers are also good candidates as taco or tortilla fillings.

3. Stir in the chilies, spices, beans, and spaghetti sauce. Cover and simmer for 20 minutes to 40 minutes, depending on how much time you have. The longer this simmers, the more blended the taste will be. Season to taste with salt.

4. Meanwhile prepare the rice. Bring 2 cups water to a boil in a medium-size saucepan. Add the rice, lower the heat, and cook the rice covered until tender, about 18 minutes.

5. Serve the chili hot over rice with the condiments.

FENNEL-FLAVORED CARROTS AND CORN OVER RICE

MAKES 4 TO 6 SERVINGS
TIME: 45 MINUTES

Sometimes we eat only this for dinner, other times along with a side dish of Porcini-Flavored Lentils or with Glazed Veal Chops (see Index for page numbers).

1 onion
¼ bulb fresh fennel
1 bell pepper, green or red
2 tablespoons vegetable oil
4 carrots
1 package (10 ounces) frozen corn kernels, thawed
¼ cup water
Salt
½ teaspoon cayenne pepper
½ teaspoon ground cumin
½ teaspoon garlic powder
½ teaspoon dried thyme
1 cup long-grain white rice
1 cup chicken broth or water
1 cup spaghetti sauce, homemade (see Index) or prepared
Freshly ground black pepper

1. Finely chop the onion and fennel. Core, seed, and finely chop the bell pepper.

2. Heat the oil in a medium-size saucepan over medium heat. Add the onion, fennel, and pepper and sauté for a minute. Cover the pan and cook over low heat until the vegetables are tender, about 5 minutes, or however long it takes to prepare the carrots.

3. Peel and thinly slice the carrots. Add them to the pan along with the corn, water, 1 teaspoon salt, and seasonings. Cover and simmer until the carrots are tender, about 10 minutes.

4. Stir the rice, broth, and spaghetti

HANDLING CHILIES

When working with hot chilies, handle them with care because the oils in the chilies can burn your skin. Be sure to wash your hands well after chopping them and be especially careful not to touch your eyes.

Some people wear rubber gloves when working with chilies, but I find this too cumbersome and awkward.

sauce into the vegetables. Season to taste with salt and pepper. Bring the liquid to a boil, then reduce the heat and simmer covered until the rice is tender, 15 to 20 minutes. Adjust the seasoning and serve hot.

VARIATIONS

■ Add ¾ to 1 pound cubed monkfish or smoked lean ham or turkey when you add the rice.
■ To turn this into a more substantial vegetarian main course, add 1 can (16 ounces) black beans or chick-peas, rinsed and drained, with the rice. Stir ½ cup grated Parmesan or Cheddar cheese into the finished dish just before serving.

SECOND TIME AROUND

WINTER VEGETABLE CURRY: Make a double batch of this curry and freeze half for another day. You can get a different second meal out of it by cooking some fresh poultry or by reheating diced leftover meat right in the vegetables.

Puréed, the leftovers make a super side dish for any meat or poultry main course.

WINTER VEGETABLE CURRY

MAKES 4 SERVINGS
TIME: 30 TO 35 MINUTES

A delicious way to round out a meal is to serve this vegetable curry alongside baked pork chops or with a thick cheese sandwich made with whole-grain bread.

1 onion
1 clove garlic
2 tomatoes
4 carrots
2 white turnips
1 small head cauliflower
1 tablespoon vegetable oil
1½ teaspoons ground cumin
½ teaspoon curry powder
¼ teaspoon ground coriander
¼ teaspoon ground cardamom
Salt and freshly ground black
    pepper

1. Finely dice the onion and mince the garlic. Dice the tomatoes, skin, seeds, and all. Peel and slice the carrots ¾ inch thick. Peel and cut the turnips into ¾-inch chunks. Break the head of cauliflower into small florets.

2. Heat the oil in a medium-size saucepan over medium heat. Add the onion and stir-fry for a minute to get it cooking. Reduce the heat to low and simmer covered until somewhat softened, about 3 minutes.

3. Stir in the spices and tomatoes thoroughly, then add the remaining ingredients. Simmer the curry covered over low heat until all the vegetables are tender, 30 to 35 minutes. Check the curry after 10 minutes of cooking; if the mixture seems dry and the vegetables don't seem to be getting tender, add about ¼ cup water. When the vegetables are done, season to taste with salt and pepper and serve hot.

ROOT VEGETABLE RAGOUT

MAKES 4 SERVINGS
TIME: 20 MINUTES WORK
45 MINUTES NO-WORK COOKING TIME

The saffron infuses this humble combination of potatoes and other root vegetables with sophisticated taste and color, while the raisins inject a sweet counterpoint. Paprika is an acceptable (cheaper) substitute for the saffron.

2 onions
6 carrots
4 small white turnips
4 medium-size boiling potatoes
2 tablespoons vegetable oil
⅛ teaspoon saffron or ¼ teaspoon paprika
½ cup dry white wine
½ cup chicken broth or water
¾ cup raisins or currants
Salt and freshly ground black pepper

1. Thinly slice the onions. Peel and slice the carrots ¼ inch thick. Peel the turnips and potatoes and cut them into ¾-inch cubes.

2. Heat the oil in a medium-size saucepan over high heat until shimmering. Add the onions and sauté until they sizzle and begin to wilt, about 2 minutes. Reduce the heat to low and cook covered until the onions are soft and begin to turn golden, about 5 minutes.

3. Stir in the vegetables, saffron, white wine, broth, and raisins. Simmer covered over low heat until the potatoes are tender, 30 to 35 minutes. Season to taste with salt and pepper and serve hot.

VARIATION

To turn this into a main-course skillet supper: Cut 1 pound smoked ham, boneless, skinless chicken breasts, or leftover roasted meat into 1-inch cubes while the vegetables are cooking. When the potatoes are tender, stir in the meat and continue to simmer until the meat is cooked or heated through, about 10 minutes. Season to taste with salt and pepper and serve hot.

SECOND TIME AROUND

ROOT VEGETABLE RAGOUT: *If there are enough leftovers, wrap them in phyllo dough as explained in Savory Strudels (see Index) and bake until heated through.*

CRACKED WHEAT A LA JAMBALAYA

**MAKES 4 TO 6 SERVINGS
TIME: 20 MINUTES WORK
30 MINUTES NO-WORK COOKING
TIME**

An authentic Southern jambalaya is made with long-grain white rice, but I prefer the nutty flavor of cracked wheat because it plays better against the zing of the cayenne and the pungent aroma of the thyme.

*1 large or 2 small onions
2 ribs celery
2 small bell peppers, preferably red
2 tablespoons vegetable oil
½ teaspoon dried thyme
½ teaspoon garlic powder
½ teaspoon cayenne pepper
1 bay leaf
1 can (14½ ounces) stewed tomatoes
1 cup cracked wheat or long-grain white rice
¼ cup dry white wine
Salt and freshly ground black pepper
1 pound skinless, boneless chicken or turkey breasts
2 scallions (green onions; optional)*

1. Preheat the oven to 350°F.

2. Finely chop the onions and celery. Core, seed, and finely chop the peppers. You can do this chopping in a food processor.

3. Heat the oil in a medium-size heatproof saucepan or casserole over medium heat. Add the onions, peppers, and celery and sauté for about a minute just to get the ingredients going. Cover the pan and simmer over low heat, stirring occasionally, until the vegetables are tender, 8 to 10 minutes.

4. Add the thyme, garlic powder, cayenne, bay leaf, tomatoes, cracked wheat, and wine. Bring the liquid to a simmer and season to taste with salt and pepper. Bake covered 20 minutes.

5. Meanwhile cut the chicken into ½-inch cubes and trim and thinly slice the scallions if using.

6. Stir the chicken into the casserole and bake covered until the poultry is just cooked through, about 10 minutes.

7. Discard the bay leaf and sprinkle the dish with the scallions, if using. Serve right away or let it stand covered up to 45 minutes; it will keep warm for that long.

VARIATIONS

■ You can turn this into a vegetarian main course by substituting 1 can (19 ounces) red or pink beans, rinsed and drained, for the poultry; don't use black beans because they'll muddy up the gorgeous color of this dish.

■ Make a seafood jambalaya by substituting 1 pound sea scallops or peeled and deveined medium-size shrimp for the poultry.

KASHA AND MUSHROOM CASSEROLE

MAKES 4 SERVINGS
TIME: 35 MINUTES WORK
25 MINUTES NO-WORK COOKING TIME

Thanks to my grandmother, I've always loved kasha, both the grain and the Russian dish in which it appears most often. My grandmother prepared it the Jewish way in *kasha varnishkes*—buckwheat stirred into a bowl of bow-tie noodles.

I've updated her dish and serve it as a pilaf. Robust in taste and hearty in nutrition, this one-pot meal will fill the emptiest of tummies, lickety-split.

1 large onion
1 large bell pepper, any color
2 cloves garlic
½ pound fresh mushrooms
2 tablespoons olive oil
1 cup kasha (roasted buckwheat kernels, medium grain)
1 egg or 2 egg whites
1 teaspoon caraway seeds
2 cups boiling chicken broth or water
¾ pound smoked or baked ham, preferably 95% or more fat free
Fresh dill for garnish (optional)
Salt and freshly ground black pepper
Sour cream or plain yogurt (optional)

1. Chop the onion. Core, seed, and chop the bell peppers. Mince the garlic. Rinse, stem, and thinly slice the mushroom caps (reserve stems for soup).

2. Heat the olive oil in a medium-size heavy saucepan over medium heat. Add the onion and bell pepper; stir-fry for a minute just to get them going. Cover the pan and simmer over medium heat until the onion and pepper are tender, 8 to 10 minutes.

3. Meanwhile, in a large saucepan, mix the buckwheat with the egg (or egg whites if you are on a no-cholesterol diet) with clean hands until each grain is coated.

CLEAN-UP TIP

Don't be embarrassed by pans left to soak overnight. Believe me, at our house any crusted-up casserole, broiler, or roasting pan gets soaked at least overnight in hot soapy water. Sometimes I don't even get to it until 24 hours later. The wonderful thing about this method is that after soaking even the grimiest pan is a snap to clean.

If the grains clump together, break them up with your fingers.

4. When the onion and pepper are soft, add the garlic and mushrooms and sauté for 30 seconds. Cover and simmer for 5 minutes over medium heat, then add the caraway seeds and broth. Bring to a boil over medium heat.

5. Place the pan with the kasha over medium-high heat. With a wooden spoon, flatten, stir, and chop the egg-coated kasha until the egg has dried and the kernels are hot and mostly separate, 3 to 4 minutes.

6. Averting your face to avoid any splattering liquid, gently ladle the boiling liquid, mushrooms, and other solids into the kasha. Bring the liquid back to a simmer, cover the pan tightly, and simmer until tender, about 10 minutes.

7. Meanwhile cut the ham into ½-inch cubes and mince the dill for garnish, if using. Remove the kasha from the heat, stir in the ham, and let the dish stand covered for 10 minutes to heat the ham through without toughening it.

8. Season the dish well with salt and pepper. Top with sour cream and sprinkle with dill.

VARIATION

For a spicer version: Substitute ¾ pound chorizo for the ham. Thinly slice the chorizo and sauté in a small skillet until somewhat crisp, 3 to 4 minutes. After the kasha is cooked, fold in the chorizo when you would have the ham. This is wonderful with sour cream.

SAFFRONED SCALLOP AND ARTICHOKE CASSEROLE

MAKES 4 TO 6 SERVINGS
TIME: 30 MINUTES WORK
30 TO 35 MINUTES NO-WORK
COOKING TIME

Although I know that cooking this casserole on top of the stove is faster, I prefer to bake it in the oven because it cooks more evenly and I like the extra time this gives me to open my mail or do a couple of chores before dinner.

If you get caught up in what you're doing, that's okay, too, because the casserole can stand covered for 30 minutes after you've taken it out of the oven. It won't be piping hot, but it will be warm enough to serve.

Precede this with a dish of warm

asparagus, tossed with a Basic or Herbed Vinaigrette or Spaghetti Squash Strands. Or you could follow it with Exotic Fruit Salad (see Index for page numbers).

1 onion
1 clove garlic
½ cup bottled sweet or roasted
   peppers, drained
2 tablespoons olive oil
1 package (10 ounces) frozen
   artichoke hearts, thawed
⅓ cup dry white wine
⅛ teaspoon saffron threads
1 cup long-grain white rice
1½ cups water, fish broth, or clam
   juice
Salt and freshly ground black
   pepper
1½ pounds firm-fleshed seafood,
   such as monkfish, sea scallops,
   or peeled and deveined shrimp
½ cup fresh parsley leaves or 4
   scallions (green onions)

1. Preheat the oven to 350°F.
2. Finely chop the onion. Mince the garlic. Chop the peppers.
3. Heat the olive oil in a medium-size ovenproof saucepan or casserole over medium heat. Add the onion and sauté, stirring occasionally, until somewhat tender, 3 to 4 minutes. Add the peppers, garlic, arti-

chokes, wine, saffron, rice, and water. Season to taste with salt and pepper and bring the liquid to a boil. Cover the pan and bake 20 minutes.
4. Meanwhile cut the fish into 1-inch pieces. (If you're using scallops, remove the tough, rubbery appendage from the side of each scallop and halve them if they're large.) Mince the parsley or trim and thinly slice the scallions.
5. Remove the pan from the oven and gently stir in the seafood. Bake covered until the seafood is cooked through, 10 to 15 minutes.
6. Remove the pan from the oven and let it stand for 10 minutes. Don't fret if the rice hasn't absorbed all of the liquid. The dish is still yummy even if it is a little soupy. Stir in the parsley or scallions and serve.

BLUEFISH AND BUCKWHEAT NOODLE CASSEROLE

MAKES 4 SERVINGS
TIME: 25 to 30 MINUTES

Chunks of bluefish, bits of carrot, and strands of buckwheat noodles come

SECOND TIME AROUND

SAFFRONED SCALLOPS: Leftovers are best tossed with a vinaigrette and served as a salad; reheating turns the rice to mush and dries out the fish.

SECOND TIME AROUND

BLUEFISH AND BUCK-WHEAT: Add more liquid—clam juice or water—to make the mixture soupy and reheat slowly so the noodles don't burn. If you don't have quite enough for a second meal, add more fish or a fresh vegetable.

together in a broth of clam juice seasoned with rice vinegar.

I like to serve dessert after this; Sautéed Apples with Currants and Cognac or Berry Shortcake makes a fine finish (see Index for page numbers).

4 carrots
2 tablespoons rice vinegar
1 teaspoon sugar
1 bottle (8 ounces) clam juice
¼ pound buckwheat noodles (soba)
Salt and freshly ground black pepper
1½ pounds bluefish, mackerel, or
    tuna fillets
4 scallions (green onions)
2 tablespoons prepared sesame and
    seaweed seasoning (optional)

1. Peel the carrots and grate in a food processor or by hand.

2. Combine the carrots, rice vinegar, sugar, and clam juice in a large saucepan. Bring the liquid to a boil over medium-high heat. Break the noodles in half and add them to the pan. Season to taste with salt and pepper. Cover and simmer until the noodles are almost cooked through, about 5 minutes.

3. Meanwhile cut the fish into 2-inch pieces.

4. Add the fish to the pan, cover, and simmer until the fish and noodles are cooked through, about 5 minutes more.

5. Meanwhile trim and thinly slice the scallions.

6. When the fish is cooked, stir in the scallions and sprinkle the top with sesame seeds if you wish. Serve hot.

VARIATION

If you can't find buckwheat noodles, substitute a thin noodle like vermicelli or capellini. The dish won't taste as distinctive, but it will still be good.

MASTER RECIPE FOR A STIR-FRIED SKILLET SUPPER

**MAKES 4 SERVINGS
TIME: 30 MINUTES**

When you're in a hurry, one of your best bets for getting dinner together fast is a stir-fry. By cutting the ingredients into tiny pieces, you cut down enormously on the time it takes to make them soft and tender. You can make your life even easier by choosing quick-cooking ingredients like snow peas, mushrooms, chicken, and shellfish.

For seasoning, rely on prepared condiments like barbecue sauce or chili paste which will enliven the dish without requiring more work from you.

By the way, stir-fries are also a terrific way to reheat and combine leftovers, turning them into a second meal.

If you don't include a starch in the skillet, make a bowl of rice or pasta to serve this with or, better yet, just serve it over some hearty whole-grain bread.

See also Anatomy of a Stir-Fry, page 188.

1 clove garlic
1 pound fresh mushrooms
1 pound boneless, skinless chicken
   breasts
2 bunches watercress
1 to 2 tablespoons Oriental sesame
   oil
2 tablespoons rice vinegar
1 tablespoon each barbecue sauce
   and chili paste, or 2 tablespoons
   barbecue sauce
Salt and freshly ground black
   pepper

1. Mince the garlic. Rinse, trim, and thinly slice the mushrooms. Cut the chicken into 1-inch chunks. Cut off the watercress stems and rinse the leaves.

2. Heat the oil in a wok or large skillet, preferably nonstick, over medium-high heat until very hot. Add the garlic and mushrooms and stir-fry for 30 seconds. Add the rice vinegar and cook over medium heat, stirring occasionally, until the mushrooms wilt, about 5 minutes.

3. Add the chicken and stir-fry for 2 minutes. Add the barbecue sauce and chili paste, cover the wok, and cook until the chicken is cooked through, 3 to 4 minutes more.

4. Uncover the skillet, add the watercress, and stir-fry until the watercress is wilted, about 1 minute. Season to taste with salt and pepper and serve hot.

VARIATIONS

■ In step 2, right after you stir-fry the mushrooms, add 1 to 2 cups of leftover diced cold potatoes or cooked grains. This addition will stretch the stir-fry into a heartier meal.
■ Substitute ½ bunch scallions (green onions), thinly sliced, or a minced shallot for the garlic.

OPEN-FACED ANYTHING

I love bread. There's nothing like knowing I have a fresh multi-grain, Italian, or French loaf waiting to accompany dinner. Bread in my house is not simply an aside; often it is an integral part of the meal. When I'm not in the mood or have no time to cook up a side of rice or pasta to serve with a dish, I spoon my stew or skillet dinner over a thick slice of warmed bread. Delicious!

■ Instead of mushrooms, use 1 pound carrots, grated; or a 10-ounce package frozen vegetables like green beans, thawed; or about 3 cups leftover parboiled vegetables like cauliflower or asparagus.

■ Substitute scallops or peeled and deveined shrimp or crabmeat for the chicken, or use a combination of all three. Leftover diced roast pork, beef, or lamb also makes a good substitute.

■ Add prepared Indian chutney, minced hot pickle, minced sun-dried tomatoes, or prepared pesto or black olive paste instead of the barbecue sauce and chili paste in step 3.

PROTEAN RATATOUILLE

MAKES 8 SERVINGS
TIME: 30 MINUTES WORK
40 MINUTES NO-WORK COOKING
TIME

This variable and eccentric ratatouille saves on time but isn't short on taste. It is endlessly useful and can take on myriad characters: Mix in chunks of chicken or fish and eat it as a main course or serve it as a side dish for sautéed lamb chops or as a sauce to toss over pasta or rice. You can eat it chilled as a salad or scalding hot as a soup, or use it as a bed on which to braise veal shoulder chops or poach a fillet of salmon.

*4 bell peppers, preferably red
    or yellow
2 medium-size onions
2 cloves garlic
¼ cup olive oil
2 pounds eggplant, about 3
    medium-size
2 cans (14½ ounces each) stewed
    tomatoes
1½ teaspoons dried thyme
2 zucchini
2 yellow squash
Salt and freshly ground black
    pepper*

1. Core, seed, and finely chop the peppers. Finely chop the onions and mince the garlic.

2. Heat the oil over high heat until almost smoking. Add the onions and peppers and stir-fry for a minute to get them cooking. Reduce the heat to low, cover, and simmer gently until somewhat tender, about 10 minutes.

3. Meanwhile cut the eggplant into ¾-inch chunks, leaving the peel on. When the peppers and onions are tender, add the garlic, eggplant, tomatoes and thyme. Break up the tomatoes with a wooden spoon; cover the pot and simmer 30 minutes.

4. Meanwhile cut the zucchini and yellow squash lengthwise into halves or quarters, depending on how thick they are. Then cut the strips into ¾-inch lengths. Add the zucchini and squash to the stew, cover, and simmer until all of the vegetables are tender, about 10 minutes more. Season to taste with salt and pepper.

VARIATIONS

■ Add 4 sliced carrots with the eggplant and finish the dish with ½ cup (tightly packed) fresh parsley or basil leaves that you have minced.

■ **For a one-pot dinner:** Stir 1 pound cubed boneless, skinless chicken breasts, ham, or shellfish into the ratatouille once it is done. Cook just long enough to cook the meat or seafood, about 15 minutes.

■ **Ratatouille Seafood Chowder:** Thin ½ recipe ratatouille with 1 cup tomato juice and stir in 1 pound seafood such as scallops, monkfish cut into small pieces, or peeled shrimp. Simmer gently until the seafood is cooked and ladle the soup over dried cubes of crusty whole-wheat bread for a bread-cum-fish main-course soup.

MULTI-COLORED BULGUR

MAKES 4 SERVINGS
TIME: 35 TO 40 MINUTES

This tasty, healthy meal, colorful with red peppers and spinach, is quite high in protein thanks to the complex carbohydrate combination of bean curd and wheat.

Nonvegetarians can substitute 1 pound diced smoked ham or 2 cups diced leftover roasted meat for the bean curd.

1 cup bulgur wheat or tabouleh grain
2 cups very hot tap water
2 red bell peppers
½ pound fresh spinach
4 firm bean curd cakes, 3 inches square and about 1 inch thick each
2 cloves garlic
2 tablespoons olive oil
2 tablespoons vinegar, white wine or cider
Salt and freshly ground black pepper

SECOND TIME AROUND

MULTI-COLORED BULGUR: It's a good idea to make this dish in double batches because the leftovers make for a terrific main-course salad. All you need to do to spruce up the bulgur is add any one of the following dressings (see the Index for page numbers): Citrus Dressing, the dressing with the Fresh Tuna and Red Pepper Salad, and the dressing with the Yellow and Orange Salad.

PAPRIKA

I use paprika a lot more than for its jolly bright color. Added in large enough amounts, it brings a deep peppery character to soups and stews and works especially well with meat and poultry. If you're a real aficionado, you can purchase paprika imported from Hungary in two forms, sweet and hot. Paprika tastes best when added to liquid off the heat. When stirred in directly over heat, it will turn bitter.

1. Place the wheat in a bowl and pour the hot water over it. Let stand 20 minutes to absorb the water, then thoroughly drain off any excess water.

2. Meanwhile core, seed, and chop the bell peppers. Stem and rinse the spinach. Cut the bean curd into ½-inch cubes. Mince the garlic.

3. Heat the olive oil in a large nonstick skillet over medium heat. Add the garlic and sauté for 30 seconds. Add the peppers, cover the skillet, and simmer until tender, about 5 minutes.

4. Add the drained wheat and the vinegar to the skillet and cook, stirring occasionally, for 5 minutes. Stir in the bean curd and spinach; simmer covered over low heat until the spinach is wilted, 5 minutes. Season well with salt and pepper and serve hot.

PAPRIKA, PORK, AND POTATO STEW

MAKES 4 TO 6 SERVINGS
TIME: 20 MINUTES WORK
30 MINUTES NO-WORK COOKING
TIME

Pork, paprika, and potatoes are familiar partners in many a Hungarian stew. I Americanized the mix by adding turnips, which harmonize merrily with all the other ingredients. You'll need 50 minutes only for dinner to be ready, from the time you begin preparing the ingredients to the time you remove the lid of the pot.

*4 medium-size boiling potatoes
    (about 1 pound)
4 medium-size white turnips (about
    1 pound)
1 to 1½ pounds boneless pork
    shoulder or picnic shoulder
1 onion
2 bell peppers, preferably red
2 tablespoons paprika
1 teaspoon caraway seeds
½ cup to 2 cups beef broth or water
    (depending on type of pressure
    cooker you own)
Salt and freshly ground black pepper
1 bunch fresh dill or mint (optional)
Plain yogurt or sour cream (optional)*

1. Peel the potatoes and turnips and cut them into 1-inch cubes. Trim the fat from the pork and cut the meat into 1½-inch cubes. Thinly slice the onion. Core, seed, and thinly slice the peppers.

2. Combine all the ingredients except for the salt, pepper, dill, and yogurt in your pressure cooker. Bring the liquid to a boil over medium-high heat. Cover the pressure cooker, lock the lid, and slowly bring to full pressure. Cook at full pressure for 10 minutes.

3. Meanwhile stem and mince the dill, if using.

4. Turn off the heat and let the pressure return to normal, naturally (this should take about 15 minutes). Release the pressure and unlock the cooker, averting your face as you do so to avoid a steam burn. Season the sauce to taste with salt and pepper.

5. Serve the dish as a thick soup, sprinkled with the dill and topped with yogurt, if you wish. Or, for a thicker, stew-like consistency, remove the solids with a slotted spoon before seasoning and boil the liquid down over high heat until it has reached the consistency you like. Return the solids to the liquid, season, and stir in the dill. Ladle the stew into bowls and top each bowlful with a dollop of yogurt.

CABBAGE, POTATO, AND CHICKEN STEW

MAKES 4 SERVINGS
TIME: 30 MINUTES

When I hanker for the taste of slowly simmered food but have little time to get dinner on the table, I turn to my pressure cooker. As my friend Lorna Sass says in her book *Cooking Under Pressure*, pressure cookers produce quick-cooking meals with "slow-cooking taste."

This meal of cabbage, potatoes, and chicken flavored with tomatoes, garlic, and fresh dill is reminiscent of a Russian soup known as "shchi."

1 medium-size onion
1 tablespoon olive or vegetable
    oil
4 medium-size carrots or parsnips
½ small head green cabbage
4 medium-size new red potatoes
1 can (14½ ounces) stewed
    tomatoes
2 cups water
6 cloves garlic
Salt
1 teaspoon sugar
4 to 8 chicken thighs
¼ cup fresh dill or parsley leaves
    (optional)
2 tablespoons lemon juice
Freshly ground black pepper

1. Finely chop the onion.
2. Heat the oil in your pressure cooker over medium-high heat until very hot. Add

PRESSURE OVER MICROWAVES

I prefer my pressure cooker over my microwave oven because, believe it or not, when making dishes that serve more than two people, the pressure cooker requires a lot less work. You just assemble the ingredients, adjust the pressure, and the cooking takes care of itself.

STEWS IN THE PRESSURE COOKER

*P**ressure-cooker stews yield marvelously-flavored juices just waiting to be sopped up by accommodating grain side dishes. Once you've got the pressure cooker stew simmering, whip up Silky Cornmeal, Kasha with Onions, or Millet with Parmesan (see Index for page numbers), all especially complementary to this shoulder of veal.*

the onion and stir it around until it is coated with the oil. Reduce the heat to low and sauté gently, stirring every now and then, until softened, 5 to 10 minutes.

3. Meanwhile peel and slice the carrots or parsnips ½ inch thick. Finely shred the cabbage. Scrub and quarter the potatoes. Add these vegetables to the pot along with the stewed tomatoes and water. Bring the liquid to a simmer over high heat. Peel the garlic but leave it whole. Add the garlic, 1 teaspoon salt and sugar (omit the sugar if you're using parsnips).

4. Remove as much of the skin and fat from the chicken as possible and add the pieces to the pot. Cover the pressure cooker, lock the lid, and bring to full pressure over medium-high heat. Cook at full pressure for 12 minutes.

5. Meanwhile mince or, easier yet, finely snip the dill, if using, with scissors.

6. Cool the pressure cooker under cold running water until the pressure is normal. Release the pressure and unlock the cooker, averting your face as you do so to prevent a steam burn. Add the lemon juice and dill to the pot, stir, and season to taste with salt and pepper.

VARIATION

Substitute an additional ½ pound carrots or parsnips for the cabbage.

SHOULDER OF VEAL WITH WILD MUSHROOMS

MAKES 4 TO 6 SERVINGS
TIME: 15 MINUTES WORK
1 HOUR NO-WORK COOKING TIME

A while back Rosh Hashanah (Jewish New Year) fell on a night during the work week. I couldn't find any time that week to make the homey pot roast I was counting on. So the night of the holiday dinner, thanks to my pressure cooker, I came up with this delicious veal shoulder roast instead. Along with take-out gefilte fish and matzoh ball soup and a dessert I had in the freezer, the cozy holiday meal I had anticipated came off in an hour.

2 onions
8 carrots
½ pound fresh wild mushrooms, such as
*   shiitake or chanterelles, or domestic*
2 cloves garlic
1 tablespoon olive or vegetable oil
1 veal shoulder roast, rolled, boned
*   and tied, about 2½ pounds*
1 cup spaghetti sauce, homemade
*   (see Index) or prepared*
1 cup water
Salt
Freshly ground black pepper

1. Finely chop the onions. Peel and cut each carrot into 3 pieces. Rinse and stem the mushrooms. Thinly slice the caps (reserve the stems for soup). Peel the garlic cloves but leave them whole.

2. Heat the oil in your pressure cooker over high heat until very hot. Add the veal roast and brown on all sides, about 5 minutes. With tongs, remove the veal to a plate.

3. Add the onions to the pressure cooker and sauté over medium heat until they just begin to wilt, about 2 minutes.

4. Add the carrots, mushrooms, garlic, spaghetti sauce, water, and 1 teaspoon salt and stir to combine. Return the browned veal to the pot and bring the liquid to a boil over high heat.

5. Cover the pressure cooker, lock the lid, and slowly bring to full pressure. Cook at full pressure for 45 minutes.

6. Turn off the heat and let the pressure return to normal, at room temperature (this takes about 15 minutes). Release the pressure and unlock the cooker, averting your face as you do so to prevent a steam burn. Season the sauce to taste with salt and pepper. Slice the meat.

VARIATION

If you have the time, you can remove the roast and other solids and boil the liquid over high heat until reduced to a thick pan sauce.

BEEF, GARLIC, AND SWEET POTATO STEW

MAKES 4 TO 6 SERVINGS
TIME: 25 TO 30 MINUTES

The sweetness of the potatoes and headiness of the garlic enhances the richness of the beef. A salad of greens or

SECOND TIME AROUND

SHOULDER OF VEAL: If you have veal left over, slice it and reheat it in leftover sauce in a microwave, on top of the stove, or in the oven.

■ *If you don't have lots of meat left, dice whatever you do have and mix it with the remains of the sauce and 1 can (16 ounces) chick-peas, rinsed and drained, to create a sauce substantial enough to turn a bowl of pasta or grains into a meal.*

broccoli or green beans would be a lovely start or finish to this meal. Or, serve this with an exotic grain dish, like quinoa or millet, to soak up the lovely stew juices.

> *4 medium-size sweet potatoes, about*
> *   1½ pounds*
> *1 to 1½ pounds beef chuck or stew*
> *   meat*
> *10 cloves garlic*
> *½ to 2 cups beef broth or water*
> *   (depending on type of pressure*
> *   cooker you own)*
> *Salt and freshly ground black*
> *   pepper*

1. Peel the sweet potatoes and cut them into 1-inch cubes. Cut the beef into 1-inch cubes. Peel the garlic cloves but leave them whole.

2. Combine all the ingredients except the salt and pepper in your pressure cooker. Bring the liquid to a boil over medium-high heat. Cover the pressure cooker, lock the lid,

and slowly bring to full pressure. Cook at full pressure for 10 minutes.

3. Turn off the heat and let the pressure return to normal, naturally (this should take about 15 minutes). Release the pressure and unlock the cooker, averting your face as you do so to prevent a steam burn.

4. Season the stew to taste with salt and pepper. If the stew is too soupy, remove the solids and boil the liquid down to the consistency you like, then season to taste with salt and pepper. Serve hot.

VARIATIONS

■ While the stew is cooking, chop ¼ cup each dried apricots and pitted prunes. Simmer them in the finished stew until they're tender and hot, 3 to 4 minutes.

■ Substitute lamb shoulder, trimmed of fat and cut into 1-inch cubes, for the beef. Add ¼ teaspoon each ground cumin, cinnamon, and coriander to the pot with the other ingredients in step 2.

GRAIN & BEAN DISHES

There can't be a living soul in the United States who hasn't heard about the healthful properties of grains and legumes and about how they should feature more prominently in everyone's diet. But for many these delightful foods are still considered drab and boring. At one time, I would have agreed, but my agreement would have come from ignorance.

Now, though, thanks to my place of work, a corporate dining room where the chairman of the board is a vegetarian who must eat food that is low in fat and cholesterol-free, I've discovered how wrong I was. In fact, healthy complementary proteins are truly delicious, and each variety of grain or legume has a distinctive individual taste.

The beans I use Monday to Friday are instantaneously available because I use only the canned variety. It also will surprise some to discover that most grains take just 15 minutes to cook, and that lentils and split peas are transformed from their dry state to a cooked one in only 30 minutes, because they need no presoaking.

For the Monday-to-Friday cook, what's exciting about working with these ingredients is that not only are they gems of nutrition—high in fiber, minerals, and vitamins—but they are also inexpensive and a superb foil for myriad other textures and flavors.

Now that I've discovered the scores of grains on the market, I no longer think of rice as the only possibility and so I wind up with variety in my everyday meals. (See Pantry chapter for information on how and where to buy grains and legumes.)

SECOND TIME AROUND

MIDDLE EASTERN CASSE-ROLE: This is well worth making in double batches because it freezes well and is a terrific side dish; it also works chilled in salads and can be added to vege-table soups as a protein boost.

■ *When making this dish in double batches, it's wise to cook it instead in a pre-heated 350°F oven for 45 minutes (step 4) so that you don't risk burning the bottom of the pot.*

■ *Leftovers or frozen por-tions can be reheated in a 350°F oven until hot, about 20 minutes.*

MIDDLE EASTERN BARLEY, LENTIL, AND RICE CASSEROLE

MAKES 4 TO 6 SERVINGS
TIME: 15 MINUTES WORK
45 MINUTES NO-WORK COOKING TIME

This is a mouth-watering spicy mix of grains and lentils, so flattering to any number of other tastes that it's well worth the effort to make this in double batches to freeze in small portions for a rainy day.

I round out this casserole with a side of Stir-Fried Cabbage and Greens or Cauliflower with Red Pepper Ribbons; meat eaters can pair this with beef, lamb, or pork.

The fresh mint brings color to the otherwise monochromatic dish, but, as far as flavor is concerned, dried mint works as well as fresh.

2 onions
3 cloves garlic
2 tablespoons vegetable or olive oil
2 teaspoons sugar
1 tablespoon vinegar, white wine or cider
1 teaspoon ground cumin
1/4 teaspoon ground cardamom
1/2 cup fresh mint leaves or 1 teaspoon dried
1/2 cup pearl barley
1/2 cup lentils
1/2 cup brown rice, long or short grain
3 cups water
Salt and freshly ground black pepper
1/2 cup currants or raisins

1. Chop the onions and mince the garlic.

2. Heat the oil in a medium-size sauce-pan over medium heat. Add the onion and sugar and sauté for about 1 minute. Reduce the heat to low and simmer covered until the onions are tender, about 5 minutes.

3. Add the vinegar, garlic, cumin, car-damom, and dried mint if you don't have fresh; sauté just to release their aroma, about 30 seconds.

4. Add the barley, lentils, rice, and water. Season to taste with salt and pepper. Bring the liquid to a boil over medium heat, then cover and simmer over low heat until almost completely tender, about 30 minutes.

5. Meanwhile mince the fresh mint, if using.

6. Stir the currants into the grains and simmer until all the grains and lentils are tender, about 10 minutes more. Adjust the seasoning and let the casserole sit off the heat for 10 minutes. Fold in the fresh mint if using and serve hot.

SILKY CORNMEAL

MAKES 4 SERVINGS
TIME: 25 MINUTES

Although most of the time I serve cornmeal purée as a main course, I sometimes use it as a side dish with roasted meat. I always make this amount and count on having leftovers, which taste great the next day. I like my purée very loose. If you like it rather firm use only 3 to 3½ cups liquid.

¼ cup corn or vegetable oil
1 cup yellow cornmeal
4 cups chicken broth or water
2 tablespoons butter (optional)
Grated Parmesan cheese (optional)
Salt and freshly ground black pepper

1. Heat the oil in a medium-size saucepan over medium heat. Add the cornmeal and sauté, whisking continuously, for 1 minute.

2. Add the broth and bring to a boil, whisking all the while. When the cornmeal comes to a boil, it will bubble up vigorously, not unlike a volcano erupting. Quickly put a lid on the saucepan, turn the heat down to really low and cook the cornmeal covered until it is soft like a purée, 20 minutes. If you wish stir in the butter and the Parmesan or both and season to taste with salt and pepper.

CORNMEAL PUREE WITH VEAL AND PEPPER SAUCE

MAKES 4 SERVINGS
TIME: 25 TO 30 MINUTES

I turn a dish of cornmeal purée into a quick meal by topping it with a hearty sauce of ground veal and peppers. Alternative toppings that go equally well are pasta sauces (see Index).

SECOND TIME AROUND

SILKY CORNMEAL: If you intend to make the cornmeal mush so that you can sauté the leftovers, you've got to make a thicker mixture. To do so, use 1½ cups of cornmeal, instead of the 1 cup.

To reheat the leftovers quickly, cut the cornmeal into strips or squares and set them in a single layer on a baking sheet. Pour some tomato sauce over the top, sprinkle with Parmesan, and bake in a 350°F oven until heated through, 10 to 15 minutes.

Italian cookbooks instruct you to make polenta by slowly adding cornmeal to boiling water and then stirring it continuously for some 30 minutes so that it doesn't lump. But in my experience, cooking the cornmeal this way invariably produces lumps of uncooked cornmeal. Upon reflecting on this culinary dilemma, a better solution occurred to me: Cook the cornmeal a bit first, before adding a liquid, just as I would a flour roux in a sauce.

So now when I make polenta or cornmeal mush, I sauté the grains first in olive oil, then add lots of liquid and bring it to a simmer, whisking all the while. After that it just requires an occasional stir to produce a lump-free smooth cornmeal dish.

¼ cup corn, olive, or vegetable oil
1 cup yellow cornmeal
4 cups chicken broth or water
2 bell peppers, red or green
2 tablespoons olive oil
1 pound ground veal or turkey
2 cups spaghetti sauce, homemade
    (see Index) or prepared
3 scallions (green onions)
2 tablespoons butter (optional)
Salt and freshly ground black pepper
Grated Parmesan cheese (optional)

1. Heat ¼ cup oil in a large saucepan over medium heat. Add the cornmeal and sauté, stirring constantly, for about a minute so that all the grains are coated with oil.

2. Add the broth and bring the liquid to a boil over medium heat, whisking all the while. When the cornmeal comes to a simmer, it will bubble vigorously, not unlike a volcano erupting. Quickly put a lid on the saucepan, turn the heat down to very low, and cook the cornmeal until it no longer tastes raw, about 20 minutes, while you make the sauce.

3. Meanwhile core, seed, and finely chop the bell peppers. Heat 2 tablespoons olive oil in a large skillet over medium heat. Add the peppers, cover the skillet and cook until tender, about 10 minutes.

4. Uncover the skillet, crumble in the ground veal, and cook, stirring frequently, until the veal is no longer pink, 4 to 5 minutes. Add the spaghetti sauce and cook uncovered over very low heat until the flavors blend, about 5 minutes.

5. Meanwhile trim and thinly slice the scallions.

6. When the cornmeal is ready, stir in the butter if using and season to taste with salt and pepper.

7. Ladle the cornmeal into deep bowls and spoon the veal and pepper sauce over the top. Sprinkle with the scallions and pass the Parmesan on the side, if you wish.

QUICK AND EASY COUSCOUS

MAKES 4 SIDE-DISH OR 2 MAIN-DISH SERVINGS
TIME: 20 TO 25 MINUTES

Couscous is as essential to my weekly menu as a basic black dress is to my wardrobe. Its flavor harmonizes with myriad tastes, it's nubby texture marries with a variety of others, and its neutral flavor makes it a hit with kids.

At times I make it the centerpiece of my meal and douse it with a meat sauce or pour a bean chili over it to round out the meal. On other days it slides into the background to accompany a lamb roast or poached salmon. Leftover couscous will bolster a variety of salads.

1 cup couscous
1¼ cups hot water from the tap
1 to 2 tablespoons olive oil or butter
Salt and freshly ground black pepper

OPTIONAL ADDITIONS (CHOOSE 1 OR MORE):
1 teaspoon dried herb, such as tarragon, oregano, or thyme
2 to 4 tablespoons minced fresh herb, such as dill, parsley, or basil
½ cup sliced scallions (green onions)
¼ cup chopped sun-dried tomatoes, packed in oil
¼ cup chopped pimientos
⅓ cup chopped green chilies
1 to 2 cups diced cooked poultry, meat, or seafood
1 package (10 ounces) frozen vegetables, such as peas or corn, thawed
1 to 2 cups leftover steamed vegetables, such as asparagus or cauliflower
1 to 2 cups chopped fresh vegetables such as bell peppers
¼ cup salad dressing

1. Place the couscous in a small bowl and cover with the hot water; let stand until the grains have swelled and are soft, about 20 minutes.

2. Break up any clumps of couscous with your fingers or a fork. The grain is now ready to be heated or used as is in a cold preparation.

3. **To heat the couscous plain:** Heat 1 to 2 tablespoons oil in a medium-size skillet over medium heat. Add the plumped couscous and sauté until the couscous is hot, about 2 minutes. Stir occasionally to make sure the couscous is not clumping together. Season to taste with salt and pepper.

To heat the couscous with dried or fresh herbs: Heat 1 to 2 tablespoons oil in a medium-size skillet and add the dried herb with the plumped couscous. Sauté as directed for plain couscous.

When using fresh herbs instead of dried, sauté the couscous plain until hot, then season to taste with salt and pepper and add the fresh herb. Stir together for a few seconds just to gently wilt the herb, then remove the couscous from the heat.

To heat the couscous with other ingredients (except the salad dressing): Heat 2 tablespoons oil in a medium-size skillet. Add whatever ingredients you wish to season the couscous with and sauté to heat through, about 1 minute. Add the plumped couscous and sauté until all ingredients are heated

COUSCOUS: A MONDAY-TO-FRIDAY BASIC DISH

Couscous is durum wheat (semolina) formed into beadlike shapes. Prepared the authentic Moroccan way, couscous is plumped up with water, steamed over a seasoned broth, raked to keep it fluffy, steamed over the broth once more, and raked a second time. After such gentle and lengthy care, the grains swell into puffy aromatic nubbins.

On occasion for company, and on a weekend, I've prepared couscous the authentic way and the results are truly marvelous. Unfortunately during the week, I don't have the time to go through all this which is how I came up with my speedy way of rehydrating couscous, much as I do bulgur wheat.

through, about 2 minutes more. Season to taste with salt and pepper.

To use the couscous in a salad: Prepare any of the salad dressings (see Index). Once the couscous has been rehydrated, it doesn't need further cooking and is ready to be combined with other ingredients in a salad. Once combined, toss with the dressing.

MILLET WITH PARMESAN

MAKES 4 SERVINGS
TIME: 30 TO 35 MINUTES

Millet is a wonderfully flavored grain that I have always found perplexing to cook. Dutifully I've followed recipes on the back of the package or in a cookbook, yet invariably the millet turns out chalky or mushy. These sad failures led me to devise a pasta-like way of cooking millet. I simply boil it in lots of water and drain it after the grain is tender.

In experimenting with millet, I found out that the grain never turns out fluffy and separate like rice; instead the texture ends up somewhere between mashed potatoes and polenta. And so,

SECOND TIME AROUND

MILLET: Cook a double batch of millet and reserve half, without the olive oil or Parmesan, for another day. To reheat it, sauté a bit of minced garlic or onion and bell pepper in oil until tender. Then add the leftover millet and sauté, stirring constantly, until the grain is hot. Season to taste with salt and pepper.

with polenta in mind, I serve it with a knob of butter or a spoonful of olive oil worked in at the end, along with a few tablespoons of Parmesan cheese.

1 cup hulled millet
2 tablespoons olive oil or butter
¼ cup grated Parmesan cheese
Salt and freshly ground black pepper

1. Bring at least 4 cups of water to a boil in a medium-size saucepan over high heat. Add the millet, reduce the heat to medium, and simmer covered until the grains are tender, 25 to 30 minutes. Drain immediately in a sieve or colander.

2. Return the drained millet to the saucepan and, off the heat, stir in the olive oil and Parmesan. Season to taste with salt and pepper (I like lots of fresh pepper with millet).

VARIATIONS

■ Stir in 2 tablespoons minced fresh basil along with the Parmesan.

■ Or, substitute 1 tablespoon olive oil, ¼ cup grated sharp Cheddar cheese, ¼ cup chopped green chili, and 2 tablespoons minced scallions for the olive oil and Parmesan. Top with sour cream.

KASHA AND ONIONS

MAKES 4 SERVINGS
TIME: 20 MINUTES

The addition of a bit of sugar to the recipe tempers the slightly bitter edge of the kasha without destroying the character. Heating the kasha with the egg helps separate the grains and makes the finished dish fluffy. Cholesterol watchers can use egg whites only; the kasha will be a little mushier and less fluffy but just as good.

This is a wonderful side dish to serve with meat or poultry or to stir into a bowl of boiled elbow macaroni.

2 medium-size onions
1 cup kasha (roasted buckwheat
* kernels), medium grain*
1 large egg or 2 egg whites
1 tablespoon vegetable oil or butter
¼ cup water
1 tablespoon sugar
1¾ cups hot water from the tap
Salt and freshly ground black pepper

1. Thinly slice the onions. Mix the kasha with the egg (or egg whites if you are on a no-cholesterol diet) with your clean hands until the grains are thoroughly coated with the egg.

2. Heat the oil in a large skillet over medium heat. Add the onions and sauté until they just begin to soften, about 2 minutes. Add the water and continue to sauté, stirring frequently, until the onions are tender and golden brown, 7 to 8 minutes.

3. Stir in the sugar and egg-coated kasha. Sauté, over low heat, until the kasha smells toasty and begins to stick to the pan, 2 to 4 minutes. Add the hot tap water (as hot as possible) to the skillet and bring the liquid to a boil. Stir and season to taste with salt and pepper. Simmer covered over low heat until the kasha is tender, about 10 minutes. Adjust the seasoning and serve hot.

NUBBLY QUINOA

MAKES 4 SERVINGS
TIME: 25 MINUTES

I love quinoa for its extraordinary nutty flavor and the texture of the round translucent grains which snap in your mouth. I also love its versatility: it's so light and fluffy you can eat it as a hot breakfast cereal as easily as you can a savory side dish. And as the mother of

QUINOA (KEEN-wah)

Quinoa is an ancient grain that comes from the Andes Mountains of South America. A staple food of the Inca civilization, it was rediscovered and popularized in the 1980s in the U.S. It is often touted as the grain of the future because it contains more protein than other grains and is unique in that it is also a complete protein, containing all essential amino acids.

SECOND TIME AROUND

NUBBLY QUINOA: The no-frills version is worth making in double batches. It reheats well in the oven, regular or microwave. It's terrific the next morning, served as a hot cereal with maple syrup and milk and it's fabulous the next night as a main course to be served with a pasta sauce or cold as the building block for a main-course tuna and red pepper salad.

Flavored leftover quinoa can be reheated as is in the oven and served as a side dish or stirred into some beans.

a picky eater who lives on carbohydrates like pasta and grains, I love its high nutritional profile.

Although the instructions on the package direct you to boil the quinoa in plain water, I prefer its flavor when simmered in broth along with some vegetables for seasoning.

Be sure to thoroughly rinse the grain under cold running water to rid it of any bitter saponin residue.

1 cup quinoa
1 onion
2 carrots
1 tablespoon vegetable or olive oil
2 cups chicken broth or water
1/2 teaspoon salt
Freshly ground black pepper

1. Place the quinoa in a sieve and rinse under cold running water for about 1 minute. Finely chop the onion and carrots.

2. Heat the oil in a medium-size saucepan over medium heat. Add the onion and carrots and sauté, stirring frequently, until the onion is translucent, 4 to 5 minutes. If the vegetables begin to stick to the bottom of the pan, add a tablespoon of water and continue to cook.

3. Add the quinoa and sauté for another minute. Add the broth, the salt, and

pepper to taste. Cover and simmer over low heat for 10 minutes. Remove the pot from the heat and let it stand covered 5 minutes longer. Adjust the seasoning and fluff up the grain with a fork before serving.

VARIATION

No-Frills, Fail-Safe Quinoa: After rinsing the grain, cook it in boiling salted water until tender, 12 to 15 minutes. Drain for at least 5 minutes before using further to ensure it won't be waterlogged. To reheat, simply sauté it in oil or butter, or dress it with 1/4 cup salad dressing of your choice (see Index) and serve it in a salad. Fluff it up with a fork before serving.

BROWN RICE, CURRANT, AND WALNUT CASSEROLE

MAKES 4 TO 6 SERVINGS
TIME: 25 MINUTES WORK
35 to 50 MINUTES NO-WORK COOKING TIME

Serve this superb blend of hot, sweet, and tangy tastes on cold nights or evenings when you need to get some work done before you can sit down to eat. The casserole slowly cooks by itself. Timing is not of the essence here: 5 minutes more or less in the oven won't make or break the dish.

It's also helpful to know that this dish will keep piping hot for at least 30 minutes if you leave it covered once you have removed it from the oven.

2 to 4 cloves garlic
½ cup dried apricots
1 tablespoon olive oil
1 cup long-grain brown or white
    rice or cracked wheat
¼ teaspoon cayenne pepper
¼ teaspoon ground coriander
¼ cup dried currants or raisins
2½ cups chicken broth or water
Salt and freshly ground black
    pepper
1 pound smoked or baked ham,
    95% or more fat free, leftover
    roast lamb, or smoked turkey
½ cup walnuts or pecans
Fresh mint or parsley for garnish
    (optional)
Sour cream or plain yogurt
    (optional)

1. Preheat the oven to 375°F.

2. Mince the garlic. Halve or quarter the dried apricots, depending on how large they are or how big you would like the pieces to be.

3. Heat the olive oil in a medium-size heatproof casserole over medium heat. Add the garlic and sauté for a few seconds until you can smell its aroma. Stir in the rice and spices, then the apricots and currants. Add the broth and bring the liquid to a boil. Season to taste with salt and pepper. Cover and bake for 35 minutes (or 20 minutes if you're using white rice or cracked wheat).

4. Meanwhile cut the ham into ½-inch cubes and coarsely chop the nuts. Mince the mint if using.

5. Remove the pan from the oven and stir in the ham. Cover and bake until the rice is tender, 15 minutes or more. Just before serving, stir in the nuts and mint. Adjust the seasoning and serve hot with sour cream or yogurt on the side, if you desire.

VARIATIONS

Vegetarians can substitute 2 cans chick-peas, drained, or 4 firm bean curd cakes, chopped, for the ham.

ESPECIALLY GOOD FOR CHILDREN

BROWN RICE CASSEROLE: *Older children usually like this dish because of the combination of savory and sweet, but when I make this for our family, I omit the cayenne and ground coriander and, to make up for this loss, stir dried red pepper flakes into the adults' portion at the end and douse the casserole with fresh mint or parsley.*

SECOND TIME AROUND

MIXED GRAINS: You can reheat this grain dish by stir-frying the leftovers with bits of vegetable, poultry, or meat.

The chilled leftovers make a fine foundation for a salad with steamed broccoli and cauliflower and bell peppers.

MIXED GRAINS ORIENTALE

MAKES 4 SERVINGS
TIME: 30 TO 35 MINUTES

The pairing of chewy short-grain rice with tender creamy millet is heavenly. This dish, flavored with sesame oil, garlic, and rice vinegar, has an Oriental tang that works well alongside Baked Fish with Vegetables (see Index), or steamed vegetables.

1 clove garlic
2 carrots
2 tablespoons Oriental sesame oil
1 teaspoon sugar
½ cup short-grain brown rice
2 tablespoons rice vinegar
2 cups water
½ cup millet
2 tablespoons prepared sesame and
*   seaweed (see Pantry Chapter; optional)*
Salt and freshly ground black pepper

1. Mince the garlic. Peel and slice the carrots ¼ inch thick.

2. Heat the sesame oil in a medium-size saucepan over medium heat. Add the garlic and carrots and sauté for a couple of minutes, stirring constantly. Add the sugar and rice and sauté for a few seconds.

3. Add the rice vinegar and water. Bring the liquid to a boil, then reduce the heat to low, cover, and simmer very gently for 10 minutes. Stir in the millet and simmer covered until both grains are tender, 25 to 30 minutes. Stir in the sesame seed condiment and taste (this condiment is salty), then season to taste with salt and pepper.

PERFECT RICE

MAKES 4 TO 6 SERVINGS
TIME: 20 TO 25 MINUTES

There is one single basic way I make a plain bowl of rice, whether the grain is long or short, brown or white, or aromatic. I set the rice in a pot, add the liquid, salt, oil or butter, and I simmer gently until tender. Any liquid not absorbed by the rice is drained away.

1 cup long-grain white rice
1¾ cups chicken broth, clam juice,
*   or water (depending on what*
*   you're serving the rice with)*
2 teaspoons oil or unsalted butter
Salt and freshly ground black pepper

1. Place the rice, broth, oil, and some salt and pepper in a medium-size saucepan. Bring the liquid to a boil over medium heat. Cover the pot and simmer over low heat until the rice is as tender as you like it, about 18 minutes.

2. If there is any leftover liquid in the pot, drain the rice in a strainer. Adjust the seasoning and serve hot.

VARIATIONS

You may, of course, use any of the suggestions below alone or in combination with one another.

■ **To flavor the rice:** In step 1 sauté 2 to 4 tablespoons chopped onion or ¼ cup chopped bell pepper and/or 1 teaspoon minced garlic in 1 tablespoon oil for a few minutes to soften it a bit. Stir in the rice, then add the liquid but not more oil. Season to taste with salt and pepper and cook as directed.

■ **To make the rice taste richer:** Stir 1 to 2 tablespoons grated Parmesan or Cheddar, butter, sour cream, or crème fraîche into the finished rice.

■ **To color the rice:** Simmer the rice in half tomato juice and half water or broth.

AROMATIC RICE WITH VEGETABLES

MAKES 4 TO 6 SERVINGS
TIME: 35 MINUTES

This recipe is a model for how to combine two parts of a meal, the starch and the vegetable, in a single pot and save on clean-up. I use Texmati rice here because I love its aroma, but you can substitute converted rice and get equally delicious results. This two-for-one idea works just as well with other grains.

Crackling Fish Fillets (see Index) or sautéed chicken breasts would be all you need to complete your dinner.

Selection of fresh vegetables, such as fennel, onions, carrots, and/or bell peppers (you will need 2 cups diced)
1 to 2 tablespoons olive oil or butter
1 cup Texmati white rice
1¾ cups chicken broth, tomato juice, or water
1 teaspoon dried herb, such as tarragon or oregano
Salt and freshly ground black pepper

TO COOK OTHER RICES

Here are the proportions of liquid to rice for other varieties. Note that for aromatic rices such as basmati, Texmati, and Wehani, both the proportion of liquid to rice and time it takes to cook each different type is usually variable. Therefore, I have included a foolproof method that includes them all.

1 cup long-grain brown rice to 2¼ cups liquid. Cook 20 to 25 minutes.

1 cup short-grain white rice to 1¾ cups liquid. Cook 20 minutes.

1 cup short-grain brown rice to 2 cups liquid. Cook 30 to 35 minutes.

1 cup aromatic rice to 4 cups liquid. White cooks in 15 to 20 minutes; brown cooks in 40 to 45 minutes. Drain immediately.

DOUBLING UP

•—————•

BASIC CRACKED WHEAT:
This is a terrific basic dish
because you can add any
number of other ingredients
to it after it's cooked. It is
fantastic with bits of poul-
try, meat, legumes, other
vegetables, and fish. For
this reason, you may want
to make a double batch and
save half for another day.
If you do, cook the dish in
a large saucepan, not a
skillet.

This type of dish is
terrific reheated in the
microwave, by the portion,
as you need it. However,
if you need to reheat the
entire dish, add a tad more
water to the skillet, cover,
and simmer gently over low
heat until heated through.
Stir the wheat every now
and then to make sure it
isn't sticking to the bottom
of the skillet.

1. Rinse and dice whatever fresh vegetables you decide to use.

2. Heat the oil in a medium-size saucepan over medium heat. Add the vegetables and sauté until they begin to soften, 2 to 3 minutes.

3. Add the rice, broth, and herb; season to taste with salt and pepper. Slowly bring the liquid to a simmer, then cover the pan and cook over low heat until the rice is tender, 15 to 17 minutes. Drain off whatever liquid isn't absorbed by the rice and serve hot.

VARIATIONS

■ Substitute converted white rice for the Texmati and increase the liquid to 2 cups.
■ To make this dish with frozen instead of fresh vegetables, omit steps 1 and 2. Place 1 package (10 ounces) frozen corn, artichokes, or lima beans, thawed, in the pot along with the rice and other ingredients and simmer as directed.
■ Stir in 1 tablespoon oil or butter just before serving.
■ Look also at the variations for Perfect Rice (preceding) to get more ideas on how to change this dish.

■ **For a more complicated two-for-one dish:** In step 1, finely chop 1 onion, 2 tablespoons sun-dried tomatoes, and 1 package (10 ounces) thawed frozen artichoke hearts instead of the fresh vegetables.

In step 2, sauté the onion in the oil until somewhat tender, about 3 minutes. Add 1 teaspoon curry powder and the sun-dried tomatoes; sauté for a minute longer to release the aroma.

In step 3, add the artichokes with the rice but omit the herb. Proceed with the recipe as directed.

BASIC CRACKED WHEAT

———

MAKES 4 SERVINGS
TIME: 35 MINUTES

This basic method of cooking cracked wheat works equally well with millet or rice. It makes for an aromatic side dish that would be good with any form of meat, poultry, or fish, but made in double batches, it can also work as the foundation for a vegetarian meal. It is easy to make and full of flavor.

The amazing thing about this dish is that innumerable heatings and reheatings don't seem to do damage to the taste or the texture.

For a no-frills way of cooking plain cracked wheat, see the boiling method for quinoa on page 231.

1 medium-size onion
2 medium-size carrots
2 tablespoons olive oil or butter
1 cup cracked wheat or millet
1½ cups chicken broth or water
Salt and freshly ground black
  pepper
2 tablespoons fresh parsley
  leaves (optional)
2 tablespoons plain yogurt
  (optional)

1. Finely chop the onion and carrots.
2. Heat the oil in a large skillet over medium heat. Add the onion and carrots and sauté, stirring constantly, until the onion is translucent, 4 to 5 minutes.
3. Add the cracked wheat and sauté for another minute just to heat it. Add the broth, and salt and pepper to taste. Cover and simmer over low heat until the wheat is tender, about 20 minutes.
4. Meanwhile mince the parsley if using.
5. When the wheat is tender, stir in the yogurt, if using, and parsley off the heat and adjust the seasoning.

CRACKED WHEAT WITH CARROTS

MAKES 4 SERVINGS
TIME: 35 TO 40 MINUTES

This is a richly flavored vegetarian dish, great served as a match for legumes, poultry, or meat or lovely served on its own, dabbed with some plain yogurt.

1 onion
2 carrots
2 tablespoons vegetable oil or butter
½ teaspoon ground cinnamon
½ teaspoon ground cumin
1 cup cracked wheat
¼ cup raisins or currants
2½ cups chicken broth or water
Salt and freshly ground black pepper

1. Mince the onion. Peel and thinly slice the carrots.
2. Heat the oil in a large skillet over medium heat. Add the onion and sauté, stirring frequently, until it is translucent, 4 to 5 minutes.
3. Add the carrots, spices, cracked wheat, raisins, and broth. Season to taste with salt and pepper.

SAVING SPACE IN THE FREEZER

An invaluable aid for maximizing the space of any size freezer is to make use of Ziploc freezer bags instead of awkwardly shaped plastic containers. You can freeze from 1 to 6 portions in a single bag and squeeze out any excess air from the package, thus saving space. The bags can be washed and reused, which also makes them ecologically sensible.

To freeze any food, first let it cool to room temperature. Ladle or spoon the contents into the freezer bags in portions most appropriate for you and your family. Press out all the air as you close the bag. Label the bag with the contents and the date, then freeze. You'll find the filled bags stack wonderfully well.

4. Bring the liquid to a boil, then reduce the heat to low and simmer covered until the wheat is tender, 15 to 20 minutes. Adjust the seasoning and serve hot.

VARIATIONS

■ Substitute 4 chopped tomatoes or 1 package (10 ounces) artichoke hearts, thawed and chopped, for the carrots.
■ To amplify the dish, stir 2 tins (3½ ounces each) smoked sardines, chopped, or 8 ounces smoked tuna or turkey into the cooked wheat and simmer until heated through, about 3 minutes more.

PORCINI-FLAVORED LENTILS

MAKES 4 SERVINGS
TIME: 5 TO 10 MINUTES WORK
25 MINUTES NO-WORK COOKING
TIME

By far this is my easiest and most favorite way to cook lentils. Deeply flavored with dried mushrooms and garlic, these earthy legumes will turn a bowlful of grains, a slice of bread, or a dish of pasta into a complete meal.

My shortcut does away with the conventional step of presoaking the mushrooms without compromising their intense flavor.

> ½ ounce dried mushrooms,
>   preferably porcini
> 2 cloves garlic
> 1 cup lentils
> 2 cups water
> 2 tablespoons olive oil (optional)
> Salt and freshly ground black
>   pepper

1. Rinse the dried mushrooms in cold water if they seem gritty. Peel the garlic, leaving the cloves whole.
2. Place the mushrooms, garlic, lentils, and water in a medium-size saucepan. Bring the liquid slowly to a boil over medium heat. Lower the heat, cover, and simmer until just tender about 25 minutes.
3. Fish out the garlic cloves, stir in the olive oil if using, and season to taste with salt and pepper. (Do not salt the lentils earlier or they will take longer to cook.) Serve hot.

SECOND TIME AROUND

PORCINI-FLAVORED LENTILS: Serve leftovers as a purée by blending them in a food processor with some water or chicken broth to loosen them up. Reheat by stirring constantly over low heat or heat in a microwave.
■ Eat the lentils cold, dressed with a vinaigrette and turned into a cold main-course salad by dicing in a red bell pepper along with 1½ cups cubed smoked turkey, cooked chicken, or ham.

VELVET PEA PUREE

MAKES 4 SERVINGS
TIME: 10 MINUTES WORK
40 MINUTES NO-WORK COOKING
TIME

A soft purée of split peas is a superb dish to serve alongside lamb or pork chops or as a rich protein sauce over brown rice or pasta.

Contrary to popular opinion, split peas don't take all day to cook and they don't need presoaking. They cook in just 40 minutes and require no tending to.

½ onion
2 carrots
1 cup (½ pound) split green peas
3 cups water
½ teaspoon dried rosemary
Salt and freshly ground black pepper
¼ cup low-fat or whole milk, or
*   heavy (or whipping) cream*

1. Mince the onion. Peel and mince the carrots.

2. Combine the onion, carrots, split peas, water, and rosemary in a medium-size saucepan. Bring the liquid slowly to a boil over medium heat. Cover and simmer over low heat until just tender, 35 to 40 minutes.

3. Stir and mash the peas with a wooden spoon against the side of the pan. Season to taste with salt and pepper. (Don't salt the split peas sooner or they'll take longer to cook.) Off the heat, stir in the milk or cream. Adjust the seasoning and serve hot.

VARIATIONS

A delicious finish is to stir into the cooked purée ½ cup minced fresh herbs; fresh mint and dill are especially terrific with split peas.

CHICK-PEAS WITH FENNEL AND ROASTED PEPPERS

MAKES 4 TO 6 SERVINGS
TIME: 30 MINUTES WORK
30 MINUTES NO-WORK COOKING
TIME

This is a refreshingly good mix of starch and vegetable that is great with grains, lamb, beef, or pork.

DOUBLING UP

CHICK-PEAS: This dish tastes terrific even after being frozen; so make it in double or triple batches and freeze in 1-, 2-, or 4-portion packages.

SECOND TIME AROUND

CHICK-PEAS: Leftovers of this chick-pea dish make a fine base for a soup. Just add enough stock, tomato juice, or water to make it soupy, bring to a boil, and serve.

2 onions
2 bulbs fennel or 4 or 5 ribs celery
1 jar (7 ounces) bottled sweet or
    roasted peppers
2 cans (16 ounces each) chick-peas
    or white kidney beans
1 tablespoon vegetable oil
1 tablespoon balsamic vinegar
½ teaspoon dried rosemary, thyme,
    or oregano
Salt and freshly ground black pepper

1. Thinly slice the onions. Discard the tops from the fennel, then core and thinly slice the bulb. Drain and thinly slice the roasted peppers. Rinse and drain the chick-peas.

2. Heat the oil in a large saucepan over medium heat. Add the onions and sauté, stirring occasionally, until tender and somewhat golden, about 5 minutes. Add the vinegar and continue to sauté until the onions are brown and wilted, about 5 minutes more.

3. Add the fennel, peppers, chick-peas and rosemary. Cover the pan and simmer until the flavors have melded, about 30 minutes. Season to taste with salt and pepper and serve hot.

VARIATIONS

To make this a one-pot meal: Add ½ pound rinsed and chopped greens, such as kale, or

1½ cups cubed leftover meat, or both, to the finished dish. Cook 10 minutes to wilt the greens or reheat the meat.

GINGERED KIDNEY BEANS WITH CAULIFLOWER

MAKES 4 TO 6 SERVINGS
TIME: 30 TO 35 MINUTES

All you need to do to get dinner ready after you've cooked this dish is to sauté a few chops or boil some millet or pasta.

1 piece (½ inch) fresh ginger
1 clove garlic
2 medium-size or large tomatoes
1 medium-size to large head
    cauliflower
1 tablespoon vegetable oil
2 tablespoons lime juice
½ teaspoon ground turmeric or
    curry powder
2 cans (16 ounces each) red kidney
    beans, white beans, or chick-peas
Salt and freshly ground black pepper

1. Peel and mince the ginger and garlic. Core the tomatoes and chop them fine or purée them in a food processor. Separate the cauliflower into florets.

2. Heat the oil over medium heat in a medium-size saucepan until very hot. Add the ginger and garlic and sauté for a few seconds, until you get a whiff of their aroma. Stir in the cauliflower, tomatoes, lime juice, and turmeric; reduce the heat to low and simmer covered until the cauliflower is softened, about 10 minutes.

3. Rinse and drain the beans and stir them into the cauliflower mixture. Simmer covered until the flavors come together, about 15 minutes. Season to taste with salt and pepper and serve hot.

TORTILLA AND RED BEAN SKILLET SUPPER FOR TWO

MAKES 2 SERVINGS
TIME: 30 MINUTES

In this original and wonderful supper, the red beans and tortillas combine to provide both protein and starch, and the peppers and tomatoes add color, taste, and more nutrition.

Hungry souls can supplement this main course with steamed broccoli or slices of avocado, and die-hard meat lovers could accompany this with a broiled lamb chop or grilled chicken.

Although I make this meal just for me and my husband, it can be doubled or even tripled.

1 onion
1 bell pepper, any color
1 tomato
4 corn tortillas
1 tablespoon olive oil
1 can (16 ounces) red kidney beans or pink beans
1 fat bunch fresh coriander or parsley
1 tablespoon lime or lemon juice
Salt and freshly ground black pepper

1. Thinly slice the onion. Core, seed, and thinly slice the pepper. Chop the tomato and cut the tortillas into 1-inch pieces or triangles.

2. Heat the olive oil in a large skillet over medium heat. Add the onion and bell peppers and sauté for a few seconds to release their aroma. Reduce the heat to low

AVOCADOS

Nothing adds the finishing touch to a meal of tortillas and beans like a perfectly ripe avocado. I prefer the Haas variety; it is pear-shaped with green-black, bumpy, alligator-type skin. When I have one ready and waiting on my windowsill, I plan my dinner accordingly. If possible, I like to sprinkle avocado slices with fresh lime juice and some fresh cilantro leaves as well.

and simmer covered until tender, about 5 minutes.

3. Uncover the skillet, add the tortillas, and sauté for a couple of minutes to give them a nuttier flavor. Add the beans with their juices, cover the skillet, and simmer 15 minutes.

4. Meanwhile, rinse, stem, and mince the coriander.

5. When the beans and vegetables are hot and the flavors have mellowed together, remove the skillet from the heat, stir in the fresh herb and lime juice, and season to taste with salt and pepper. Serve hot.

SWEET-AND-SOUR RED BEANS

MAKES 4 SERVINGS
TIME: 30 MINUTES

This is a study in contrasting tastes and textures. The sting of the vinegar and cayenne with the bite of the capers and garlic counterpoints the gentleness of the sweet plums and beans. Serve this full-flavored side dish with a chewy grain like short-grain rice or quinoa or with plain roasted meats or poultry.

1 can (16 ounces) purple plums
2 cloves garlic
2 cans (16 ounces each) red kidney
*   beans*
1 tablespoon vegetable oil
¼ teaspoon cayenne pepper
1 tablespoon capers
1 tablespoon balsamic or sherry
*   wine vinegar*
Salt

1. Drain the plums, remove the pits, and coarsely chop. Finely mince the garlic. Rinse and drain the beans.

2. Heat the oil in a medium-size saucepan over medium heat. Add the garlic and plums and sauté for a minute until you can smell their aroma.

3. Add the beans, cayenne, capers, and vinegar. Cover and simmer until the beans are very hot and the flavors have come together, about 20 minutes. Season to taste with salt and serve hot.

VARIATIONS

For other lovely fruit and bean combinations: Substitute ½ cup chopped dried apricots or pitted prunes, or ½ cup canned unsweetened pineapple chunks for the plums. If the dried fruit doesn't soften enough, add ¼ cup water and cook a few minutes more.

WHITE BEANS PROVENCAL

MAKES 4 SERVINGS
TIME: 10 MINUTES WORK
30 MINUTES NO-WORK COOKING
TIME

Olive oil, beans, garlic, and tomato is a surefire Mediterranean combination guaranteed to wake up the sleepiest of palates. Easy to make on any hectic night of the week, this pot of beans can simmer gently as you prepare the rest of your meal or simply put up your feet before dinner.

In winter I like serving this with sautéed veal chops and in summer with slices of grilled eggplant.

2 cloves garlic
2 cans (16 ounces) white cannellini
    beans or chick-peas
1 tablespoon olive oil
1/4 teaspoon fennel seeds
1/4 teaspoon dried thyme
1 can (14 1/2 ounces) Italian-style
    stewed tomatoes
Salt and freshly ground black
    pepper

1. Mince the garlic. Rinse and drain the beans.

2. Heat the oil in a medium-size saucepan over medium heat. Add the garlic, fennel seeds, and thyme and sauté for a few seconds until you can smell their aroma.

3. Add the beans and tomatoes. Season to taste with salt and pepper. Simmer uncovered until you're ready to serve, at least 15 or up to 30 minutes. If too much liquid is evaporating, remove the pan from the heat and reheat the beans covered just before serving.

CURRIED BEANS WITH SPINACH

MAKES 4 SERVINGS
TIME: 30 MINUTES

Here's a dish for times when you begin thinking about dinner ten minutes *after* you've come home from work; you don't even have to defrost the spinach—it thaws in the stew as it cooks.

I make a dinner of this by serving it with slices of thick whole-grain bread. Heartier eaters (whose week allowed

SECOND TIME AROUND

WHITE BEANS PROVENCAL: *This is wonderful to make in double or even triple batches; it freezes superbly well and has that sophisticated yet unfussy flavor that makes it a welcome companion to all sorts of other grain, meat, and poultry dishes.*

Leftovers can be reheated as is or turned into a soup by adding some chicken broth. If you do turn this into a soup, it is grand with fresh spinach leaves and diced fresh chicken tossed in at the end of cooking time.

AN ASIDE ON KETCHUP

The birth of our daughter changed and enriched our lives in many ways, plenty of them unexpected. The most humorous is the liberty I now allow myself in cooking. Her childhood eccentricities rid me of any culinary pretensions I might have had.

One of my discoveries has been the seasoning properties of ketchup. Our child, not an especially big eater nor an adventuresome one, could be enticed at age three to eat almost anything if it was coated in ketchup. After a while I began to cook with ketchup, without my daughter in mind. I found that adding a tablespoon here and there, as I once did tomato paste, brought a delicious tang to stews and sautés.

for a little planning) could accompany it with Herbed Lamb Chops, Crackling Fish Fillets, or Nubbly Quinoa (see Index for page numbers).

1 onion
1 clove garlic
1 to 2 tablespoons vegetable oil
2 packages (10 ounces each) frozen chopped spinach
1½ teaspoons ground cumin
½ teaspoon ground ginger
½ teaspoon ground cardamom
1 teaspoon ground turmeric or paprika (for color)
1 can (4 ounces) chopped green chilies
2 cans (16 ounces each) small white beans or chick-peas
1 tablespoon ketchup or 1 tablespoon tomato paste and 2 teaspoons cider or wine vinegar
Salt and freshly ground black pepper

1. Thinly slice the onion and mince the garlic.

2. Heat the oil in a large saucepan over medium heat until very hot. Add the onion and sauté, stirring occasionally, until somewhat softened, 3 to 5 minutes.

3. Add the garlic, spinach, spices, and chilies. Cover and simmer over very low heat

for 5 minutes to partially thaw the spinach. Break up the spinach as best you can with a wooden spoon, then simmer covered until the spinach is completely thawed, 5 to 10 minutes more. Be sure to check on the spinach every now and then to make sure it's not burning.

4. Rinse and drain the beans and stir them into the spinach. Simmer covered until heated through, about 5 minutes more. Stir in the ketchup (for a touch of sour and sweet) and season to taste with salt and pepper. Serve hot.

THREE BEAN STEW WITH VEGETABLES

MAKES 4 SERVINGS
TIME: 20 MINUTES WORK
45 MINUTES NO-WORK COOKING TIME

This dish is so easy to make it's hard to believe it could taste as good as it does. Turn it into dinner by serving it over a bowlful of pasta, rice, or cornmeal purée.

2 small onions
2 carrots
1/2 cup sun-dried tomatoes, packed
    in oil (optional)
2 pickled jalapeño peppers (optional)
2 tablespoons vegetable oil
1 package (10 ounces) frozen corn
    kernels
1 can (16 ounces) black beans
1 can (16 ounces) red kidney beans
1 can (16 ounces) chick-peas
1 can (4 ounces) chopped green chilies
1/4 cup balsamic or sherry wine vinegar
Salt and freshly ground black pepper

1. Finely chop the onions. Peel and slice the carrots 1/4 inch thick. Chop the sun-dried tomatoes, and, if you like your food hot and spicy, seed and mince the jalapeños.

2. Heat the oil in a medium-size saucepan over medium heat. Add the onions and carrots, reduce the heat to low, and simmer covered until somewhat tender, about 3 minutes.

3. Add the sun-dried tomatoes, jalapeños, corn (frozen or thawed), the beans with their juices, and chilies. Cover and simmer for as little as 20 minutes just to heat the ingredients or for as long as 45 minutes for a more mellow flavor. Check and stir the beans every now and then to make sure they are not scorching; add a few tablespoons of water if they are.

4. Add the vinegar and simmer 5 minutes longer. Season to taste with salt and pepper and serve hot.

BEAN CURD AND VEGETABLE STIR-FRY

MAKES 4 SERVINGS
TIME: 20 TO 25 MINUTES

You need only serve this dish alongside some baked fish or as a sauce on top of pasta or a soft grain like Silky Cornmeal to make it a dinner. Gorgeous red or yellow peppers glamorize the look besides adding to the range of flavors.

2 bell peppers, preferably red or yellow
1 pound fresh mushrooms,
    preferably 3/4 domestic and 1/4
    shiitake
1 tablespoon Oriental sesame oil
1/8 teaspoon dried orange peel
2 tablespoons orange or lemon juice
4 firm bean curd cakes, 3 inches
    square and about 1/2 inch thick
    each
8 leaves romaine lettuce
Salt and freshly ground black pepper

SECOND TIME AROUND

THREE BEAN STEW: Leftovers make an excellent tortilla or taco filling topped with sour cream.

1. Core, seed, and cut the peppers into long, thin strips. Rinse, stem, and coarsely chop the mushroom caps (reserve the stems for soup).

2. Heat the oil in a deep, large skillet over medium heat. Add the peppers and sauté until somewhat tender, about 2 minutes. Add the mushrooms and sauté for another minute to get them hot. Add the orange peel and juice. Reduce the heat to low and simmer covered until the vegetables are cooked through, about 10 minutes.

3. Meanwhile cut the bean curd cakes into ½-inch squares. Rinse and coarsely chop the romaine lettuce.

4. When the peppers and mushrooms are tender, stir in the bean curd and lettuce. Sauté, stirring constantly, until the bean curd is hot and the lettuce is wilted; about 2 minutes. Season to taste with salt and pepper and serve hot.

VARIATIONS

■ One can (19 ounces) beans or chick-peas, rinsed and drained, can be substituted for the bean curd.

■ Carnivores could substitute 1 pound diced fresh poultry or ham for the bean curd. Sauté until the meat is cooked or heated through, about 10 minutes.

VEGETABLE ASIDES

I've assembled these side dishes for the cook who can't get away with serving one-pot meals every night of the week. After all, people who can't stand to have different ingredients mushed together as they are in stews, as well as people who don't believe they've eaten a proper dinner unless they've had a piece of protein with a couple of separately cooked sides are entitled to their fair share of good recipes too.

Although I realize vegetables can be cooked in lots of different ways, for this book I selected one or two basic methods for each because they're delicious yet easy and/or fast. I've also included, for almost each vegetable, those spices, herbs, and condiments that best complement it.

STOCKING UP ON VEGETABLES

There are two vegetable categories I always have in the house, even if I haven't the foggiest notion what or when I'm going to cook that week. First there are vegetables whose flavor I rely on to season almost every dish I make. Second there are the vegetables I load up on because they keep for a long time without spoiling. What's convenient for me, small apartment dweller that I am, is that most of the vegetables in one category overlap into the other category, thus saving me storage space.

THE SEASONING VEGETABLES

Every week, I fill in on two or three of my seasoning vegetables like onions, garlic, carrots, bell peppers, and mushrooms. Most folks would also include celery, but I don't because I happen to dislike its taste. Your seasoning list could be quite different depending on your own family's idiosyncracies and tastes.

VEGETABLES THAT SAVE ON SHOPPING TIME

In addition to my seasoning vegetables, I stock up on ones that have a long shelf life. This way I can be assured that whatever vegetables I've bought at the beginning of the week are still usable by the end if I need them.

The winter tubers and roots like potatoes, onions, carrots, turnips, beets, cabbages, and winter squashes stand up the best over time.

TO SAVE ON SHOPPING TIME

Learn these pointers on how to buy and store vegetables, and I guarantee you'll get more flavor out of your cooked vegetables as well as cut down on spoilage and, thus, have to shop less frequently.

■ Fresh vegetables sold by the pound will taste far better than those that have been prepackaged.

■ Except for the long-lasting winter roots and tubers, vegetables don't keep well in the refrigerator for more than 3 days, so don't buy more than you'll need within that time frame.

■ If you're unsure of what your cooking schedule is going to be like during a given week, don't buy anything that you know will spoil. Just load up on your seasoning or long-lasting varieties and rely also on your cache of frozen vegetables.

SHOP FOR VEGETABLES IN SEASON

Any seasonal vegetable, locally grown or vine ripened, is ideal for the Monday-to-Friday cook. The fanciest of dishes painstakingly prepared don't measure up to a simple bowl of steamed spring asparagus dabbed with butter or slices of scarlet juicy tomatoes dusted with basil.

Vegetables that are in season will be at the peak of their flavor and won't need more than the simplest and easiest cooking methods to release their good taste.

As seasonality varies from one part of the country to the other, check your local newspaper food section to find out what's in season, cheap, and fresh that week.

HOW FRESH AND GOOD-TASTING VEGETABLES SHOULD LOOK AND FEEL

Fresh vegetables should look "alive." Their good taste depends on them being firm and plump, free of blemishes, spots, or scars, and bright and vividly colored.

■ Fruit vegetables like avocados, cucumbers, eggplants, summer squashes, peppers, and tomatoes should be without bruises and feel heavy for their size.

■ Leafy vegetables and fresh herbs should look bright and moist, never wilted. Avoid lettuces that have rust or brown spots on their edges and stay clear of fresh herbs that look dead.

■ Roots and tubers like potatoes, beets, turnips, carrots, and should be firm, heavy, and plump without scars. Avoid potatoes that are soft or have sprouting "eyes."

■ Cabbages, broccoli, and cauliflower should be compact, with moist-looking heads and tightly closed florets. The florets should be free of yellow buds in broccoli and free of brown or grayish patches in cauliflower. Brussels sprouts should be vivid and each one tightly packed without yellow outer leaves.

■ Members of the onion family like garlic, shallots, and all types of onions should feel heavy, tight, and firm, never damp or soft.

ON STORING VEGETABLES

In the end you'll save on shopping time, to say nothing of money, if you learn to store vegetables properly to preserve and prolong their life.

■ Keep uncut raw vegetables in open plastic bags in the crisper drawer of the fridge, if possible. This allows moisture to escape and prevents the vegetables from spoiling and becoming limp. Don't pack them too tightly in the plastic bags because they need room to breathe so that they don't rot.

■ If you're lucky and have a cool dark pantry or cellar, use it to store root vegetables or tubers and save on precious refrigerator space needed for more perishable items. Onions, potatoes, winter squashes, and root vegetables, each kind stored separately in bins, keep well in a cool dark place. However, they must be kept in a refrigerator if you live, as we do, in an overheated city apartment.

■ If the leafy tops are still attached to the root vegetable, cut them away because the sap continues to flow to the leaf at the expense of the root; store the green tops as you would leafy greens.

■ To get the most out of leafy greens, wrap them in a dampened towel and

place them in an open plastic bag in the crisper drawer in the refrigerator.

■ Fresh herbs will keep in the refrigerator for a week with the stems in 2 inches of water in a tall glass or jar and the tops covered loosely with a plastic bag.

VEGETABLES THAT SHOULD BE STORED AWAY FROM EACH OTHER

Vegetables continue to give off certain gases after they've been picked. Because of these gases, some vegetables and fruits, when stored together, react adversely to each other causing a change of flavor or even hastening spoilage.

■ Carrots turn bitter when stored alongside apples.

■ Potatoes rot more quickly when stored with onions.

■ Leafy greens tend to spoil more quickly when stored with fruit vegetables such as eggplants or tomatoes.

ARTICHOKES

MAKES 4 SERVINGS
TIME: 5 MINUTES WORK
12 TO 20 MINUTES NO-WORK
COOKING TIME

Skip this recipe if you don't own a microwave oven. Before I bought one, I'd indulge my love of fresh artichokes only on weekends when I had the time to prepare them for cooking, boil them, and then clean up the huge cooking pot.

Now that I've discovered how uncomplicated and unmessy it is to cook artichokes in a microwave, I can have them any day of the week. In 10 to 20 minutes (depending on how many artichokes I'm cooking at once), my artichokes are cooked beautifully tender, aromatic, and unsoggy. Serve them with any of the sauces suggested below.

1 medium (8 to 10 ounces) artichoke per person, or 2 medium if you're making a meal of them

1. With a sharp knife, cut the stem and the top 1 inch of leaves from each artichoke. Wrap each artichoke in microwave-proof plastic wrap and set them in a circle on a microwave-proof dish.

2. Cook at full power: 2 medium artichokes will take 10 to 12 minutes; 3 or 4 artichokes, 15 minutes; and 6 artichokes, 20 minutes.

3. Remove them from the oven and unwrap them carefully (the plastic is very hot). Serve them right away or set them upside down on a plate to cool.

SAUCY ACCOMPANIMENTS

If you're going to serve the artichokes hot, while they're cooking, whip up a saucy accompaniment to dip them in.

■ Stir-fry ¼ teaspoon minced garlic and ⅛ teaspoon crushed black pepper in ½ cup olive oil for a couple of minutes to release their aroma. Dip the leaves in this flavored olive oil.

■ Heat ⅓ cup olive oil and stir in 2 tablespoons black olive paste or pesto, or ¼ cup finely chopped sun-dried tomatoes.

■ Heat ½ cup olive oil until hot. Remove it from the heat and stir in ½ cup minced fresh herbs of your choice.

■ If you're going to serve the artichokes chilled or at room temperature, you can turn them into a meal by serving two per person and by accompanying them with ricotta cheese that you can use as a dip.

■ Another good sauce to serve with cold artichokes is made by mixing ¼ cup mayonnaise, ¼ cup ketchup, 1 teaspoon Dijon mustard, and 2 tablespoons red or white wine vinegar.

ASPARAGUS

MAKES 4 SERVINGS
TIME: 10 MINUTES

I remember the day Mimi Sheraton, then the food critic of *The New York Times*, visited me to review my cooking class for her annual evaluation of New York City's cooking schools. This was the first course I had ever taught and I was feeling, to put it mildly, quite sick to my stomach.

In that particular class I was teaching my students the proper way to cook asparagus. I made sure they snapped the stems, peeled the stalks, and tied the asparagus in neat bundles. They then set the asparagus upright in a tall pot so the stems would cook standing in a couple of inches of boiling water, while the delicate tips steamed gently above. Preparing the asparagus for cooking took about 30 minutes, and finding a pot tall enough to accommodate those standing asparagus was no small task. I got an excellent review for the class, and having proved to myself I was an acceptable cook, I promptly changed my asparagus cooking techniques so that I can enjoy them quickly and easily without lots of fussy preparation.

Now I snap off the tough stem ends, rinse the asparagus under warm water, and lay them flat in a large skillet to cook until done in an inch of boiling water. Season them simply with salt and pepper or in one of the ways described below.

2 pounds asparagus or 6 to 8 spears
per person
Salt and freshly ground black
pepper

1. Hold the stem end of each asparagus spear and bend it. Wherever it snaps off is fine; discard this stem bottom. Rinse the asparagus in warm water to remove any grit.

2. In a skillet large enough to accommodate the asparagus in a single layer, soak in water to a depth of about 1 inch. Bring it to a boil over medium heat. Add a pinch of

SEASONING POSSIBILITIES

*W*hile the asparagus is cooking, heat 2 to 4 tablespoons of butter or olive oil in a small saucepan over medium heat. Add 2 tablespoons lemon or orange juice or rice vinegar and/or 2 tablespoons minced scallions (green onions), chives, dill, or parsley. Remove the pan from the heat and pour the sauce over the cooked asparagus.

■ *Toss hot cooked asparagus with 2 tablespoons prepared pesto or black olive paste and 1 tablespoon lemon juice.*

■ *Lightly sprinkle asparagus with drops of rice vinegar and scatter prepared sesame and seaweed seasoning (see Pantry chapter) over top.*

SECOND TIME AROUND

AVOCADO SALAD: Avocados, once cut, don't age well under any circumstances, but when the avocado is mixed with citric acid, it turns an especially sad shade of brown green. However, the taste of the avocado is still delicious; so camouflage its less than perfect appearance in a sandwich or use it as a topping for tacos. Before storing any avocado leftovers, wrap well with airtight plastic wrap. Don't keep leftovers longer than a day or they will develop a "refrigerator" taste.

salt and add the asparagus in a single layer. After the water comes back to a simmer, boil uncovered until just tender, 4 to 5 minutes.

3. Remove asparagus with tongs and pat dry with towels before serving. Season to taste with salt and pepper.

AVOCADO SALAD

MAKES 4 TO 6 SERVINGS
TIME: 10 MINUTES

I know that avocados are fattening, but they taste so delicious. On days when I'm feeling thin, I indulge in an avocado in lieu of a salad.

What's so nice about the avocado is that you can halve and pit it, then chop up the flesh and dress it right in its own skin, avoiding the cleaning of a salad bowl. On days when I'm feeling less lazy, I remove the flesh from the skin, chop it up, and dress it with tomatoes, coriander, and lime juice. This can serve as a salad or as a guacamole dip for raw vegetables, Potato Chips (see Index), and tacos or tortillas, or you can serve it as a sandwich stuffer with slices of leftover meat or poultry.

Choose pear-shaped Hass avocados with black-green skin that offer little resistance when pressed gently.

2 medium-size avocados
2 ripe medium-size tomatoes
1 fat bunch coriander
1 to 2 tablespoons lime juice
Salt and freshly ground black
*   pepper to taste*

1. Halve each avocado. Remove the skin and pit, coarsely chop the flesh, and place it in a salad bowl. Don't overchop.

2. Cut the tomatoes in half, scoop out the seeds with a spoon, and chop the remaining flesh; and into the bowl.

3. Remove the coriander leaves from the stems, then rinse, stem, and mince the leaves.

4. Toss the coriander and the remaining ingredients together with the vegetables in the salad bowl.

VARIATION

Chopped roasted red peppers mixed with lemon juice is a lovely topping for avocado halves as is minced dill, coriander, or parsley.

GRATED BEETS

MAKES 4 TO 6 SERVINGS
TIME: 15 MINUTES

This is an instant and delicious way to prepare beets provided you have a food processor on hand. This recipe can be made with or without the green tops.

> 6 medium-size beets, with or
>   without green tops
> 1/2 cup fresh dill or parsley leaves
> 2 tablespoons vegetable oil or butter
> Salt and freshly ground black
>   pepper
> 1 cup plain nonfat yogurt

1. If the beets have their green tops, remove them and set aside. Peel the beets and grate them with the shredding disk of a food processor. If you have beet greens, rinse and coarsely chop them. Mince the dill or parsley.

2. Heat the vegetable oil in a large skillet over medium heat. Add the grated beets (and greens if you have them) and sauté for a minute or so to heat them up.

3. Cover the skillet and simmer over medium heat until tender, 3 to 4 minutes. Remove from the heat and stir in the dill. Season to taste with salt and pepper.

4. With a slotted spoon, transfer the beets to a serving dish or plate. Top each individual portion with yogurt.

VARIATION

Grated beets with apple: Peel, core, and grate 2 apples and sauté them along with the beets.

BAKED BEETS

MAKES 4 SERVINGS
TIME: 1 1/4 HOURS NO-WORK
COOKING TIME

Beets are the perfect bake-along when you're already roasting meat or cooking a casserole. Not only is this the easiest way I know to cook beets, it's also the most delicious because the slow cooking releases and intensifies the natural sweetness of the vegetable.

> 1 1/2 pounds beets, with or without
>   green tops
> Salt and freshly ground black
>   pepper
> Butter for serving

LAID-BACK BEETS

If I'm cooking something else in the oven that takes longer to cook than an hour, I simply leave the beets in the oven until the other dish is done; no harm will come to them.

HOW TO KEEP GREEN VEGETABLES BRIGHT

*T*he green in green vegetables, created by chlorophyll, changes from bright to drab when it comes into contact with an acid like lemon juice, vinegar, or white wine. The color also grays when you cover the vegetable as you cook it, because the vegetable releases a volatile acid into the water which then condenses on the pot, lid and falls back into the pot changing the color. For this reason you should always cook a green vegetable uncovered if you want to keep the color bright.

When you're making a broccoli salad, add the dressing at the last minute to preserve the vivid color for as long as possible.

---

1. Preheat the oven to 375°F.

2. Scrub the beets under running water, trim their bottoms, and remove the green tops (if you're saving the greens, stir-fry them; see page 264).

3. Place the beets on a baking sheet and bake until they're tender, 1 hour at least.

4. Remove the beets from the oven and let them cool until you can handle them, about 10 minutes. When cool enough to handle, remove the skin with the help of a knife. Cut them into quarters or eighths and serve seasoned with salt, pepper, and butter.

VARIATIONS

■ While you're letting the beets cool, heat 2 tablespoons oil or butter in the same pan you baked the beets (the heat of the pan will warm up the oil or melt the butter, no need to set the pan on the burners). Add ¼ cup minced fresh herbs, such as mint, dill, chives, or parsley, and 2 tablespoons orange or lemon juice. Toss this mixture with the beets and season with salt and pepper.

■ Or you can simply add 1 tablespoon Dijon mustard to the warmed oil or butter and then add the beets. Season with salt and pepper.

EMERALD BROCCOLI

MAKE 4 SERVINGS
TIME: 10 MINUTES

Of all the winter vegetables, broccoli boiled until just tender most frequently takes center stage in our winter meals. It looks great, tastes terrific, and happens to be healthy to boot.

Boiling is the simplest way to cook broccoli and the best way to keep its color a vivid green.

Salt
1 bunch broccoli
Freshly ground black pepper
Lemon wedges

1. Bring a medium-size pot of salted water to a boil. Cut 3 to 4 inches off the thick stems and save for another day. Separate the remaining broccoli into pieces of about equal size.

2. Add the broccoli to the boiling water and cook uncovered until just cooked through, 3 to 4 minutes.

3. Drain the broccoli thoroughly in a colander. Serve hot dusted with pepper and sprinkled with fresh lemon juice.

VARIATIONS

To add some more flavor to the broccoli, while it is draining in the colander:

■ Add 2 tablespoons of olive oil or butter, off the heat, to the pan in which you boiled the broccoli. The heat of the pan will warm the oil or gently melt the butter. Swish the cooked stalks in the oil, in the pan, off the heat.

■ If desired, add 1 to 2 tablespoons prepared mustard, lemon juice, or black olive paste to the warmed oil or butter. Or add 1 tablespoon prepared pesto and 1 tablespoon lemon juice, then swish in the cooked stalks.

■ A delicious and low-calorie seasoning that marries well with cooked broccoli is a fine dusting of Japanese prepared sesame and seaweed seasoning (see Pantry chapter).

BRUSSELS SPROUTS ROUNDS

MAKES 4 SERVINGS
TIME: 15 MINUTES

This quick-cooking method leaves these miniature cabbages crunchy and a bright vivid green.

1 to 2 pints Brussels sprouts
1 tablespoon vegetable oil
¼ cup chicken broth or water
¼ cup fresh herb leaves, such as parsley or dill, or 1 teaspoon dried herb, such as tarragon, thyme, or oregano
1 tablespoon butter (optional)
Salt and freshly ground black pepper

1. With a sharp knife, trim the bottoms of the Brussels sprouts and peel off any discolored or yellowing outer leaves. Slice the sprouts crosswise about ¼ inch thick, so that you end up with little disks.

2. Heat the vegetable oil in a large skillet over medium heat. Add the Brussels sprouts and sauté, stirring frequently, for about a minute to just get them hot.

3. Add the broth, reduce the heat to low, and simmer covered until the sprouts are tender yet still crunchy, about 5 minutes.

4. Meanwhile mince the fresh herb.

5. Add the herb and butter, if using, to the sprouts and simmer a minute longer until the butter has melted and everything is hot. Season to taste with salt and pepper and serve immediately.

VARIATIONS

■ Mince 1 clove garlic or 1 piece (½-inch)

HOW TO RELEASE THE MOST FLAVOR FROM VEGETABLES

Mild-tasting vegetables, like mushrooms and summer squash, are best cooked in a minimum of liquid and for a short time only.

Strong-tasting vegetables, like cauliflower and broccoli, are best cooked in lots of liquid to dilute their strong flavor. But, they should be cooked for a short time only; if you cook them too long, you intensify their pungent aroma.

Members of the onion family are the exception to this rule—cooking them for a long time turns their harsh and bitter taste into one that is both sweet and mild.

GARLIC

Here's a tip on how to make the job of peeling garlic a little easier (especially useful when you've lots of garlic to chop at once). Place the flat end of a chef's knife on a garlic clove and with your fist pound the knife. You'll flatten the clove and the skin will separate from the clove within.

In general remember that if you are making a slow-cooking dish, you don't have to mince garlic as fine as you would were you making a quick-cooking dish, because garlic, when simmered for a long time, loses its harsh edge and becomes mild.

of fresh ginger or both and sauté it in the oil (before adding the sprouts) for a few seconds until you can smell the aroma. Proceed as directed but don't use dill with ginger—the two flavors aren't good together.

■ Another way to vary this recipe is to grate about ¼ cup Parmesan cheese, add it after you've added the butter, and then season to taste.

FRAGRANT STIR-FRIED CABBAGE AND GREENS

MAKES 4 SERVINGS
TIME: 30 MINUTES

This dish of bright greens interwoven with pearly strands of light green is a delicious as well as a handsome way of making the most of leftover cabbage. The cabbage and greens are gently sweetened with the sweet fruity tang of applesauce.

Those of you with baby food on hand can substitute a jar of strained pears or peaches for the applesauce.

2 cloves garlic
½ small head green cabbage
1 pound greens, such as kale, turnip or mustard greens, or romaine lettuce
2 tablespoons olive oil
½ cup applesauce or 1 jar (4½ ounces) baby applesauce or strained pears or peaches
1 teaspoon caraway seeds
Salt and freshly ground black pepper

1. Mince the garlic. Core and shred the cabbage. Stem and rinse the greens, then coarsely chop the leaves.

2. Heat the olive oil in a large nonstick skillet over high heat until very hot. Add the garlic, cabbage, applesauce, and caraway seeds and stir-fry for a few seconds just to release the aroma of the garlic.

3. Cover the skillet, reduce the heat to medium, and simmer until the cabbage is somewhat tender, 5 to 10 minutes.

4. Add the chopped greens to the skillet along with any water that clings to the leaves. (If all the greens don't fit into the skillet at once, add about half and stir-fry until somewhat wilted, then add the second half.) With tongs stir the greens around. Cover the skillet and simmer over low heat until the greens and cabbage are tender to the bite but still have some crunch, 5 to 10 minutes. They still should look bright and vivid. Season to taste with salt and pepper.

GARLICKY CABBAGE AND NEW POTATOES

MAKES 6 SERVINGS
TIME: 15 MINUTES WORK
50 MINUTES NO-WORK COOKING
TIME

Although this takes about 50 minutes to cook, it is easy to assemble and cooks on its own. It makes sense to serve this with a main course like baked chicken or veal chops that take about the same time to cook as the cabbage.

½ medium-size head green or
  Chinese cabbage or 2 small
  heads bok choy
2 tablespoons olive oil
1 tablespoon paprika
1 cup dry white wine
1 cup water
1 teaspoon caraway seeds
3 medium-size or 6 small cloves
  garlic
2 pounds new potatoes
Salt and freshly ground black pepper

1. Core and finely shred the cabbage.
2. Heat the olive oil in a medium-size saucepan over medium-high heat. Add the cabbage and stir-fry until it just begins to wilt, 2 to 3 minutes.
3. Stir in the paprika, wine, water, and caraway seeds. Cover and simmer over low heat for about 5 minutes.
4. Meanwhile chop the garlic.
5. Add the garlic to the cabbage and continue to simmer over low heat while you peel the potatoes and cut them into quarters or eighths, depending on their size (you want to end up with pieces that are about 1½ inches wide).
6. Add the potatoes to the pan and season to taste with salt and pepper. Cover and simmer until the potatoes and cabbage are tender, about 45 minutes. Adjust the seasoning and serve hot.

CARROT THREADS WITH TARRAGON LIMAS

MAKES 4 SERVINGS
TIME: 20 MINUTES

I had begun to make this recipe for dinner one night but then realized that I had forgotten to thaw the limas. I discovered, however, there was no need to

SECOND TIME AROUND

***GARLICKY CABBAGE:** To turn the leftovers into a soup, purée them with enough chicken broth or tomato juice to make them soupy. Reheat for 15 minutes and serve with a dollop of yogurt and a sprinkling of snipped fresh dill.*

If you started this recipe with a whole head of cabbage, you can turn the remaining half into coleslaw: Just shred it and toss with a Basic or Herb Vinaigrette (see Index) and chopped scallions. Or use the remaining half in the preceding recipe for Fragrant Stir-fried Cabbage and Greens.

defrost them first because they thawed right in the skillet as the carrots cooked.

1 package (10 ounces) frozen lima
    beans or petite peas
4 large carrots
2 tablespoons butter or vegetable oil
½ teaspoon dried tarragon
¼ cup plain nonfat yogurt or sour
    cream (optional)
Salt and freshly ground black
    pepper

1. Remove the wrapper from the lima beans or peas. Set them aside to thaw. Peel the carrots, then grate them with the shredding disk in a food processor or slice them wafer thin.

2. Melt the butter in a large skillet over medium heat until very hot. Add the carrots and sauté, stirring frequently, until they begin to soften, about 2 minutes.

3. With your fingers, break up the frozen lima beans as best you can as you add them to the skillet. Add the tarragon, cover the skillet, and simmer over low heat until the limas are hot and the carrots are tender, about 5 minutes. Check the vegetables and stir them around after a couple of minutes to make sure the carrots aren't burning.

4. Remove the vegetables from the heat, stir in the yogurt, and season to taste with salt and pepper.

ORANGE-JUICE-STEAMED CARROTS

MAKES 4 SERVINGS
TIME: 15 TO 20 MINUTES

This is a tasty way to prepare carrots quickly.

8 medium-size carrots
½ cup orange juice
¼ cup fresh dill or parsley leaves
1 teaspoon sugar
1 tablespoon butter (optional)
Salt and freshly ground
    black pepper

1. Peel the carrots and cut them into ½-inch chunks or slices. (If you know how, you could also cut them into Chinese "oblique" shapes.)

2. Place the carrots and orange juice in a large skillet. Bring the liquid to a boil over medium heat, then reduce the heat, cover, and simmer for 5 minutes.

3. Meanwhile mince the herb.

4. Sprinkle the carrots with the sugar and cook uncovered over medium heat until all the liquid has evaporated and the carrots begin to stick to the pan, 3 to 4 minutes.

5. Remove the skillet from the heat, stir in the herb and butter if using, and season to taste with salt and pepper.

CAULIFLOWER WITH RED PEPPER RIBBONS

MAKES 4 SERVINGS
TIME: 10 TO 15 MINUTES

Although my first choice for cauliflower is an addition of roasted red peppers, you can flavor it with a variety of condiments and seasonings.

1 head cauliflower
1 tablespoon lemon juice or white
*   wine vinegar*
2 tablespoons roasted red peppers
*   or pimientos, cut into ribbons,*
*   or chopped olives, or*
*   1 tablespoon prepared pesto*
*   or black olive paste*
1 tablespoon olive oil or butter
*   (optional)*
Salt and freshly ground black pepper

1. Cut the core from the cauliflower and separate the head into florets.

2. Bring a medium-size pan of water to a boil and add the lemon juice (to prevent discoloration of the cauliflower) and then the florets. Boil until the cauliflower is cooked through yet firm, 3 to 4 minutes.

3. Drain the cauliflower well, then toss with the roasted peppers, or other flavoring and olive oil if you wish. Season to taste with salt and pepper and serve hot.

VARIATIONS

■ The cooked cauliflower can also be dusted with grated Parmesan or Cheddar cheese instead of the peppers.

■ Dip room-temperature or chilled cooked cauliflower in a dressing made by mixing ½ cup sour cream or plain yogurt with 2 teaspoons Dijon mustard, or by blending ⅓ cup mayonnaise with a small tin of anchovies and seasoning this with a teaspoon or two of lemon juice.

■ Minced herbs that go well with cauliflower are parsley, dill, chives, and scallions.

ESPECIALLY GOOD FOR CHILDREN

CAULIFLOWER: I've discovered that by turning boiled vegetables into soup purées I can get my daughter to eat just about any of them, even the ones she ordinarily rejects. I did that with the Garlicky Cabbage and New Potatoes dish earlier in this chapter (see the accompanying Second Time Around sidebar, page 257) and with leftover cauliflower. To turn cauliflower into a soup: Sauté an onion until soft in a tablespoon or so of oil, then add the chopped florets, 1 quart of liquid (water, chicken broth, tomato juice, or a combination of 2 or 3 of these) and ⅓ cup of long grain white rice. Simmer until the cauliflower is soft, about 30 minutes. Purée in a blender with 1 cup of milk and season with salt. It's creamy and delicious.

RECYCLING SWEET POTATOES

If you can't find chestnuts, you can still make use of this recipe — it is a wonderful way to recycle plainly baked sweet potatoes. Peel the sweet potatoes and cut them into small dice and substitute them for the chestnuts. About 4 medium-size sweet potatoes will equal the amount of chestnuts called for in this recipe.

CHESTNUT, ONION, AND PEAR SAUTE

MAKES 4 SERVINGS
TIME: 20 TO 25 MINUTES

This sweet-savory winter dish of roasted chestnuts, onions, and fresh pears is wonderful with meats that are rich in flavor, like lamb or pork.

1 onion
2 jars (8 ounces each) whole
    chestnuts, roasted or plain
2 pears, preferably Comice
1 tablespoon butter
⅓ cup dry red wine
Salt and freshly ground black
    pepper

1. Mince the onion and chop the chestnuts. Core and peel the pears, then cut them into ½-inch dice.

2. Melt the butter in a large skillet over medium heat until golden brown. Add the onion and sauté for a minute or so just to get them going. Add the red wine and cover the skillet. Simmer over low heat until the onion is tender and soft, about 5 minutes. Add the chestnuts and simmer covered 5 minutes more.

3. Uncover the skillet, add the pears, and sauté for a minute or two until the pears are just heated through. Don't overcook the pears or you will lose all their crunch. Season to taste with salt and pepper and serve hot.

PERFECT CORN

MAKE 2 EARS PER SERVING
TIME: 15 MINUTES

For my money the absolutely perfect and only way to cook freshly picked corn is to boil it for a few minutes until done.

I read in one of Jean Anderson's cookbooks never to add salt to the water in which you boil corn, but, if it isn't as fresh as you'd like, add a tablespoon of sugar to the water to sweeten the corn. Thanks, Jean Anderson, for that terrific advice.

2 ears corn per person
1 quart water for every 2 ears corn
1 tablespoon sugar (optional)
Salt and freshly ground black
    pepper
Butter or olive oil for serving

1. Shuck the corn, removing all the silks.

2. Bring the water to a boil over high heat, adding the sugar if the corn isn't tip-top fresh.

3. Add the corn to the water, cover the pot, and cook at a rolling boil until the kernels are just tender, 3 to 6 minutes, depending on how fresh the corn is (the fresher it is, the quicker it cooks) and how big the ears are.

4. With tongs, remove the corn from the water and season with salt and pepper. Let each person spread some butter or, for cholesterol watchers, olive oil on each ear.

MEXICAN CORN AND SWEET POTATO SAUTE

MAKES 4 SERVINGS
TIME: 10 TO 15 MINUTES WORK
25 MINUTES NO-WORK COOKING TIME

The natural sweetness of the corn and sweet potatoes provides an intriguing contrast to the hot jalapeños and the tang of lime juice. This makes a good side dish to serve with richly flavored meats like beef, pork, and lamb. Stir in leftover pieces of meat to make a meal of this dish.

1 sweet potato
2 green bell peppers
2 ripe tomatoes
2 tablespoons vegetable oil
1 package (10 ounces) frozen corn kernels, thawed
2 pickled jalapeño peppers
½ cup fresh coriander leaves
6 scallions (green onions)
2 tablespoons lime juice
Salt and freshly ground black pepper

1. Peel the sweet potato and cut into ½-inch cubes. Core and seed the bell peppers, then cut them into small dice. Halve the tomatoes and remove the seeds with a spoon; chop the remaining flesh into small dice.

2. Heat the oil in a large skillet over medium heat. Add the sweet potatoes, peppers, tomatoes, and corn. Cover, reduce the heat to low, and cook, stirring occasionally, until the sweet potatoes are tender, about 20 minutes.

3. Meanwhile seed the jalapeño peppers and mince. Mince the coriander. Trim and thinly slice the scallions.

4. Add the jalapeños, lime juice, and coriander to the skillet and continue

THOSE LOW-FAT SALSAS

If you're on a serious fat-restricted diet, think salsa. And relishes and vinaigrettes. These flavorful condiments make wonderful accompaniments to plainly cooked poultry and fish dishes.

to cook uncovered until almost all the liquid has evaporated, about 5 minutes. Add the scallions and season to taste with salt and pepper. Serve hot.

CORN AND TWO-PEPPER RELISH

MAKES ABOUT 2 CUPS
TIME: 5 MINUTES

Not only is this a terrific condiment with lamb chops, roast chicken, and hamburgers, it is also a surefire way to wake up a baked potato, enliven a pot of beans, or dress up a ham sandwich. It couldn't be simpler to make and, when refrigerated, it keeps well for over a week.

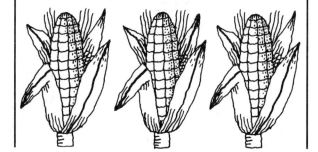

1 package (10 ounces) frozen corn
  kernels, thawed
1 jar (4 ounces) pickled sweet red
  peppers
1 jar (3 ounces) cocktail onions
2 pickled jalapeño peppers
Salt

1. Place the corn kernels in a serving dish.

2. Put the remaining ingredients except the salt in a food processor and process with a couple of short bursts until chopped. Don't overdo this step or you'll lose all the texture. Stir this mixture into the corn and season to taste with salt. Cover and keep refrigerated until ready to serve.

GREEN CHILI and JALAPENO SALSA

MAKES ABOUT 1½ CUPS
TIME: 10 MINUTES

This condiment of chilies is delicious served with lamb, pork, or black beans.

2 ripe small tomatoes
3 scallions (green onions)
2 jalapeño peppers, fresh or pickled
1 can (4 ounces) chopped green chilies
2 teaspoons lime or lemon juice
Salt

1. Chop the tomatoes. Trim and thinly slice the scallions. Mince the jalapeños.

2. Combine all the ingredients in a bowl and season to taste with salt. Cover and refrigerate until ready to serve.

SUNDAY BAKED EGGPLANT

MAKES 4 TO 6 SERVINGS
TIME: 10 MINUTES WORK
1 HOUR NO-WORK COOKING TIME

This is an extremely easy way to make eggplant—you don't even have to salt it first. It does, however, take an hour to bake; so plan to serve it with another dish like Roast Leg of Lamb, No-Work Filet of Beef (see Index for page numbers), or poultry that takes at least as long to cook.

2 pounds eggplant
1 clove garlic
1 can (14½ ounces) stewed
  tomatoes
2 tablespoons olive oil
Salt and freshly ground black
  pepper

1. Preheat the oven to 375°F.

2. Trim the stem ends of the eggplants, cut lengthwise in half, then slice crosswise ½ inch thick. Mince the garlic.

3. Spoon a third of the stewed tomatoes over the bottom of a 13 x 9-inch baking pan. Arrange half the eggplant slices over the top; sprinkle with half the garlic and olive oil. Season to taste with salt and pepper. Repeat the layers, finishing with the last third of the stewed tomatoes. Cover the pan with aluminum foil and bake until tender, about 1 hour.

VARIATION

To turn this into a main course, at the end of baking time, arrange ¼ pound thinly sliced mozzarella cheese on top of the eggplant, drizzle with more olive oil, and continue to bake uncovered just until the cheese melts.

SECOND TIME AROUND

BAKED EGGPLANT: Serve leftovers at room temperature, splashed with an herb vinaigrette and a teaspoon of black olive paste. Crusty bread is a must.

**BRAISED FENNEL
SAUCE**

Just as salsas and relishes make good sauces to serve over plainly cooked meats, fish, and poultry, so do puréed cooked vegetable dishes. Leftover braised fennel is terrific thinned with stewed tomatoes, and puréed in a blender until smooth. It goes well with turkey, lamb or a lively flavored fish like bluefish.

BRAISED FENNEL

MAKES 4 SERVINGS
TIME: 30 MINUTES

This deliciously flavored dish of fresh fennel braised with tomato is a terrific adjunct to roast or sautéed lamb, pork, and poultry and is a fine side dish for well-flavored fish like mackerel, swordfish, bluefish, and tuna. Celery can be substituted for the fennel.

4 bulbs fennel
2 ripe tomatoes
1 cup fresh parsley leaves
2 tablespoons vegetable oil or butter
½ teaspoon dried tarragon
½ cup chicken broth or water
Salt and freshly ground black pepper

1. Trim and discard the feathery tops from the fennel. Cut each bulb in half from top to bottom and cut out the triangular core. Slice each half crosswise, about ½ inch thick. Cut each tomato in half and remove the seeds with a spoon; finely chop the flesh. Mince the parsley.

2. Heat the oil in a large skillet over medium heat until sizzling. Add the fennel and tomatoes; sauté for a minute or so to coat with the oil. Add the tarragon, broth, and salt and pepper to taste. Cover and simmer until the fennel is tender, about 20 minutes.

3. Remove the lid from the skillet. Add the parsley. If there is too much liquid in the skillet, boil it away over medium-high heat until most of it evaporates. Adjust the seasoning and serve hot.

STIR-FRIED GREENS

MAKES 4 SERVINGS
TIME: 15 TO 25 MINUTES

Nutritionists exhort us to add turnip, beet, dandelion, and mustard greens, kale, spinach, broccoli rabe, and Swiss chard to our weekly diet because they are so healthy. I love them though, not for their salubrious effect, but their lusty flavor. Unfortunately the more exotic types of greens are not that easy to find, but I never substitute the frozen variety (except for spinach) for the fresh, because frozen greens are wilted and taste bitter.

2 pounds fresh greens
3 or 4 cloves garlic
1 to 2 tablespoons olive oil
Salt and freshly ground black pepper

1. Cut the stems from the greens and coarsely chop the leaves. Rinse the leaves under cold water and place them with any water that clings to them in a large bowl. Mince the garlic.

2. Heat the oil in a large skillet over high heat until hot and shimmering. Add the garlic and greens along with any water that clings to the leaves. If all the greens won't fit into the skillet at once, add half and cook until there's room for the remaining half. The greens will sizzle and sputter loudly as the water on the leaves hits the oil, but the racket dies down quickly.

3. With tongs, stir the greens around. Cover the skillet and simmer over low heat until the leaves are tender but not over-cooked, 5 to 15 minutes, depending on the type of green. Check after 5 minutes of cooking and add a few tablespoons of water if the leaves are beginning to stick to the bottom of the skillet. When properly done, the leaves will be vivid green and just tender to the bite but not soggy. The cooking time varies depending on the type of greens you're cooking and on how you like to eat them. Season to taste with salt and pepper and serve hot.

LEMON GREEN BEANS

MAKES 4 SERVINGS
TIME: 10 MINUTES

I find that fresh green beans for most of the year are woody and tough. However, I discovered that cutting them into small pieces before boiling dissipates some of their stringy texture and that it's crucial to boil them hard for 5 minutes. Summer is their natural season and the best time to buy green beans.

1 pound green beans
Salt
1 tablespoon butter (optional)
1 tablespoon lemon juice
Freshly ground black pepper

1. Trim the stem ends and cut the green beans into ½- to ¾-inch lengths.

2. Bring a large pot of salted water to a boil, over high heat. Toss in the beans and boil hard, uncovered, until the beans are tender, about 5 minutes.

3. Drain the beans and return them to the pot they were cooked in, off the heat. Toss with the butter, if using, and lemon juice; season to taste with salt and pepper. Serve hot.

SECOND TIME AROUND

LEMON GREEN BEANS: I'm not terribly fond of re-heated cooked green beans. However, chilled and dressed, they form the basis of a wonderful side or main course salad.

For instance, combine the beans with diced boiled potatoes, chopped fresh tomatoes, and an herb vinaigrette that includes plenty of fresh dill or parsley. They are also terrific tossed with a dice of plain cooked chicken and a mustard vinaigrette or one that has been seasoned with chopped pickles and capers. Just use your imagination — and whatever you have in the refrigerator.

DOUBLING UP

SAUTEED MUSHROOMS WITH CORN: You can make a double batch using 2 skillets if you have to. If there are any leftovers (hard to imagine), use them the following day in a bean soup or stew or wrapped in phyllo dough or tortillas.

SAUTEED MUSHROOMS WITH CORN

MAKES 4 SERVINGS
TIME: 15 TO 20 MINUTES

My favorite mushrooms are wild, and my favorite way to cook them is to sauté them in olive oil with garlic. However, because they're so expensive, I stretch the wild mushrooms with the domestic variety and corn kernels as well. The result is a delicious dish.

1 pound fresh domestic mushrooms
½ pound fresh wild mushrooms, such as shiitake or chanterelles
1 clove garlic
1 package (10 ounces) frozen corn kernels, thawed
1 tablespoon olive oil
Salt and freshly ground black pepper

1. Clean the mushrooms by wiping them with a damp paper towel; don't rinse them with water unless they're very sandy, otherwise they'll get waterlogged. Remove the stems from the mushrooms and cut the caps in halves or in quarters. (Reserve the stems from the domestic mushrooms for soups, stews, stir-fries, or casseroles.) Mince the garlic and make sure the corn is thawed.

2. Heat the oil in a large skillet over medium heat. Add the mushrooms, corn, and garlic and sauté, stirring constantly, until the mushrooms begin to soften, about 5 minutes. If the mushrooms begin to stick to the pan, add a few tablespoons water to the skillet and proceed. After another 2 or 3 minutes, when the mushrooms are wilted, season to taste with salt and pepper and serve immediately.

BRAISED PEAS AND LETTUCE

MAKES 4 SERVINGS
TIME: 5 MINUTES WORK
15 MINUTES NO-WORK COOKING
TIME

An utterly simple yet delicious dish I remember from my childhood in Belgium are sweet peas stewed in butter with tender leaves of Boston lettuce. This is a perfect adjunct to sautéed chops, steaks, and poultry.

1 large head Boston lettuce
1 package (10 ounces) frozen petite
   peas, thawed, or 2 cups freshly
   shelled young peas
6 to 8 cocktail onions or 1 clove
   garlic, minced
2 tablespoons butter or olive oil
Salt and freshly ground black
   pepper

1. Finely shred the lettuce and place it with the peas, onions, and butter in a medium-size saucepan.

2. Bring the ingredients to a simmer over medium heat, then reduce the heat to low and simmer covered, stirring occasionally until the ingredients are tender and the flavors are blended, about 20 minutes. Season to taste with salt and pepper and serve hot.

TRI-COLORED PEPPERS

**MAKES 4 SERVINGS
TIME: 20 MINUTES**

A light touch of vinegar or lemon juice brings out the flavor of the peppers.

4 to 6 bell peppers, preferably a
   combination of colors
1 to 2 tablespoons olive oil
1 to 2 tablespoons red wine
   vinegar or lemon juice
Salt and freshly ground black
   pepper

1. Core, seed, and cut the peppers into long thin slices.

2. Heat the oil in a large nonstick skillet over high heat until hot and almost smoky. Add the peppers and stir-fry for a couple of minutes to begin their cooking.

3. Reduce the heat to low and simmer covered until the peppers are soft, about 10 minutes. Remove the skillet from the heat, add the vinegar, and stir to mix. Season to taste with salt and pepper.

VARIATIONS

■ Add 1 minced clove of garlic with the peppers in step 3.
■ Or mince 1 clove garlic and ¼ cup fresh basil leaves separately. Sauté the garlic with the peppers. Stir in the basil after you add the vinegar.
■ Anything from the onion family blends exceedingly well with peppers: Try sliced onions or scallions (green onions) or minced chives.

WHEN YOU CAN'T FIND A BELL PEPPER RAINBOW

If you like the looks of a multi-colored bell pepper dish, but can only find them in green, proceed with the recipe but substitute jarred thinly-sliced roasted red peppers or pimientoes for the other colors. The taste is different, but still good, and you'll get a nice effect as well.

BAKED POTATOES

*E*ven though I serve baked potatoes as a side dish, I usually serve them with a variety of toppings as a main course. Because of this I thought it more fitting to place them prominently in the Omnium Gatherum chapter than in this chapter on side dishes. To find out how to bake a potato, see Index.

HERBED NEW POTATOES

MAKES 4 SERVINGS
TIME: 5 MINUTES WORK
25 MINUTES NO-WORK COOKING TIME

Steaming is the fastest as well as tastiest way to cook new potatoes; cooked this way, they're free of the waterlogged texture boiling produces.

If you're as much of a potato maven as I, you'll enjoy an entire plateful of these, joined by a bowl of cool yogurt on the side, for dinner.

1 pound new potatoes
2 tablespoons olive oil or butter
1 bunch chives, ½ bunch scallions (green onions), or ½ cup fresh parsley leaves
Salt and freshly ground black pepper

1. Scrub the potatoes and halve the large ones. Place the potatoes in a steamer and place the steamer in a pot. Add about an inch of water to the pot or as much water as you can without having the bottom of the steamer come in contact with the water.

2. Place the pot over medium heat. When the water comes to a boil, cover the pot, reduce the heat a bit, and steam until the potatoes are tender, 20 to 25 minutes.

3. Meanwhile place the olive oil or butter in the bottom of a serving dish. Mince the chives, scallions, or parsley and add it to the dish.

4. When the potatoes are tender, place them in the serving dish, halving or quartering them as you go. Toss the potatoes with olive oil and herb right in the bowl and season to taste with salt and pepper.

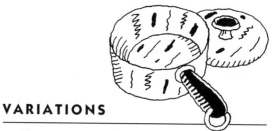

VARIATIONS

■ The more carefree way of cooking new potatoes is to boil them, but they won't be as flavorful as steamed and they might be waterlogged if you boil them too long. Nevertheless, here's how: After you scrub and halve the potatoes, place them in a saucepan and cover with cold water. Bring the water to a boil and simmer until tender, 20 to 25 minutes. Drain well and proceed as directed.

■ Substitute chopped basil or bottled roasted peppers for the chives and mix with olive oil (not butter).

POTATO CHIPS

MAKES 2 TO 4 SERVINGS
TIME: 40 TO 45 MINUTES

This recipe is for potato lovers, for crispy-food aficionados, for people who love "feeling stuffed," *and* for people who are on strict fat-free diets.

Cookie-mogul and food-lover David Liederman, who fits the above description, devised this recipe when he was trying to lose what has now become a legendary 100 pounds.

These chips are very easy to make, but they do need some watching after; so make use of the time you have to spend in the kitchen by making other parts of your meal. Chances are, too, that they'll bake somewhat unevenly, but this is to be expected because most ovens have hot spots. Sweet potatoes can also be baked this way but won't become as crisp.

Beware: these are addictive.

*2 medium-large Idaho baking
    potatoes or sweet potatoes
Salt
Freshly ground black pepper or ¼
    teaspoon dried red pepper flakes
    (optional)*

1. Preheat the oven to 375°F.
2. Scrub the potatoes well, then slice no thicker than ⅛ inch. Place the slices in a single layer on 2 large nonstick baking sheets. Bake for 25 minutes.
3. Remove any slices that have browned deeply. Turn the remaining slices over and bake for another 5 to 15 minutes, depending on how even your oven heat is and how brown you like them.
4. Remove the potatoes from the oven and season to taste with salt and pepper or dried red pepper flakes. If you make them ahead of time, keep them warm in a 200°F oven up to 20 minutes and they'll continue to crisp up. Beyond that point, serve them at room temperature.

GRATED ROOT VEGETABLES

MAKES 4 TO 6 SERVINGS
TIME: 20 MINUTES

Stir-frying is a great quick method of cooking root vegetables that are traditionally baked and take forever to

ALMOST HASH BROWNS

Another delicious way of getting crispy potatoes (although not as crunchy as these potato chips) is to spread out on a baking sheet roughly chopped boiled potatoes which you have tossed with some olive oil and salt. Bake at 400°F, uncovered, for up to an hour, tossing them every now and then. Season with pepper after baking; pepper burns when exposed to high heat for a long time.

GLAZED ROOT VEGETA-BLES: Leftovers from this dish are best added to meat or poultry stir-fries. You could also toss the leftovers in a casserole or in a sauce that you'll serve over pasta or grains.

cook. Serve this medley with lamb, veal, pork, or poultry.

> 2 carrots
> 2 white turnips
> 2 parsnips
> Or 1½ pounds of any one of the
>   above root vegetables
> 2 cloves garlic
> 2 tablespoons vegetable oil
> ¼ teaspoon ground ginger
> ½ teaspoon fresh grated lemon or
>   orange zest or ¼ teaspoon dried peel
> ½ teaspoon sugar
> ¼ cup lemon juice
> Salt and freshly ground black pepper

1. Peel the vegetables. Cut the parsnips lengthwise in half; if they have wide inner cores, cut them out because they are woody.

2. Grate all the root vegetables with the shredding disk of a food processor. Mince the garlic.

3. Heat the oil in a large skillet over medium heat. Add the garlic and stir-fry for a few seconds to release the aroma. Add the vegetables, ginger, lemon zest, sugar, and lemon juice. Sauté, stirring constantly, until the vegetables are barely wilted, 3 to 5 minutes. Remove the skillet from the heat and season the vegetables to taste with salt and pepper.

GLAZED ROOT VEGETABLES WITH GINGER AND GARLIC

MAKES 2 MAIN-COURSE OR 4 SIDE-DISH SERVINGS
TIME: 15 MINUTES WORK
30 MINUTES NO-WORK COOKING TIME

For dinner I serve a portion of these sweet soy-glazed vegetables along with kasha or lamb chops.

Although I like to cook different root vegetables together, purists can stick to a single variety if they wish.

> 1 piece (1 inch) fresh ginger
> 1 clove garlic
> 2 sweet potatoes
> 2 white turnips
> 2 parsnips
> 4 carrots
> 1 small celery root
> 1 tablespoon Oriental sesame oil
> 1 tablespoon soy sauce
> ½ cup water
> 2 teaspoons sugar
> Salt and freshly ground black
>   pepper

1. Peel and mince the ginger and garlic. Peel all the vegetables and cut them into ¾-inch cubes.

2. Heat the sesame oil in a large skillet over medium-high heat until very hot. Add the ginger and garlic and stir-fry for 10 seconds just to release their aroma.

3. Add the soy sauce, water, and sugar along with the vegetables. Cover the skillet and simmer over low heat until the vegetables are tender and have absorbed the liquid, 20 to 30 minutes. Season to taste with salt and pepper and serve hot.

VARIATION

Substitute vegetable oil instead of sesame oil and omit the soy sauce. Add ½ teaspoon dried tarragon (especially flattering to carrots) with the vegetables.

SNAPPY SNOW PEAS

MAKES 4 SERVINGS
TIME: 7 TO 10 MINUTES

This uncomplicated recipe would add a bright crunch and a snappy color to any sort of meat, poultry, fish, or salad dinner.

Salt
1 pound snow peas

1. Bring a medium-size saucepan of salted water to a boil over medium heat. As the water comes to a boil, snap off the stem ends of the snow peas and pull off the strings; discard any yellow or bruised ones.

2. Add the snow peas. Bring the water back to a boil and drain the snow peas immediately; this will keep them firm and bright.

3. Serve immediately or, if you want them cold, run them under cold water to stop them from cooking further.

MAPLE AND CINNAMON ACORN SQUASH

MAKES 4 SERVINGS
TIME: 5 MINUTES WORK
1 HOUR NO-WORK COOKING TIME

I've sustained so many little knife nicks trying to split recalcitrant acorn squash in half that I now bake them whole. After baking, I halve them, scoop out the seeds, and season with butter, maple

SNAP UP SNOW PEAS

Snow peas are terrific cold as a salad. I like to squeeze lemon or lime juice over them and sprinkle on lots of minced chives or chopped scallions, dill, basil, or parsley. When I feel like eating something with a bit more of an Asian influence, I sprinkle them with rice vinegar and scatter prepared sesame seed and seaweed dressing (see Pantry chapter) on top.

DOUBLING UP
•

SQUASH: You can cook twice as many squash and have lovely vegetable leftovers to stir into a soup or stew or to reheat in a stir-fry. You also can reheat any seeded and seasoned squash halves, covered with foil, in a 350°F degree oven until heated through, about 20 minutes.

syrup, or honey and a dash of cinnamon. Although they take longer to cook this way, I no longer cut myself and, at the same time, I preserve more of their flavor.

By the way, don't be alarmed by slight popping sounds you'll hear from the oven. It's simply the steam building up in the squash and then escaping. Rest assured that if you've pricked your squashes before baking, they won't explode.

2 acorn squash, about 1 pound each
Salt and freshly ground black
 pepper
Butter (optional)
Maple syrup, brown sugar, or
 honey
Ground cinnamon, allspice, or
 mace

1. Preheat the oven to 400°F.

2. Scrub the squash, place them on a baking sheet, and prick each one in several places with a sharp knife.

3. Bake until tender, about 1 hour.

4. Remove the squash from the oven, cut them in half (use a towel to hold them), and scoop out the seeds. Season each cavity with salt and pepper, butter if you wish, a teaspoon of the sweetener of your choice, and a sprinkling of spice.

BAKED BUTTERNUT SQUASH

MAKES 4 SERVINGS
TIME: 5 MINUTES WORK
1 HOUR NO-WORK COOKING TIME

As with acorn squash, I also bake butternut squash whole, then cut it in half, seed it, and serve. A squeeze of lime juice complements the sweet flavor and mealy texture of the squash.

1 butternut squash, 2 to 3 pounds
1 to 2 tablespoons lime juice
Salt and freshly ground black
 pepper

1. Preheat the oven to 375°F.

2. Scrub the squash, place it on a baking sheet, and prick it in a few places with a sharp knife. Bake until tender, about 1 hour.

3. Remove the squash from the oven, split it in half (hold it in a towel), and scoop out the seeds. Season each half with some lime juice and salt and pepper to taste. Cut each half in half again and serve.

VARIATIONS

■ While the squash is baking, melt 2 tablespoons butter in a small skillet over low heat. Stir in ½ teaspoon spice, such as ground cardamom, cloves, cinnamon, or cumin, and, if you like, 1 tablespoon brown sugar. Brush the butter mixture over each portion of squash before serving.

■ Or heat 2 tablespoons olive or vegetable oil in a small skillet until hot, stir in ¼ cup minced herbs, like parsley or dill, and drizzle over each portion right before serving.

SPAGHETTI SQUASH STRANDS

MAKES 4 SERVINGS
TIME: 10 MINUTES WORK
1 HOUR NO-WORK COOKING TIME

Spaghetti squash is an amusing alternative to butternut or acorn squash. After baking you rake the cooked flesh of the squash, and the vegetable naturally separates into "spaghetti" strands, which taste like a cross between nutty winter squashes and grassy summer squash. Don't be alarmed by the firm texture of the strands after baking, they're supposed to be that way.

The sturdy crunch of the spaghetti squash makes it a terrific vegetable for main-course salads It is also an excellent side dish to serve when you're cooking a roast or baking some chops. Because cooking and preparing this vegetable takes some doing, I like to serve it as a main course, as I would pasta, simply tossed with a vegetable or meat sauce.

1 spaghetti squash, 2 to 3 pounds
2 tablespoons olive oil
1 to 2 tablespoons lemon juice
Salt and freshly ground black pepper

1. Preheat the oven to 375°F.

2. Place the spaghetti squash on a baking sheet and prick it in a few places with a sharp knife. Bake until the flesh yields when pressed with your finger, 45 to 60 minutes.

3. Remove the squash from the oven, split it in half, and scoop out the seeds. (This is a little tedious to do as the seeds seem to get caught in the strands of squash.) With a fork, begin to rake the squash, separating it in strands. Stop raking when the fork hits the shell. Transfer the strands of squash to a bowl and toss with the oil and lemon juice. Season to taste with salt and pepper.

PAN-STEAMED YELLOW SQUASH

MAKES 4 TO 6 SERVINGS
TIME: 15 MINUTES

I make summer squash this way when I'm too lazy to take out my food processor and make it the other easy way (see Zucchini Sauté, page 277).

> 2 pounds yellow summer squash or
>   zucchini (about 3 to 4 medium-
>   size)
> 4 scallions (green onions) or ½ cup
>   fresh herb leaves of your choice
> ½ cup chicken broth or dry white
>   wine
> 1 tablespoon butter (optional)
> Salt and freshly ground black pepper

1. Rinse the squash and trim the ends. Cut the squash lengthwise into quarters and cut away most of the seeds. Cut the remaining flesh into ½-inch chunks. Trim and thinly slice the scallions or mince the herb.

2. Pour the broth into a large skillet and bring it to a boil over high heat. Add the squash, reduce the heat to medium, and simmer covered until just cooked through, about 3 minutes.

3. Uncover the skillet, add the scallions or herb, and evaporate the liquid over high heat until the squash begins to stick to the pan, about 1 minute. Remove the pan from the heat and swirl in the butter if using. Season to taste with salt and pepper. Remove the squash with a slotted spoon and serve immediately.

ORANGE-FLAVORED SWEET POTATOES

MAKES 4 SERVINGS
TIME: 30 MINUTES

By sautéing sweet potatoes instead of baking them, you can appreciate their fresh taste more than when you prepare them in the traditional ways. And, of course, sautéing takes less time.

> 4 medium-size sweet potatoes or yams
> 1 tablespoon vegetable oil
> ½ cup orange juice
> ¼ teaspoon dried orange peel
> 1 tablespoon brown sugar (optional)
> 1 tablespoon butter (optional)
> Salt and freshly ground black pepper

SECOND TIME AROUND

ORANGE-FLAVORED SWEET POTATOES: These are best reheated by sautéing them some more in a skillet either alone or in the company of some other grated vegetable like carrots or other root vegetable.

1. Peel the sweet potatoes and grate them with the shredding disk in a food processor.

2. Heat the oil in a large skillet over medium-high heat. Add the sweet potatoes and stir-fry for about 30 seconds just to get them cooking.

3. Add the orange juice and peel. Cover the skillet and simmer over low heat for 20 minutes. Stir the potatoes every now and then to make sure they're not sticking to the bottom of the pan.

4. Add the sugar if you like the potatoes sweeter; sauté uncovered until the potatoes begin to get a little crisp, 3 to 4 minutes.

5. Remove the skillet from the heat and swirl in the butter if using. Season well with salt and pepper and serve immediately.

MINTED CHERRY TOMATOES

MAKES 4 SERVINGS
TIME: 20 MINUTES

Baked cherry tomatoes seasoned with olive oil, scallions, and herbs bring a splash of color and taste to any poultry, fish, or meat main course. The sugar in the recipe brings out the flavor of the tomatoes without sweetening them.

2 pints cherry tomatoes
2 tablespoons olive oil
1/2 teaspoon sugar
1/4 cup fresh mint, basil, parsley, or dill leaves, or 1 teaspoon dried mint, oregano, or tarragon
Salt and freshly ground black pepper
2 scallions (green onions; optional)

1. Preheat the oven to 350°F.

2. Rinse and stem the cherry tomatoes. Set the tomatoes in a 9-inch square baking pan and toss them with the olive oil, sugar, dried herbs if you are not using fresh, and salt and pepper to taste.

3. Pop the tomatoes in the oven 15 minutes before you plan to eat.

4. As they're baking, mince the fresh herb and trim and thinly slice the scallions if using. Toss the baked tomatoes with the fresh herb or scallions or both and serve hot.

SECOND TIME AROUND

MINTED CHERRY TOMA-TOES: Leftovers should be chopped up and added to soups, stews, relishes, or pasta sauces, or puréed with some chicken broth and served as a fresh tomato pasta sauce.

SECOND TIME AROUND

YAM AND APPLE SAUTE: I like to reheat leftovers mixed with other sautés of vegetables or in a bean soup or stew.

YAM AND APPLE SAUTE

MAKES 4 SERVINGS
TIME: 30 MINUTES

This rather speedy dish provides a lovely contrast in flavors with the tang of the apple against the sweet of the yams. I usually serve this alongside Cornish game hens, turkey, lamb, ham, or pork.

*4 medium-size yams or sweet
    potatoes
1 to 2 tablespoons vegetable oil
2 tablespoons lemon juice
½ cup water
4 Granny Smith apples
1 bunch scallions (green onions)
Salt and freshly ground black pepper
1 tablespoon butter (optional)*

1. Peel the yams and cut them into ½-inch cubes.

2. Heat the oil in a large skillet over medium heat. Add the yams and stir-fry them for a minute just to get them hot.

3. Add the lemon juice and water, reduce the heat, cover the skillet, and simmer gently until the yams are just tender, about 15 minutes. Stir the yams every now and then to make sure they don't stick to the bottom of the skillet. If they do begin to stick, add another tablespoon of water and continue to cook.

4. While the yams are cooking, core, peel, and cut the apples into ½-inch cubes. Trim and thinly slice the scallions, including 2 inches of the green tops.

5. When the yams are tender, add the apples and simmer covered until heated through, about 5 minutes. Stir in the scallions and season to taste with salt and pepper. If you wish, blend in the butter off the heat for a mellow finish.

SUMMER SALAD VEGETABLE STIR-FRY

MAKES 4 SERVINGS
TIME: 15 MINUTES

Radishes, cucumbers, and tomatoes, usually thought of only as summer salad vegetables, here take center stage in a light and breezy stir-fry.

This is easy to prepare and wonderful when served with Chinese Chili Scallops (see Index).

1 large cucumber
1 bunch radishes
2 ripe tomatoes
2 scallions (green onions)
1 tablespoon vegetable or Oriental
    sesame oil
2 teaspoons rice vinegar
2 teaspoons soy sauce
1 teaspoon sugar
Salt and freshly ground
    black pepper

1. Peel the cucumber, cut it in half, and scoop out the seeds with a teaspoon. Cut the flesh into ¾-inch cubes. Thinly slice the radishes. Cut the tomatoes in half, scoop out the seeds and juice with a teaspoon, and dice the flesh. Thinly slice the scallions.

2. Heat the oil in a large skillet over medium heat. Add the cucumbers and radishes and stir-fry until they're hot, about 1 minute. Add the tomatoes and stir-fry another minute to heat them up. Add the rice vinegar, soy sauce, sugar, and scallions; stir-fry until the vegetables are glazed, about 30 seconds. Season to taste with salt and pepper and serve hot.

ZUCCHINI SAUTE

MAKES 4 TO 6 SERVINGS
TIME: 10 MINUTES

This is the easiest way I know to cook zucchini and other summer squashes. Grate the zucchini with the help of a food processor and then sauté it over high heat. You can sauté the vegetable plain or with shallots and fresh herbs (my favorite is tarragon).

In the classic French version, the zucchini is first salted for 30 minutes to rid the vegetable of excess water, then drained and squeezed dry before cooking. I don't have time for this during the week, so I sauté the vegetable at high heat and for 2 minutes only.

1 pound zucchini or yellow squash
    (about 3 medium-size)
2 tablespoons fresh herb leaves,
    such as tarragon, parsley, or dill
    (optional)
1 shallot or 2 scallions (green
    onions; optional)
2 tablespoons vegetable oil or
    butter
Salt and freshly ground black
    pepper

SECOND TIME AROUND

ZUCCHINI SAUTE: If you're going to serve the zucchini later, drain it and reheat it uncovered for 1 minute in a microwave oven. Or sauté it again until hot, about 1 minute.

1. Rinse the zucchini, trim the ends, and grate with the shredding disk of a food processor. Mince the herb and shallot, if using (trim and thinly slice the scallions).

2. Heat the oil in a large skillet over high heat. Add the shallot, if using, and sauté for 1 minute. Add the grated zucchini and sauté, stirring constantly, for 2 minutes. Add the herb and scallions, if using, and sauté for 15 seconds. Season to taste with salt and pepper.

3. With a slotted spoon, remove the zucchini to a serving dish or plates and serve immediately.

SALADS

MONDAY-TO-FRIDAY NO-FUSS QUICK FIXES

Many, many years ago, the term "salad" referred to the edible parts of various herbs or plants that were dressed only with salt. More recently the word salad has come to mean a mix of greens or an assembly of more robust ingredients, cooked or raw, coated with a dressing of some sort and usually served chilled or at room temperature.

Monday-to-Friday salads are mostly main-course mixes that include the standard dinner trio — protein (either meat, cheese, or legume), maybe a starch, and at least one vegetable. A few other salads in this chapter are light compositions of greens or raw vegetables, just ample enough to round out a hearty soup, a light stew, or a hefty sandwich. Salads, too, are my way of using leftover lean meat, poultry, or fish that would otherwise dry out with reheating.

A welcome bonus in these salads is that they require little clean-up.

Basically everything is made, assembled, and served in one bowl. I find that glass or ceramic bowls fit the bill best; you just need to choose one that is large enough to mix the ingredients together and attractive enough to bring to the dinner table. Simply mix your dressing first in the bottom of the bowl, then cut whatever ingredients you're using right over the dressing, toss, and serve.

Salads also come to mind whenever I need to make supper on a night I know that my daughter, husband, and I will be eating dinner at three different times. These meals can be assembled hours before eating and keep wonderfully well covered in the refrigerator up to a couple of days. They even last long enough so that on especially hurried weeks you can stretch one salad into two meals. They are also the solution to what to bring to the potluck supper or company softball game. And, by the way, remains of salad suppers can be further recycled into sandwich stuffers for bag lunches.

You'll find that salads are great not only on sweltering summer nights but also any night of the year when you're in need of a quick dinner without a lot of work or clean-up afterwards.

MATCHING DRESSINGS TO SALADS

Although there are no formal rules that govern the pairing of dressings with specific salads, I've discovered that light vinegar or citrus dressings are best over light vegetable side salads or whenever I'm counting calories. Thicker, richer dressings—those made with tofu, mayonnaise, or yogurt—are wonderful in sturdier salads that need something to bind the heftier ingredients together.

SMOKED MUSSEL, PEA, AND COUSCOUS SALAD

MAKES 4 SERVINGS
TIME: 30 MINUTES

The sweetness of the peas provides delightful contrast to the smokiness of the mussels. If you think you might be hungry after this meal, precede it with Bean Minestrone or Chunky Peasant Vegetable Soup, or follow it with a rich dessert like Apple-Nut Layered Pound Cake (see Index for page numbers).

1½ cups couscous
1½ cups water
1 package (10 ounces) frozen
    petite peas, thawed
2 or 3 cans (3 ounces each) smoked
    mussels, clams, or oysters
    packed in olive oil
3 to 4 tablespoons lemon juice
Salt and freshly ground black pepper

1. Soak the couscous in the water in a serving bowl for 30 minutes. Rake the couscous with your fingers to break up any clumps.

2. Add the peas, smoked mussels with their oil, and the lemon juice to the couscous and toss to combine. Season to taste with salt and pepper. Serve at room temperature or chilled.

SMOKED SEAFOOD SALAD

MAKES 4 SERVINGS
TIME: 10 TO 15 MINUTES

This salad is a veritable contrast in textures, colors, and tastes. Because it is slightly on the skimpy side, it probably won't be enough for dinner. Precede it with a hearty bean or vegetable soup and you'll have plenty to eat.

1 bunch watercress
1 bunch parsley, preferably Italian
    (flat leaf)
1 can (8 ounces) sliced bamboo shoots
1 can (8 ounces) water chestnuts
2 cans (3½ ounces each) smoked
    mussels, clams, or oysters
    packed in olive oil
1 to 2 tablespoons lemon juice,
    preferably fresh

1. Rinse the watercress and parsley, and slice the stems from each bunch. Put the watercress in a salad bowl. Mince the parsley (you should have about ¼ cup packed); add it to the salad bowl.

2. Drain the bamboo shoots and the water chestnuts. Thinly slice the water chestnuts and add them along with the bamboo shoots to the salad bowl. Open the cans of mussels and add them, as is, to the salad bowl; the oil they are packed in will be sufficient to dress the salad. Toss the ingredients together and refrigerate covered until serving time.

3. Right before serving, add the lemon juice and toss again. The lemon juice should be added at the last moment to prevent the greens from turning a dark olive green.

SCALLOPS WITH FUSILLI

MAKES 4 SERVINGS
TIME: 20 TO 25 MINUTES

The sharp edge of the lime juice makes for a lovely contrast to the smooth richness of both the scallops and pasta. You can pick up speed and save on cleanup if you cook the scallops along with the pasta. If you use shrimp instead, buy them already peeled and deveined.

Salt
1 pound fusilli or penne
1 pound sea scallops, peeled and deveined shrimp, or crabmeat
1 large bunch parsley
⅓ cup lime juice
⅓ cup olive oil
1 clove garlic
Freshly ground black pepper
2 cups cut raw vegetables, such as peppers, tomatoes, carrots, or fennel (optional)

1. Bring a large pot of salted water to a boil in a pot. Add the pasta and boil 7 minutes.

2. Meanwhile remove the tough, rubbery appendage from the side of each sea scallop. (Or pick over and remove any cartilage from the crab.) Add the shellfish to the pasta and continue to simmer until the pasta and the fish are cooked through, about 3 minutes.

3. Meanwhile rinse and stem the parsley. Process the parsley leaves, lime juice, oil, and peeled garlic in a food processor or blender until smooth. Season to taste

HOW MUCH DRESSING IS ENOUGH?

Most of my salad mixes are gently enrobed with just enough dressing to moisten them, give them flavor, and pull them together. However, I realize this is my particular quirky nature; there are people who like juicier, tangier salads with dressing to spare into which they can dunk their bread. Those hearty souls should feel free to double the amount of dressing I recommend.

with salt and pepper.

4. Drain the pasta and scallops well. Place them in a large serving bowl and toss with the dressing. Adjust the seasoning. Serve the salad at room temperature or chilled. If you wish, mix the raw vegetables into the salad before serving.

SPICY CABBAGE SALAD WITH MACKEREL

MAKES 4 SERVINGS
TIME: 15 TO 20 MINUTES

High in protein and loaded with taste as well as vitamins, this assembled dinner is quick to prepare and makes good use of a leftover half head of cabbage. Make it on an evening when you've not eaten anything substantial during the day and your blood sugar level is telling you that you need some protein — fast. If other members of your family plan to eat later, this dish keeps wonderfully in the refrigerator.

You can substitute two 7-ounce cans tuna or salmon, drained, for the mackerel, if you wish.

¼ cup mayonnaise or plain nonfat yogurt
2 tablespoons rice or tarragon vinegar
⅛ teaspoon cayenne pepper
½ teaspoon sugar
½ small head green cabbage
1 green bell pepper
2 scallions (green onions)
¼ cup fresh dill or parsley leaves
1 can (15 ounces) mackerel packed in water
Salt and freshly ground black pepper
Salad greens or sliced tomatoes for serving (optional)

1. Whisk the mayonnaise, vinegar, cayenne, and sugar together in a serving bowl.

2. Core the cabbage, finely shred, and add it to the bowl. Core, seed, and chop the green pepper; trim and slice the scallions; mince the fresh herb. Add these to the bowl as well and toss to combine.

3. Drain the mackerel, break it into pieces, and blend it into the salad. Season to taste with salt and pepper. Serve immediately or cover and refrigerate until later. If you wish, serve it over salad greens or sliced tomatoes.

VARIATIONS

Here are some other goodies I might toss in

the bowl, depending upon my mood and what I have on hand:

- 1 avocado, pitted, peeled, and chopped
- 1 McIntosh apple, cored and chopped (with the peel)
- ½ cup chopped walnuts
- 1 cup leftover steamed vegetable, such as green beans or snow peas
- 1 cup leftover grains, such as kasha, couscous, or rice.

MY SALAD NICOISE

MAKES 4 SERVINGS
TIME: 40 TO 45 MINUTES

For lots of reasons, this is a most sensible Monday-to-Friday meal: It's substantial, delicious, and uncomplicated to make, and, because the salad is assembled, dressed, and served in one bowl, clean-up is kept to a minimum. This is also the perfect solution for nights when you're not sure when you'll be eating, for the salad can stand at room temperature for several hours before serving.

This classic combination of tuna, potatoes, and green beans hardly needs

improvement, but the addition of red peppers and chives does add a pretty touch.

1 pound new red potatoes
½ cup Basic Vinaigrette (see page 308) or Yogurt-Parsley Dressing (see page 310)
2 red bell peppers
2 or 3 ripe tomatoes
¼ cup pitted black olives, preferably imported
2 scallions (green onions) or 1 small bunch fresh chives
2 cans (7 ounces each) tuna or 1 can (15 ounces) mackerel packed in water
1 package (10 ounces) frozen French-cut green beans, thawed
1 tablespoon capers
Salt and freshly ground black pepper
8 to 10 salad greens, such as romaine or Boston lettuce (optional)

1. Lightly scrub the potatoes. Boil them in water to cover until tender, 17 to 20 minutes. Drain and pat them dry.

2. While the potatoes are cooking, prepare the vinaigrette in a serving bowl.

3. Core, seed, and dice the peppers and add them to the bowl. Quarter the tomatoes and remove the seeds with a spoon;

SECOND TIME AROUND

MY SALAD NICOISE: Leftovers look wilted but still taste excellent, so I camouflage them in a pita sandwich.

SALAD SANDWICH STUFFERS

I've said earlier on that leftover dressed salads are good as sandwich stuffers. In addition to pita pockets lots of other types of bread are delicious carriers. Pumpernickel and rye breads are terrific with bean, grain, meat, and fish salads. Whole wheat, multigrain, and oat breads are wonderful with vegetable and fish salads, and crusty French, Italian, or sour doughs go with absolutely every salad imaginable.

dice the tomato flesh and add it to the bowl. Mince the olives, trim and thinly slice the scallions or mince the chives, and add these to the bowl. Drain the tuna and pat dry the green beans. Add them along with the capers to the tuna.

4. When the potatoes are cool enough to handle, cut them into halves or quarters, depending upon their size, and add them to the bowl.

5. Toss the ingredients well and season to taste with salt and pepper. Cover the salad until serving time. If you wish, rinse and dry some greens and arrange them on dinner plates. Spoon the salad attractively onto the greens.

WHITE BEAN AND TUNA SALAD

MAKES 4 TO 6 SERVINGS
TIME: 10 MINUTES

This is a lovely, light summer dinner that is as nourishing to eat as it is speedy to make.

1/4 cup prepared pesto or 1/4 cup olive oil plus 1/2 cup fresh basil leaves
2 cans (16 ounces each) white cannellini beans or chick-peas
3 cans (7 ounces each) tuna packed in water
1/4 cup lemon juice
4 ripe tomatoes
Salt and freshly ground black pepper
1 bunch watercress

1. If you don't have prepared pesto on hand, first mix the olive oil with the basil in a blender or food processor. Drain and rinse the beans. Drain the tuna.

2. Combine the lemon juice with the pesto in a mixing bowl, then add the beans and tuna.

3. Quarter the tomatoes, spoon out the seeds, and finely chop the flesh. Add the tomatoes to the bowl. Toss the ingredients together and season to taste with salt and pepper.

4. Rinse the watercress. Chop the watercress leaves into the salad or serve the salad over sprigs of watercress.

VARIATIONS

My friend Dana Jacobi, food writer, consultant, and connoisseur, suggested a delicious combination of white beans with smoked tuna fish. With the few changes outlined below, the above salad accommodates the smoked fish rather nicely.

Omit the pesto. Finely mince 1 shallot, 2 scallions (green onions), or a bunch of fresh chives. Also mince ½ cup fresh parsley leaves. Dice 1 pound smoked tuna.

Combine ¼ cup olive oil and ¼ cup lemon juice and add the minced shallot, scallions or chives, and parsley. Add the drained beans, smoked tuna, and tomatoes. Toss well, season, and serve over watercress.

LIGHT TUNA OR SALMON SALAD

MAKES 1 SERVING
TIME: 10 MINUTES

Commercial tuna salads are often peculiar concoctions held together with gobs of mayonnaise. They have a pasty texture relieved every now and then with odd bits of celery.

This version is spritely, crisp, and delicious and makes a perfect sandwich to serve as a meal in summer months, along with a green or vegetable salad.

Proportions are for one serving, but you can double or quadruple the quantities as needed.

> *1 cucumber, 1 carrot, or ¼ bulb*
> *fresh fennel*
> *½ cup fresh parsley, basil, or dill*
> *leaves, or 1 scallion (green*
> *onion)*
> *1 can (7 ounces) tuna or salmon*
> *packed in water*
> *1 tablespoon capers*
> *1 tablespoon olive oil*
> *2 tablespoons lemon or lime juice*
> *Salt and freshly ground black*
> *pepper*

1. Peel the cucumber, cut lengthwise in half, and scoop out the seeds with a spoon. Cut the cucumber into small dice. (Or peel and cut the carrot or fennel into small dice.) Mince the fresh herb or trim and thinly slice the scallion. Drain the tuna or salmon.

2. Combine all the ingredients in a small bowl and season to taste with salt and pepper.

SALMON, CORN, AND CHILI SALAD

MAKES 4 SERVINGS
TIME: 10 MINUTES WORK
UP TO 1½ HOURS NO-WORK CHILLING TIME

All you need to turn this into a meal is to stuff it into pita bread or add diced leftover potatoes, pasta, or rehydrated grains, like couscous or bulgur wheat.

Be sure to mix the salmon in last or you'll end up with a flaked fish paste.

> 8 sun-dried tomatoes packed in olive oil
> 6 tablespoons lemon juice
> 2 cans (4 ounces each) chopped green chilies
> 2 packages (10 ounces each) frozen corn kernels, thawed
> 4 cans (6½ ounces each) boneless, skinless pink salmon packed in water
> Salt and freshly ground black pepper

1. Mince the sun-dried tomatoes and place them in a serving bowl. Add the lemon juice, chilies, and corn and mix well.

2. Drain the salmon and mix it gently into the corn, trying to leave the salmon in somewhat large chunks. Season to taste with salt and pepper.

FRESH TUNA AND RED PEPPER SALAD

MAKES 4 SERVINGS
TIME: 15 TO 20 MINUTES WORK
1 TO 1½ HOURS NO-WORK CHILLING TIME

Although I've usually got no quarrel with tuna from the can, the fresh baked tuna in this salad transforms the commonplace into something grand. The salad tastes so special, it is worthy to serve on weekends for company. This is super served with room-temperature rice dressed with a Basic Vinaigrette (see Index).

If you don't like your fresh tuna rare, don't bother using the fresh fish.

FOR THE SALAD:
1 pound fresh tuna steaks, about
    ½ inch thick
2 red bell peppers

FOR THE DRESSING:
2 tablespoons vegetable or Oriental
    sesame oil
2 tablespoons rice vinegar
1 bunch fresh coriander or
    parsley
Salt
¼ to ½ teaspoon dried red
    pepper flakes

1. Preheat the oven to 375°F for 10 minutes.

2. Place the tuna in a baking dish and bake for 5 to 7 minutes for fish that is rosy red in the center; 10 to 12 minutes for fish that is just cooked through. Remove from the oven and let cool while you make the rest of the salad.

3. Core, seed, and coarsely chop the red peppers.

4. With a fork mix the oil and vinegar in a serving bowl. Rinse, stem, and mince the coriander.

5. Cut the cooked tuna into 1-inch chunks. Toss the bell peppers, coriander, and tuna with the dressing. Season to taste with salt and red pepper flakes. You can serve the salad immediately or refrigerate covered up to 1½ hours.

FRESH SALMON, RICE, AND PEPPER SALAD

MAKES 4 SERVINGS
TIME: 25 MINUTES

The texture and taste of freshly poached salmon is rich and luxurious, totally unlike the canned variety. So even though this salad takes the effort of poaching the salmon and cooking the rice first, the result is really worth it.

If you're making this for only two people, be sure to halve the recipe. Leftover refrigerated rice is hard and unpleasant tasting.

4 fresh salmon or halibut steaks,
    about 1½ pounds
1 cup long-grain white rice
2 cups water
Salt
4 red bell peppers
1 small bunch dill
4 tablespoons mayonnaise
4 tablespoons tarragon or white
    wine vinegar
Freshly ground black pepper

1. Set the salmon steaks in a skillet

SUBSTITUTE FRESH
FISH

Although many of my fish salads call for canned tuna, salmon, mackerel, and sardines, don't forget to refer to these concoctions when you have leftover baked fresh fish. It is always better to use this extra fish in a chilled salad because reheating tends to dry it out. Also, if you dress the fish when it has just been cooked, it will have time to absorb the flavors of the dressing and will taste better the following night.

SECOND TIME AROUND

FUSILLI SALAD: These salad leftovers can be stretched out with cubed fresh mozzarella cheese and romaine lettuce, hand torn into uneven pieces. (Greens like romaine should be torn, not cut with a knife. Cutting gives them a metallic taste and their edges will turn brownish.)

large enough to accommodate them in a single layer and just cover them with water. Slowly bring the water to a simmer over medium heat, cover the skillet, and cook gently until the fish is cooked through, about 10 minutes. Remove the steaks from the skillet and let them cool for a bit on a plate.

2. Meanwhile combine the rice, the water, and salt to taste in a medium-size saucepan. Bring to a boil, then reduce the heat and simmer until the rice is tender, about 18 minutes. Drain it immediately.

3. While the salmon and rice are cooking, core and seed the peppers. Cut 2 of them into small dice. Remove the dill leaves from the stems.

4. Put the other 2 peppers in a blender or food processor, add the dill, mayonnaise, and vinegar, and process until smooth. Season to taste with salt and pepper and scrape the dressing into a salad bowl.

5. Add the rice and dried peppers to the dressing and toss to combine. Remove the skin from the salmon steaks and break them in half to remove the inner bones. Set the salmon pieces over the rice and peppers and serve at room temperature.

FUSILLI, FENNEL, AND HAM SALAD

MAKES 4 SERVINGS
TIME: 25 TO 30 MINUTES

At last, a terrific pasta salad with tomatoes. This can be made when you come home and eaten any time after that—warm, at room temperature, or chilled.

Salt
½ pound fusilli, penne, or elbow macaroni
2 small or 1 large bulb fennel or 4 ribs celery
½ bunch scallions (green onions)
1 large bunch Italian (flat-leaf) parsley (2 cups loosely packed leaves)
1 bunch fresh dill (1 cup loosely packed leaves)
1 tablespoon capers
¼ cup olive oil
3 to 4 tablespoons balsamic vinegar
¾ pound smoked, baked, or boiled ham, preferably 95% or more fat free
Freshly ground black pepper

1. Bring a large pot of salted water to a boil over high heat. Add the pasta and boil until just tender, 10 to 12 minutes.

2. Meanwhile, cut the feathery tops from the fennel and discard; core and cut the bulb into small dice or chop the celery. Place the fennel in a large serving bowl.

3. Trim and thinly slice the scallions and add them to the bowl. Rinse the parsley and dill, stem, and mince the leaves. Add the scallions and herbs to the bowl along with the capers, olive oil, and vinegar.

4. When the pasta is tender, drain it well and add it to the bowl. Toss all the ingredients together thoroughly.

5. Dice the ham and add it to the salad. Season the salad to taste with salt and pepper and mix the ingredients once more.

RICE, HAM, AND DATE SALAD

MAKES 4 SERVINGS
TIME: 20 TO 25 MINUTES

This sweet summer supper of ham, rice, oranges, and dates evokes the exotic flavors of Morocco.

1 cup long-grain white rice
2 cups water
Salt
1 recipe Citrus Dressing (see page 310)
¼ teaspoon ground cinnamon
1 pound smoked or boiled ham, preferably 95% or more fat free
2 navel oranges
8 pitted dates
1 bunch watercress
Freshly ground black pepper

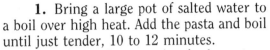

1. Combine the rice, the water, and salt to taste in a medium-size saucepan. Bring the liquid to a boil over medium heat, then reduce the heat and simmer partially covered until the rice is tender, about 18 minutes.

2. Meanwhile make the citrus dressing in a serving bowl. Mix the cinnamon into the dressing. Cut the ham into ½-inch pieces and add them to the bowl. Peel the oranges. Cut the oranges and dates into ½-inch pieces and add them to the bowl. Rinse the watercress, stem, and set aside.

3. Drain the rice well, add it to the bowl, and toss with the dressing and other ingredients. Season to taste with salt and pepper.

4. Serve this salad warm or at room temperature over the watercress leaves.

SWEET AND SAVORY TOUCHES

The Rice, Ham, and Date Salad is a wonderful example for me to use to show you how to compose a dish. For this dish, I started out with a neutral tasting rice because it is so adaptable to other flavors. The first dose of taste is the ham—a smoky and assertive flavor. In this salad, I decided to add something sweet, the dates, to contrast with the ham. However, after putting those flavors together I still needed to balance the whole to make sure the sweetness of the dates did not overwhelm the salad. So, I introduced an acidic taste by adding the Citrus Dressing, which works as well with dates as it does with ham.

*S*oft tasting grains like
couscous, bulgur, and
rice form the building
blocks of my grain salads
even though the ones with
stronger flavors, like millet
and kasha, work well too.
When you have some left-
overs of these robust
grains, be sure to pair
them with other equally
assertive ingredients like
smoked ham or fish, and
coat them with lively
dressings. The Apple-Dill
Dressing is terrific with
kasha and smoked chicken
chunks whereas the Spicy
Tart Pepper Dressing is
fabulous with millet. Both
dressings appear at the end
of this chapter.

BULGUR, HAM, AND RED PEPPER MELANGE

MAKES 4 SERVINGS
TIME: 30 MINUTES

In a colorful and cozy-tasting salad, you have all that's needed for an easy, nutritious meal.

2 cups bulgur wheat or 2 boxes (5¼
　ounces each) Near East tabouleh
　(reserve the seasoning packet for
　another use)
2 cups hot water
1½ teaspoons dried tarragon
2 teaspoons Dijon mustard
3 tablespoons vegetable oil
¼ cup white wine, tarragon, or rice
　vinegar
Salt and freshly ground black pepper
1 pound smoked, boiled, or baked
　ham, preferably 95% or more
　fat free
4 bell peppers, preferably red

1. Soak the bulgur wheat in the water in a serving bowl, for 30 minutes. After 30 minutes drain the wheat in a sieve and squeeze out any excess water from the grains with your hands. Dry the serving bowl and return the bulgur to it.

2. Add the tarragon, mustard, oil, and vinegar to the bulgur and toss to combine. Season to taste with salt and pepper.

3. Cut the ham into small pieces and add it to the bowl. Core, seed, and dice the peppers and add them as well. Combine all the ingredients well and adjust the seasoning.

SUMMER BORSCHT SALAD

MAKES 2 TO 4 SERVINGS
TIME: 15 TO 20 MINUTES WORK
1½ HOURS NO-WORK CHILLING TIME

This dish is named for the chilled Russian soup of beets and sour cream.

FOR THE DRESSING:
1 cup plain nonfat yogurt
1 tablespoon prepared horseradish
Salt and freshly ground black pepper

FOR THE SALAD:
1 jar (16 ounces) pickled sliced beets
2 bunches watercress
¾ to 1 pound boiled, smoked, or
　baked ham, preferably 95% or
　more fat free

1. Whisk the yogurt and horseradish together in a serving bowl. Season to taste with salt and pepper.

2. Drain the beets, add them to the dressing, and toss to coat.

3. Holding the bunches of watercress by the stem ends, rinse them under cold running water, shake, and then pat dry with towels. Slice off the stems with a sharp knife and add the watercress leaves to the bowl.

4. Cut the ham into ½-inch pieces and add them to the bowl. Toss the ingredients together. You can serve the salad immediately or refrigerate up to 1½ hours.

A MODERN CHEF'S SALAD

MAKES 4 SERVINGS
TIME: 20 TO 25 MINUTES WORK
1 TO 1½ HOURS NO-WORK CHILLING TIME

Instead of the traditional salami and Swiss cheese one expects in a chef's salad, you'll enjoy the modern combination of lean smoked ham and fresh mozzarella dressed with a sun-dried tomato vinaigrette.

FOR THE DRESSING:
4 sun-dried tomatoes packed in oil
8 fresh basil leaves
2 scallions (green onions)
3 to 4 tablespoons balsamic vinegar
2 tablespoons olive oil (optional)
Salt and freshly ground black pepper

FOR THE SALAD:
8 romaine lettuce leaves
4 to 6 ounces boiled ham,
*   preferably 95% or more*
*   fat free*
4 to 6 ounces smoked turkey breast
4 ounces fresh mozzarella (fior di
*   latte) packed in water*
1 cucumber

1. Chop the sun-dried tomatoes, mince the basil, and trim and slice the scallions. Combine these ingredients with the remaining ingredients for the dressing in a serving bowl. Season to taste with salt and pepper.

2. Rinse the romaine leaves and pat dry. Coarsely tear them and add to the salad bowl. Cut the ham and turkey into ½-inch cubes or into thin strips and add them to the bowl. Drain the mozzarella and pat dry, then cut into ½-inch cubes. Peel, seed, and chop the cucumber.

3. Toss all the ingredients together. Adjust the seasoning. Serve immediately or refrigerate 1½ hours at most.

MONDAY-TO-FRIDAY
M · E · N · U

See a Minimalist Summer Menu in The Monday-to-Friday Menu Sampler in the Appendix for a week long meal plan using A Modern Chef's Salad and other salads in this chapter.

SECOND TIME AROUND

SALAD OF SMOKED TUR-KEY: Freshen up leftovers with sliced water chestnuts, chopped fresh watercress leaves, diced smoked ham (which will go with chicken or turkey but not smoked tuna); make additional dressing if needed.

SALAD OF SMOKED TURKEY AND BULGUR DRESSED JAPANESE STYLE

MAKES 4 SERVINGS
TIME: 30 TO 35 MINUTES

This salad of intriguing textures and tastes makes for a plentiful cold supper.

1 cup bulgur wheat or Near East tabouleh (reserve the seasoning packet for another use)
1 cup hot water
6 tablespoons rice vinegar
3 tablespoons soy sauce
1 tablespoon prepared white horseradish
1 big bunch fresh coriander or parsley
4 scallions (green onions)
4 cucumbers
Salt and freshly ground black pepper
¾ pound smoked turkey or chicken breast or smoked tuna

1. Combine the bulgur with the hot water in a mixing bowl and let sit until the bulgur has softened and absorbed the water, 30 minutes at least.

2. Meanwhile combine the vinegar, soy sauce, and horseradish in a serving bowl.

3. Rinse, stem, and chop the coriander; trim and slice the scallions; peel, seed, and chop the cucumbers. Add all these ingredients to the serving bowl. Mix well and season to taste with salt and pepper.

4. Cut the turkey into ½-inch cubes and add it to the bowl.

5. Drain the bulgur in a sieve and squeeze out the excess water by pressing down on the grain with your hand. Add the bulgur to the other ingredients and toss well. Serve immediately or refrigerate covered until serving time. This will keep for a couple of days.

BULGUR SALAD WITH PEANUTS

MAKES 4 SERVINGS
TIME: 30 TO 35 MINUTES

Peanuts give this tangy salad an Indonesian cachet. If, because of health concerns, you must omit the nuts, then do so, even though the salad will lose some of its appeal. It keeps wonderfully well covered in the refrigerator for 2 to 3 days.

> 1 cup bulgur wheat or 1 box
> (5¼ ounces) Near East tabouleh
> (reserve the seasoning packet for
> another use)
> 1 cup hot water
> 1 bell pepper, preferably red
> ¼ cup lemon or lime juice
> ⅓ cup unsalted peanuts
> ⅓ cup (tightly packed) fresh
> coriander or parsley leaves
> ¼ cup vegetable oil
> Salt and freshly ground black pepper
> 3 firm bean curd cakes, about 4
> ounces each
> 4 ripe tomatoes, quartered, or 2
> large bell peppers, preferably
> red, sliced (optional)

1. Combine the bulgur wheat with the hot water in a large serving bowl and let sit until the bulgur has softened and absorbed the water, 30 minutes at least. Drain the bulgur in a sieve and squeeze out any excess water by pressing down on the grain with your hand.

2. Meanwhile core, seed, and cut the bell pepper into large pieces. In a food processor or blender, process the pepper, lemon juice, peanuts, coriander, and oil until smooth; season to taste with salt and pepper. Add the dressing to the bulgur.

3. Cut the bean curd into ½-inch cubes and add them to the bulgur. Toss all the ingredients together well. Serve the salad at room temperature with tomato quarters or slices of raw pepper if you like.

BARLEY, BEAN, AND CORN SALAD

MAKES 4 SERVINGS
TIME: 30 TO 35 MINUTES

This colorful and fresh-tasting mix is perfect for vegetarians as well as for diners mindful of their diets.

> 1 cup pearl barley
> 3 cups water
> ¼ cup vegetable oil
> ¼ cup balsamic vinegar
> 1 cup fresh parsley leaves
> Salt and freshly ground black
> pepper
> 1 can (16 or 19 ounces) red kidney
> beans
> 1 package (10 ounces) frozen corn
> kernels, thawed

SECOND TIME AROUND

BARLEY, BEAN, AND CORN SALAD: Leftovers can be amplified with diced roasted pork, lamb, and beef. Add romaine lettuce torn into medium-size pieces and make a mayonnaise dressing with mustard to really change its character.

SALAD IN WINTER

Don't forget that salads are a terrific main course dish—even in winter. Any season of the year they are quick and easy. Even if you are used to having certain types of ingredients hot, serving them chilled or at room temperature in no way takes away from their nutritional value nor from how good they taste.

1. Place the barley in a medium-size saucepan and add the water. Bring the liquid to a boil over medium heat, then simmer, partially covered, until tender, about 30 minutes.

2. Meanwhile prepare the dressing in a bowl: Combine the oil and vinegar. Mince the parsley and add it to the dressing. Season to taste with salt and pepper.

3. Drain the kidney beans and add them to the bowl along with the corn.

4. When the barley is done, drain it in a sieve and add it to the bowl. Toss all the ingredients together and adjust the seasoning. Serve this salad warm or at room temperature.

YELLOW AND ORANGE SALAD

MAKES 4 SERVINGS
TIME: 35 MINUTES

The yellow in the title of this recipe refers to the couscous; the orange, the navel oranges and grated carrots.

Whatever the title, the taste is terrific, fresh and unexpected. To supplement this salad and round out the meal, make a second salad of either beans, sliced smoked turkey, or salmon, dressed with a Basic Vinaigrette (see page 308).

FOR THE SALAD:
1 box (10 ounces) or
* 1¾ cups couscous*
2 cups water
4 navel oranges
6 carrots

FOR THE DRESSING:
1 cup fresh parsley or mint leaves
¼ cup vegetable oil
¼ cup lime juice
¼ teaspoon ground cardamom
Salt and freshly ground black
* pepper*

1. In a large bowl soak the couscous in the water for 30 minutes while you prepare the rest of the ingredients.

2. Peel the oranges, making sure you remove all the white pith, cut the sections into ½-inch pieces and add them to the dressing. Grate the carrots with the shredding disk in a food processor and add them to the bowl.

3. Mince the parsley or mint. Whisk all the ingredients for the salad dressing together in a serving bowl and season to taste with salt and pepper.

4. Drain the couscous of any water it

has not absorbed and add it to the bowl. Mix the ingredients thoroughly and adjust the seasoning.

VARIATION

Instead of the couscous, you can make this salad with 2 cups cooked pasta or grains, like millet, quinoa, and, as always, rice.

A MANHATTAN SALAD: MOZZARELLA, TOMATOES, AND RICE

MAKES 4 SERVINGS
TIME: 20 TO 25 MINUTES

In New York City, in the 80s, salads of sliced tomatoes and fresh mozzarella were as ubiquitous as Big Macs. But in spite of how familiar this combination is, I continue to love it. By adding rice to this well-loved mix, I turned a favorite salad

into a favorite summer meal.

To complete the meal and perk up the look, you can add chopped arugula or watercress.

1 cup long-grain white rice,
    preferably Texmati
1¾ cups water
8 to 12 ounces (depending upon
    your appetite and mood) fresh
    mozzarella cheese (packed in
    water, not just wrapped in
    plastic)
4 small or 2 large tomatoes
¾ cup fresh basil leaves
1 bunch arugula or watercress
    (optional)
¼ cup vinegar, such as balsamic or
    other fruity wine vinegar
6 tablespoons olive oil
Salt and freshly ground black
    pepper

1. Place the rice and water (2 cups if you are using ordinary long-grain white rice) in a medium-size saucepan. Bring the water to a boil, over medium heat, then reduce the heat and simmer covered until the rice is tender, about 18 minutes.

2. While the rice is cooking, cut the mozzarella into ½-inch cubes. Quarter the tomatoes and scoop out the seeds. Cut the pulp into small dice. Rinse and mince the

FLAVORED VINEGARS

Flavored vinegars can change hum-drum salads into fare you pay attention to. Here is how you can whip up a batch.

Transfer to a jar 1 cup of an excellent quality vinegar like red wine, white wine, tarragon, or rice. Flavor red wine vinegar with a couple of cloves of garlic and a tablespoon of crushed dried thyme, or caraway, anise, and fennel seeds. I like to beef up tarragon vinegar with chopped stems or tired looking leaves of fresh mint, parsley, and dill. White wine vinegar takes to all of the above and rice vinegar is lovely flavored by a handful of star anise.

Be sure to strain the vinegar when you pour it so that you don't get bits of seed or herbs in your dressing. Keep vinegar, covered, in the refrigerator.

basil. Rinse and stem the arugula, if using. In a serving bowl, whisk together the vinegar, olive oil, and basil.

3. When the rice is done, drain it well in a sieve, if necessary, then add it to the mixing bowl along with cheese, tomatoes, and arugula. Toss all the ingredients together and season to taste with salt and pepper. Serve this salad warm or at room temperature.

PARSLIED RICE AND PEPPER SALAD

MAKES 4 TO 6 SERVINGS
TIME: 20 TO 25 MINUTES

*P*erk up your tired taste buds with this salad on a warm spring or summer evening. Serve it as a side dish to sautéed chicken breasts or veal scaloppine, or turn it into a complete meal by blending in diced cooked or smoked poultry, fish, or ham. Allow a half cup per person.

It's best to eat this salad warm or at room temperature, instead of chilled, because rice hardens when refrigerated.

2 cups long-grain white rice
4 cups water
Salt
1/4 cup vinegar, such as balsamic or
    other fruity wine vinegar
2 tablespoons olive oil
Freshly ground black pepper
2 bell peppers, preferably red or
    green
2 scallions (green onions)
1/2 cup fresh parsley leaves

1. Place the rice, water, and some salt in a medium-size saucepan and bring the liquid to a boil over medium heat. Cover the pan, reduce the heat, and simmer, partially covered, until the rice is tender, about 18 minutes.

2. Meanwhile combine the vinegar and oil in a serving bowl and season to taste with salt and pepper.

3. Core, seed, and finely dice the peppers. Trim and thinly slice the scallions. Mince the parsley. Add these to the bowl.

4. When the rice is tender, drain it well in a sieve and add it to the bowl. Mix the ingredients thoroughly and adjust the seasoning.

QUINOA, CUCUMBER, AND CURRANT SALAD

MAKES 4 SERVINGS
TIME: 20 MINUTES

Quinoa has a unique crunchiness which makes it a pleasing grain to use in salads. The combination of cucumbers and currants is unexpected, fresh, and delicious.

1 cup quinoa
4 cups water
3 tablespoons vegetable oil
3 tablespoons balsamic or sherry
    wine vinegar
2 to 3 drops Tabasco sauce
    (optional)
½ cup currants or raisins
2 cucumbers
Salt and freshly ground black pepper

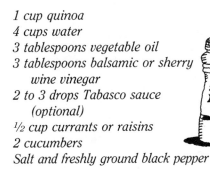

1. Place the quinoa in a sieve and rinse it under running water; drain. This will rid the grain of any saponin residue which would make it taste bitter.

2. Bring the water to a boil in a medium-size saucepan over medium heat. Add the quinoa and simmer uncovered until tender, 10 to 15 minutes.

3. Meanwhile mix the oil, vinegar, and Tabasco if using in a serving bowl. Add the currants. Peel, seed, and cut the cucumbers into small dice; add them to the bowl.

4. When the quinoa is tender, drain it well and add it to the bowl. Toss all the ingredients together while the grain is still warm. Season to taste with salt and pepper and serve at room temperature or chilled.

VARIATION

For a main course, add ½ pound crumbled feta or ricotta salata. The contrast of the tangy cheese and sweet raisins is terrific.

CHICK-PEAS AND BITTER GREENS

MAKES 4 SERVINGS
TIME: 20 MINUTES

If a portion of this salad alone doesn't seem like it will fill you up, serve it alongside room-temperature rice, tabouleh, pasta, or couscous, or with slices of cold roasted pork, chicken, or beef.

MONDAY-TO-FRIDAY M · E · N · U

See the Winter Menu for a Hectic Week in The Monday-to-Friday Menu Sampler in the Appendix for a week long meal plan using the Quinoa, Cucumber, and Currant Salad and other salads in this chapter.

ADDITIONAL DRESSINGS

Although there is a small section at the end of this chapter devoted to different salad dressings, don't forget that there are a number of additional dressings scattered through the Salad chapter. Each one of these is made for a specific salad but would work equally well with a host of other ingredients. The dressing made for the Chick-Peas and Bitter Greens salad, for example, would work just fine with the Bulgur Ham, and Red Pepper Melange or salads made from leftover meats and poultry.

FOR THE DRESSING:
¼ cup vegetable oil
¼ cup lemon juice
2 tablespoons ketchup
1 teaspoon Dijon mustard
½ teaspoon ground cumin
¼ teaspoon cayenne pepper
Salt and freshly ground black
pepper

FOR THE SALAD:
2 cans (16 ounces each) chick-peas
1 pound fresh escarole or romaine lettuce, or 2 bunches watercress
1 medium bell pepper, preferably red or yellow
1 cucumber
6 radishes

1. Whisk all the ingredients for the salad dressing together in a serving bowl. Season to taste with salt and pepper.

2. Rinse and drain the chick-peas under cold running water and shake dry. Add them to the bowl and toss with the dressing. Thoroughly rinse the greens and coarsely chop the leaves. Add the greens to the bowl.

3. Core, seed, and finely dice the pepper. Peel, seed, and chop the cucumber. Slice or chop the radishes. Add these vegetables to the bowl and toss well. You can serve the salad immediately or refrigerate it, covered, up to 1½ hours.

VARIATIONS

■ You can stretch the protein value of the salad by adding 2 cans (6 or 7 ounces each) salmon or tuna, drained; be sure to double the dressing so that you have enough.

■ Red kidney beans can be substituted for the chick-peas; white beans are too soft and black beans muddy the color of other ingredients. This also would be nice with some cooked lentils instead of chick-peas.

ELBOWS AND CHICK-PEAS A LA CHINESE NOODLES

MAKES 4 SERVINGS
TIME: 20 TO 25 MINUTES

A favorite appetizer of mine is Chinese sesame noodles. Inspired by that dish, I came up with this lovely main-course salad by combining the salient Chinese seasonings with pasta, chick-peas, and vegetables.

Salt
2 cups short tubular pasta, such as elbows, tubetti, or penne
2 tablespoons sesame paste
2 tablespoons Oriental sesame oil
¼ cup vegetable or peanut oil
¼ cup peanuts, preferably unsalted
1 clove garlic
1 teaspoon chili paste with soy bean
2 tablespoons soy sauce
3 tablespoons rice vinegar
Freshly ground black pepper
1 can (16 ounces) chick-peas
2 cucumbers or 2 cups cubed cooked vegetable, such as green beans or broccoli

1. Bring a large pot of salted water to a boil. Add the pasta, and cook until just tender, about 10 minutes.

2. Meanwhile combine the sesame paste, sesame oil, vegetable oil, peanuts, peeled garlic, chili paste, soy sauce, and rice vinegar in a blender or food processor. Process for a few minutes until smooth. Season to taste with salt and pepper.

3. Rinse and drain the chick-peas and place them in a serving bowl. Peel, seed, and dice the cucumber; add it to the chick-peas.

4. Drain the pasta thoroughly and add it to the chick-peas along with the sesame dressing. Toss well, adjust the seasoning, and serve at room temperature or chilled.

BLACK BEAN, ORANGE, AND CUCUMBER SALAD

MAKES 4 SERVINGS
TIME: 10 TO 15 MINUTES

Don't ask me what in the world possessed me to first put these three ingredients together, but who cares! The result is a delectable combination of colorful, fabulous textures and tastes. And not only does it taste terrific, you don't even have to cook to bring it together.

The salad also keeps well at room temperature, with nothing in it to spoil or turn sour.

Although this recipe serves four, I have tripled it successfully and can't think of any reason why it wouldn't work multiplied any number of times.

SECOND TIME AROUND

ELBOWS AND CHICK-PEAS: *Leftovers make wonderful sandwich stuffers, especially in pita bread along with sliced tomato.*

¼ cup vegetable oil
2 tablespoons lemon juice
2 cans (16 ounces each) black beans
2 cucumbers
4 navel oranges

1. Whisk the oil and lemon juice together in a serving bowl.

2. Drain the black beans, rinse them well, then drain again. Place them in the bowl.

3. Peel, seed, and dice the cucumbers; add them to the black beans. Peel the oranges, removing all the white pith, then dice the sections and add them to the bowl.

4. Toss the ingredients together (not too roughly; you don't want to burst all the beans and splatter their black hue over those great orange and pale green colors). Cover the salad and refrigerate until serving time.

SECOND TIME AROUND

THREE BEAN SALAD: If you have about a cup of this salad left, purée it with some plain yogurt to a nice, thick consistency. Use the dressing as a dip for strips of raw fresh vegetables, steamed asparagus, or artichokes.

THREE BEAN SALAD WITH RED ONION

MAKES 4 SERVINGS
TIME: 20 MINUTES

By adding grains to a traditional bean salad, you can turn a light salad into a substantial meal. This is great to make on a summer night when you want to go for a run before supper, because you can make it before your jog and keep it refrigerated until dinner time. It will improve as it stands for the beans will absorb more of the flavors in the dressing.

FOR THE SALAD:
¾ cup rice, quinoa, or millet
1½ cups water
Salt and freshly ground black pepper
½ pound fresh green beans or 1
*   package (10 ounces) frozen*
*   French-cut green beans, thawed*
1 small red onion
1 can (16 ounces) chick-peas
1 can (16 ounces) pink or red
*   kidney beans*

FOR THE DRESSING:
2 tablespoons olive oil
2 to 3 tablespoons black olive paste or
*   1 to 2 tablespoons prepared pesto*
¼ cup lemon juice

1. If you're using quinoa, rinse it well under cold running water. Place the grain and 1½ cups water in a small pan. Bring the water to a boil over medium heat, season with salt and pepper, and cook covered until the grain has absorbed the water, 10 to 15 minutes. If there's excess water, drain it off.

2. Meanwhile boil the fresh green beans in 6 cups boiling water just until tender, 3 to 4 minutes, or cook the frozen beans according to package directions. Drain well.

3. Finely chop the red onion. Rinse and drain the chick-peas and kidney beans under cold running water and shake dry.

4. Whisk all the ingredients for the salad dressing in a serving bowl. Add all the prepared ingredients to the dressing and toss well. Adjust the seasoning.

VARIATIONS

■ For more texture add 1 to 2 cups chopped bell peppers, seeded cucumber, zucchini, celery, or fennel.

■ Instead of the black olive paste or pesto in the dressing, you could add ¼ cup minced fresh dill, parsley, or mint leaves.

BREAD SALAD

MAKES 2 SERVINGS
TIME: 30 MINUTES WORK
30 MINUTES NO-WORK MARINATING
TIME

Don't ever throw out that delicious stale sourdough or Italian whole-wheat bread. Use it instead in this tasty bread-salad dinner. In Italy, wondrous salads are made from stale bread, which is rejuvenated in hot water, squeezed dry, and coupled with fresh tomatoes and a lively anchovy dressing. To turn this into a substantial meal, I've added chopped crunchy vegetables and slices of fresh mozzarella.

Don't substitute white cottony bread in this salad, because you need a sharp yeast flavor which, in an honest good loaf, will come through even after the bread gets a soaking.

Those with hearty appetites could supplement the meal with soup first or a dessert last.

Large chunks of stale bread: crusty
*   sourdough, French, or Italian,*
*   about 6 cups*
2 ripe tomatoes
2 to 4 tablespoons olive oil
¼ cup tarragon, rice, or balsamic
*   vinegar*
2 teaspoon capers
2 to 8 canned anchovies
1 sliver fresh garlic (optional)
Salt and freshly ground black pepper
1 bell pepper, preferably red
1 cucumber
4 ounces fresh mozzarella (optional)

SECOND TIME AROUND

BREAD SALAD: Leftover bread salad is good minced and served as a garnish in bowls of bean soup. The starchiness of beans, split peas, and lentils couples well with such tangy accompaniment.

You could also purée a bit of the salad and use it to thicken a vinaigrette. Serve the dressing with vegetable or green salads.

SECOND TIME AROUND

Never throw out dressed salad. I know that the remains get soggy, but it's precisely that tart softness of leftover salad that is so wonderful in sandwiches, especially ones made with slices of smoked ham or roasted chicken or beef in pockets of pita bread.

1. Soak the bread in warm water to cover for about 20 minutes. Core the tomatoes.

2. Meanwhile process the oil, vinegar, capers, anchovies, tomatoes, and garlic in a blender or food processor until smooth. Season to taste with salt and pepper. Pour the dressing into a serving bowl.

3. Squeeze the excess water from the bread with your hands. Break up the bread into the dressing and mix.

4. Core, seed, and chop the bell pepper. Peel, seed, and chop the cucumber. Thinly slice the mozzarella. Add these ingredients to the bowl and combine. Let sit for 30 minutes before serving.

ABOUT MONDAY-TO-FRIDAY GREEN SALADS

I always order a green salad—arugula or spinach, preferably—in a restaurant because I'm happy to pay them to do all the dreary work of cleaning, rinsing, and drying!

At home my green salads are more red and white than green. They contain few green leaves and only those that need little washing and care. Hard-to-clean lettuces like Boston, red leaf, arugula, field lettuce, and spinach are usually out. They take forever to rinse and I never succeed in getting rid of all the sand. Also, these soft lettuces usually wind up slightly soggy unless the leaves are meticulously dried.

(I do have a salad spinner, but it's always more trouble to dig out than it is to towel dry the greens.)

Instead my "green" salads are composed of a few leaves of romaine (about 2 leaves per person), which are hardy and don't catch too much water in the rinsing, and some watercress leaves, which need only a rapid rinse. If available, I'll use hydroponically grown Boston lettuce because to clean it you need only remove the root end of the lettuce. On occasion I might throw in some chopped endive, a few pieces of torn radicchio leaves, shredded head cabbage or Chinese cabbage, or sliced bell pepper.

A time-saving clean-up trick is to make your salad dressing right in the bowl in which you are going to toss your salad.

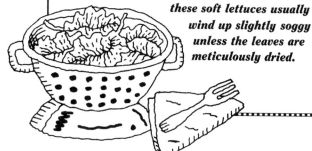

BLUEPRINT FOR A BASIC VEGETABLE SALAD

MAKES 2 MAIN-COURSE OR 4 SIDE-DISH SERVINGS
TIME: 15 TO 20 MINUTES

Make a vegetable salad for dinner when you're too hot to cook, or not very hungry because you've over-eaten at a business lunch, or when you're feeling just plain lazy.

The recipe below is meant to be a working model for you to embroider on or change according to your tastes. By adding some protein to the salad, you can stretch it into a filling and refreshing dinner.

Basically count on 2 cups cut-up vegetables and 2 tablespoons dressing per person.

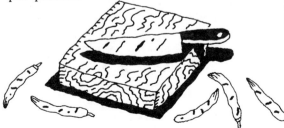

*Double recipe Apple-Dill Dressing
   (see page 309)*
*1 package (10 ounces) frozen
   French-cut green beans, thawed,
   or 2 cups parboiled fresh green
   beans*
2 cucumbers
1 yellow squash
1 zucchini
1 bunch radishes
Salt and freshly ground black pepper

1. Prepare the salad dressing in a salad bowl. Towel dry the thawed green beans and add them to the salad bowl.

2. Peel and halve the cucumbers lengthwise. With a spoon, remove the seeds, then dice the cucumber and add it to the bowl.

3. Rinse the squash and zucchini. Cut each in half lengthwise and scoop out and discard the seeds. Dice the flesh and skin of both squashes and add them to the bowl.

4. Thinly slice the radishes and add them to the bowl. Toss the ingredients together; season to taste with salt and pepper.

VARIATIONS

■ To save on time, you can chop the cucumber, squash, and zucchini without seeding them first.

■ You can add the following vegetables to

SECOND TIME AROUND

BASIC VEGETABLE SALAD: Any remaining vegetables should be finely diced or minced and used as a garnish for hot steaming soups. The contrast of the raw chilled crunch is de-lightful against the warmth of the cooked ingredients.

the salad bowl without having to parboil them first: Bell peppers, zucchini, yellow squash, cucumbers, carrots, celery, fennel, tomatoes, and cabbage. Some people enjoy the flavor of raw mushrooms, but I find them too earthy tasting. Other thawed frozen vegetables that work are petite peas and corn kernels.

■ Vegetables that I don't think taste good raw (even though many a gourmet store will include these in their house salads) are onions, broccoli, cauliflower, and asparagus.

■ Canned or pickled beets work well, too.

■ To turn the salad into a more substantial meal, add, per person, 3 to 4 ounces drained canned tuna, salmon, mackerel, or lean ham, or 2 cups chick-peas or diced tofu. You could also toss in a cup of leftover cooked grain, such as couscous, bulgur, or rice, or accompany the salad with a scoop of cottage cheese.

SECOND TIME AROUND

CABBAGE AND PEPPER SLAW: Small amounts of leftovers are delicious on pumpernickel or rye bread with slices of cold meat.

CABBAGE AND PEPPER SLAW

MAKES 6 SERVINGS
TIME: 10 TO 15 MINUTES

This recipe came into being on a night when I was musing about what type of salad I should bring to a school potluck supper that would take place two nights later. I was making coleslaw at the time when I realized I could triple the recipe and save most of it for the night of the potluck because the longer this salad stands, the better it tastes. This keeps well for about a week even though the color will then look a little drab.

To save some time on the night I was making the salad, I turned our portion into a complete meal by tossing in about ½ cup of tuna per person. Other ingredients that would do as well would be chick-peas, leftover roast beef, or smoked ham.

½ cup mayonnaise, regular or low-fat
2 tablespoons Dijon mustard
⅓ cup cider, white wine, or
*   tarragon vinegar*
½ bunch scallions (green onions)
½ bunch fresh parsley
½ head green cabbage
2 bell peppers, preferably red
Salt and freshly ground black pepper

1. Whisk together the mayonnaise, mustard, and vinegar in a large serving bowl.

2. Trim and thinly slice the scallions. Rinse, stem, and mince the parsley leaves.

Add both to the bowl and mix them into the mayonnaise.

3. Core and thinly shred the cabbage. Add it to the salad bowl. Core, seed, and thinly slice the peppers and add them to the bowl.

4. Thoroughly mix all the ingredients together and season to taste with salt and pepper. Serve immediately or refrigerate covered until later.

SPINACH SALAD WITH ORANGES AND RICOTTA

MAKES 4 SERVINGS
TIME: 20 TO 25 MINUTES

The unusual combination of spinach with silky ricotta, tangy orange, and sharp radish makes for a light and refreshing meal. Serve the salad with a side of whole-grain bread or a bowl of chilled grains like rice, couscous, or bulgur.

1 pound fresh spinach
8 radishes
4 navel oranges
2 tablespoons vegetable oil
1 cup walnuts (optional)
Salt and freshly ground black pepper
2 cups ricotta cheese or 4 cups part-
 skim ricotta or low-fat cottage
 cheese

1. Stem, rinse, and coarsely chop the spinach leaves. Thinly slice the radishes. Peel the oranges, removing all the white pith, and cut the sections into small chunks. Place all these ingredients in a serving bowl and toss with the oil.

2. If you wish, chop the walnuts and toss them in. Season to taste with salt and pepper. Serve the ricotta cheese on the side or fold it into the salad.

CUCUMBER SALAD

MAKES 4 SERVINGS
TIME: 10 MINUTES

In our house, this is a standard Monday-to-Friday salad that I love to make in double or in triple batches because its flavor improves with standing. It goes well with anything you serve, and there's practically no work involved.

> 1 teaspoon sugar
> 1/4 cup rice or tarragon vinegar
> 2 tablespoons vegetable oil
> 1/4 cup fresh herb leaves, such as dill
>   or mint (optional)
> 4 small cucumbers, preferably
>   Kirbys
> Salt and freshly ground black pepper

1. Mix the sugar, vinegar, and oil in a serving bowl. Mince the herb if using and add it to the bowl.

2. Peel and thinly slice the cucumbers and add them to the bowl. Season to taste with salt and pepper and thoroughly mix the ingredients together.

WATERCRESS, WATER CHESTNUT, AND RED PEPPER SALAD

MAKES 4 SERVINGS
TIME: 10 TO 15 MINUTES

This salad is as lovely before main-course soups and pastas as it is served as a side dish alongside White Bean and Tuna Salad or Elbows and Chick-Peas à la Chinese Noodles (see Index for page numbers).

> FOR THE DRESSING:
> 1/4 cup olive or vegetable oil
> 2 tablespoons balsamic or
>   sherry wine vinegar
> 1 teaspoon Dijon mustard
> Salt and freshly ground
>   black pepper

> FOR THE SALAD:
> 2 bunches watercress
> 2 red bell peppers
> 1 can (8 ounces) sliced
>   water chestnuts

1. Whisk all the ingredients for the salad dressing together in a serving bowl. Season to taste with salt and pepper.

2. Holding the watercress bunches by the stem ends, rinse the leaves under cold running water. Shake them and pat dry with towels. With a sharp knife slice off as much of the stems as you can in one fell swoop; add the watercress leaves to the bowl.

3. Core, seed, and finely dice the peppers; add them to the bowl. Drain and rinse the water chestnuts and add them as well.

4. Toss the ingredients together thoroughly. You can serve the salad im-

SECOND TIME AROUND

EITHER WATERCRESS SALAD: Leftovers are good on sour dough, French, or Italian bread with sliced ham or turkey.

mediately or refrigerate covered up to 1½ hours.

Watercress Salad with Ricotta Pecorina

MAKES 2 SERVINGS
TIME: 5 TO 10 MINUTES

Fifteen years ago I worked as part-time chef at a (now-defunct) small funky Upper West Side restaurant named Ruskay's. In those days three of us women shared the job as chef. Each of us had the responsibility of cooking two or three nights of the week, and the challenge was to cook a different menu every night.

Happily Ruskay's was located close to Lincoln Center and we were blessed with an "artsy" sophisticated clientele. Occasional visits were made to the restaurant by Yoko Ono, John Lennon, and Zero Mostel, while Perry Ellis, Michael Bennett, and Peter Martins were "regulars." We were given free reign with the food and could indulge our fanciful and eclectic tastes.

This zany place also had guest chefs, and one such guest—a wonderful man named Gerald Busby, a pianist and composer—introduced me to this fantastic salad of watercress and ricotta pecorina. While at the restaurant I used to serve small portions of this salad as an appetizer, at home I eat a big portion of it for dinner. If you can't get ricotta pecorina, then substitute a dry goat cheese.

Serve a bean, lentil, or split-pea soup, either before or alongside this salad.

2 tablespoons vegetable oil
1½ tablespoons lemon juice
Freshly ground black pepper
6 ounces ricotta pecorina, feta, or
*   dry goat cheese*
1 bunch watercress

1. Combine the oil and lemon juice in a serving bowl and season well with pepper.

2. Crumble the cheese and add it to the dressing. Holding the watercress by the stem ends, rinse the leaves under cold running water. Shake them and pat dry, then cut the bottom 2 inches from the stems. Add the watercress to the bowl. Toss the ingredients together and serve immediately before the watercress wilts.

SECOND TIME AROUND

RICOTTA CHEESE WITH FRUIT: Turn leftovers of this salad into a dessert filling. Purée it with some fruit jam for sweetness and sandwich the purée between slices of pound cake or spread onto plain cookies.

RICOTTA CHEESE WITH FRUIT

MAKES 2 SERVINGS
TIME: 10 MINUTES

A bowlful of fruit blended with ricotta cheese makes for a delightful and refreshing supper. Creamy sweet ricotta is best with fruit, but dieters and calorie watchers may substitute cottage or pot cheese.

> 1 Granny Smith apple
> 1 cup seedless red grapes
> 1 cup strawberries or blueberries or
>   1 ripe peach or Comice pear
> 1 container (15 ounces) ricotta
>   cheese, whole or part skim,
>   preferably unsalted

1. Core and cut the apple (with the peel) into ½- to ¾-inch chunks. Rinse and dry the grapes. Stem the berries and halve them if large. If using a peach, just pit it and dice; or peel the pear, core, and dice.

2. Toss the ingredients together and serve immediately or refrigerate up to several hours.

BASIC VINAIGRETTE

MAKES 2 CUPS OR ENOUGH FOR 8 TO 10 SERVINGS
TIME: 5 MINUTES

The ratio of oil to vinegar in a classic vinaigrette is 3 parts oil to 1 part vinegar, but my basic vinaigrette is leaner with just 2 parts oil to 1 part vinegar. If you follow my recipe, be sure to use a mild-tasting vinegar like balsamic, sherry wine, or raspberry.

I also use this dressing sparingly because it is tarter than most. Two to four tablespoons is enough to gently coat the greens. Leave the garlic clove whole to perfume the dressing.

> ⅔ cup olive oil
> ⅔ cup vegetable oil
> ⅔ cup balsamic vinegar
> 2 teaspoons Dijon mustard
> 1 clove garlic, peeled
> Salt and freshly ground black
>   pepper to taste

Combine all the ingredients in a glass jar and shake until well combined. Store covered in the refrigerator. This dressing keeps forever.

VARIATION

Herb Vinaigrette: To the above ingredients add ½ teaspoon dried tarragon, oregano, or dill seed, or ¼ cup tightly packed minced fresh herb leaves, such as parsley, basil, dill, coriander, or mint, or a combination of 2 or 3.

APPLE-DILL DRESSING

MAKES 1 CUP OR ENOUGH FOR 4 SERVINGS
TIME: 10 MINUTES

This dressing has a wonderful fresh sweet flavor — good with beets or a vegetable salad. If you do not have an apple on hand, stir a tablespoon of apple-sauce into the dressing instead.

1 McIntosh apple
¼ cup fresh dill or parsley leaves
¼ cup mayonnaise, regular or low fat
2 tablespoons rice, sherry wine, or balsamic vinegar
Salt and freshly ground black pepper to taste

Peel, core, and chop the apple. Process all the ingredients in a blender or food processor until smooth. Store covered in the refrigerator up to 1 week.

SPICY TART PEPPER DRESSING

MAKES ABOUT 3 CUPS OR ENOUGH FOR 12 SERVINGS
TIME: 5 TO 10 MINUTES

This marvelous dressing is great with all kinds of things — cold fish and bean salads, shredded cabbage, chilled artichokes, and steak sandwiches to name just a few.

2 bell peppers, preferably red or yellow — they look great
½ cup mayonnaise, regular or low fat, or 1 small cake soft tofu
¼ cup tarragon or other herb vinegar
1 teaspoon caraway seeds
2 tablespoons Dijon mustard
Salt and freshly ground black pepper to taste

SALAD DRESSING MARINADE

Marinate boneless skinless chicken or turkey breasts or fish steaks overnight (covered) in leftover salad dressing. The following evening, bake in a 350°F preheated oven until the poultry or fish is cooked through. The flavor imparted will be complex yet the method is easy.

CREATING DRESSINGS

·——·

When you have only a spoonful of black olive paste, mustard, pesto, or even Indian pickle left, simply add right in the jar, 2 or 3 tablespoons of oil to 1 tablespoon of vinegar. Shake the jar vigorously and you've created a seasoned salad dressing, especially good for main course salads.

A small handful of walnuts, pecans, and almonds are also efficiently and deliciously used up when puréed into a vinaigrette. These "nut" dressings are lovely with grain, legume and poultry salads.

Core, seed, and coarsely chop the bell peppers. Process all the ingredients in a blender or food processor until smooth. Store covered in the refrigerator up to 1 week.

YOGURT-PARSLEY DRESSING

MAKES ½ CUP OR ENOUGH FOR 4 SERVINGS

TIME: 5 MINUTES

The no-cholesterol answer to salad dressings. Fresh mint or dill, instead of the parsley, is wonderful with the yogurt as well.

½ cup plain nonfat yogurt
½ cup fresh parsley leaves
1 tablespoon vegetable oil
1 tablespoon lemon juice
Salt and freshly ground black
   pepper to taste

Process all the ingredients in a blender or food processor until the parsley is chopped. Store covered in the refrigerator up to 4 days.

CITRUS DRESSING

MAKES ½ CUP OR ENOUGH FOR 4 SERVINGS

TIME: 5 TO 10 MINUTES

The fruity and spicy character of this dressing mixes as happily with ham or poultry as it does with grain and bean salads.

¼ cup fresh orange juice
1 tablespoon lemon juice
¼ cup vegetable oil
¼ teaspoon dried orange peel
⅛ teaspoon ground cinnamon
Salt and freshly ground black
   pepper to taste

Process all the ingredients in a blender or food processor until smooth. Store covered in the refrigerator up to 1 week.

1

1311

OMNIUM GATHERUM

A HODGEPODGE OF LOVELY RECIPES FOR GUILT-FREE DINNERS

I think it's time that I, professional cook and working mother, fess up to the secret that on many a night my family and I don't have a "proper" meal. I'm not ashamed of this fact; in fact, I want to go on record as saying that I think it's perfectly all right. People, women especially, should not feel they are failing their families if they don't manage to cook a three-course dinner every night of the week.

When circumstances take over, dinner often ends up being a robust sandwich, a quick pizza, or a couple of scrambled eggs—anything that is assembled in an instant and satisfies hunger. These dinners, like the recipes assembled in this chapter, might not meet the old-fashioned standards of what makes for a sound and healthy dinner, but who cares? Just as long as it is fairly easy to prepare, tastes good, and is reasonably healthy, you shouldn't feel guilty about what form it takes—sandwiches, baked pota-toes, eggs, tortillas, tacos, even a bowl of cereal are all perfectly lovely alternatives to a dinner of starch, protein, and vegetable gathered together on a single plate.

In preparing to write this book, I asked the women at my gym what they ate for dinner most nights during the week. What struck me most about their replies was that they all felt somewhat guilty about what they really ate for supper—no matter how good it seemed—and expressed relief when I described the odd and eclectic dishes that appear regularly on my dinner table. Although they are all savvy about food and nutrition, none of the women I spoke to cooked a "proper" dinner regularly for themselves or for their families.

I recognize my little sample is not a random national poll, but it is enough to convince me that all those dinner-in-30-minutes cookbooks and magazine articles hardly reflect how people really and truly cook and eat.

And so, armed with a notion of what *is* going on in America's kitchens, I felt I ought to give everyone who makes a baked potato for dinner a nod and a wink and say "Hey, look—it's all right—you're not alone."

HAND-HELD LEFTOVERS

Tacos, tortillas, and pizzas make fabulous disguises for just about any kind of leftover dish (sorry — soups and desserts don't work here). In addition to the obvious ground meat, poultry, and bean dishes, and pasta sauces, don't forget to think of tacos, tortillas, and pizzas as a way to recycle the less obvious remainders like fish and vegetable dishes, relishes, and smidgeons of dressings.

MUCHOS TACOS

MAKES 12 TACOS OR ENOUGH FOR 4 TO 6 SERVINGS
TIME: ABOUT 5 MINUTES TO ASSEMBLE; SEE BELOW FOR FILLING AND TOPPING TIMES

The scenario runs a bit like this. One kid needs to eat early and the other can't be home before 7. Dad comes home early and hungry, but Mom won't be home until after 9. These are the nights you need tacos for dinner.

The night before, prepare a taco filling of your choice and all kinds of toppings. Cover them all and refrigerate overnight.

As each person comes home and is ready for dinner, reheat the taco shells, a portion at a time in a microwave, or several together in a toaster oven or 350°F regular oven. Reheat the filling in a skillet — it can be heated, reheated, and warmed through yet another time without any damage — and finish with whatever topping each person likes.

I prefer this bean filling, but a Ten-Minute Chili, Sloppy Mike's, or a vegetable filling like Quick and Basic Vegetable Curry (see Index for page numbers) will do as well. Other appropriate filling are leftover roast chicken, veal, or pork, chopped and tossed with spaghetti sauce, or leftover grains with bits of ham or even Barbecued Black Beans and Rice.

Note that all these toppings are terrific served over baked potatoes as well (see page 318).

1 box (12) tacos
1 recipe Taco Filling (recipe follows)
4 to 6 Taco Toppings (suggestions
   follow)

1. Heat the tacos in a microwave oven at full power for 1 minute or in a toaster oven or regular oven at 350°F for 5 to 7 minutes. The tacos can be heated a few at a time or altogether, depending on your family's eating schedule.

2. Heat the filling in a large skillet over medium heat, stirring occasionally to keep it from sticking, 10 minutes.

3. Set out or prepare the taco toppings, if you haven't prepared them the night before.

4. Let each family member assemble their tacos whenever they're hungry. Dig in.

TACO FILLING

MAKES 3 CUPS
TIME: 35 MINUTES

1 onion
2 cloves garlic
1 can (16 ounces) black beans or
   red kidney beans
2 tablespoons vegetable or olive oil
1 tablespoon chili powder
1 teaspoon dried oregano
1 package (10 ounces) frozen corn
   kernels, thawed
1 can (4 ounces) chopped green
   chilies
¾ cup spaghetti sauce, homemade
   (see Index) or prepared
Salt and freshly ground black pepper

1. Mince the onion and the garlic. Rinse and drain the beans.

2. Heat the olive oil in a large skillet over medium heat. Add the onion and garlic and sauté until tender, about 5 minutes.

3. Add the beans, chili powder, oregano, corn, and green chilies; sauté for a couple of minutes just to heat them through. Add the spaghetti sauce and season to taste with salt and pepper. Cover the skillet and simmer over medium-low heat for 10 to 15 minutes to heat the filling through and blend the flavors. The filling is now ready to be used or reheated later.

TACO TOPPINGS

MAKES: SEE BELOW FOR AMOUNTS
TIME: 7 TO 10 MINUTES

FOR CRUNCH:
About 1 cup shredded cabbage or
   iceberg lettuce, or chopped bell
   peppers

HOT AND SPICY:
½ cup sliced nacho jalapeños, 1 to
   2 seeded and minced fresh
   chilies, or 1 bunch sliced
   scallions (green onions), or drops
   of hot sauce or Tabasco

COOL AND CREAMY:
About 1 cup ricotta, cottage cheese,
   sour cream, plain yogurt, or
   slices of ripe avocado

OTHER POSSIBILITIES:
1 to 2 chopped ripe tomatoes, ½
   cup chopped fresh coriander or
   parsley, 1 lemon or lime cut into
   wedges, or about 1 cup shredded
   sharp Cheddar or Monterey Jack
   cheese

THE POTATO SKIN TACO SHELL

O ur daughter loves the insides of baked potatoes taken out of the skins, mixed with milk and butter, and beaten to a creamy smoothness. On the other hand, I prefer to eat the crunchy skins almost like a taco, with whatever filling and toppings I have chosen. So to make us both happy, I bake the potatoes at a higher temperature than ordinarily recommended: 500°F. The very hot oven yields an outer skin that is crispier and thicker than the one produced when the potato is baked at a lower temperature. I'm happy; she's happy.

Prepare 2 or 3 of the suggested toppings, depending on what you have on hand and the mood you're in. Just keep in mind you want something for crunch, something for hotness or spice, something for a creamy cool contrast, and something else just for fun.

STUFFED ROLLED TORTILLAS

MAKES 12 TORTILLAS OR 4 TO 6 SERVINGS
TIME: 25 MINUTES

One of the best ways I know of serving a dish the second time around is to dress up the leftovers in tortillas, bake them in a spaghetti sauce, and top them with crunchy stuff. Even a picky kid might not recognize last night's dinner.

You can use the same fillings and toppings you would with tacos or try some others.

ESPECIALLY GOOD FOR CHILDREN

I think most parents would agree that when tacos, tortillas, and pizzas are on the menu, there is very little kid-resistance to dinner. I find that tortillas, cut into taco-chip-like wedges and heated in a toaster oven also make a good pre-dinner snack. Top with a favorite condiment or set out a little dish of salad dressing as a light dip.

*FOR THE FILLING (see Index for
    page numbers):*
3 to 4 cups filling such as:
Monday-to-Friday Gumbo
*Chick-peas with Fennel and Roasted
    Peppers*
*Leftover grains or legumes mixed
    with steamed vegetables*
*Leftover shredded roast chicken, turkey,
    pork, or ham mixed with grains*

*FOR THE ASSEMBLY AND
    COOKING:*
12 corn or flour tortillas
1 cup ricotta or cottage cheese
*2 cups spaghetti sauce, homemade
    (see Index) or prepared*
*½ cup shredded cheese, such as
    Cheddar or mozzarella*

FOR THE GARNISHES:
(Use two or three of the following)
*About 1 cup shredded cabbage or
    iceberg lettuce, or chopped bell
    peppers*
*½ cup sliced nacho jalapeños, 1 to
    2 seeded and minced fresh
    chilies, 1 bunch sliced scallions
    (green onions), or drops of hot
    sauce or Tabasco*
½ cup chopped fresh coriander or parsley
1 lemon or lime cut into wedges

1. Preheat the oven to 375°F.

2. Spread about ¼ to ⅓ cup of the filling on each of the tortillas, then dot the filling with 2 tablespoons of the ricotta. Roll the tortillas up into tight cylinders.

3. Spread ¾ cup of the spaghetti sauce over the bottom of a baking dish large enough to hold the tortillas in a single layer. Set the tortillas, seam side down, on the sauce. Spread the remaining sauce over the tortillas and top with the shredded cheese. Bake until the filling is hot and the cheese has melted, about 20 minutes.

4. Meanwhile prepare the garnishes. Serve the tortillas hot and pass the garnishes.

HOMEMADE PIZZAS

MAKES 1 SMALL PIZZA
TIME: 10 TO 15 MINUTES

My friend Tikki Halperin turned me on to this way of making pizzas with pita bread. They taste a lot more authentic than those made with English muffins, and you can top them with bits and pieces of whatever ingredients you have on hand. Each pizza can bear a different topping, thereby satisfying the most eclectic bunch of eaters.

I wrote this recipe for just one serving because it's a handy solution for dining alone, but, if you're feeding a family, a dozen are almost as easily made as one.

2 tablespoons spaghetti sauce,
    homemade (see Index) or prepared
1 round white-flour pita bread,
    about 6 inches across (I use a
    brand called "Toufayan's")
½ cup leftover cooked meat,
    poultry, fish, or vegetables
½ cup shredded mozzarella cheese
1 to 2 teaspoons olive oil
Pinch of oregano

1. Preheat the oven to 400°F. If you are baking a single pizza, use a toaster oven; don't bake it in a microwave oven because the crust will be soggy.

2. Spread the spaghetti sauce over the pita (don't split it). Top with whatever leftovers you're using, and then the cheese. Sprinkle with olive oil and the seasoning. Set the assembled pizza on a baking sheet and bake until the crust is crisp, the topping is hot, and the cheese is melted, 7 to 10 minutes.

VARIATIONS

Following are examples of how to assemble

ENTERTAINING TIP

*P*ita pizzas cut into *wedges make good Monday-to-Friday appetizers to serve alongside drinks. Keep the toppings simple so they don't overwhelm the rest of the dinner.*

different pizzas; each example is a single pita bread. Spread the ingredients on the pita in the order in which they appear in the list.

- 2 tablespoons spaghetti sauce, ½ cup shredded mozzarella, pinch dried oregano, ½ teaspoon olive oil
- 2 tablespoons spaghetti sauce, 2 tablespoons ricotta or cottage cheese, ½ cup shredded mozzarella, 1 teaspoon minced fresh basil or parsley, 2 or 3 anchovy strips, ½ teaspoon olive oil
- 1 tablespoon olive oil, ¼ cup finely diced smoked ham, ¼ cup sliced fresh mushrooms, 2 tablespoons spaghetti sauce
- 1 tablespoon olive oil, ¼ cup drained canned minced clams, large pinch each garlic powder and thyme
- ½ cup drained black beans or leftover bean or meat chili, 1 tablespoon chopped green chilies, and shredded or wafer-thin slices of sharp Cheddar cheese
- 1 tablespoon black or green olive paste, ½ cup drained flaked tuna, 2 to 3 chopped sun-dried tomatoes
- 2 tablespoons spaghetti sauce, ¼ cup chopped drained sardines, 1 tablespoon drained capers, generous pinch garlic powder, 2 teaspoons olive oil
- ½ cup leftover cooked vegetables, 1 teaspoon olive oil, 1 tablespoon minced fresh basil or parsley, 2 chopped anchovy fillets
- ¼ cup ricotta or cottage cheese or crumbled goat cheese, 2 tablespoons chopped

pimientos or roasted peppers, ¼ cup shredded mozzarella, 1 teaspoon olive oil
- 1 tablespoon prepared pesto, 2 tablespoons ricotta or cottage cheese, ½ cup seeded and chopped ripe tomato

PICNIC LOAF

**MAKES 2 TO 3 SERVINGS PER LOAF
TIME: 25 MINUTES
2 TO 24 HOURS NO-WORK
MARINATING TIME**

The first time I ate a picnic loaf was on a freezing cold afternoon when my friend Rolly Woodyatt brought it to a beach picnic held on what was supposed to have been a warm afternoon, some Memorial Day weekend.

Rolly had hollowed out a large round Italian loaf, splashed it with olive oil, and filled it with layers of salami, prosciutto, provolone, black olives, and other ingredients that I forget. A wedge was served to each, and we all partook of the ideal picnic sandwich—a meal wrapped in bread.

This idea has now become a mainstay in my weekly summer repertoire. It's especially handy because it can be made a couple of days in advance and gets better with time. Think of making this for a Friday night supper — to eat in the car as you're leaving for a weekend or to have when you reach your destination. It's also great just for a midweek late dinner. You can make the loaf when you come home from work and let it sit in the refrigerator while you go for a run, do some errands, or just relax with a book or newspaper.

Quantities listed below are enough for two 6-inch loaves; each bread is ample enough to serve two.

> *2 round white or whole-wheat loaves, 6 to 7 inches in diameter (they should feel heavy and have a tough chewy crust)*
> *2 bunches watercress*
> *2 ripe tomatoes*
> *4 to 6 sun-dried tomatoes, packed in olive oil*
> *1 jar (4 ounces) roasted peppers*
> *4 to 8 anchovy fillets*
> *1 can (16 ounces) chick-peas*
> *¼ cup prepared pesto or olive paste, green or black*
> *1 can (2 ounces) smoked mussels*
> *4 teaspoon capers*

1. With a sharp serrated knife, cut out a circle in the top of the bread and remove it (this will be the cap). With your fingers, remove as much of the bready interior as possible. Repeat with the other bread. (Save the bread to dry and pulverize into bread crumbs.)

2. Rinse and stem the watercress. Slice the tomatoes. Coarsely chop the sun-dried tomatoes and roasted peppers. Mince the anchovies. Rinse and drain the chick-peas.

3. Now you're ready to assemble the loaves: Spread 1 tablespoon pesto around the inside of one hollowed-out bread. Scatter a quarter of the sun-dried tomatoes on the bottom and then ½ cup of the chick-peas over that. Top with a quarter of the roasted peppers, smoked mussels, and anchovies, 1 teaspoon capers, a few tomato slices, and a quarter of the watercress leaves.

4. Repeat the layers, beginning with the pesto. Place the bread cap over the filled bread and wrap the bread in aluminum foil. Repeat the entire procedure with the other loaf and wrap it as well.

5. Refrigerate the loaves for an hour at least; the longer the loaves sit, the better they taste because the flavors get a chance to mingle and blend with each other.

6. To serve, unwrap the loaves and cut each one into 4 thick wedges.

MINI LOAVES

Make individual picnic loaves by layering fillings inside pita pockets. Spoon in ham with a vinaigrette and roasted peppers or chick-pea purée with watercress and sliced fresh tomatoes. Wrap the mini loaves in plastic wrap and refrigerate overnight or until wonderfully flavorfully soggy and ready to eat.

NO MORE FOIL-WRAPPED POTATOES

*D*on't wrap baking potatoes in aluminum foil before baking—it makes them steam and the outside won't be crisp.

BAKED-FOR-DINNER POTATOES

MAKES 4 SERVINGS
TIME: 15 MINUTES WORK
1¼ HOURS NO-WORK BAKING TIME

The starch of a baked potato is comfortingly filling, its aroma a soothing experience, and its sweet fluffy texture mixes and matches with just about anything. This vegetable stir-fry is my favorite topping because it yields natural juices which the potatoes just sop up. See more suggestions at the end of the recipe.

Although this usually suffices for dinner, sometimes I precede it with a vegetable salad or, on days when I'm feeling hungrier, a lentil, split-pea, or bean soup.

4 Idaho baking potatoes
4 bell peppers, any color
1 pound fresh mushrooms
1 to 2 tablespoons olive oil
1 tablespoon black olive paste
    (optional)
Salt and freshly ground black pepper
Plain nonfat yogurt (optional)

1. Preheat the oven to 425°F.
2. Scrub the potatoes thoroughly so that you can feast on the crisp and crunchy skin once the potatoes are cooked. Pierce each potato in a couple of places with a sharp knife and place them directly on a rack in the oven. Bake until the potatoes are tender when pierced with a fork, 1 to 1¼ hours.
3. Meanwhile make the vegetable topping: Core, seed, and cut the bell peppers into thin strips. Clean, trim, and thinly slice the mushrooms.
4. Heat the oil in a large skillet over medium heat. Add the peppers, reduce the heat to low, and cook covered until tender, about 5 minutes.
5. Add the mushrooms and cook covered until all the vegetables are very soft, about 10 minutes more. Stir in the olive paste if you wish and season to taste with salt and pepper. Keep the vegetables covered, off the heat, until dinner time.
6. When the potatoes are done, split them with a knife almost all the way to the bottom and squeeze up some of the potato flesh. Spoon the vegetables over and around the potatoes. Top with yogurt if you wish and dig in!

VARIATIONS

Quantities are appropriate for 4 servings. For recipe page numbers, see the Index.

■ 4 cans (3 ounces each) smoked mussels or clams mixed with 1 bunch scallions (green onions), thinly sliced

■ 2 cups cottage cheese blended with ¼ cup minced sun-dried tomatoes and 1 tablespoon prepared pesto

■ Olive oil, lots of fresh peppers, and grated Parmesan or Cheddar cheese

■ Bean or Ten-Minute Chili

■ Stir-Fried Cabbage and Greens

■ Protean Ratatouille

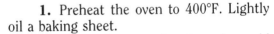

STRUDEL YOUR WAY

MAKES 2 TO 4 SERVINGS
TIME: 20 MINUTES WORK
35 MINUTES NO-WORK COOKING
TIME

I came up with this sauerkraut and ham strudel one night when I had nothing else in the refrigerator. This is how I discovered that wrapping leftovers in phyllo dough is a clever way of serving them in a new guise the following night.

You'll need 3 to 4 cups leftovers per strudel, and all sorts of leftovers are appropriate. Try a bean stew or cubed roasted meat mixed with leftover vegetables. Depending upon the filling, one strudel can serve 2 people as a main course or 4 people as a side dish. If you are serving this as a main course, accompany it with a salad.

1 cup sauerkraut (either from a barrel
or bagged; do not buy canned)
3 to 4 ounces cooked ham, poultry,
or other leftover meat
¼ pound fresh mushrooms
½ cup part-skim ricotta cheese
Freshly ground black pepper
6 sheets packaged phyllo (filo) dough
2 to 3 tablespoons olive oil or
melted butter
Dijon mustard for serving

1. Preheat the oven to 400°F. Lightly oil a baking sheet.

2. Rinse the sauerkraut under cold water and squeeze it dry.

3. Cut the leftover meat into small dice. Clean, stem, and thinly slice the mushrooms. Combine the sauerkraut, meat, mushrooms, and ricotta in a mixing bowl and season well with pepper.

4. Place 3 sheets of phyllo dough on a kitchen towel. Dip a pastry brush or your fingers in the olive oil and spread it over the

PHYLLO PIE

Repackage leftovers in phyllo to create something that looks a bit like a pie. Spread the leftovers in a baking pan. Set 1 phyllo sheet over the filling and brush with olive oil. Crimp the outside edges so that they fit inside the baking pan and don't hang over the edges. Layer with about 5 or 6 more sheets phyllo dough, oiling each one, and bake until the leftovers filling is reheated and the top sheets are crunchy, 30 minutes.

top sheet. Place the remaining 3 sheets of phyllo over the oiled sheet, then brush the top one with more oil.

5. Place the sauerkraut filling in a strip along the longer side of the phyllo closest to you, leaving a 1-inch border at the ends and side. Fold the borders in, then, using the towel, lift the filling and the dough and roll it up like a jelly-roll. Place the strudel, seam side down, on the prepared baking sheet.

6. Brush the remaining olive oil over the top of the dough. With a sharp knife, make 4 diagonal slashes on top of the strudel. Bake until the dough is crispy and golden and the filling is hot, 30 to 35 minutes. Cut into thick slices and serve accompanied by mustard.

CHICK-PEA PUREE

MAKES 4 SERVINGS
TIME: 10 MINUTES

A purée of chick-peas fits the bill on nights when I come home late, am facing an evening of work, and need to eat something quickly that is light enough so I don't fall asleep at my desk but nutritious enough to sustain me.

This aromatic and spunky mash of chick-peas mixed with watercress and coriander is not unlike a tangy hummus. Stuff the mix into whole-wheat pita bread, serve with sliced red peppers, and dinner's done.

> *2 cans (16 ounces each) chick-peas*
> *1 to 2 bunches fresh coriander or Italian (flat-leaf) parsley*
> *1 bunch watercress*
> *2 or 3 scallions (green onions)*
> *1 clove garlic*
> *1 to 2 tablespoons tahini (optional)*
> *4 to 6 tablespoons lemon or lime juice*
> *Salt and freshly ground black pepper*

1. Rinse and drain the chick-peas under cold water and place them in a food processor.

2. Rinse the coriander and watercress, cut off the stems, and add the leaves to the food processor. Trim, then cut the scallions into large pieces. Peel the garlic and add to the food processor with the scallions and tahini if using.

DOUBLING UP

CHICK-PEA PUREE: Make this in a double batch to have as a quick snack when you come home feeling starved and need a nibble to get you through until dinner time. It keeps well in the refrigerator up to 4 days.

3. Process the mixture, adding the lemon juice as you go, until it is as smooth as you want it to be. Season to taste with salt and pepper.

GIANT FRITTATA

MAKES 4 SERVINGS
TIME: 30 TO 35 MINUTES

Think about making a frittata for dinner on a night when you come home late from a stressful day at the office or from a cocktail party where you've had too much to drink and too little to eat. I can't think of a quicker way to get some sound and good-tasting nutrition under your belt.

In this version, a mess of vegetables and potatoes come together in a pancake of eggs. Quickly assembled and cooked, the frittata is served hot or at room temperature. You can reheat it the next day or serve it cold sandwiched between bread. You can round out the meal by serving a salad alongside it or a dessert after it, and it's always wonderful accompanied by a hearty whole-grain bread.

This is a handy way to use up odd bits of leftovers, and, as you'll see below, there are myriad ways you can make this.

1 small to medium-size onion or
2 cloves garlic
1 green or red bell pepper or
1 medium-size carrot
1 white potato or sweet potato
1 package (10 ounces) frozen vegetables, such as chopped spinach, artichokes, corn kernels, or lima beans, thawed
8 whole eggs or 4 eggs mixed with 4 egg whites or 8 egg whites
2 tablespoons seasoning, such as barbecue or chili sauce, green or black olive paste; or minced fresh herbs, such as parsley or basil; or minced sun-dried tomatoes, pimientos, chopped scallions (green onions), or canned green chilies
Salt and freshly ground black pepper
2 tablespoons olive oil

1. Chop the onion or mince the garlic (or you can use a bit of both). Core, seed, and finely chop the bell pepper or peel and finely chop the carrot. Peel and cut the potato into ½-inch cubes. If you're using frozen spinach, make sure to drain it well. If you're using artichokes, cut them into small dice.

AN ASIDE ABOUT EGGS

Eggs have gotten a lot of bad press of late. These days most folks seem convinced that if they ingest a whole egg, yolk and all, a heart attack will be waiting just around the corner.

Well, I still hold the egg in high esteem. In my book, an egg is still an incredibly nutritious and wonderfully filling food. I can't think of a faster way to get a more delicious and nutritious dinner on the table than a couple of eggs turned into an omelet, a frittata, or scrambled into a mess of vegetables.

Even cholesterol-watchers can join in—simply substitute 2 egg whites for a whole egg. The end result may not look as great, nor hold together as well, but the nutrition, ease of preparation, and quickness remain the same.

2. In a mixing bowl, whisk the eggs (or eggs and whites) with half of your chosen seasoning. Season lightly with salt and pepper.

3. Heat the olive oil in a large non-stick skillet over medium heat. (If you don't have a nonstick skillet, increase the oil to 4 tablespoons.) When the oil is very hot, add the onion, pepper, and potatoes and sauté for a minute or so just to get them cooking. Cover the skillet and simmer over low heat until the potatoes are tender, 15 to 20 minutes. Add the spinach and sauté for a minute to heat. Add the remainder of your chosen seasoning and season to taste with salt and pepper.

4. Stir the eggs into the vegetables, cover, and cook over low heat until the eggs have set, about 5 minutes. Cut into 4 wedges and serve.

CURRIED SCRAMBLED EGGS

MAKES 1 SERVING
TIME: 20 MINUTES

Scrambling a couple of eggs over vegetables is the perfect dinner for one. I serve it for myself over a toasted English muffin so that I also get my starch and grain. Sometimes I make a watercress salad to serve alongside it.

You can double the quantities to serve two people, but be sure to use a 9- or 10-inch skillet instead. If you are making eggs for more than 2 people, use the frittata recipe that precedes this one. And as with the frittata, this recipe is merely a guide for turning eggs into dinner. For variations, use your imagination and what your cupboard has to offer.

If you're scrambling egg whites only, the color of the dish will be a little odd, but not the taste.

1 ripe tomato or bell pepper, any color
2 scallions (green onions) or ¼ cup fresh herb leaves
2 whole eggs or 1 egg mixed with 1 egg white or 3 egg whites
½ teaspoon curry powder, ground cumin, or chili powder
Tabasco sauce or freshly ground black pepper
Salt
1 English muffin
2 teaspoons vegetable oil
½ package (10 ounces) frozen corn kernels, petite peas, or green beans, thawed

1. Quarter the tomato, scoop out the seeds, and dice the flesh. (Or core, seed, and dice the bell pepper.) Trim and thinly slice the scallions or mince the fresh herb (or use both).

2. In a small bowl whisk the eggs with the curry powder. Season to taste with Tabasco and salt. Split and toast the English muffin.

3. Heat the oil in a small skillet, preferably cast-iron, over medium heat until very hot. Add the tomato and corn and season to taste with salt and Tabasco. Sautè for a few minutes until hot or tender. Add the scallions or herbs along with the eggs. Scramble for a minute or so until the eggs are set. Adjust the seasoning and serve hot over the toasted muffin.

VARIATIONS

■ Substitute 1 teaspoon prepared pesto, black olive paste, grainy mustard, or chili or barbecue sauce for the curry powder.

■ Substitute 2 or 3 sausage links for the tomato and frozen vegetable. Sauté them in the oil until done, then remove them from the pan and slice. Return the slices to the pan and scramble the eggs on top.

■ Substitute a cupful of leftover beans or grains for the tomato and frozen vegetable, sauté, and then scramble the eggs on top.

■ Instead of the tomatoes and vegetable, sauté ¼ cup minced onion and ¼ cup chopped bell pepper until tender. Add ¼ cup cubed leftover chicken or fish and sauté until hot, then scramble the eggs over this mixture.

SAVORY OMELET

MAKES 1 SERVING
TIME: 10 TO 15 MINUTES

For the quickest dinner fix of all, try a filled omelet. Instead of sautéing bits and pieces of vegetables or leftovers first, you simply flavor some cottage cheese or ricotta with whatever you have on hand and use it to fill a pancake of eggs. As with the scrambled eggs, this makes the most sense when you're just making dinner for yourself. I always help myself to bread and a salad or raw peppers and cabbage and round out my dinner.

Sorry, dieters — I've tried making this with egg whites only, but it just doesn't work.

EGG TIP

If you've lost track of when you bought the eggs sitting in your refrigerator, there is an easy ways to test their freshness. Crack an egg open onto a plate. If the white hugs the yolk and the yolk is round and plump, the egg is fresh. If the white spreads out all over the plate and the yolk looks flat, the egg is not fresh.

When I used to teach cooking, the egg lesson always included a dessert omelet even though it always seemed somewhat ridiculous to me to serve a dessert that was so protein rich after a full dinner. However, a dessert omelet does make sense if you turn it into your main course, satisfying your need for nourishment as well as the needs of your sweet tooth. Serve a salad before and your dinner's done. To make one, just follow the directions for the savory omelet but fill it with 3 to 4 tablespoons of a sweet filling like apricot jam mixed with chopped nuts or perhaps with some leftover fruit dessert like poached pears or sautéed apples.

¼ cup pimientos or sun-dried
   tomatoes packed in olive oil
1 scallion (green onion) or a small
   piece fresh bell pepper or 2
   tablespoons fresh herb leaves
¼ cup ricotta or cottage cheese
Salt or freshly ground black pepper
3 whole eggs or 2 eggs mixed with
   1 egg white
2 teaspoons vegetable oil
About 1 tablespoon spaghetti sauce

1. Chop the pimientos or sun-dried tomatoes. Trim and slice the scallion or mince the bell pepper or herb. Place these ingredients in a small bowl. Add the cheese and stir to combine. Season to taste with salt and pepper.

2. In another small bowl whisk the eggs together and season them to taste with salt and pepper.

3. Heat the oil in a small skillet, preferably cast-iron, over medium heat. Add the eggs and scramble them very lightly. Cover the skillet, reduce the heat to low, and let the eggs set for a minute.

4. Drizzle the spaghetti sauce over half the eggs and cover with the cheese filling. Cover the skillet and cook over low heat for another minute until the eggs are set. With a spatula fold the unfilled omelet half over the filled half and slide it out of the skillet onto a plate. Serve immediately.

EGGS OVER BEANS

MAKES 4 SERVINGS
TIME: 30 MINUTES

How do you make an egg dinner for more than 2 people? Well, eggs and potatoes are popular, right? So why not eggs and beans? You, of course, may make this with potatoes, provided you have some already cooked in your refrigerator.

1 small onion
1 tablespoon vegetable or olive oil
1 can (16 to 19 ounces) black beans
1 package (10 ounces) frozen corn
   kernels, thawed
2 tablespoons sliced nacho
   jalapeños (optional)
Salt and freshly ground black
   pepper
4 to 8 eggs

1. Finely chop the onion. Heat the oil in a large nonstick skillet over medium heat. Add the onion and sauté until translucent, 3 to 4 minutes.

2. Rinse and drain the beans, and add them, plus the corn and nacho peppers if using, to the skillet. Cover and simmer over low heat until the beans and corn are tender and hot, about 10 minutes. Season to taste with salt and pepper.

3. Meanwhile carefully break the eggs into a shallow soup plate. After the beans have cooked for 10 minutes, slide the eggs over the top of the beans. Cover the skillet again and cook until the egg whites are completely set (the egg yolks will be a bit tender in the center), about 10 minutes more. Serve immediately.

RED AND YELLOW PANCAKES

MAKES 8 TO 10 PANCAKES OR 4 SERVINGS
TIME: 15 TO 20 MINUTES

A delectable meal can be made of these delicious corn pancakes accompanied by a portion of a favorite bean dish, a slice of Cheddar cheese, or a plate of stir-fried vegetables. The pancakes can be made in advance and reheated for 10 minutes in a 350°F oven or for a minute in the microwave.

1 red bell pepper
2 scallions (green onions)
1 package (10 ounces) frozen corn
   kernels, thawed
1 cup yellow cornmeal
1/2 teaspoon baking powder
1 egg
1/3 cup hot water
1 teaspoon salt
Freshly ground black pepper to taste
1 to 4 tablespoons vegetable oil

1. Core and seed the bell pepper. Trim and cut the scallions into large pieces. Place the pepper, scallions, and corn kernels in a food processor and process until smooth. Add the remaining ingredients except the oil and process again until smooth, about 1 minute. If you don't own a food processor, use a blender; chop the pepper, slice the scallions, and mix all ingredients together by hand (the pancakes will be chunkier and might fall apart when you cook them).

2. Heat 1 tablespoon vegetable oil in a nonstick skillet over medium heat. Drop about 1/4 cup of the batter into the hot skillet for each pancake. Cook 4 to 5 minutes per side. Repeat, adding more oil as needed to cook the pancakes.

VARIATION

For cholesterol watchers: Make the batter

PANCAKE REDUX

If you find you've made too many pancakes, here's how you can use them the following night as the basis for another dish.

In a baking pan, layer the pancakes with rinsed and drained black beans, sliced scallions (green onions), and shredded Cheddar cheese. Top with another layer of pancakes and spoon some spaghetti sauce over all. Cover the baking pan with aluminum foil and bake at 350°F until very hot, about 20 minutes.

without the egg; then beat 2 egg whites until stiff and fold it into the batter right before cooking the pancakes. These pancakes might be more crumbly, but they should still hold together.

A SWEET MAIN COURSE

To make sweet pancakes as a main course, beat 1 cup low-fat small curd cottage cheese with ⅓ cup all-purpose flour, 1 egg, 2 tablespoons sugar, and 1 cup rinsed and drained strawberries (hull them first), raspberries, or blueberries. Proceed to cook the pancakes as instructed in the recipe for Cottage Cheese and Vegetable Pancakes, step 5 (beginning with heating the oil).

Precede the pancakes with a plateful of freshly steamed vegetables or a vegetable salad and your dinner is set.

COTTAGE CHEESE AND VEGETABLE PANCAKES

MAKES 8 PANCAKES OR 2 SERVINGS
TIME: 35 MINUTES

The rich taste of these cheese pancakes belie their healthful qualities. I'm too lazy to go to the trouble of making pancakes for more than 2 people, but, if you wish to serve 4, double the recipe and use 2 skillets. The sugar in this recipe doesn't really sweeten the pancakes, it merely makes them taste more mellow.

I like to serve these after a fish soup of some sort or before a hefty salad.

1 small onion
1 bell pepper, any color
1 tablespoon olive oil
½ cup fresh parsley leaves
1 cup low-fat small-curd cottage cheese
⅓ cup all-purpose flour
1 egg
¼ teaspoon sugar
½ teaspoon salt
Freshly ground black pepper to taste
2 tablespoons vegetable oil

1. Mince the onion. Core, seed, and finely chop the bell pepper.

2. Heat the olive oil in a medium-size nonstick skillet over medium heat. Add the onion and pepper, reduce the heat immediately, and simmer covered until the vegetables are tender, about 10 minutes.

3. Meanwhile mince the parsley.

4. Remove the vegetables from the heat and let them cool while you assemble the batter: In a mixing bowl mix the cheese, flour, egg, sugar, salt, pepper, and parsley with a fork until well-blended. When the vegetables have cooled somewhat, add them to the batter and blend well.

5. Wash out the skillet in which you cooked the vegetables to cook the pancakes. Heat 1 tablespoon vegetable oil in the cleaned skillet over medium heat. Drop about ¼ cup batter into the hot skillet for each pancake and flatten them out with a spoon. Cook until golden brown, 4 to 5 minutes per side. (If the pancakes are too hard to flip over, cover the skillet and cook the pancakes for 4 to 5 minutes more on the same side.) Repeat, adding more oil as needed to cook the pancakes.

VARIATION

For cholesterol watchers: Instead of blending a whole egg into the batter, whip 2 egg whites until stiff and fold them into the batter.

SAVORY FARINA

MAKES 4 TO 6 SERVINGS
TIME: 35 MINUTES

I bet that after one look at the title of this recipe either you'll be intrigued enough to read on or perplexed enough to pass over it. Well, don't skip it. This is a wonderful version of an "uppama," which is a fabulous savory farina dish served for breakfast in the south of India.

The texture is like that of cream of wheat or soft polenta, but the spicing is Indian—hot and pungently aromatic. To make the dish more appropriate for dinner, I've added peppers and cauliflower.

I love to eat a bowl of this for dinner with nothing else, but you could accompany it with plain yogurt. You could also serve this as a side dish to Roasted Chicken or precede it with Basic Vegetable Salad or follow it with a dessert of Broiled Bananas (see Index for page numbers).

1 small head cauliflower
2 small red bell peppers
1 piece (½ inch) fresh ginger
1 fresh green chili (optional)
½ cup roasted cashews, preferably
  unsalted
¼ cup vegetable oil
1 teaspoon cumin seeds or ground
  cumin
1 teaspoon ground coriander
½ teaspoon turmeric or paprika
1¼ cups water
1 cup plain nonfat yogurt
¾ cup farina
Salt and freshly ground black
  pepper

1. Core the cauliflower, break it into florets, and cut them into ½-inch chunks. Core, seed, and cut the peppers into small

FARINA TOASTS

If you've made too much farina or cream of wheat for breakfast, don't throw it out. Refrigerate until dinnertime, then cut the solidified leftovers into slices, if possible (if not, cubes will do). Sauté the slices in a little olive oil until lightly browned on all sides. Spoon onto plates, top with a mild tomato sauce, and you have a makeshift polenta.

chunks. Mince the ginger. Seed and mince the chili, if using. If you're using salted cashews, rinse them under cold running water.

2. Heat the oil in a large skillet over medium heat. Add the cumin, coriander, and turmeric and stir-fry for a few seconds to release their aroma. Add the ginger, peppers, and chili; sauté for about a minute just to get them cooking. Add the cauliflower and ¼ cup of the water. Cover the skillet and simmer, stirring frequently, over low heat until the cauliflower is tender, about 15 minutes.

3. Meanwhile mix the remaining 1 cup water with the yogurt and set it aside until later.

4. Uncover the skillet and cook until any liquid has evaporated. Add the cashews and farina to the skillet and mix well. Slowly add the yogurt mixture and bring the liquid to a simmer over low heat, stirring constantly with a wooden spoon. The farina tends to stick to the pan, so you need to keep stirring. Then cover the skillet and simmer until the farina is cooked, 3 to 4 minutes. Remove the pan from the heat and let stand covered for 5 minutes. Season to taste with salt and pepper and fluff it up with a fork before serving.

VARIATIONS

■ **Tex-Mex Farina Supper:** In step 1, omit the ginger and cashews. Instead, finely chop 1 can (4 ounces) green chilies and mince 1 cup fresh coriander leaves.

In step 2, substitute ½ teaspoon each ground cumin, coriander, chili powder, and oregano for the spices. Add the green chiles after you've added the peppers.

In step 3, substitute 1 cup chicken broth or stewed tomatoes mixed with 1 cup water for the yogurt mixture.

In step 4, add the coriander and 1 tablespoon lime juice after you remove the skillet from the heat. Proceed as directed.

■ If you're too chicken to eat spicy cereal, substitute for the farina 1 cup bulgur or couscous plumped in 1½ cups water, or use 2 cups leftover cooked grains, like rice or millet.

DESSERTS
SPECIAL WAYS TO END A
MEAL MONDAY-TO-FRIDAY STYLE

During the week, dessert in our house is most often ice cream spooned straight from the carton or a plain piece of fresh fruit from the fridge, so that when I do go to the trouble of making a dessert Monday to Friday, I want it to be gussied up—just enough to make me feel pampered.

Some of my desserts, like the fruit ones, are healthy; while others, like the whipped cream and chocolate cookie cake, are outrageously caloric. And whereas a daily dose of thick hot fudge or a brownie topped with whipped cream is a bit extreme, I think every one needs and deserves the occasional indulgence.

If you are entertaining during the week, many of these desserts can be made a day or so in advance and kept refrigerated until the evening of your party. All, even the soufflés and mousses, look festive and seem labor intensive, but like the other recipes in this cookbook, are child's play to prepare.

For entertaining purposes or celebratory times—I don't mean just birthdays, but for any times there's good news—there are a few supplies I like to keep on hand, which give even the plainest desserts an elegant face. Serve a plain store-bought cake on a doilie or a pretty china plate, for example, and it suddenly looks impressive. If you're short of doilies or fancy plates, dress up a dessert with fresh berries or even a few fresh flowers. Pink or yellow roses are particularly nice on a chocolate cake.

If ice cream, sherbert, or frozen yogurt is the ending for your special meal, assemble a selection of easy toppings, and let everyone create their own ice cream sundaes. Freshly whipped cream, puréed berries sweetened with jam and thinned with a tablespoon of liqueur or lemon juice, chopped up nuts or bananas, and some chocolate shavings all make for festive endings to Monday-to-Friday meals.

SAUTEED APPLES WITH CURRANTS AND COGNAC

MAKES 4 SERVINGS
TIME: 25 MINUTES

What's handy about this recipe is that you can make it as easily for 2 people as you can for 6. Divide or multiply the recipe, using the following proportions: each person should get the equivalent of 1 large apple, 1 tablespoon currants, and ½ tablespoon each butter, brown sugar, and Cognac.

Relentless in my pursuit of shortcuts, I tested this recipe with unpeeled apples but with poor results. The texture just wasn't right.

In the fall, Comice pears make a fine substitute for the apples.

4 large or 5 medium-size McIntosh apples
1 or 2 tablespoons butter
2 tablespoons brown sugar
¼ cup currants or raisins
2 tablespoons Cognac, brandy, or white wine, or lemon juice if kids are among your diners

1. Core, peel, and quarter the apples, then cut them into ¼-inch slices.

2. Melt 1 tablespoon butter in a large nonstick skillet over medium-high heat. Add the apples and sprinkle with the sugar. Sauté, stirring constantly using a wooden spoon in each hand, until the apples begin to get tender, 2 to 3 minutes.

3. Add the currants and sauté for another couple of minutes to heat them through and continue to cook the apples.

4. Remove the skillet from the heat, stir in the Cognac, and swirl the apples around until it is absorbed. If you wish, swirl in the remaining 1 tablespoon butter to finish the flavor.

BROILED BANANAS

MAKES 4 SERVINGS
TIME: 10 MINUTES

This dessert, which requires no time nor culinary expertise, is nonetheless sophisticated because of the intriguing play between the sweet of the fruit and the sugar and the tang of the lime juice. Sour cream, for those who can afford the calories, adds yet another dimension, the play of cool against hot.

Because broiling bananas is not messy, and this recipe is so good, it's worth making an exception to my rule of never broiling.

4 bananas, not too ripe
¼ cup (packed) brown sugar
1 tablespoon lime juice
Sour cream (optional)

1. Preheat the broiler.

2. Peel the bananas and slice crosswise ½ inch thick. Mix the brown sugar and lime juice and toss it with the banana slices.

3. Spread the bananas in a shallow baking pan and broil until the sugar has melted into a glaze, 3 to 5 minutes. Serve immediately, with sour cream if you wish.

FRESH FRUIT SALAD

MAKES 4 TO 6 SERVINGS
TIME: 10 MINUTES

Here's a popular during-the-week dessert. It's healthy, refreshing, light, and easy to prepare. I've described the combinations I especially like either because of the color, the textural contast, or the meld of flavors. For balance I try to mix acidic fruit with mellow ones. The fruits I dislike in salads are apples, grapefruit, and pears; I'd rather eat them whole. And, finally, you can make a fruit salad more festive by setting it on top of slices of pound cake.

1 pint strawberries
1 small cantaloupe
2 bananas
¼ cup fresh mint leaves (optional)

1. Rinse, hull, and halve the strawberries, and place them in a serving bowl. Halve and seed the cantaloupe. Cut it into thick wedges and remove the rind. Cut the fruit into pieces about the size of the strawberries. Add the cantaloupe to the bowl. Peel and slice the bananas into the bowl, and mince and sprinkle in the fresh mint, if using.

2. Toss the fruit salad and serve immediately. If you are making this salad in advance, it keeps for up to 3 hours in the refrigerator. But, don't add the bananas until right before serving. Bananas discolor in the refrigerator.

VARIATIONS

■ ½ pint raspberries, 1 small honeydew, and 2 kiwi

■ 4 navel oranges, 2 bananas, and ⅛ tea-

RIPENING UNDERRIPE FRUIT

Pears, peaches, mangoes, and bananas are all harvested underripe and are often sold that way. If you purchase underripe fruit, keep it in a partially closed paper bag, in a cool place (by an open window, for example). The paper bag entraps some of the ethylene gas the fruit emits, and this gas helps the fruit to ripen. Since bananas and apples give off more of this gas than other fruits, keeping one or the other in a paper bag with slower-ripening fruit will speed up the process.

CREATE A WEEKEND
CULINARY EFFECT
WITH MINIMAL
WEEKDAY EFFORT

A fruit salad can seem like the most humdrum dessert imaginable—but you can turn this ordinary salad into an exotic dessert by selecting unusual fruits and mixing them with an unexpected spice or two.

A fruit salad made with oranges, grapefruit, and apples is reminiscent of cafeteria fare; whereas chunks of mangoes, pineapple, or papaya tinged with a few raspberries takes on a festive glow and exciting aura. You can further heighten the glamour by bathing it with an easy dessert sauce of citrus juice, sugar, and a hint of exotic spice, like anise, clove, ginger, cardamom, or even fresh pepper.

spoon vanilla extract
- 1 pineapple and 1 pound seedless red grapes

EXOTIC FRUIT SALAD

MAKES 4 SERVINGS
TIME: 15 MINUTES

The combination of exotic fruit with Oriental spices makes for an exciting dessert that has a splendid and festive character but is accomplished with a minimum of work.

> 2 tablespoons confectioners' sugar
> 1 to 2 tablespoons lemon or lime
>   juice or ¼ cup orange juice
> ½ teaspoon vanilla extract
> ¼ teaspoon Chinese five-spice
>   powder or ⅛ teaspoon each
>   ground anise, cloves, and ginger
> 4 kiwi
> 2 mangoes or papayas or 1 pineapple
> 2 bananas
> ½ pint raspberries or 1 small
>   cantaloupe

1. Whisk together the sugar, lemon

juice, vanilla, and spice powder in a serving bowl.

2. Add each fruit to the bowl as you peel and cut it and toss it with the sauce. Peel the kiwi and cut it into thin rounds. Peel and dice the mangoes or papayas, or peel, core, and dice the pineapple. Peel the bananas and thinly slice. Rinse the raspberries under cold water and pat dry but don't add them to the bowl yet, or peel, seed, and cut the rind from the melon, and cut the fruit into small dice; add it to the bowl.

3. Toss the fruit (except for the berries) with the sauce.

4. If you're using raspberries, place them on top of the fruit salad and toss gently. Serve immediately so that the berries don't get smashed and bleed their color over the other fruit. If you are making this salad in advance, it keeps for up to 3 hours in the refrigerator. But, don't prepare and add the bananas until right before serving. Bananas discolor in the refrigerator. Add them before the raspberries.

Melon with Rum, Lime, and Ginger Sauce

MAKES 4 SERVINGS
TIME: 10 MINUTES

Make this dessert before you start on the other parts of your dinner so that the melon has time to marinate in the sauce and pick up a maximum of flavor. This somewhat Caribbean mixture works wonderfully also with diced mango, papaya, and banana.

2 tablespoons superfine or
  confectioners' sugar
1 to 2 tablespoons dark rum,
  brandy, or orange juice
1 tablespoon fresh lime juice
⅛ teaspoon ground ginger
1 medium-large honeydew or
  Crenshaw melon or 2 small
  cantaloupes (about 4 cups diced
  fruit)
¼ cup fresh mint leaves (optional)

1. Whisk together the sugar, rum, lime juice, and ginger in a serving bowl.
2. Cut the melon in half and scoop out the seeds. Cut it into thick wedges and remove the rind. Cut the fruit into ½-inch cubes and toss it with the ginger sauce. Cover the bowl and refrigerate until ready to eat, up to 3 hours. If you want to add more tang, mince the fresh mint and sprinkle it over the fruit right before serving.

Sliced Oranges and Vanilla

MAKES 4 SERVINGS
TIME: 15 MINUTES

Texture is what takes this dessert out of the ordinary. By slicing away all of the peel and white pith from the oranges, you eliminate the unpleasant stringy texture of sliced oranges in ordinary fruit salads.

I have seasoned the oranges here with vanilla but at other times have substituted a tablespoon of port or Grand Marnier or another orange-flavored liqueur.

5 or 6 navel oranges
1 to 2 tablespoons sugar
1 to 2 teaspoons vanilla extract

EATING ORANGES

Navel oranges are the best oranges for eating; Valencias and Temples are best used for juice. Citrus fruits contain tiny sacs of bitter oil at the surface of the rind and in the white pith below the skin. This is why you should pare this white pith away when you peel oranges. Also, when grating citrus fruit for its zest, avoid grating the white part, otherwise it will be bitter.

1. With a sharp knife, pare away all the peel and white pith from the oranges. Cut each orange in half from navel to stem end. With your fingers, pull away any white pith in the center, then slice the orange halves.

2. Toss the oranges with the sugar and vanilla to taste in a serving bowl. Serve right away if you wish or, better yet, cover and chill up to 24 hours.

VARIATIONS

■ **Minted Oranges and Bananas:** Substitute ¼ cup fresh mint leaves, minced, for the vanilla and slice in 1 ripe banana.

■ **Oranges and Raspberries:** Thaw 1 package (10 ounces) frozen raspberries in "lite" syrup. Toss the orange slices with the raspberries and their syrup instead of the sugar and vanilla.

SECOND TIME AROUND

WINE-BRAISED PEARS: If you have only leftover syrup, save it in a covered jar in the refrigerator; it's a great sauce to spoon over fresh fruit, ice cream, and pound cake.

WINE-BRAISED PEARS

MAKES 4 TO 6 SERVINGS
TIME: 20 TO 25 MINUTES

Poached pears is a classic dessert. It's elegant enough to serve to company but also easy enough to serve to your family during the week.

You can change the flavor of this dessert each time you make it by seasoning the sugar syrup with either wine, coffee, or green tea. When I poach the pears in wine, I use red rather than white, because it makes the pears look more attractive. This dish is best prepared in the fall, when the pears are in season.

2 cups water
2 cups dry red or white wine, strong coffee, or strong green tea
1½ cups sugar
2 whole cloves, 1 teaspoon dried orange peel, or ½ teaspoon ground cinnamon (optional)
4 to 6 pears, preferably Comice, not too ripe

1. Bring the water, wine, sugar, and cloves if using to a boil in a medium-size saucepan. Lower the heat and allow the wine mixture to simmer.

2. Meanwhile, if you own an apple corer, first core the pears, otherwise leave them whole. With a sharp knife peel each pear and drop it into the wine mixture. (This is to save you the step of rubbing the pears with lemon juice so that they do not discolor during the time it takes to bring the wine and sugar to a boil.)

3. When all the pears are in, cover the pan and continue simmering until tender, 10 to 15 minutes. (Timing depends on how firm the pears are; just take care not to overcook them.)

4. Remove the pears from the liquid with a slotted spoon. If you're in a rush, serve them now—hot with a spoonful of sauce. If you have more time, cool the pears to room temperature and, during this time, boil down the cooking liquid over medium heat until reduced by half or more; this will intensify the flavor of the syrup and thicken it as well.

SAUTEED CHESTNUTS AND PINEAPPLE

MAKES 4 SERVINGS
TIME: 15 TO 20 MINUTES

The sweet starch of the chestnuts makes a perfect foil for the moist tang of the pineapple. This is such a richly textured dessert and so exquisite in taste that you could serve it even for a fancy weekend meal.

*1 can or jar (8 ounces) roasted
  whole chestnuts
2 cans (8 ounces each) crushed
  pineapple packed in its own juice
2 tablespoons butter
2 tablespoons brown sugar
¼ cup currants or raisins
1 tablespoon dark rum*

1. Drain and coarsely chop the chestnuts; thoroughly drain the pineapple.

2. Right before serving dessert, melt the butter in a large skillet over medium heat until it is golden brown. Add the chestnuts and sugar; cook, stirring constantly, until the sugar melts, about 2 minutes.

3. Add the drained pineapple, currants, and rum. Bring to a simmer and cook until the mixture just begins to stick to the pan, 2 to 3 minutes more. Remove the pan from the heat and spoon the dessert into deep bowls. Serve hot.

BUYING FRESH FRUIT

Fruit, like vegetables, are at their best when at their seasonal peak and, if possible, when grown locally. However, seasonality varies from one part of the country to the other. Check your newspaper's food pages to see what fruit is in season in your neck of the woods; it will probably be at its most fragrant and delicious.

BROWN-SUGAR-GLAZED PINEAPPLE

MAKES 4 TO 6 SERVINGS
TIME: 15 MINUTES

This is one of my favorite speedy desserts. Slices of fresh pineapple are
blanketed with brown sugar and broiled
until the sugar caramelizes into a gently
crackling crust. This is one of few times
I make use of my broiler, because it
doesn't get too messy by this dessert.

1 or 2 medium-size fresh pineapples
About ¼ cup (packed) dark brown
* sugar*
Port (optional)

1. Preheat the broiler.
2. With a sharp knife cut the skin
from the pineapple, making sure to cut away
enough so that you get rid of those prickly
"eyes" as well. Slice the remaining pineapple
into thin rounds.
3. Place the slices in a single layer on
a broiling pan and thickly coat each slice
with a thin layer of brown sugar. Place the
pan under the broiler as close to the heat as
possible and broil until the sugar is brown
and caramelized, about 3 minutes.

4. Remove the pan from the broiler
and, with a spatula, place the pineapple
slices on dessert plates. Serve immediately—
plain or each slice sprinkled with drops of
port if you wish.

VARIATION

Toss 4 cups sliced fresh fruit, such as
peaches, mangoes, plums, pears, or papayas,
with 2 tablespoons port and ¼ cup crushed
cookie crumbs. Spread the mixture on a
baking sheet. Top with ¼ cup (packed)
brown sugar and broil until the sugar is
caramelized, about 2 minutes.

CRANBERRY-PEAR MOUSSE

MAKES 8 SERVINGS
TIME: 20 MINUTES WORK
45 MINUTES TO 2 HOURS NO-WORK
CHILLING TIME

In a weak moment a while back, I invited a few people over for dinner in
the middle of the week. On my way
home from work, I realized I had forgotten to make dessert the night before, so
I was going to have to come up with

something that looked festive but was fast and easy to make.

Pears were in season and a pear mousse with egg whites would be easy enough to whip up in a few minutes. Then the vision of 8 individual beige mousses danced before my eyes. Luckily some leftover Thanksgiving cranberries in the freezer saved the day. I puréed them along with the pears and thus was born this delicious and pretty concoction.

If you can afford the calories, fold in a cup of whipped cream instead of beaten egg whites. *En famille*, omit the egg whites and serve the puréed fruit as an uncooked sauce over store-bought pound cake. Halve the recipe if you need dessert for only 4 people.

2 very ripe pears, preferably Comice
2 cans (8 ounces each) pears packed in water or "lite" syrup
2 cups raw cranberries
2 tablespoons Cognac or Poire Williams
4 egg whites or 1 cup heavy (or whipping) cream
⅔ cup sugar

1. Peel and core the fresh pears, then place them in a food processor. Drain the canned pears and add them along with the cranberries and Cognac. Process until smooth and pour this mixture into a bowl. Refrigerate until ready to serve.

2. Beat the egg whites or heavy cream until somewhat stiff, then gradually beat in the sugar and continue to beat until the whites are stiff and glossy or the cream holds soft peaks.

3. With a rubber spatula fold half the whites or cream into the fruit purée, then fold this mixture back into the remaining whites or cream and continue to fold until well blended.

4. Spoon the mixture into 8 dessert bowls or wine glasses. Serve immediately or refrigerate up to 45 minutes if using egg whites or 2 hours if using cream.

PRUNE AND COCOA MOUSSE

MAKES 6 SERVINGS
TIME: 10 MINUTES WORK
45 MINUTES TO 3 HOURS NO-WORK CHILLING TIME

Prunes with chocolate might sound odd but the tastes are terrific together. What you notice most is the flavor

FOLDING IN EGG WHITES

In order to incorporate beaten egg whites into a base, you must first lighten the heavier mixture. Do this by first folding in about one-quarter of the egg whites. Place the whites on top of the batter. Using a large rubber spatula, gently cut through the whites and batter at the center of the bowl. Lift up the batter and lightly deposit it on top of the beaten whites. Turn the bowl as you continue to fold. Add the remaining whites and fold them in until no traces of whites remain. Work fast in order not to deflate the egg whites.

of the chocolate and the liqueur with only a hint of prunes in the background. The prunes give body and texture to the dessert without unnecessary fat.

1 package (12 ounces) pitted prunes
2 tablespoons unsweetened cocoa powder
¼ cup Armagnac, Cognac, or brandy
1 cup evaporated skim milk
4 egg whites
¼ cup sugar

1. In a food processor or blender purée the prunes, cocoa, Armagnac, and evaporated milk until smooth. Transfer the purée to a mixing bowl.

2. Beat the egg whites until almost stiff, then gradually beat in the sugar and continue to beat until the egg whites are stiff and glossy. Fold the egg whites into the prune purée.

3. Spoon the mousse into 6 dessert bowls or large wine glasses. Cover each bowl with plastic wrap and refrigerate until dinner time, at least 45 minutes but no longer than 3 hours.

VARIATION

For a more caloric and festive version, substitute 1 cup heavy (or whipping) cream for the egg whites. Whip the cream with the sugar, fold it into the purée, and proceed as directed.

RASPBERRY MOUSSE

MAKES 4 SERVINGS
TIME: 20 MINUTES WORK
45 MINUTES TO 3 HOURS NO-WORK CHILLING TIME

This berry mousse is refreshing and fairy, perfect for summer nights. The cookies help give it body; use 4 to 8 cookies, depending upon your taste and how large they are.

1 package (10 ounces) frozen raspberries in "lite" syrup, thawed
4 to 8 shortbread or butter cookies
½ pint fresh raspberries or blackberries
4 egg whites
¼ cup sugar

1. In a food processor or blender purée the thawed raspberries with their syrup and the cookies. Transfer the purée to a mixing bowl.

2. Rinse the fresh berries.

3. Beat the egg whites until almost stiff, then gradually beat in the sugar and continue to beat until very stiff and glossy. Fold the egg whites into the raspberry purée, then fold the purée into the fresh berries.

4. Spoon the mousse into 4 dessert bowls or large wine glasses. Cover each bowl with plastic wrap and refrigerate until dinner time, at least 45 minutes but no longer than 3 hours.

RHUBARB AND STRAWBERRY DESSERT

MAKES 4 TO 6 SERVINGS
TIME: 25 MINUTES

Rhubarb is a natural for a workweek dessert because it takes all of 5 minutes to cook. And when cooked, rhubarb dissolves into a purée, creating a natural base that I sweeten with jam and texturize with chopped fresh strawberries.

*1 pound fresh rhubarb stalks, green
   leaves removed
6 tablespoons sugar
1/4 cup water
1/4 teaspoon ground cinnamon
1 pint strawberries
2 tablespoons strawberry jam
Light cream (optional)*

1. Peel the rhubarb stalks if they're woody. The easiest way to do this is to cut 1/8 inch deep into the stalk with a knife and then, in strips, pull away the fibrous outer layer. Cut the stalks into 1-inch lengths.

2. Stir the sugar into the water in a medium-size noncorrosive saucepan. Add the cinnamon. Dissolve the sugar in the water over low heat. Add the cut rhubarb, cover the pan, and simmer gently until the rhubarb is just tender, 3 to 5 minutes.

3. Meanwhile rinse, hull, and halve or quarter the strawberries.

4. When the rhubarb is tender, remove the pan from the heat and stir in the jam and the strawberries. Spoon the rhubarb mixture into 4 to 6 dessert bowls and refrigerate uncovered until cool. Cover the bowls with plastic wrap if you plan to refrigerate the dessert longer.

5. If you can afford the cholesterol and calories, pour some light cream over each portion; the blend of mellow cream against the tart fruit is delightful.

RHUBARB LEAVES

Although rhubarb stalks are usually sold without their leaves, if you buy stalks with leaves be sure to cut them off entirely. Rhubarb leaves are never eaten because they are poisonous.

SECOND TIME AROUND

SAUTE OF SUMMER FRUIT: Any leftovers are good stuffed between layers of pound cake.

SAUTE OF SUMMER FRUIT

MAKES 4 TO 6 SERVINGS
TIME: 10 MINUTES

A sauté of fruit is a terrific, easy, and unusual dessert; the unexpected hotness of the fruit is a delicious surprise. For those who can afford the calories, the addition of cold vanilla ice cream adds to the textural contrast.

2 peaches
4 dark plums
½ pint blueberries or raspberries
2 tablespoons butter
¼ cup red currant or other jelly
Vanilla ice cream (optional)

1. With a sharp knife cut the peaches in half, remove the pits, and thinly slice. Pit and quarter the plums. Rinse the berries.
2. Melt the butter in a large nonstick skillet over medium-high heat. Stir in the jelly, then add the peaches and plums. Continuing to stir, sauté until the fruit is hot and the jelly syrupy, about 1 minute. Add the berries and remove the skillet from the heat. Serve immediately, with ice cream if you wish.

VARIATION

For a lower-calorie version, omit the butter. Instead melt the jelly in the skillet and simmer the peaches and plums in the jelly until hot.

EARLY FALL COMPOTE

MAKES 4 TO 6 SERVINGS
TIME: 15 MINUTES

This is an unusual combination I came up with when I gathered together whatever fruit I could find in my refrigerator. The peaches that day were hard and needed some simmering to tenderize them; the rest followed naturally.

3 peaches
¼ cup sugar
¼ cup dry white wine
¾ cup water
1 cup (packed) dried apricots
3 dark plums
½ pint blueberries
½ cup sliced blanched
*   almonds (optional)*

1. With a sharp knife peel, pit, and cut the peaches into 1-inch chunks.

2. Bring the sugar, white wine, and water to a simmer in a medium-size saucepan over medium heat. Add the peaches and apricots to the pan and simmer covered until tender, 3 to 5 minutes.

3. Meanwhile halve and pit the plums; quarter them if they're very large.

4. Add the plums to the fruit and simmer for a minute more to heat them through. Remove the pan from the heat and add the blueberries. Let the fruit cool to room temperature before serving, then sprinkle with the almonds if you wish.

PORT-SOUSED FRUIT WITH YOGURT

MAKES 4 SERVINGS
TIME: 20 MINUTES

This comforting dried fruit combination is rich in calories and flavor. If your waistline permits, substitute sour cream or crème fraîche for the yogurt.

I don't halve the fruit before poaching, but you could do so to make the dessert look more delicate.

1 cup (packed) dried apricots
1 cup (packed) pitted prunes
½ cup good-quality port or Madeira
2 or 3 whole cloves
1 cup plain yogurt

1. Place the dried fruit in a small skillet with the port and the cloves.

2. Slowly bring the liquid to a boil over low heat, then reduce the heat even further and simmer until the fruit is barely tender, about 2 minutes. Remove the skillet from the heat and cool the fruit to room temperature.

3. Fish out the cloves (although they are visible enough for your diners to fish out for themselves). Spoon the fruit with its juices into 4 dessert bowls and top each portion with ¼ cup yogurt.

CHERRY CLAFOUTI

MAKES 4 TO 6 SERVINGS
TIME: 10 MINUTES WORK
45 MINUTES NO-WORK BAKING TIME

During the week when I've invited company for dinner, I always try to make my dessert the night before, but some weekdays I don't have even a mo-

SECOND TIME AROUND

PORT-SOUSED FRUIT: Leftovers without the yogurt and puréed make an excellent filling to spread between layers of storebought pound cake.

HOW TO MAKE THE MOST OF CANNED AND FROZEN FRUIT

■ *Frozen raspberries and strawberries make wonderful substitutes for fresh berries; they're great in soufflés, mousses, or in puddings or custards. Frozen blueberries, however, are too firm and frozen melon is too watery.*

■ *Canned pears make the most of pear flavor, but peaches are too sweet and mushy. When poached fresh peaches are called for, I substitute apricots. I also find canned cherries acceptable but always avoid canned citrus fruits.*

■ *Canned fruit puréed with a touch of cream or plain yogurt makes a speedy fruit sauce that is great on pound cake, ice cream, or over fresh fruit.*

ment to plan ahead. That's when I resort to this unfussy clafouti—a good example of how one can dress up common ingredients in fancy clothes with delicious results.

An authentic French clafouti is a mixture of fruit (fresh or poached) mixed with an egg batter and baked for 1½ hours, which results in a tender pancakelike fruit pudding. During the week I don't have time to poach fruit, so I use canned or frozen fruit instead, and I mix it with a firmer batter that bakes in half the time. A touch of cornmeal adds unexpected crunch.

2 cans (16 to 17 ounces each) canned fruit packed in "lite" syrup, such as pitted cherries, pears, or apricots
¼ cup all-purpose flour
2 tablespoons cornmeal
½ teaspoon baking powder
⅛ teaspoon ground cinnamon or cloves
2 eggs
¼ cup granulated sugar
Confectioners' sugar for garnish (optional)

1. Preheat the oven to 375°F.
2. Drain the canned fruit, reserving ½

cup of the syrup. If the fruit is in large pieces, cut it into pieces the size of cherries.

3. In a mixing bowl blend the flour, cornmeal, baking powder, and cinnamon. Lightly beat the eggs, then add them, plus the granulated sugar and the reserved fruit syrup. Whisk the ingredients together and stir in the chopped fruit.

4. Pour the batter into an 8-inch square baking pan or 10-inch pie plate and bake for 45 minutes. Serve hot, warm, or at room temperature. Sprinkle the confectioners' sugar over the top if you wish to make it look more attractive.

VARIATIONS

■ **Clafouti with Berries:** Substitute 2 packages (10 ounces each) thawed, frozen raspberries or strawberries packed in "lite" syrup, for the canned fruit. Drain the fruit, reserving ½ cup of the syrup. Proceed as directed, increasing the sugar to ⅓ cup because the berries are tarter.

■ If you're on a cholesterol-free diet, you can make this dessert with egg whites only: Substitute 4 egg whites for the 2 whole eggs and beat them until almost stiff. Gradually beat in ¼ cup sugar and continue to beat until the egg whites are white and glossy. Mix the dry ingredients with the reserved fruit syrup, then mix in the fruit. Fold the beaten egg whites into the batter and pour it into the baking pan. Bake for 45 minutes.

BROWN BETTY PEACHES

MAKES 4 SERVINGS
TIME: 15 MINUTES WORK
1 HOUR NO-WORK BAKING TIME

Even though this takes a long time to bake, it is a snap to make thanks to the help of store-bought cookies. While the dessert is baking, make some soup or just relax.

When peaches are in season and especially sweet, this dessert becomes so irresistible, I sheepishly confess to having had a couple portions of it for dinner. To assuage my guilt, however, I ate it with a nutritious cup of low-fat ricotta, which, by the way, makes for a delicious mix with the peaches. This recipe is my exception to the never-use-canned-peaches rule.

1 package (7 to 8 ounces)
  shortbread or butter cookies
  (I love Pepperidge Farm)
6 ripe peaches
1 can (16 ounces) peaches or
  apricots packed in "lite" syrup
1 tablespoon vanilla extract

1. Preheat the oven to 375°F.

2. Smash the cookies in their package with your hands or with a rolling pin. Or transfer the cookies to a Ziploc bag, then smash them on the counter until you have cookie crumbs.

3. Peel (or not, as you wish) and pit the peaches, then cut them into 1-inch chunks. Cut the canned peaches into matching chunks. In a large bowl combine the fresh peaches, canned peaches with their syrup, and the vanilla.

4. Spoon half the peach mixture in the bottom of an 8-inch square baking pan (or another medium-size baking pan) and top with half the cookie crumbs. Repeat with the remaining peaches and cookies. (This dish can be prepared in advance to this point. It will keep up to 24 hours, covered, in the refrigerator.)

5. Cover the baking pan with aluminum foil and bake for 35 minutes. Uncover the pan and bake until the peaches are soft, 20 to 25 minutes longer. Remove the pan from the oven and serve hot, warm, or at room temperature.

VARIATION

This is a delicious dessert for company, and it can be made a day ahead and reheated in a 350°F oven for 15 minutes. For company, top each portion with whipped cream to make it look attractive.

PARING FRUIT

When paring pears and peaches, use a stainless steel knife so that the flesh doesn't turn brown as quickly.

STORING AND SOFTENING DRIED FRUITS

I often add raisins or other dried fruits to crisps, fruit salads, and puddings. I keep my dried fruit, well wrapped, in the refrigerator; it keeps better that way.

If you have dried fruit in the pantry or refrigerator that has hardened and turned to stone, don't throw it out. Instead, cover it with Port, Madeira, wine, or warm water. After a short time it will soften enough so you can use it in favorite dishes.

FALL FRUIT CRISP

MAKES 6 SERVINGS
TIME: 10 MINUTES WORK
40 MINUTES NO-WORK BAKING TIME

A crisp is a crisp is a crisp—simply a mix of fruit baked underneath some doughlike topping. I can't think of many other ways that can turn humdrum fruit as quickly and easily into a festive dessert.

This crisp recipe can be put together in innumerable ways and is great any season of the year. In winter use cranberries; in summer, fresh berries.

4 peaches or nectarines
4 pears
1 tablespoon lemon juice
½ cup (packed) brown sugar
½ cup all-purpose flour
½ cup old-fashioned rolled oats
¼ cup vegetable oil or
*   melted butter*
1 cup plain low-fat yogurt
*   or sour cream (optional)*

1. Preheat the oven to 350°F.
2. Peel and pit or core the fruit, then cut it into 1-inch chunks. Set the fruit in a 9-inch square noncorrosive baking pan and toss it with the lemon juice.
3. In a mixing bowl mix the sugar, flour, oatmeal, and oil with your fingers until the mixture is moist and crumbly. Sprinkle this topping over the fruit.
4. Bake until the fruit is tender, 30 to 40 minutes. Serve warm or at room temperature, with yogurt or sour cream if you like for a cool, tart contrast.

VARIATIONS

■ Instead of the combination of pears and peaches, use just one or the other.
■ **Berry Crisp:** Use 4 cups raspberries, blueberries, or blackberries. If you use berries frozen in syrup, drain them first of any liquid. Omit the lemon juice and cut the sugar back to 6 tablespoons in the topping.
■ **Cranberry Crisp:** Combine 4 cups cranberries, ¼ cup brown sugar, and ¼ cup water in a small saucepan. Bring the mixture to a boil, then transfer it to the baking pan. Make the topping as directed, decreasing the sugar to ¼ cup.
■ **For a change in the topping,** substitute ¼ cup cornmeal for the oats and increase the flour to ¾ cup. Or, instead of mixing flour and the oats, use 1 cup of one or the other.

CHOCOLATE-WALNUT PUDDING

MAKES 4 SERVINGS
TIME: 15 MINUTES WORK
1 HOUR NO-WORK CHILLING TIME

Sometimes for dinner I just want a big salad and a rich dessert. On those days or on days when I have company during the week, I prepare this chocolate pudding. It's surprisingly nutritious (as well as delicious) because it's made from farina.

2 tablespoons unsweetened cocoa
    powder, preferably Droste's
1/2 cup sugar
2 cups milk, low fat or whole
1 teaspoon vanilla extract
1/3 cup farina
1/2 cup walnuts

1. Place the cocoa and sugar in a small saucepan. Add the milk and vanilla and whisk until smooth. Slowly bring the milk to a simmer over low heat, whisking as you heat it.

2. When you see little bubbles beginning to form on the surface of the milk, pour the farina in a steady stream into the milk. Cook over low heat, stirring constantly with a wooden spoon, until it no longer tastes raw, 3 to 4 minutes.

3. Remove the pudding from the heat and let it stand while you chop the walnuts. Fold the walnuts into the pudding and spoon it into four 1/2-cup custard dishes or ramekins. Let it cool to room temperature, then refrigerate until dinner, at least 45 minutes (this dessert can be made up to a day ahead of time).

UNBELIEVABLE CHOCOLATE-CHESTNUT PUREE

MAKES 4 SERVINGS
TIME: 10 MINUTES WORK
1 HOUR NO-WORK CHILLING TIME

I named this concoction "unbelievable," because it tastes unbelievably rich and chocolatey even though it has little fat in it and no cholesterol. In addition it takes all of 10 minutes to make. Unbelievable, no?

The texture, as dense as fudge, comes from the chestnuts puréed with cocoa. If you can afford the calories and the cho-

WHIPPING CREAM

Before making whipped cream be sure the cream, bowl, and beaters are well chilled. If the cream is warm, it will not whip and will tend to clump into butter more quickly. Heavy cream is a mixture of butterfat emulsified in milk. When you whip cream, you're building up protein and fat walls which then enclose the tiny bubbles of air created by beating. The more you whip, the stronger the walls. If you overbeat, however, the fat molecules cling together, the protein walls collapse releasing water, and you're left with clumps of homemade butter instead of whipped cream!

WHIPPED CREAM TIPS

■ *Don't add flavoring or sugar until the cream is almost completely whipped or you won't be able to get quite as much air into the cream.*

■ *If you make whipped cream in advance, store it in a cheesecloth-lined sieve placed over a bowl. Cover the bowl with plastic wrap. This way, any excess liquid will seep out of the cream into the bowl and you'll be left with a lovely stiff whipped cream, even a day after you have whipped it.*

lesterol, then by all means indulge your-selves and top this with whipped cream or fold some whipped cream into the mixture before refrigerating it.

This is best served after a main-course soup or salad.

> 1 can (15½ ounces) whole chestnuts
> ½ cup unsweetened cocoa powder,
>   preferably Droste's
> ½ cup confectioners' sugar
> 2 tablespoons dark rum
> ¼ cup evaporated skim milk
> 1 cup heavy (whipping) cream
>   (optional)

1. Drain the chestnuts and rinse them under cold water. Place the chestnuts and all the other ingredients except the cream in a food processor and process for a minute. With a rubber spatula scrape down the sides and process until the chestnuts are puréed and light, about 1 minute more.

2. If you wish, whip the cream and fold it into the chestnut purée.

3. Spoon the purée into four ½-cup custard dishes or ramekins. Cover each one with plastic wrap and refrigerate until din-ner time, at least 1 hour (this dessert can be made up to a day ahead of time).

SWEET COUSCOUS

MAKES 4 SERVINGS
TIME: 25 MINUTES

I love this dessert so, perhaps I should have included it in the main-course grains chapter—on more than one occa-sion I have eaten double portions of this instead of dinner.

Because the dessert is made with a filling grain, it's perfect to have after a scrambled egg, soup, salad, or sandwich.

> 1 cup couscous
> 1 cup water
> 2 tablespoons butter
> 2 tablespoons sugar, brown or white
> ½ cup unsalted peanuts
> Sour cream or plain yogurt (optional)

1. Soak the couscous in the water for at least 15 minutes. Right before sautéing it, break up any clumps of couscous with your fingers.

2. Melt the butter in a medium-size skillet over medium heat. Stir in the cous-cous, sugar, and peanuts; sauté for a minute or two until all the ingredients are hot. Serve immediately with or without sour cream.

VARIATIONS

For a richer gussied-up version, substitute chopped walnuts or almonds for the peanuts.

Soak ⅓ cup currants or raisins and ⅓ cup diced dried apricots in 2 table-spoons port for at least 15 minutes. Add the steeped dried fruit to the couscous right after you add the sugar.

RASPBERRY RICE PUDDING

MAKES 4 SERVINGS
TIME: 25 MINUTES WORK
25 MINUTES NO-WORK
COOKING TIME

On days when I am in need of comfort more than of sustenance, I'll eat starch on starch: a large bowl of capellini noodles tossed with butter and then two to three helpings of this dessert. Sometimes I even have just this for dinner!

Rice pudding made the traditional way is loaded with fat and can take up to an hour to cook. My version, though, is done in half the time and, while rich tasting, is light and not too caloric.

1 cup white short-grain or Texmati long-grain rice
1¾ cups water
½ pint raspberries or strawberries
⅓ to ½ cup sugar (depending on how sweet you like dessert)
½ cup evaporated skim milk

1. Place the rice and the water in a small saucepan. Bring the liquid to a boil over low heat, then simmer covered until the rice is tender, about 18 minutes.
2. Meanwhile rinse and dry the berries. Hull and cut up the strawberries to raspberry size, if using.
3. When the rice is tender, stir in the sugar and evaporated milk. Simmer covered until the rice is mushy and the mixture tastes rich, 5 to 10 minutes.
4. Remove the pan from the heat and fold in the berries. Spoon the pudding into 4 dessert bowls and let sit at room temperature until dessert time, up to 3 hours.

VARIATIONS

■ Dissolve 2 teaspoons instant coffee in the

milk before adding it to the rice. Omit the berries.

■ Or dissolve 1 tablespoon unsweetened cocoa powder in the milk before simmering. Keep the berries in.

APRICOT SOUFFLES

MAKES 6 SERVINGS
TIME: 10 MINUTES WORK
30 MINUTES NO-WORK BAKING TIME

The word "soufflé" probably conjures up an image of a kitchen beset with dirty pots, whisks, and mixing bowls and a frazzled cook too terrified to open the oven door to find out if the soufflé has fallen. Hardly an image I'd like to visualize on an ordinary week night.

Fear not, my soufflés are simple and quick to make. This one, a purée of dried fruit is thickened by apricots instead of a cooked roux, and then folded into egg whites that have been beaten with sugar. To save time, I don't even bother to grease the little molds in which they bake.

It's worth the extra step of baking the soufflés in a bain marie (water bath)

—they won't rise as high, but neither will they collapse as quickly.

2 cups (packed) dried apricots
¼ cup Grand Marnier or Cognac
½ cup evaporated skim milk
4 egg whites
½ cup sugar

1. Preheat the oven to 400°F.

2. In a food processor purée the apricots with the liqueur and milk. Transfer the mixture to a large bowl.

3. Beat the egg whites until somewhat stiff, then gradually beat in the sugar and continue to beat until stiff and glossy. With a rubber spatula fold half the egg whites into the fruit purée, then fold the purée back into the remaining egg whites; fold until well blended.

4. Spoon the mixture into six ½-cup ovenproof ramekins or custard cups. Set the cups in a deep baking pan and pour about an inch of very hot water, straight from the tap, into the baking pan. Place the pan in the oven. Bake for 30 minutes and serve immediately.

VARIATION

Child's-Play Soufflés: Make a paste of 2 tablespoons cornstarch, 1 tablespoon liqueur of your choice, and 1 tablespoon milk. Stir into

WATER BATH

A water bath may sound like some fancy food preparation technique but, in fact, it is an easy no-clean-up method of preparing delicate foods. Placing a soufflé or custard in a water bath keeps it from cooking at a heat that is too high and prevents it from curdling or breaking down.

this paste 3 jars (6 ounces each) or 4 jars (4½ ounces each) of baby fruit purée (pear, apple, apricot, or peach). Beat 3 egg whites with ½ cup sugar as directed and proceed.

FRESH FRUIT SOUFFLES

MAKES 6 SERVINGS
TIME: 10 MINUTES WORK
30 MINUTES NO-WORK BAKING TIME

Another easy soufflé, this time using fresh fruit and a thickener of cornstarch.

4 or 5 ripe peaches or pears or 1
   pint berries
2 tablespoons cornstarch
2 tablespoons milk, lemon juice, or
   liqueur, such as Grand Marnier
   or Cognac
3 egg whites
½ cup sugar

1. Preheat the oven to 400°F.
2. Peel and pit the peaches or peel and core the pears or rinse and dry the berries. Cut the peaches or pears into large chunks; if using berries stem or hull them.
3. In a food processor purée the fruit. You should have 2 cups.
4. In a mixing bowl, mix the cornstarch with the milk to form a paste. Add the fruit purée and mix well.
5. Beat the egg whites until somewhat stiff, then gradually beat in the sugar and continue to beat until stiff and glossy. With a rubber spatula fold half the egg whites into the fruit purée, then fold the purée back into the remaining whites; fold until well blended.
6. Spoon the mixture into six ½-cup ovenproof ramekins or custard cups. Set the cups in a deep baking pan and pour very hot water, about an inch deep, straight from the tap, into the baking pan. Place the pan in the oven. Bake for 30 minutes and serve immediately.

CHOCOLATE SOUFFLES

MAKES 6 TO 8 SERVINGS
TIME: 10 MINUTES WORK
25 MINUTES NO-WORK BAKING TIME

These puffs of chocolate air rise high, taste intense, and are a snap to make. It's hard to believe anything so easy to

PERFECT PEARS

My favorite eating pears are Comice which appear in the late fall and early winter. Bartletts, too, are good eating pears. They appear in late summer.

LAYERING POUND CAKES

Store-bought pound cake can be turned into a delicious and festive-looking dessert almost instantly.

First, slice the cake horizontally into 3 thin layers. Spread the bottom layer with seedless raspberry jam, then spoon over applesauce, puréed peaches or pears, or leftover fruit salad. Sprinkle with chopped nuts. Top with another cake layer and repeat with jam, fruit mixture, and nuts. Top with the final cake layer. Slice the cake crosswise and serve with whipped cream.

prepare can be so wonderful to eat. Once you get hooked, even on weekends when you have time to fuss over dinner, you'll never go back to making chocolate soufflés the old-fashioned way.

Calorie counters and cholesterol watchers should use evaporated skim milk and leave the cream to the hedonists.

This recipe makes 6 to 8 individual soufflés, depending on how well you beat the egg whites and if you manage to incorporate them into the chocolate base without deflating them too much.

As with the Apricot Soufflés, baking these in a bain marie (water bath) will keep them moist and from collapsing as quickly or as much.

¼ cup unsweetened cocoa powder, preferably Droste's
2 tablespoons cornstarch
1 cup evaporated skim milk or heavy (whipping) cream
1 tablespoon liqueur (Kahlúa is nice)
4 egg whites
½ cup sugar

1. Preheat the oven to 375°F.
2. In a small bowl whisk together the cocoa and cornstarch. Add a little of the milk and whisk to make a smooth paste, then whisk in the remaining milk and the liqueur. The mixture will be especially soupy with the skim milk.

3. Beat the egg whites until somewhat stiff. Gradually beat in the sugar and continue to beat until stiff and glossy.

4. With a whisk fold a quarter of the egg whites into the chocolate mixture. (This is more of a folding and stirring motion at this point.) Fold in another quarter of the whites, then pour this mixture into the remaining egg whites and fold until well blended.

5. Spoon the soufflé batter into six to eight ½-cup ovenproof ramekins or custard cups. Set the cups in a deep baking pan and pour very hot water, about an inch deep, straight from the tap, into the baking pan. Place the pan in the oven. Bake for 25 minutes and serve immediately. The centers should be a little runny.

BERRY SHORTCAKE

MAKES 4 SERVINGS
TIME: 10 MINUTES WORK
1 HOUR NO-WORK CHILLING TIME

The particular combination of butter cookies with berries is scrumptious and irresistible with or without the whipped cream. This dessert is also terrifically easy to assemble, and the more ahead of time you make it, the longer it has to set in the refrigerator and become mushy. I prefer this made with fresh summer berries, but I like it in winter, too, when I substitute bananas and peeled and sliced oranges for the berries.

½ cup heavy (whipping) cream
  (optional)
1 tablespoon confectioners' or
  superfine sugar (optional)
½ teaspoon vanilla extract
  (optional)
1 package (10 ounces) frozen
  raspberries in "lite" syrup,
  thawed
½ pint fresh blueberries,
  raspberries, or blackberries
½ package (7 to 8 ounces)
  shortbread or butter cookies, or
  2 to 3 cookies per person

1. Beat the cream until somewhat stiff, add the sugar and vanilla, and continue to beat until stiff. Set the whipped cream aside in the refrigerator. (If you're on a diet, you can omit this step.)

2. In a food processor or blender purée the thawed raspberries with their syrup and set aside.

3. Stem and rinse the fresh berries.

4. Crumble 2 to 3 cookies in the bottom of each of four 1-cup dessert bowls. Top with the raspberry purée and then the fresh berries. Finish it off with the whipped cream. Cover each bowl with plastic wrap and refrigerate until dinner, at least 1 hour (this dessert can be made up to a day ahead of time).

VARIATION

If you're making this in winter, substitute 2 oranges and 2 bananas for the fresh berries. You'll still need the frozen raspberries to moisten the cookies and create that instant "cakey" feel to the dessert.

INSTANT CHOCOLATE AND WHIPPED CREAM CAKE

**MAKES 8 TO 10 SERVINGS
TIME: 20 MINUTES WORK
UP TO 24 HOURS NO-WORK
CHILLING TIME**

This "instant cake" is from my childhood. It is really nothing more than a

DECORATING THE CAKE

If you're entertaining during the week and have bought a store-bought, plain cake, gussy it up. Place a paper doily on top of the cake (I know that having a doily in the house and being a Monday-to-Friday cook might be antithetical, but anyway . . .) and sift some confectioners' sugar, through a strainer, over the doily. Remove the doily and its pattern will stay on the cake, making it look very festive.

SECOND TIME AROUND

CHOCOLATE AND WHIPPED CREAM CAKE: Leftovers (not the berry variation) can be frozen, then thawed in the re-frigerator before serving again.

confection of plain chocolate wafers layered with whipped cream, but I think it is great during-the-week party fare. It is best made a day in advance, and the longer it stands, the softer the cookies become, so that their texture resembles that of cake.

I prefer to make this cake with plain round chocolate wafers, but, when I can't find them, I substitute chocolate cookies shaped like teddy bears or dino-saurs — it works.

Every now and then I strew fresh raspberries in between the layers to give it a more sophisticated flavor but, made this way, the cake must be eaten within a few days because it doesn't freeze as well as the simpler version.

> *1 cup heavy (whipping) cream*
> *¼ cup confectioners' or superfine*
> *   sugar*
> *2 teaspoons vanilla extract*
> *About ½ pound plain chocolate wafers*

1. Beat the cream until somewhat stiff, add the sugar and vanilla, and continue to beat until stiff.

2. Crumble a quarter of the cookies in a 9-inch pie plate. With a spoon or spatula spread a fifth of the cream over the cookies. Arrange another quarter of the cookies whole over that layer of cream and spread with another fifth of the whipped cream. Re-peat the layers of whole cookies and cream, ending with a layer of whipped cream.

3. Cover the pie plate with plastic wrap and refrigerate at least 8 hours but pre-ferably overnight.

VARIATION

Use a 10-inch pie plate and strew fresh raspberries over each layer of whipped cream in between the cookie layers; you'll need about ½ pint berries.

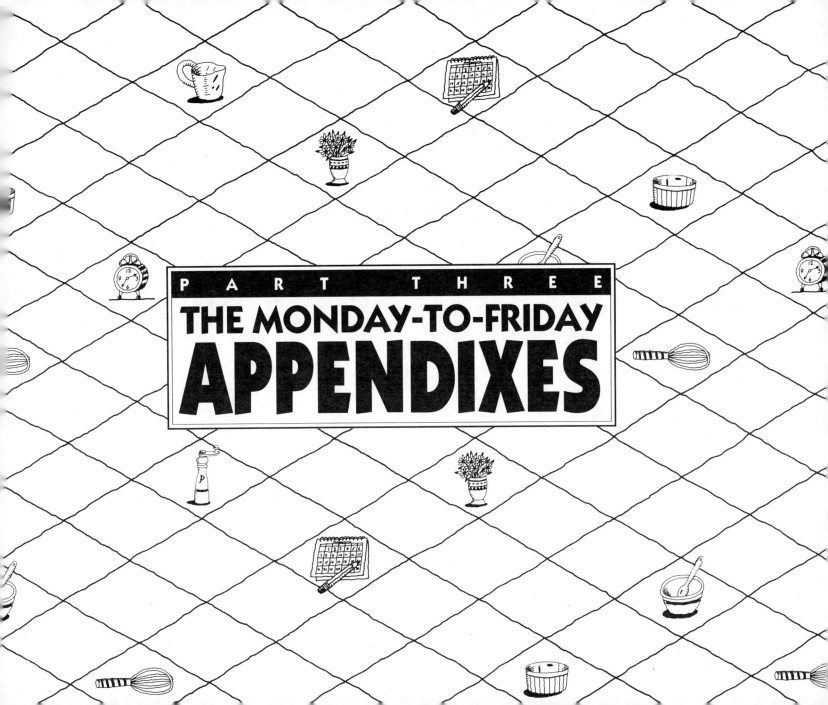

PART THREE
THE MONDAY-TO-FRIDAY
APPENDIXES

QUICK-REFERENCE RECIPE LISTINGS

Company's coming for dinner—which dishes make good entertaining fare? Or, which are sure-fire vegetarian hits? Or which are particularly well-suited to a child's taste? These reference lists were devised to help you meet your dinnertime menu needs quickly.

ESPECIALLY GOOD FOR ENTERTAINING

If you're expecting company for dinner during the week, any of these easy dishes should fit the bill.

ESPECIALLY GOOD FOR CHILDREN

These Monday-to-Friday recipes are well-suited to children's tastes or are easily adaptable.

ESPECIALLY GOOD FOR SINGLES

These dishes are particularly suitable for singles, or even couples without children (see also the Salad chapter).

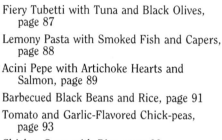

ESPECIALLY QUICK DISHES

These dishes are done, start to finish, in 30 minutes or less (see also the Salad chapter).

ESPECIALLY GOOD FOR VEGETARIANS

Here is a selection of dishes that are mostly complex carboyhydrates main courses. The recipes don't include fish, poultry, or meat, but do include eggs and dairy (see also the Grain & Bean Dishes chapter).

EATING SERIATIM

In addition to the recipes in the Soup, Pasta, One-Pot Meals, Salad, and Omnium Gatherum chapters, these dishes are perfect to make when you don't know when family members will be home for dinner. Some dishes can be reheated by the portion, others can be cooked to order or simply eaten at room temperature.

DISHES FOR SPRING OR SUMMER DAYS

Many of the veal, chicken, fish, and of course salad dishes in The Monday-to-Friday Cookbook are appropriate for warm or hot spring and summer nights. But here are some others that you should also keep in mind.

Festive Mackerel Salad, page 78

Tangy Beet Salad with Smoked Sardines, page 80

Sunny Couscous, page 85

Lemony Pasta with Smoked Fish and Capers, page 88

Soup with Tuna and Summer Vegetables, page 105

Gazpacho, page 113

Monkfish in Miso Sauce, page 150

Muchos Tacos, page 312

Picnic Loaf, page 316

Red and Yellow Pancakes, page 325

Egg dishes (any recipe), pages 321–324

COZY DISHES FOR FALL AND WINTER

Hearty roasted meats are especially suitable for cold winter days, as are all the recipes in the One-Pot Meals Chapter. Here are a few of my favorite comforters.

Sweet-and-Sour Ham Casserole, page 81

Curried Fish with Rice, page 85

Creamy Lentil casserole with Dried Apricots, page 90

Barbecued Black Beans and Rice, page 91

Chunky Peasant Vegetable Soup, page 103

Barley-Vegetable Chowder, page 106

Savory Thick Greens Soup, page 108

Corn, Tortilla, and Split Pea Soup, page 109

Split Pea Soup with Cauliflower and Sausage, page 110

Bean Minestrone, page 111

Pork Chops Baked in a Pear Sauerkraut, page 199

Winter Seafood Stew, page 206

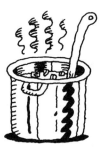

Asian Lentils with Potatoes and Chicken, page 207

Kasha and Mushroom Casserole, page 213

A MONDAY-TO-FRIDAY MENU SAMPLER

T his collection of some of my menus will give you a good idea of how I plan my weekday dinners. If there's time, I try to get a jump on the week by preparing a Sunday start-up dish or two. But there are plenty of times when this isn't possible, so Monday becomes the start-up day. I have also included a menu for a week when guests are coming for dinner. Although you certainly don't have to follow any of these to the letter, I think you'll find them useful in planning out your own strategies.

A ROASTED CHICKEN SUNDAY START-UP MENU

SUNDAY START-UP

ROASTED CHICKEN (prepare 2).

BASIC VEGETABLE SALAD (prepare a double batch of vegetables; dress only half)

FRESH FRUIT

MONDAY

POLENTA SOUP (prepare a double batch)

HAM SANDWICHES

WATERCRESS SALAD

MADEIRA-SOUSED FRUIT (prepare a double batch).

TUESDAY

STIR-FRIED VEGETABLES (from Sunday)

HERBED LAMB CHOPS

MADEIRA-SOUSED FRUIT (from Monday)

WEDNESDAY

AROMATIC EGGPLANT AND CHICKEN WITH PASTA (prepared with chicken from Sunday)

FRESH FRUIT OR ICE CREAM

THURSDAY

GAZPACHO

THREE BEAN SALAD WITH RED ONION

SWEET COUSCOUS

FRIDAY

POLENTA SOUP (from Monday)

ACINI PEPE WITH ARTICHOKE HEARTS AND SALMON

BAKERY COOKIES

A ROAST BEEF SUNDAY START-UP MENU

SUNDAY START-UP

NO-WORK ROAST BEEF, about 3½ pounds

HERBED NEW POTATOES (prepare a double batch)

ORANGE-JUICE-STEAMED CARROTS

CRANBERRY-PEAR MOUSSE (prepare a double batch)

MONDAY

SALAD OF ROAST BEEF, NEW POTATOES, (from Sunday), and green or red bell pepper strips

SPICY TART PEPPER DRESSING (prepare a triple batch)

CHERRY CLAFOUTI (prepare a double batch)

TUESDAY

SALSA-BAKED BLUEFISH (prepare a double batch)

AROMATIC RICE WITH VEGETABLES (prepare a double batch)

CRANBERRY-PEAR MOUSSE (from Sunday)

WEDNESDAY

Salad combining **BLUEFISH** and **RICE** (from Tuesday) with **SPICY TART PEPPER DRESSING** (from Monday). Add fresh diced fennel, bell peppers, or cucumbers, if you wish.

FRESH FRUIT

THURSDAY

BEEF AND NOODLE SOUP A LA VIETNAMESE with cubed beef (from Sunday)

CHERRY CLAFOUTI (from Monday)

FRIDAY

ELBOWS WITH TUNA AND SUN-DRIED TOMATOES

STEAMED BROCCOLI or **ASPARAGUS,** served either hot or cold and dressed with **SPICY TART PEPPER DRESSING** (from Monday)

BROILED BANANAS or **BROWN-SUGAR-GLAZED PINEAPPLE**

A BRAISED VEAL SUNDAY START-UP MENU

SUNDAY START-UP

BRAISED VEAL

BAKED SWEET POTATOES

PROTEAN RATATOUILLE (prepare a double batch)

MONDAY

WHITE BEANS PROVENCAL STYLE (prepare a double batch) Add 2 cups cubed veal (from Sunday) to half the beans; reheat for tonight.

CRUSTY BREAD

BROILED BANANAS

TUESDAY

CHILLED PROTEAN RATATOUILLE (from Sunday)

FESTIVE MACKEREL SALAD

PRUNE AND COCOA MOUSSE (prepare a double batch)

WEDNESDAY

SPAGHETTI TOSSED WITH OLIVE OIL AND GARLIC

SUMMER BORSCHT SALAD made with remaining 2 cups of leftover veal (prepare extra beets for Friday)

FRESH FRUIT

THURSDAY

WHITE BEAN SOUP made from the remaining beans (from Monday; see Second Time Around with recipe) thinned with chicken broth and freshened with ½ pound spinach and, if you wish, cubed chicken or fish.

WHOLE GRAIN BREAD

PRUNE AND COCOA MOUSSE (from Tuesday)

FRIDAY

PAN-BROILED STEAK WITH SALSA

SHREDDED BEETS (from Wednesday)

CRUSTY BREAD

ICE CREAM

❁

·····

A ROAST LEG OF LAMB START-UP MENU

SUNDAY START-UP

BEAN MINESTRONE (prepare a double batch)

ROAST LEG OF LAMB

BASIC VEGETABLE SALAD (prepare a double batch of vegetables) with a dressing of your choice (prepare a double batch at least)

MONDAY

EGG RIBBON SOUP

CHEESE AND TOMATO SANDWICHES

SLICED ORANGES WITH VANILLA

TUESDAY

CUBED LAMB (from Sunday) tossed with dressing or anchovy mayonnaise. Toss in remaining vegetables from Sunday.

FRUIT SALAD

WEDNESDAY

BEAN MINESTRONE (from Sunday) thinned with water, chicken broth, or tomato juice, and reheated with cubed lamb.

PEPPER AND CABBAGE SLAW

BROWN BETTY PEACHES OR PEARS (prepare a double batch)

THURSDAY

PASTA PRIMAVERA made with cauliflower or broccoli

FISH IN AN HERB BLANKET

BROWN-SUGAR-GLAZED PINEAPPLE

FRIDAY

TANGY BEET SALAD WITH SMOKED SARDINES

WHOLE-GRAIN OR FRENCH BREAD

BROWN BETTY PEACHES OR PEARS (from Wednesday)

A Monday Start-Up Menu

MONDAY

MEATY CHILI WITHOUT THE MEAT (prepare a double batch)

PERFECT RICE

STORE-BOUGHT POUND CAKE LAYERED WITH FRUIT AND NUTS

TUESDAY

STIR-FRIED GREENS

WOODSY MUSHROOM AND SCALLOP SOUP (prepare a double batch)

STORE-BOUGHT POUND CAKE (from Monday)

WEDNESDAY

MY SALAD NICOISE

WHOLE-GRAIN BREAD

CHERRY CLAFOUTI

THURSDAY

MILLET WITH PARMESAN with **WOODSY MUSHROOM AND SCALLOP SOUP** (from Tuesday) as a sauce

MONDAY-TO-FRIDAY GREEN SALAD (prepare a double batch of greens, but don't dress extras)

APPLE-DILL DRESSING (prepare a double batch)

FRIDAY

MONDAY-TO-FRIDAY GREEN SALAD with **APPLE-DILL DRESSING** (from Thursday)

MEATY CHILI WITHOUT THE MEAT (from Monday)

FRESHLY COOKED PASTA

STORE-BOUGHT COOKIES or **ICE CREAM**

A Really Limited Cooking Time Menu

MONDAY

SWEET-AND-SOUR HAM CASSEROLE

WHOLE-GRAIN BREAD

FRESH FRUIT OR STORE-BOUGHT DESSERT

TUESDAY

SAUTEED CHICKEN BREASTS (your favorite variation; prepare a double batch)

FRESH BROCCOLI OR CAULIFLOWER (prepare a double batch)

SAUTEED CHESTNUTS AND PINEAPPLE (prepare a double batch)

WEDNESDAY

FESTIVE MACKEREL SALAD (prepare a double batch)

WHOLE-GRAIN BREAD

EXOTIC FRUIT SALAD (prepare a double batch)

THURSDAY

Salad combining **SAUTEED CHICKEN BREASTS** and **BROCCOLI** or **CAULIFLOWER** (from Tuesday). Add thawed frozen corn kernels, if you wish.

OR

Sauce from Tuesday's leftovers. Chop then sauté them in ¼ cup olive oil with 1 clove minced garlic. Serve over pasta, baked potato or rice.

EXOTIC FRUIT SALAD (from Wednesday)

FRIDAY

FESTIVE MACKEREL SALAD (from Wednesday; second time around version)

FRENCH OR ITALIAN BREAD

SAUTEED CHESTNUTS AND PINEAPPLE (from Tuesday)

MENU FEATURING A MID-WEEK DINNER PARTY

SUNDAY START-UP

MONDAY-TO-FRIDAY GREEN SALAD
(prepare a double batch of dressing)

ASIAN LENTILS WITH POTATOES AND CHICKEN (prepare a double batch)

MONDAY

NO-WORK SALMON CHOWDER

SPINACH SALAD WITH ORANGES AND RICOTTA

INSTANT CHOCOLATE AND WHIPPED CREAM CAKE (for Wednesday)

TUESDAY

ASIAN LENTILS WITH POTATOES AND CHICKEN (from Sunday; second time around variation)

FRESH FRUIT or **STORE-BOUGHT DESSERT**

Prepare **HERBED COTTAGE CHEESE** sauce (for pasta) and **WINTER SEAFOOD STEW,** up to point where you add seafood (both for Wednesday)

WEDNESDAY

(company's coming)

CAPPELINI WITH HERBED COTTAGE CHEESE

WINTER SEAFOOD STEW

FRENCH BREAD

INSTANT CHOCOLATE AND WHIPPED CREAM CAKE

THURSDAY

(recover from Wednesday's dinner)

WATERCRESS, RED PEPPER, AND WATER CHESTNUT SALAD

BAKED-FOR-DINNER POTATOES with smoked mussels and scallion topping

INSTANT CHOCOLATE AND WHIPPED CREAM CAKE (from Wednesday)

FRIDAY

BULGUR SALAD WITH PEANUTS with dressing (from Sunday)

SAUTE OF SUMMER FRUIT WITH ICE CREAM (as a treat for making it to end of the week)

A MINIMALIST SUMMER MENU

It's the middle of July and the whole week is forecasted as hot and muggy. Plus, you have little time left after work to cook.

SUNDAY START-UP

PICNIC LOAVES (prepare 2 to 3)

INSTANT CHOCOLATE AND WHIPPED CREAM CAKE

MONDAY

GAZPACHO (prepare a double batch)

A MODERN CHEF'S SALAD

RHUBARB AND STRAWBERRY DESSERT (prepare a double batch)

TUESDAY

GAZPACHO (from Monday)

PICNIC LOAF (from Sunday)

INSTANT CHOCOLATE AND WHIPPED CREAM CAKE (from Sunday)

WEDNESDAY

STEAMED ASPARAGUS OR ARTICHOKES

THE BEST AND EASIEST SOFT-SHELL CRABS

SOUR DOUGH BREAD

RHUBARB AND STRAWBERRY DESSERT (from Monday)

THURSDAY

SALAD OF SMOKED TURKEY AND BULGUR dressed Japanese Style

MONDAY-TO-FRIDAY GREEN SALAD or **BASIC VEGETABLE SALAD** (prepare extra vegetables for Friday)

FRIDAY

(off for a summer week-end; for the car trip)

PICNIC LOAF (from Sunday)

CUT UP RAW VEGETABLES (from Thursday)

FRESH FRUIT and **STORE-BOUGHT COOKIES**

WINTER MENU FOR A HECTIC WEEK

Salads in winter are especially handy when you are pressed for time.

MONDAY

HERBED LAMB CHOPS (prepare a double batch)

CARROT THREADS WITH TARRAGON LIMAS

BROILED BANANAS

TUESDAY

QUINOA, CUCUMBER, AND CURRANT SALAD tossed with strips of chilled lamb (from Monday),

FRESH FRUIT SALAD

WEDNESDAY

SLOPPY MIKES

BASIC VEGETABLE SALAD (prepare a triple batch of dressing)

PUMPERNICKEL BREAD

PRUNE AND COCOA MOUSSE (prepare a double batch)

THURSDAY

EGG RIBBON SOUP

A MANHATTAN SALAD

SLICED ORANGES AND VANILLA

FRIDAY

A MANHATTAN SALAD (from Thursday)

STIR-FRIED BEEF WITH SCALLIONS

PRUNE AND COCOA MOUSSE (from Wednesday)

INDEX

G

S

W